Pueblo Bonito

Pueblo Bonito

Center of the Chacoan World

Edited by
Jill E. Neitzel

Smithsonian Books
Washington and London

Copy editor: Jane Kepp

Production editor: E. Anne Bolen

Designer: Brian Barth

Library of Congress Cataloging-in-Publication Data

Peublo Bonito: center of the Chacoan world / edited by Jill E. Neitzel.

   p.   cm.

  Includes bibliographical references and index.

  ISBN 1-58834-106-2—ISBN 1-58834-131-3 (pbk.)

    1. Pueblo Bonito Site (N.M.).   2. Pueblo Indians—New
Mexico—Chaco Canyon—Antiquities. 3. Pueblo architecture—
New Mexico—Chaco Canyon.   4. Excavations (Archaeology)—
New Mexico—Chaco Canyon—History. 5. Chaco Culture
National Historical Park (N.M.)—Antiquities.   I. Neitzel, Jill E.

E99.P9 P82 2003

978.9′82—dc21   2002030597

British Library Cataloguing-in-Publication Data are available

Manufactured in the United States of America

10 09 08 07 06 05 04 03   1 2 3 4 5

On the title page: Threatening Rock in 1901, four decades before its
collapse. Photograph by Charles F. Lummis, courtesy Museum of New
Mexico, Palace of the Governors, neg. no. 6153.

For Rueben, Judson, Hannah, and Isaac

Contents

Figures

Tables

Contributors

Nancy J. Akins, Office of Archaeological Studies, Museum of New Mexico, Santa Fe, New Mexico

Wendy Bustard, Chaco Culture National Historical Park, Department of Anthropology, University of New Mexico, Albuquerque, New Mexico

James D. Farmer, Department of Art History, Virginia Commonwealth University, Richmond, Virginia

Dabney Ford, Chaco Culture National Historical Park, U.S. National Park Service, Nageezi, New Mexico

Richard Friedman, Computer and GIS Services, County of McKinley, Gallup, New Mexico

Anne Lawrason Marshall, Department of Architecture, University of Idaho, Moscow, Idaho

Frances Joan Mathien, U.S. National Park Service, Santa Fe, New Mexico

Mary P. Metcalf, Clinical Tools, Inc., Chapel Hill, North Carolina

Jill E. Neitzel, Department of Anthropology, University of Delaware, Newark, Delaware

John R. Stein, Chaco Protection Sites Program, Navajo Nation Historic Preservation Department, Window Rock, Arizona

Thomas C. Windes, U.S. National Park Service, Santa Fe, New Mexico

Preface

The preparation of this volume has been a lengthy but rewarding experience. When I first began to study Pueblo Bonito in 1984, I was full of optimism about the site's research potential. The 1980s were an exciting time in Southwestern archaeology—a time of new questions about how prehispanic Southwestern societies were organized, new methods for addressing such questions, and heated debates about how to interpret results. The focus of these debates was the issue of complexity: Were prehispanic Southwestern societies egalitarian, as their ethnographically known descendants seemed to be? Or were some hierarchically organized?

For several reasons it seemed to me that Pueblo Bonito was an ideal site for attempting to answer these questions. It was the largest structure in the cluster of contemporaneous, multistory buildings located in central Chaco Canyon. This preeminent position made Pueblo Bonito one of the likeliest places in the entire Southwest where evidence for complexity might be present. Furthermore, it was one of the few very large Southwestern sites to have been almost completely excavated and perhaps the only one of those few sites to have intact collections with accompanying provenience information available for study.

As I began to investigate Pueblo Bonito's unique database over the next decade, I increasingly began to feel as if I were being buried by data. The more I worked, the more questions I identified. As I did a little bit of research on this question and a little bit on that one, I seemed never to finish anything. I just burrowed farther and farther into a seemingly endless mass of information. Clearly, Pueblo Bonito's research potential was not going to be fulfilled by my continuing to work on my own.

I first had the idea for this book in 1995 when I realized that the following year was Pueblo Bonito's archaeological centennial—100 years previously, the first large-scale excavations at the site had begun. I thought that a productive way to commemorate this anniversary would be a collaborative effort to take stock of how much had been learned about Pueblo Bonito after a century of research. My idea was to invite archaeologists who were working on various aspects of the site's database to present their research in a symposium at the 1996 annual meeting of the Society for American Archaeology. After the symposium, the participants agreed to revise their papers for publication, and two other researchers, Nancy Akins and John Stein, were asked to contribute papers as well.

The preparation of the volume was facilitated by the efforts of many. Bruce Smith of the Smithsonian Institution initially encouraged the idea of a Pueblo Bonito centennial volume. At Smithsonian Books, Daniel Goodwin got the project started and Scott Mahler kept it going. The critical comments of two anonymous reviewers were extremely helpful in making the completed volume much more focused. The efforts and understanding of two researchers, Jonathan Reyman and David Hurst Thomas, whose chapters were cut when the volume's focus changed, are also acknowledged.

Production of the completed manuscript was carried out with great skill and patience by Maripat Metcalf, Linda Clifton, and Nova McKernan. Juan Villamarin and Karen Rosenberg, successive chairpersons of the Department of Anthropology at the University of Delaware, generously allowed department resources to be used in preparing the manuscript. Getting the manuscript to press was aided by the perseverance of Emily Sollie, the supervision of Anne Bolen, and the expertise of other staff members at Smithsonian Books. The quality of the volume was vastly improved by the thorough copyediting of Jane Kepp.

The strength of this volume lies in the collaboration that produced it. Each of the contributors presents significant insights into his or her particular topic, but it is the combination of all the individual chapters that creates an image of Pueblo Bonito as the powerful center of the Chacoan world. Furthermore, this combined research provides clear, redundant evidence that the society the inhabitants of Pueblo Bonito dominated was hierarchically organized.

In no way does this volume exhaust Pueblo Bonito's research potential. All of the topics addressed in the following chapters can be investigated further, and there are undoubtedly other topics that have not yet begun to be explored. In putting this book together, I have recognized that my original optimism about investigating Pueblo Bonito was well founded. Researchers working at the site in its second century of archaeological study will find that there is still much to be learned.

I

Three Questions about Pueblo Bonito

Jill E. Neitzel

Even in ruin Pueblo Bonito stands as a tribute to its unknown builders. It is one
of the most remarkable achievements of all the varied Indian peoples who
dwelt within the present United States in prehistoric times.

—NEIL M. JUDD

"Everyday Life in Pueblo Bonito"

Approximately 1,000 years ago, there arose in the northern part of what is now the southwestern United States a place of unprecedented power. That place was Chaco Canyon
(Fig. 1.1), and at its center stood the structure known today as Pueblo Bonito. An enormous
building, Pueblo Bonito rose four stories tall, held perhaps as many as 800 rooms, and encompassed almost three acres. Its occupants ruled not just the canyon in which they lived but
also much of the surrounding region. Their power was political, economic, and, perhaps most
importantly, religious. It provided the unifying force for Chacoan society, one of the most complex societies ever to develop in the prehispanic Southwest.

At its peak, Pueblo Bonito must have been a spectacular, awe-inspiring sight. Today, abandoned and in ruin, the structure continues to overwhelm all who see it (Fig. 1.2). As the largest
building in a remote, desolate canyon, Pueblo Bonito has been the subject of much specula-
tion and ongoing scientific study. This book presents the results of the most recent archaeological investigations at the site. The conclusions drawn by the authors are significant not only
for what they contribute to our understanding of Pueblo Bonito itself but also for what they
imply about the society that the inhabitants of Pueblo Bonito dominated.

In this first chapter I offer a short history of previous archaeological investigations at Pueblo

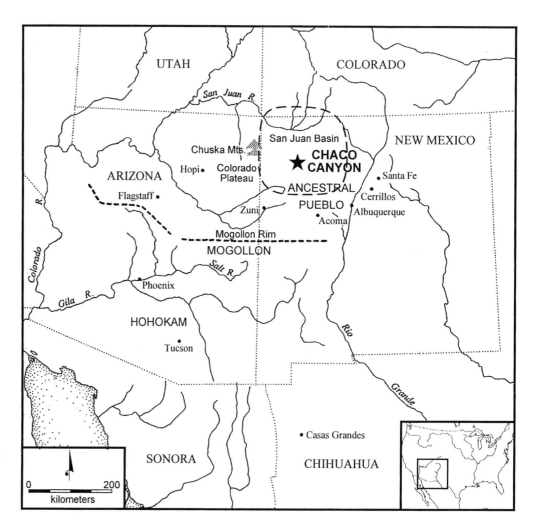

Figure 1.1. Location of Chaco Canyon in the southwestern United States.

Bonito and how they fit into the broader study of Chacoan society. Then I consider three questions about Pueblo Bonito that have been topics of ongoing and sometimes heated debate among Chacoan archaeologists and that provide the unifying theme for this volume: How were the people who built and used Pueblo Bonito organized? What was this enormous structure used for? And how many people lived in the building?

HISTORICAL BACKGROUND

Archaeologists have been investigating Chacoan remains for more than a century (see Lister and Lister 1981 for a detailed history). Large-scale archaeological research in Chaco Canyon began at Pueblo Bonito, where two major excavation projects uncovered almost the entire ruin (Fig. 1.3). Together, the Hyde Exploring Expedition (1896–1899) and the National Geographic Society Expedition (1920–1927) produced a detailed site map, reconstructed the building's complex architectural history, and unearthed rich burials and hundreds of thousands of artifacts. Pueblo Bonito's burials are among the most elabo-

rate from any Southwestern site, and its artifacts include the largest quantity of turquoise ever excavated by archaeologists. In addition to the nonlocal turquoise, excavations revealed numerous other imported goods, such as shell from the Gulf of California and the Pacific coast and macaws from Mesoamerica, as well as a variety of unusual and exotic items such as bone objects inlaid with turquoise and jet, cylindrical ceramic jars, and wooden flutes. The results of these excavations are summarized in three volumes (Judd 1954, 1964; Pepper 1920) and a series of journal articles (Judd 1921, 1922, 1923a, 1923b, 1924, 1925a, 1925b, 1925c, 1926, 1927a, 1927b, 1928a, 1928b, 1930a, 1930b, 1955; Pepper 1899, 1905, 1906, 1909). These publications emphatically confirm conclusions about Pueblo Bonito's importance among prehispanic Southwestern sites, both Chacoan and non-Chacoan, that were first suggested by its enormous size.

The initial focus of Chacoan archaeology on Pueblo Bonito was subsequently broadened to include other sites, both large and small. Although some of this later research involved excavations (e.g., Breternitz et al. 1982; Irwin-Williams and Shel-

Figure 1.2. Unexcavated Pueblo Bonito, 1896. Courtesy American Museum of Natural History Library, neg. no. 17772, photograph by Granger, Wortman Paleontological Expedition.

Figure 1.3. Detail of aerial photograph of excavated Pueblo Bonito taken by Charles Lindberg in 1929. Note the location of Threatening Rock at upper center. Courtesy Museum of New Mexico, Palace of the Governors, neg. no. 130232 (no. L55) (no. 70.1/182).

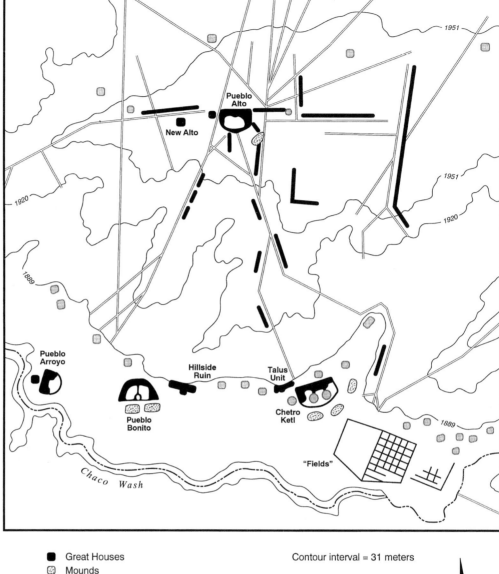

Figure 1.4. Downtown Chaco (adapted from Holley and Lekson 1999:40).

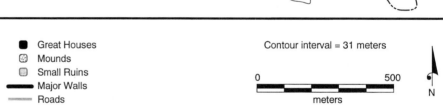

■ Great Houses
▣ Mounds
▢ Small Ruins
▬ Major Walls
═ Roads

Contour interval = 31 meters

0   500
meters

N

ley 1980; Judd 1959a; McKenna 1984; Morris 1919, 1921, 1924; Roberts 1929; Truell 1992; Vivian and Mathews 1965; Windes 1987a, 1987b, 1993a), the emphasis eventually shifted to surveys. Systematic survey projects were undertaken to document all sites located in Chaco Canyon (Hayes et al. 1981) as well as the distribution of Chacoan structures outside the canyon (Marshall et al. 1979; Powers et al. 1983). The goals of these surveys were to investigate how Chacoan society was organized and to explain why it developed the way it did.

Surveys of the canyon and its surrounding region have allowed archaeologists to consider individual Chacoan sites such as Pueblo Bonito within their broader social context. For example, researchers now recognize that Pueblo Bonito was

not an isolated, independent structure (Fig. 1.4). Instead, it sat in the middle of a cluster of at least five multistory buildings, which archaeologists call Chacoan great houses.[1] This cluster, sometimes referred to as the Pueblo Bonito complex or "downtown Chaco," makes up a very large, possibly proto-urban settlement (Holley and Lekson 1999:40; Lekson 1984:70–71, 1999:12; Neitzel 1989a:512–513). Elsewhere in the canyon were at least eight more great houses (Fig. 1.5), numerous small sites, and a variety of other features, including roads.[2]

At an even broader scale, more than 100 great houses have been located throughout the San Juan Basin of northwestern New Mexico and beyond (Fig. 1.6). These so-called Chacoan outliers mark the extent of Chaco Canyon's influence, and con-

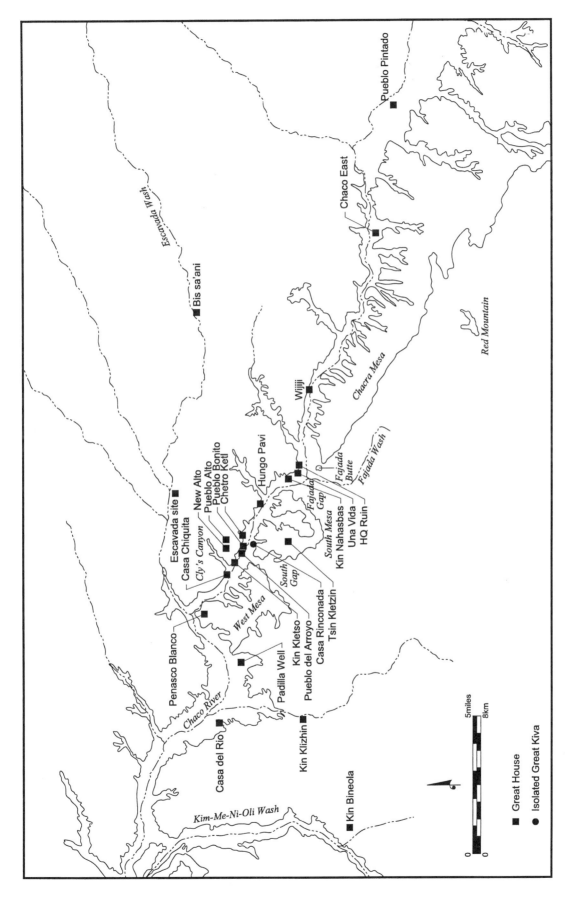

Figure 1.5. Locations of major Chaco Canyon sites. Courtesy National Park Service.

Pueblo Pintado

Chaco East

Bis sa'ani

Escavada Wash

Wijiji

Red Mountain

Chacra Mesa

Hungo Pavi

New Alto
Pueblo Alto
Pueblo Bonito
Chetro Ketl

Escavada site
Casa Chiquita
Cly's Canyon

Penasco Blanco

West Mesa

South Gap

Fajada Gap

Fajada Butte

Fajada Wash

South Mesa

Kin Nahasbas
Una Vida
HQ Ruin

Kin Kletso
Casa Rinconada
Tsin Kletzin

Padilla Well
Pueblo del Arroyo

Chaco River

Casa del Rio

Kin Klizhin

Kim-Me-Ni-Oli Wash

Kin Bineola

5 miles
8 km
0
0

■ Great House
● Isolated Great Kiva

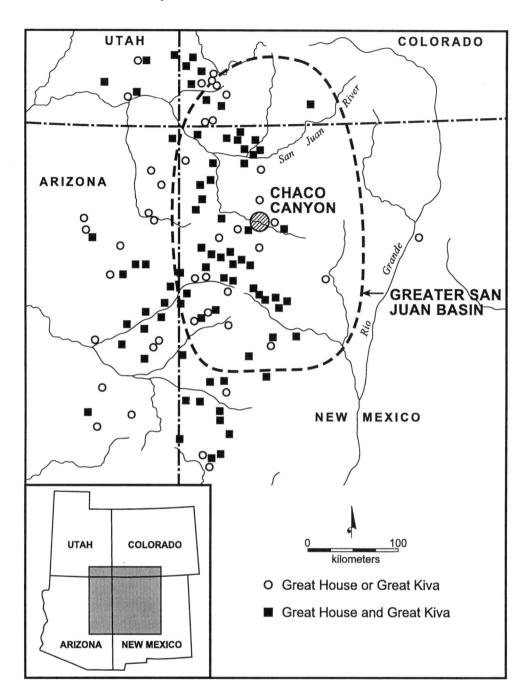

Figure 1.6. Locations of Chacoan great houses in the northern part of the southwestern United States (adapted from Lekson 1991:47).

sequently Pueblo Bonito's influence, in the northern Southwest (Lekson 1991). The varying sizes of the outliers also indicate that Chacoan society was hierarchically organized (Neitzel 1989a, 1994, 1999; Powers et al. 1983; Schelberg 1984).

These conclusions about the extent of Chacoan influence and the organization of Chacoan society have raised new, and as yet unanswered, questions. For example, does the widespread distribution of Chacoan outliers represent the limits of a single society or those of multiple societies that were interacting in some way? What kind of control did Pueblo Bonito exert from its position at the apex of the Chacoan settlement hierarchy? How much of Pueblo Bonito's power was political, economic, and religious? How strong was its domination of its society? If multiple Chacoan societies existed, what was the nature and strength of Pueblo Bonito's power over societies other than its own?

Additional questions are raised by efforts to evaluate proposed explanations for the extent of Chacoan influence and the hierarchical organization of Chacoan society. Early explanations emphasized economic and environmental factors (Altschul 1978; Grebinger 1973; Judge 1979). Their proponents interpreted the distribution of Chacoan outliers and their hierarchical organization as adaptations to temporal and spatial resource variability in a marginal environment. More recent explanations have emphasized ideological factors, interpreting the presence of great kivas at Chacoan outliers as evidence of a widely shared religion (Lekson 1991; Stein and Lekson 1992).

The impetus for this volume is the idea that efforts to resolve current questions in Chacoan archaeology may be aided by a new look at Pueblo Bonito. Obviously, data from Pueblo Bonito cannot clarify the extent of Chacoan influence or tell us whether outlying great houses encompassed one or multiple societies. But a more thorough understanding of the site that occupied the top of the Chacoan organizational hierarchy may provide insights into the kinds of power that held Chacoan society together.

Pueblo Bonito is presently part of Chaco Culture National Historical Park, which is administered by the U.S. National Park Service. Because the Park Service's policy is to preserve Pueblo Bonito, no significant excavations have been conducted at the site since the end of the National Geographic Society Expedition in 1927. Further digging has been limited to extremely small-scale excavations done in conjunction with ruins stabilization (Vivian 1940; Windes 1993b) and the collection of wood samples for tree-ring dating (Windes and Ford 1996).

Despite the absence of new fieldwork, Pueblo Bonito has continued to be investigated through specialized analyses of its existing database. These studies have focused on dating the site's construction sequence (Lekson 1986; Windes and Ford 1996) and documenting its architectural patterning (Baxter 1980; Bernardini 1999; Bustard 1996; Cooper 1995; Fritz 1987; Metcalf 1997), its astronomical significance (Reyman 1976, 1978a, 1978b, 1979; Sofaer 1997; Stein et al. 1997; Williamson 1977, 1978; Zeilik 1984, 1986), its burials (Akins 1986; Palkovich 1984; Reyman 1978b; Turner and Turner 1999), and its artifacts (Cameron 2001; Mathien 1981a, 1981b, 1984, 1997, 2001; Neitzel and Bishop 1990; Reyman 1990; Toll 1990, 2001). Thus, although much of Pueblo Bonito's data was collected more than a century ago, it continues to generate new research results.

The three questions about Pueblo Bonito that provide the unifying theme for this volume all have implications for the broader study of Chacoan society. First, how were the people who built and used Pueblo Bonito organized? Given Pueblo Bonito's preeminence among Chacoan settlements, as measured by its great size, rich burials, and enormous quantities of unique and imported artifacts, conclusions about its organization can contribute to our understanding of how Chacoan society as a whole was organized. Second, what was the huge structure used for? Determining whether Pueblo Bonito was an elite residence, a ceremonial center, or both affects interpretations about the kinds of power Pueblo Bonito exerted over its society. And third, how many people lived in this building? If the structure was a residence, whether its inhabitants were few or many has implications for its other, nonresidential functions and thus for the nature of Pueblo Bonito's rule over Chacoan society. The remainder of this chapter provides background on each of these questions.

ORGANIZATION

The one question that has dominated Chacoan research in recent years is that of how the society that constructed great houses such as Pueblo Bonito was organized. The few archaeologists who thought about Chacoan social organization prior to the 1970s generally assumed that Chacoan society was similar to historic Pueblo Indian society—in other words, it was egalitarian (Vivian 1970). This view was subsequently challenged after a few archaeologists (e.g., Cordell and Plog 1979) suggested that some prehispanic Southwestern societies, including that centered on Chaco Canyon (Altschul 1978; Grebinger 1973; Judge 1979), might have been hierarchically organized. The result was heated archaeological debates during the 1980s about issues related to organizational complexity and its presence in the prehispanic Southwest (see Feinman et al. 2000; Lightfoot and Upham 1989; McGuire and Saitta 1996).

The general consensus among archaeologists today is that Chacoan society was hierarchically organized with an intermediate degree of complexity (e.g., Akins 1986; Earle 2001; Fish 1999; Lekson 1991; Neitzel 1989a, 1999; Peregrine 2001; Schelberg 1984; Sebastian 1992b; cf. Vivian 1990; Wilcox 1999). The evidence supporting this view is diverse and redundant. It includes settlement patterns, mortuary data, trade goods, and labor costs. Each type of data indicates that not all Chacoan sites and not all Chacoan people were socially equivalent. Instead, a moderately developed social hierarchy held sway.

Data from Pueblo Bonito contributed significantly to this conclusion. The site's massive architecture, rich burials, and huge quantities of unique and imported goods have suggested to many researchers that its residents had high status. Yet the data from Pueblo Bonito cannot be truly appreciated in isolation. Because Chacoan society encompassed numerous settlements, conclusions about its organization must be drawn from evidence on a regional scale (Feinman 1992; Neitzel 1989a, 1999). It is through comparisons with other sites that Pueblo Bonito's preeminent position in the Chacoan settlement hierarchy, its disproportionate quantity and quality of imported and unique artifacts, and the richness of its burials can be seen.

FUNCTION

The question of Pueblo Bonito's function relates to current efforts to determine what kinds of connections formed the basis of Chacoan society. Some see Pueblo Bonito and the other great houses as having functioned primarily as elite residences (Akins 1986; Kantner 1996; Schelberg 1982; Sebastian 1992b; Tainter and Gillio 1980; Vivian 1990; Wills 2000). Others argue that they functioned primarily as ceremonial centers (Judge 1989; Renfrew 2001; Stein and Lekson 1992; Toll 1985).

These views are not mutually exclusive. Most advocates of the elite residence position would probably agree that important ceremonies took place at Pueblo Bonito, and most advocates of the ceremonial center position would probably acknowledge that Pueblo Bonito also functioned as a residence. What distinguishes the two positions is which function they identify as primary and how they interpret Pueblo Bonito's residential population size. Generally, those who see Pueblo Bonito as primarily an elite residence accept the site's highest population estimates (e.g., Sebastian 1992a). Those who see Pueblo Bonito as a ceremonial center advocate the site's lowest population estimates, noting that the few priestly elite residents might have been joined periodically by large numbers of religious pilgrims (e.g., Judge 1989).

To support their positions, both elite residence and ceremonial center advocates compare Pueblo Bonito with other ancestral and historic Puebloan sites. Elite residence proponents emphasize similarities in the residential function of pueblos throughout the northern Southwest (e.g., Judd 1964; Vivian 1990). They argue that great houses such as Pueblo Bonito are essentially big pueblos (thus the name "great house") and probably served the same residential function as smaller pueblos—the major difference being that the bigger pueblos housed more people (for another perspective on the residential function, see Wills 2000).

Ceremonial center proponents emphasize differences between Chacoan great houses and other pueblos (Bustard 1996; Fowler and Stein 1992; Wilcox 1993). They argue that great houses are qualitatively different, not only in size but also in layout and appearance. Furthermore, they claim that Pueblo Bonito's paucity of hearths indicates a small resident population (Windes 1984), and they cite a variety of evidence to argue that Pueblo Bonito's primary function was as a ceremonial center (see Lekson et al. 1988). This evidence includes the site's numerous kivas and great kivas; the large size, accessibility, and contents of its storage rooms (Lekson 1986; Windes 1987a, 1987b); its enormous quantities of broken pottery (Toll 1985; cf. Wills 1991); and its surrounding ritual landscape (Fowler and Stein 1992; Stein and Lekson 1992).

Proponents of the elite residence and ceremonial center positions also rely on comparisons with non-Southwestern cultures. The elite residence view is derived primarily from ex- tensive archaeological and ethnographic data on the function of big sites in intermediate-level societies (Feinman 1995; Feinman and Neitzel 1984:66–67; Lekson 1985; Naroll 1956). Cross-cultural comparisons indicate that such sites generally house substantial populations that include the ruling elites, their families, and their retainers.

The non-Southwestern referent for the ceremonial center position has been a single archaeological case, that of the Maya (e.g., Judge 1989:241–243). Until the 1970s, many Mayan archaeologists interpreted their extremely large sites with monumental architecture as the remains of empty ceremonial centers (see Sabloff 1990). These centers were thought to have housed only a small number of priestly elites who periodically conducted ceremonies for large numbers of visitors. Few Mayanist archaeologists now accept this interpretation, because large-scale surveys have documented substantial populations surrounding several major Mayan centers (e.g., Coe 1967; Willey and Leventhal 1979). This does not mean, however, that Pueblo Bonito could not have been an empty ceremonial center. The question of Pueblo Bonito's function will ultimately be answered using data from Pueblo Bonito and other Chacoan sites and not by analogy with sites in other areas.

POPULATION

While all archaeologists agree that Pueblo Bonito is a huge site, they hold markedly divergent opinions about whether or not its physical size correlates with a large residential population. Population estimates for the site at its peak range from a low of 70 people (Bernardini 1999) to a high of 1,200 (Pierson 1949). Between these extremes, others have estimated Pueblo Bonito's peak population to have been 100 persons (Windes 1984), 500 (Drager 1976), 800 (Hayes 1981), 950 (Neitzel 1999), and 1,100 (Judd 1954, 1964).

The reasons for these diverse population estimates lie in the data and methods used to produce them. The highest were derived by measuring some aspect of Pueblo Bonito's size (e.g., room count or area) and then applying some population conversion factor to that figure. This approach has been applied in demographic studies of the ethnographically known pueblos (e.g., Hill 1970:75; Roberts 1956:9, 43, 78; Stubbs 1950) and of other ancestral Puebloan sites (e.g., Colton 1936; Hantman 1983; Larson and Michaelson 1990), including those in Chaco Canyon (Pierson 1949). One of several problems with the archaeological applications is their failure to consider changes in site size through time, which can result in inflated peak population estimates (see Blake et al. 1986:452; Plog 1975; Schacht 1981, 1984; Schlanger 1988:781; Sullivan and Schiffer 1978:176). This problem would be exacerbated at Pueblo Bonito if the site's function was primarily ceremonial. The various population conversion factors were derived from residential sites, which presumably housed more people than did ceremonial sites.

Pueblo Bonito's lowest population estimates have been derived from analyses of residential rooms alone, as indicated by the presence of domestic features such as hearths. This approach has been criticized by those who argue that Pueblo Bonito might have had more hearths and other domestic features than are indicated in the site's excavation reports (e.g., Reyman 1987a, 1989). Furthermore, most hearths were probably located in upper-story rooms or on roofs and would have been destroyed as the structure collapsed after abandonment. If this inference is correct, then population estimates based on rooms with domestic features are too low.

Questions about how many people lived at Pueblo Bonito throughout its more than 300-year occupation are inextricably linked to questions about Chaco Canyon's population during this same interval. At one extreme, Windes (1984:84) has used the results of his hearth-based estimates for Pueblo Bonito and two nearby great houses to propose a peak canyon population of 2,000 people. This figure is slightly lower than Lekson's (1986:272) estimate of 2,100–2,700 people for downtown Chaco alone. Other size-based population estimates for the entire canyon are 3,669 persons (Schelberg 1982), 4,100 (Lekson 1981), 4,400 (Pierson 1949), 5,000 (Neitzel 1999), 5,652 (Hayes 1981), and 6,000 (Drager 1976). As with the size-based Pueblo Bonito estimates, variation in the size-based canyon estimates is due to a reliance on different aspects of site size and different conversion factors.

Regardless of which of the proposed peak population estimates are accepted for Pueblo Bonito and Chaco Canyon, the question of population trends over time is only just beginning to be addressed (Neitzel 1999:196–197; Vivian 1992:53). This question raises the issue of chronology and for Pueblo Bonito requires that methods of demographic reconstruction be applied to each stage in the site's construction sequence.

THIS VOLUME

A millennium ago, Pueblo Bonito was the most important settlement in the Puebloan world. Its residents ruled Chaco Canyon and the surrounding region, and their influence extended even further. Their unprecedented power was never equaled by leaders of later Puebloan societies. Pueblo Bonito's power provided the unifying force for one of the most complex societies ever to develop in the prehispanic Southwest.

What was the power that enabled Chacoan society to become so complex and that gave Pueblo Bonito its preeminent position? At least a partial understanding of this power can be achieved by investigating the three questions about Pueblo Bonito that provide the unifying theme for this volume: How were Pueblo Bonito's builders and users organized? What was the structure's function? And how many people lived there?

Not all of the chapters in this volume are relevant to all three of these questions. But each chapter has implications for at least one of them, if not more. We begin with a consideration of Pueblo Bonito's location and then continue with discussions of various aspects of the site's architecture—its chronology, appearance, astronomical alignments, labor investment, and layout. Later chapters describe the site's burials, its artifact distributions, and the significance of its imported goods. The final chapter synthesizes the various authors' conclusions about Pueblo Bonito's organization, function, and population. These conclusions provide the most complete picture to date of life at Pueblo Bonito. In doing so, they also contribute to a better understanding of Pueblo Bonito's role in Chacoan society.

ACKNOWLEDGMENTS

Thanks to Jonathan Reyman for locating the quotation at the beginning of this chapter, to Joan Mathien for helping me compile references on previous Pueblo Bonito research, to Tom Windes for providing both a base map for Figure 1.5 and further references, and to Wendy Bustard and Tom Rocek for offering useful suggestions on an earlier version of this chapter.

NOTES

1. Counts of the number of great houses making up downtown Chaco vary, depending on how the limits of this dispersed, proto-urban settlement are defined. Lekson (in Holley and Lekson 1999:40) includes Pueblo Bonito and its closest great-house neighbors: Pueblo del Arroyo, Chetro Ketl, Pueblo Alto, and New Alto. Neitzel (1989a:513) also includes Kin Kletso and Casa Chiquita. Elsewhere, Lekson (1999:12) defines downtown Chaco's limits as encompassing all of central Chaco Canyon.

2. Counts of the number of great houses in the rest of the canyon vary, depending on how the limits of both downtown Chaco and Chaco Canyon are defined.

2

The Siting of Pueblo Bonito

Anne Lawrason Marshall

The builders of Pueblo Bonito chose to site it on the north side of Chaco Canyon, opposite a break in the mesas to the south and beneath what we now call Threatening Rock, an enormous, fractured portion of the sandstone cliff that eventually fell and crushed part of the pueblo (Figs. 1.3, 2.1). Why was Pueblo Bonito built where it was?

One approach to answering this question is to examine those characteristics of the natural environment that were critical for human survival—characteristics such as temperature, precipitation, water sources, soil fertility, and vegetation. Another is to consider the possible religious significance of prominent natural features. For contemporary Native Americans, including Puebloan groups of the northern Southwest, the earth and its prominent features, such as unusual rock formations, buttes, mountains, lakes, and springs, are sacred (Bunzel 1932:483–487; Ferguson and Hart 1985:51; Loftin 1991:xvi, 9; Minge 1991:121; Silko 1995:155–169; Stevenson 1887:539; Swentzell 1997; White 1932:66, 142–146). Considering the archaeological and ethnographic evidence linking the modern-day Hopi, Zuni, and Acoma people to Chaco Canyon (Stoffle et al. 1994; Wozniak et al. 1993), it is fair to assume that the canyon's prehispanic occupants also revered the earth's features. Thus, because the Chacoans depended on their natural environment for survival and because natural features probably held religious significance for them, knowledge of their landscape is essential for understanding why their settlements were located where they were. I begin this chapter with a description of Chaco Canyon's natural environment and then compare the siting of Pueblo Bonito with the siting of other Chacoan great houses in relation to the landscape.

THE NATURAL ENVIRONMENT

Chaco Canyon is a wide, shallow canyon located in the relatively flat central portion of the San Juan Basin in northwestern New Mexico (Fig. 1.1). It was cut by Chaco Wash, an ephemeral stream that runs from southeast to northwest and flows only after downpours and spring thaws. The wash is entrenched more than 9 m below the canyon floor today (Vivian 1990:34), and although its channel perpetually undergoes cycles of cut and fill, it was at least 4 m deep at the time Pueblo Bonito was built (Bryan 1954; Judd 1964; Love 1977). The canyon floor is quite flat as a result of erosion and subsequent soil deposition from the wash. Its elevation at Pueblo Bonito is 1,866 m above sea level.

The central portion of Chaco Canyon contains the greatest concentration of cultural remains (Fig. 1.5). This part of the canyon is about 14 km long and from 0.5 to 1 km wide. Its north edge is a vertical wall of Cliff House sandstone rising 30 m to a gently sloping terrace or bench and then again to the top of the plateau 100 m above the canyon floor (Fig. 1.3). This wall is notched only by short canyons and does not afford easy access or a clear view to the north. In contrast, Chaco Canyon's southern edge is breached by two major gaps—South Gap, across from Pueblo Bonito, and Fajada Gap, dominated by the solitary Fajada Butte (Fig. 1.5). The canyon's south edge is an eroded Menefee shale talus slope overlaid with a series of small Cliff House sandstone terraces leading up to the mesa top (Hayes 1981:2–4; Vivian 1990:31–35).

Chaco Canyon's climate is quite harsh, both for humans and for the crops they might try to grow. Between 1941 and 1970, measured temperatures ranged from 38.9° C to –38.9° C, with an average annual temperature of 9.9° C (Vivian 1990:21). The canyon floor has an average of 150 frost-free days per year (Hayes 1981; Vivian and Mathews 1965), but between 1950 and 1970, Love (1977) observed a decline from 140 to 110. Chaco Canyon's mean annual precipitation is 22.1 cm. However, precipitation is highly variable. Vivian and Mathews (1965) found a range between 8.5 and 45.7 cm during a 28-year period. Seeps on both sides of the canyon provide additional water, and bedrock potholes and reservoirs on the north bench and plateau retain rainwater and snow. The only constant source of standing water is saline pools near the Escavada Wash (Vivian 1990:34). Paleoenvironmental reconstructions indicate numerous long- and short-term precipitation fluctuations, with a predictability average and range similar to those of the recent past (Cordell 1984:200; Gillespie 1984:39; Vivian 1990:22–24). Dean (1992:38–41) has suggested that intermittent alluviation periodically renewed the soil and that high alluvial groundwater levels provided a water source more reliable than the highly variable precipitation. These two characteristics may have made farming more predictably successful during some periods of prehispanic occupation.

Plant life on the canyon floor includes grasses and small shrubs in sandy areas near canyon mouths, four-wing saltbush and greasewood where there is less sand, and cottonwoods, willows, and tamarisks (an introduced species) along the wash. The plateau to the north is a mixed grassland with small

Figure 2.1. Threatening Rock in 1901, four decades before its collapse. Photograph by Charles F. Lummis, courtesy Museum of New Mexico, Palace of the Governors, neg. no. 6153.

shrubs. South Mesa and West Mesa are mixed grasslands with scattered, gnarled pinyon and juniper. Chacra Mesa has enough pinyon and juniper on its north slopes to be considered a woodland (Vivian 1990:35).

The prehispanic Chacoans employed at least three methods of floodwater farming. Sand dunes retained water at drainage mouths on the canyon's south side. Sandy soil on the canyon's north wall benches was watered by runoff from the cliff edge. And diversion dams, channels, and ditches delivered water from cliff tops and side canyons to gridded gardens on the canyon floor (Vivian 1992:51).

SITING

All of the great houses built on the central canyon floor are located on the canyon's north side.[1] This northern location offered several advantages. The canyon's vertical north wall shielded the great houses from northerly winter winds and allowed them to benefit from direct and reflected solar energy. Thus, south-facing Pueblo Bonito, stepping down from five floors on the north (cf. Stein et al., Chapter 4), functioned as a monumental passive solar collector. The northern location also provided closer access to water holes, reservoirs, seeps, and springs on the north wall benches and plateau and allowed for direct visual communication to signaling stations on mesas to the south (Hayes 1981:42, 61; Vivian 1983:3-13–3-14). The major disadvantages of being located on the canyon's north side were the higher temperatures from solar radiation in the summer and a greater danger of flooding than on the south side (Cordell 1984:255–256; Hayes 1981:61).

Pueblo Bonito's specific location is notable for two reasons.

The first is that together with the virtually adjacent great houses of Pueblo del Arroyo and Chetro Ketl, Pueblo Bonito was built directly opposite South Gap, one of the two major gaps breaching the south side of central Chaco Canyon. Second, Pueblo Bonito was constructed beneath an immense sandstone monolith known as Threatening Rock.

Pueblo Bonito's position opposite South Gap afforded several advantages. South Gap allows the low sun to enter Chaco Canyon, providing that portion of the canyon with more daylight and solar energy. South Gap's flat floor also provides an unimpeded transportation route to the south. With its back to a vertical wall and a view to the south as well as up and down the canyon, Pueblo Bonito's position would have allowed excellent surveillance and made the site defensible except from the cliff edge to the north (Bickford 1890:903). Infilling of doors on the structure's perimeter walls suggests that for at least part of its occupation, defense might have been an important consideration (Judd 1925a:245, 1964:34).

Another potential advantage of building opposite South Gap is the possibility of a framed view. With precise positioning, the gap could be used as a visual gate to enhance the appearance of Pueblo Bonito from the south or the view of the landscape from Pueblo Bonito. In order to achieve this effect, however, Pueblo Bonito should have been built a bit to the west. Stein and Lekson (1992:Fig. 8-9) suggested that construction of a pair of rectangular mounds to the south of Pueblo Bonito fabricated a framed view oriented toward the great kiva Casa Rinconada (Fig. 1.5; see Farmer, Chapter 5, for further discussion). This interpretation is an interesting possibility. But if the Chacoans had enough awareness of this visual technique to stage it, why did they not implement it with the existing natural feature of South Gap?

The reason may be the most notable characteristic of Pueblo Bonito's location—its construction beneath an enormous, precariously balanced, sandstone monolith. The Navajo name for Pueblo Bonito was reported by Holsinger (1901:19) as Sa-bah-ohn-nei, "the house where the rocks are propped up," by Judd (1925a:260) as Tse-biya hani ahi, "Place-of-the-braced-up-cliff," and by Wozniak et al. (1993:15) as Tsé Bíyah 'Anii'ahi, "Rock under Which Something Extends Supporting It." These names all indicate that the most significant characteristic of Pueblo Bonito for Navajos was its position relative to Threatening Rock. For Navajos living outside of Chaco Canyon, the name of the rock has been extended to include the entire canyon (Wozniak et al. 1993:14–15). The approximately 22,000-metric-ton, 30-m-high, 43-m-long rock dominated the landscape of the central canyon (Keur 1933:1, 8; Pinkley 1938). Why was Pueblo Bonito built beneath it? The site's builders must have noticed the rock's ominous potential for obliterating a large portion of any community constructed beneath it. But despite this danger, the Chacoans specifically chose to build there. The reasons may have been religious.

With its size and impressive appearance, Threatening Rock was a spectacular geological feature. If the prehispanic Chacoans were similar to their modern-day descendants (e.g., Hopi, Zuni, Acoma) in their beliefs about the natural world, then they might have considered the rock to be sacred. Although the location was hazardous, the earth beneath Threatening Rock might have been deliberately chosen as a building site because proximity to this sacred place was auspicious. This proximity might in turn have added to the sacredness that eventually came to be associated with Pueblo Bonito itself.

In examining Pueblo Bonito and its relation to Threatening Rock, we must consider that Pueblo Bonito was built in at least seven stages over several centuries (see Windes, Chapter 3; Lekson 1986:Fig. 4.20). Its earliest construction was a Pueblo I roomblock dated to the A.D. 860s and 890s (see Windes, Chapter 3; Windes and Ford 1996). It was built to the west of Threatening Rock and was not damaged when the rock eventually fell in 1941 (King 1941; McKinney 1941). Perhaps the original roomblock was carefully placed near enough to Threatening Rock to have a symbolic relationship with the sacred natural feature, yet far enough away to be in no direct danger.

During successive renovations and additions, Pueblo Bonito grew to the point that its easternmost portion sat directly beneath Threatening Rock. Given the obvious danger should the rock fall, it is possible that the builders deliberately chose to expand the site in this direction because they knew that the structure would eventually be crushed—in other words, Pueblo Bonito was intended to be a monumental architectural sacrifice. I propose this possibility of ritual destruction as a large-scale version of the ritual smashing of pottery that took place in the historic Hopi and Zuni pueblos (Cushing 1920:615; Talayesva 1942:315) and that Toll and McKenna (1987:178–181, 1997:214) have suggested happened at the nearby great house of Pueblo Alto. Whatever their ultimate intentions were, the Chacoans did make efforts to stabilize Threatening Rock in order to prevent or postpone its collapse. They jammed supporting pine timbers beneath the footing and built huge stone and earth platforms and buttresses (Holsinger 1901:19–20; Judd 1959b; 1964:141; Lister and Lister 1981:121; Schumm and Chorley 1964; also see Stein et al., Chapter 4).

Pueblo Bonito is not the only great house to be constructed near a distinctive rock formation. Casa Chiquita was built in central Chaco Canyon (Fig. 1.5) beneath an eroded cliff face with anthropomorphic rock pinnacles. This location is adjacent to Cly's Canyon, which would have been a source of water and an access point to the north mesa. I think these practical advantages were secondary to religious concerns. As significant natural features on the landscape, the anthropomorphic pinnacles were probably viewed as sacred. Their symbolic meaning might have been analogous to that of the rock in the contemporary Hopi pueblo of Walpi around which Snake dances are performed or to that of the Mother and Father pinnacles near To-wa-yäl län-ne (Corn Mountain), where Zunis leave offerings (Stevenson 1887:539–540).[2]

Another great house constructed near a distinctive rock formation is Kin Bineola. Located 17 km southwest of central Chaco Canyon on the edge of the Kim-me-ni-oli floodplain, Kin Bineola is surrounded on the north and east by earth and sandstone bluffs. These bluffs have eroded into sandstone-capped earth buttes that create a strikingly eerie landscape. There may have been a practical advantage to locating Kin Bineola in front of these bluffs, such as providing protection from the wind. But as extremely unusual features on the landscape, their primary attraction might have been that the Chacoans viewed them as sacred.[3]

In addition to the great house itself, a number of features have been found at Kin Bineola. They include a large earthen dam to divert water for irrigation agriculture, several shrines, a stone circle, an atypical great kiva, a mound, a series of parallel walls, a linear swale, and a line of upright stone slabs that might have marked a canal or a road segment (Marshall et al. 1979:57–68; Van Dyke and Powers n.d.). Apart from the dam, few of these features have been interpreted with any certainty, but some might have had ritual functions that were associated with the sacred character of the eroded buttes.

CONCLUSION

Practical considerations certainly affected the siting of Chaco Canyon's great houses. All of those on the central canyon floor were built on the canyon's north side, where they received greater solar exposure, were closer to water sources, and were visible to signaling stations. Pueblo Bonito and the adjacent great houses of Chetro Ketl and Pueblo del Arroyo were located opposite South Gap, where they could take advantage of additional sunlight as well as a view and an unimpeded path to the south. But practical considerations cannot explain why Pueblo Bonito was built beneath the spectacular geological feature Threatening Rock. Considering that contemporary Native Americans view significant natural features as sacred, I propose that Threatening Rock was a sacred site for the Chacoans and that they deliberately selected the ground beneath this sacred but hazardous feature for their largest and most elaborate piece of architecture. If Pueblo Bonito was located next to Threatening Rock because the rock was considered sacred, then it seems likely that Pueblo Bonito itself was a center of ceremony and power.

A larger question is, Why was central Chaco Canyon chosen as the place in which to build the largest and most spectacular prehispanic Puebloan structures? Perhaps the canyon's relatively favorable environment in a generally inhospitable region (Dean 1992:38; Vivian 1990:33) influenced people to build there. Another attraction might have been that Chaco Canyon is one of the two most significant geological features (the other is Chacra Mesa) on a relatively featureless plain (Vivian 1990:16). As such, the canyon might have been viewed as a sacred place. This sacredness could only have been enhanced by the canyon's central location in the San Juan Basin. Could it be that Chaco Canyon was known as the *sipapu,* the earth navel (Loftin 1991), the place where Puebloan people emerged from beneath the earth into this world? Members of Santa Ana Pueblo believe that prehispanic Chacoans settled in the canyon "because they were searching for a place of high religious and spiritual meaning, what they considered to be the center of the universe" (Stoffle et al. 1994:27). As the symbolic center of the world, Chaco Canyon might have become a pilgrimage destination for people throughout the surrounding region (Malville and Malville 2001). Perhaps this regional system emanated from Pueblo Bonito and its location beneath Threatening Rock.

NOTES

1. By great house, I mean the 12 buildings included in *Great Pueblo Architecture of Chaco Canyon, New Mexico* (Lekson 1986). Eight of the great houses are on the canyon floor, two are on the plateau immediately to the north, and two are on overlooking mesas to the south. Between 40 and 50 sites within Chaco Canyon have core-and-veneer masonry, a hallmark of great houses, and these sites are located on both sides of the canyon, with a cluster near Pueblo Bonito (Truell 1986:291–295).

2. The rock at Walpi can be seen in historic photographs of the pueblo. Offerings to the rock were described by Bourke (1962 [1884]:152–153), and Snake dances around it were described by Mindeleff (1891:65). I witnessed dances around the rock in 1989, but at my last visit to the Hopi reservation, in 1995, visitors were not allowed to watch the dances at Walpi.

3. For more information on the siting of Kin Bineola and other great houses outside Chaco Canyon, see *Anasazi Great Houses,* by Anne Lawrason Marshall, 1998–2003, http://www.its.uidaho.edu/chaco/.

3

This Old House

Construction and Abandonment at Pueblo Bonito

Thomas C. Windes

An understanding of Pueblo Bonito's chronology is a prerequisite for addressing questions about how the people who built the structure were organized, what the building's function was, and how many people lived there. Pueblo Bonito was occupied for at least five centuries from the A.D. 800s into the 1200s, and unraveling the spatial and temporal complexities of the site throughout this span is a daunting task. In this chapter I focus on several key chronological issues: the site's beginnings, its architectural development, remodelings, and reuse, and its final period of Puebloan activities.

The sequence I present for Pueblo Bonito's growth through time is similar to sequences outlined previously by Lekson (1986) and Windes and Ford (1996). The major differences lie in what I now think happened in the twelfth and thirteenth centuries, for which architectural styles are muted and tree-ring dates scarce. Besides reviewing how Pueblo Bonito developed, I look at its progressive disuse and abandonment. Although people sometimes perceive Pueblo Bonito as having constantly expanded, much of the site was in disrepair and abandoned even as new construction took place.

DATING TECHNIQUES USED AT PUEBLO BONITO

Among the chronological techniques that are informative for unlocking Pueblo Bonito's long and complex history, dendrochronology figures prominently. The site's construction stages can also be delineated through analyses of changing masonry styles. A relatively new technique, archaeomagnetic dating, has also proven useful, although it has not been widely used at the site. Finally, ceramics provide key temporal clues to Pueblo Bonito's final use and abandonment.

Dendrochronology

Pueblo Bonito offers an extreme case of building complexity and use, for which dendrochronology can provide an important but incomplete understanding. Unfortunately, the site's massive wood structural material was unknowingly frittered away for new building construction, souvenirs, and fuel during the early years of archaeological research and later during repair and stabilization. A structure that might once have incorporated as many as 25,000–50,000 trees in its construction was left with a paltry 2,947 original elements in situ by 1986, when the first systematic analysis of the wood was undertaken. By archaeological standards, happily, this is still a considerable number of potential tree-ring samples.

Judd (1964) first delineated Pueblo Bonito's construction sequence, and Lekson (1986) later refined it, using 168 dates from 342 tree-ring samples collected between 1895 and 1979. Between 1980 and 1998, 1,500 additional tree-ring samples were taken from Pueblo Bonito, mostly as part of the Chaco Wood Project, which started in 1985, resulting in nearly 450 new dates. A recent synthesis of this information (Windes and Ford 1996) is updated here to include architectural details described by Judd (n.d., 1964) and Lekson (1986) and new kiva and upper-story tree-ring samples.

Dendrochronology is best suited for illuminating when each of Pueblo Bonito's construction episodes began and for marking some subsequent repairs and remodelings. The technique provides, however, only a partial record of the site's chronology. Whereas tree-ring dates indicate a minimal occupation span of 268 years, from A.D. 860 to 1128, other chronometric data indicate that the building was used over a span of more than 1,800 years. We know that Pueblo I structures, built in the 700s or 800s, exist under the plaza (Judd 1964), that there was use of the building in the 1200s, and that later Athabascans and finally Euro-Americans used the building for storage, shelter, and building materials. Analogous situations of long occupation with extensive reuse of structural wood can be seen at the historic pueblos of Walpi (Ahlstrom et al. 1991) and Zuni (Ferguson and Mills 1988).

Architectural Masonry Styles

Much of Pueblo Bonito's construction can be dated using masonry veneer styles (Fig. 3.1) that have been correlated with tree-ring dates (Hawley 1934; Judd 1964:Pl. 10). These styles vary in the kinds of stones used and in the ways they are arranged. Early styles favored hard, dark brown sandstone of uniform size. Later styles used multicolored, softer, tabular stones of greater size variability. The latest style commonly incorporated large, soft, yellowish blocks, often ground smooth on the exposed surface.

In all, four masonry veneer styles were defined and dated by Judd (1964). Pueblo Bonito's earliest construction is associated with Judd's Type I masonry, dating in the 800s and 900s. Masonry types II–IV are associated with tree-ring dates in the 1000s. Pueblo Bonito's latest construction is in McElmo-style masonry (Lekson 1984), dating in the early 1100s or later, and a mixture of unclassified types.

Dating based on masonry styles is not without problems, which stem from the nature of the site itself as well as from classification of the various styles. One difficulty is that much of Pueblo Bonito's construction involved the reuse of earlier building stone (Judd 1964:114, 135, 170), diluting the accurate resolution of masonry types. Compounding this problem is that large areas of deteriorated masonry veneer were replaced during stabilization by the National Park Service in the 1930s. Moreover, the five defined styles are not all equally reliable for temporal interpretation. The least reliable is Type IV, which incorporates not only the classic small tabular blocks found in the southeastern roomblock and dated to 1081–1082 but also a mix of other styles that Judd (1964) misclassified. This problem is especially noticeable in kivas, a fact recognized by Judd (1964:125, 135, 165), who lamented that his type assignments were not precise. Nevertheless, his masonry veneer style assignments, when interpreted with caution, are effective tools for dating Pueblo Bonito's construction.

Archaeomagnetic Dating

Seven archaeomagnetic dates have been obtained from Pueblo Bonito (Table 3.1, Fig. 3.2). Although they add little to Pueblo Bonito's chronology, they do provide valuable clues to at least partial destruction of certain site areas.

Archaeomagnetic dating relies on the magnetic properties of clay. When baked under sufficient heat, clay forms a weak magnetic field that orients with the earth's changing magnetic field at the time of baking (see Weaver 1967 for a popular account). This phenomenon is useful for dating the baked clays in firepits or burned buildings. Samples from firepits normally coincide with either the initial use of the firepit or the last time firing exceeded 700° C (DuBois 1989). In a well-used firepit it is impossible to be sure whether the sample represents the first, the last, or an in-between firing. Nevertheless, archaeomagnetic dating is often the only tool available for dating a catastrophic fire that terminated a structure's use.

The proveniences of Pueblo Bonito's archaeomagnetic samples are a firepit in Kiva L, three very large ovens in Rooms 215, 220, and 221, respectively, and thick, highly oxidized wall plasters in Rooms 85, 108/109, and 298. The ovens, which are similar in size, shape, and construction, were built at different floor levels in rooms adjacent to Kivas A and B in the roomblock separating Pueblo Bonito's two plazas. Although only a few tree-ring construction dates came from this section of Pueblo Bonito, Lekson (1986:141–142) believed it was built after 1085.

Figure 3.1. Five masonry veneer styles used at Pueblo Bonito. From earliest to latest: *top left,* Type I; *top right,* Type II; *middle left,* Type III; *middle right,* Type IV; *bottom,* McElmo. Courtesy National Park Service, Chaco Culture National Historical Park, respective neg. nos. 20009, 19960, 19987, 19994, 19981; photographs by Stephen Lekson.

Table 3.1

Archaeomagnetic Results from Pueblo Bonito

Feature	ESO Lab No.	No. Specimens[a]	Demag Level	Declin.	Inclin.	Major Axis Pole	Minor Axis Pole	k[b]	VGP Paleo-Lat.	VGP Paleo-Long.	Alpha 95	Dubois Date (A.D.)	Wolfman Date (A.D.)	Latest Tree Ring Date	Date: Accept/Reject
Rm. 108/109 2d story, SE wall	1826	8/8	50G	342.6	61.9	1.4	1.8	2272	76.4	-167.3	1.2	1130 ± 12	1130–1170 1110–1150[c] 1155–1200[c]	1080	A
Rm 14/85 1st story, N wall	1827	8/8	150G	350.6	61.2	1.4	1.8	2176	80.4	-154.0	1.2	1100 ± 12	1015–1025 1195–1305 1030–1070[c] 1210–1255[c]	864	A
Rm 298 2d story, W wall	1828	8/8	150G	355.8	60.5	0.5	0.7	16452	83.6	-137.7	0.4	1030 ± 04	1320–1340 1360–1385 1000–1020[c,d] 1345–1360[c,d]	1047[e]	A
Rm 221, fl.1															
Firepit 4	1683	9/8	150G	342.6	61.7	5.8	7.5	130	75.0	-165.6	4.9	1120 ± 49	No date	1113[f]	A
Rm 215, fl.5															
Firepit 2	1684	8/8	200G	345.8	57.2	3.6	4.9	275	78.5	175.5	3.3	1140 ± 33	1125–1190[c]	1113[f]	A
Rm 220, fl.3															
Firepit 1	1688	10/7	200G	346.2	61.8	1.2	1.5	3724	77.2	-160.5	1.0	1110 ± 10	1070–1175 1180–1225[c]	1113[f]	A
Kiva L firepit	0018	9/7	150G	356.7	55.5	3.8	5.3	262	87.4	163.3	3.7	990 ± 37	No date	1083	A
NE foundation complex:															
Firepit 1	1731	8/8	50G	313.8	49.5	16.8	25.3	9	57.3	167.2	19.0	No date	No date	—	—
Firepit 2	1735	8/7	150G	236.0	71.0	18.2	20.9	26	13.1	-136.9	12.0	No date	No date	—	—

Note: Site longitude: –108.0°; latitude: 36.0°; declination: 13.6°. Wolfman laboratory number: add prefix DBCC to Earth Sciences Observatory (ESO #), University of Oklahoma, Norman. Plots made on the Wolfman 1990 Southwestern VGP curve. DuBois dates as of 2002.

[a] Number of specimens: number collected/number used at this demagnetization level.

[b] A measure of point dispersion on a sphere, employing Fisher's distribution. The higher the number, the tighter the point perimeter (i.e., the better the precision).

[c] Date given that fell on Wolfman's polar curve.

[d] Oval did not intersect polar curve; date given is to nearest point of curve at central point.

[e] Tree-ring date is from adjacent Room 296, originally built coeval with Room 298.

[f] Tree-ring date is from adjacent Great Kiva A.

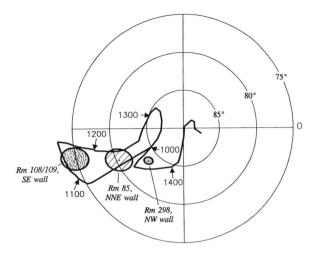

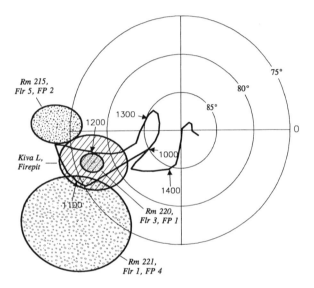

Figure 3.2. Archaeomagnetic plots of samples from Pueblo Bonito. *Top,* burned rooms; *bottom,* firepits. The heavy black line represents the changing position of the magnetic north pole from A.D. 1000 to 1500 in the Southwest. The magnetic pole is plotted on the Northern Hemisphere showing latitudes (concentric circles) and longitudes (straight lines) that converge on the center point at the true North Pole.

The archaeomagnetic dates support the time frame suggested by ceramics and tree-ring dates. The wall plasters that provided archaeomagnetic dates came from rooms with early Type I masonry, indicating initial construction in the 800s or 900s. Ceramics from these rooms suggest that they were used into the early 1100s. This use ended with intense fires that burned these rooms as well as others elsewhere at the site. For burned Room 108/109, whose latest tree-ring date is 1080, this destruction probably occurred in the mid- to late 1100s. The destruction of adjacent Rooms 85, 296, and 298, which probably burned simultaneously, may have occurred at the same

time or later. Whole vessels found in Room 298 (Judd 1954:Pl. 51) indicate last use at least in the 1100s, and the archaeomagnetic results (Table 3.1) suggest that the burning occurred in the 1300s.

Ceramics

The primary evidence attesting to Pueblo Bonito's last use—with emphasis on last use of the uppermost prepared first-story floor—rests with ceramics, including both whole vessels and bulk sherds. Nearly 1,000 whole vessels, mostly restorable, were uncovered by Pepper (1920:Table 2) and Judd (1954:186–217). Of these, 325 from 67 provenienced rooms and 11 kivas have been classified using current typology. The depositional contexts of these vessels, on the floor or fallen from the roof, provide clues to the final use of structures. That is, they help reveal whether the vessels were left in situ on the floors or roofs of rooms abandoned near the end of site occupancy or whether the vessels were deposited in abandoned rooms as trash resulting from nearby activities.

Unfortunately for archaeologists today, with the exception of a few sherds, both Pepper and Judd discarded their bulk ceramics. Information on Pepper's sherds is completely lost, because he kept no records (Windes 1997; cf. Reyman 1989). Judd maddeningly reburied most of his sherds in the west mound. Fortunately, Frank H. H. Roberts, a doctoral student at the time, tallied these materials from the site surface down to the uppermost floor for many rooms and kivas (Roberts n.d.; tallies on file with author). His tallies provide clues to the last use of approximately half the site (Fig. 3.3).

Ceramic type descriptions of the early twentieth century were less temporally meaningful than today's, but Roberts's (1927) work was excellent and can be compared, for the most part, to present ceramic chronologies (see Windes 1985, 1987b:624–634). There is no way, of course, to reestablish the vertical deposition of the latest ceramics except from the few subfloor tests. Even with subfloor results, one must be cautious, because Judd did not note intrusive ceramics resulting from rodent activity, remodeling, or subfloor pits. Sherds collected in recent years from reexcavated rooms (Windes 1993b) allow comparison with Roberts's findings.

Several attributes are critical for identifying the latest ceramic types found at Pueblo Bonito. Perhaps most important is the kind of paint used to decorate black-on-white ceramics. In contrast with pre-1100 ceramics, black designs on post-1100 ceramics were often applied with carbon paint. In his analyses, Roberts segregated his types primarily by design and slip, although he was cognizant that Mesa Verdean ceramics and, "in large measure," Chaco–San Juan vessels were decorated with carbon paint (Roberts 1927:180). He was clear in his separation of the critical types that he called Chaco–San Juan Black-on-white, which belongs to the Chacoan Cíbola White Ware

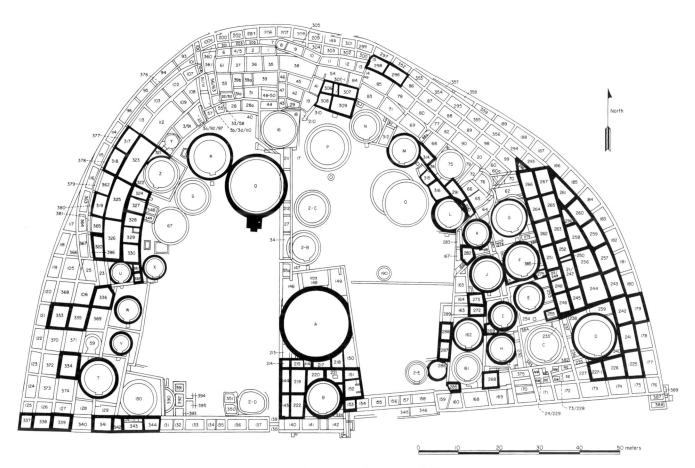

Figure 3.3. Selected proveniences for which Roberts's (n.d.) ceramic tallies are available.

tradition, and McElmo and Mesa Verde Black-on-white, later types of the Mesa Verde White Ware tradition. The last two types were prominent in the mid- to late 1100s and 1200s. They differ from Chaco–San Juan Black-on-white in their slip (thick pearly grayish white), decoration (absence of a narrow band of slip paint around the exteriors of bowls just below the rim but often with designs painted in black), and form (mostly bowls).

Ceramics attesting to use in the late 1100s are generally lacking in excavated Chaco Canyon sites (see McKenna 1991). Very few of Roberts's reclassified sherds at both Pueblo Bonito and Pueblo del Arroyo were McElmo or Mesa Verde Black-on-white. Roberts recognized 930 Mesa Verde Black-on-white sherds at Pueblo Bonito (0.4% of the total), almost all of them from bowls (94% of 300 listed by form). There is little doubt that these sherds represent true Mesa Verde Black-on-white or classic, late McElmo Black-on-white in both design and form. Mesa Verde Black-on-white pottery clusters in a few spots at Pueblo Bonito, primarily in kiva refuse, under upper kiva floors, and in rooms adjacent to kivas. Thus, some site use in the late 1100s or early 1200s is evident.

In his tabulations, Roberts (1927) found Pueblo Bonito's second most popular painted pottery to be what he called Chaco–San Juan Black-on-white (6.6% of 203,188 sherds). Only

recently has this material received type status as Chaco-McElmo Black-on-white (Franklin and Ford 1982; Windes 1985), although some of Roberts's Chaco–San Juan material includes types from the Chuska, Cíbola, Mesa Verde, and Tusayan white-ware traditions. Nevertheless, a similar preponderance of Roberts's Chaco–San Juan Black-on-white (5.6%) at nearby Pueblo del Arroyo has shown after reanalysis that indeed the vast majority can be safely equated with Chaco-McElmo Black-on-white (Windes 1985:Table 1).

Identifying the temporal range and period of dominance for Chaco-McElmo Black-on-white is critical to assessing much of Pueblo Bonito's latest use. I argued elsewhere (Windes 1985) that the type appeared by the very late 1000s and was the dominant type of the early 1100s. Since then, numerous tree-ring-dated samples in the 1100–1130 period from Kin Kletso, Pueblo del Arroyo (Windes et al. 1994), and Pueblo Bonito (Windes and Ford 1996), all with late deposition of masses of Chaco-McElmo, have affirmed this stance. Additional supporting evidence comes from Pueblo Alto (Toll and McKenna 1987; Windes 1987a) and Bis sa'ani (Breternitz 1982:Table 3).

Red wares, too, provide temporal clues to Pueblo Bonito's last use. Roberts (n.d., 1927) identified two types: early red

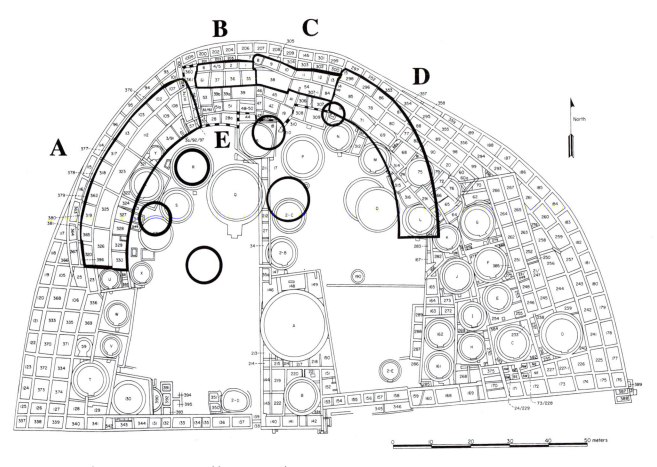

Figure 3.4. Early construction units at Pueblo Bonito. *A,* about A.D. 860; *B,* pre-860; *C,* 890; *D,* 900s; *E,* 900s?

("Indian" Red) and late red ("Cherry" Red). At least four red-ware traditions may be subsumed under these categories. However, Roberts's (1927:113) descriptions of late red as having "a deep, dark tint with soft appearance like that of a ripe fruit" and seeming "to have reached the Chaco at the same time as the Chaco–San Juan and to be closely connected with it" confirms its identity as primarily White Mountain Red Ware. This type is associated with assemblages of the early 1100s in Chaco Canyon (Toll and McKenna 1987:157; Windes 1987a:248). Overall, few red-ware vessels of any period were unearthed at Pueblo Bonito.

THE RISE AND ABANDONMENT OF PUEBLO BONITO

The kinds of chronometric data outlined in the previous section can be used to reconstruct the rise and abandonment of Pueblo Bonito. I summarize Pueblo Bonito's chronology in terms of five periods: the A.D. 800s, 900s, 1000s, and early 1100s and the years from the mid- to late 1100s to the 1200s. For each period I discuss the evidence for new construction, repairs, and remodeling. For the last three periods I also present the evidence for disuse and abandonment.

The A.D. 800s

Tests by Judd (1964:129, 131–132, Fig. 7) revealed two Pueblo I pit structures buried deep in Pueblo Bonito's West Court. Neither was thoroughly investigated, and no tree-ring dates were obtained, although a ponderosa pine had started growing in the West Court by the early 700s. This tree, undoubtedly an important symbol at Pueblo Bonito, may have become embedded in later construction themes at the site (see Stein et al., Chapter 4). Pueblo Bonito's earliest dated construction event is marked by a cluster of dates at 860–862 and 891. The earliest cutting dates, which fall between 828 and 862, are concentrated in the western and northwestern parts of the site (Fig. 3.4) and are associated with early Type I masonry construction, although some of these dates may come from beams that were robbed from earlier structures. No clustering of early dates within specific rooms can be observed, because of the widespread use of cottonwood and juniper. These species are difficult to tree-ring date, which leaves few early dated specimens from any specific room.

A second cluster of dates at 891 is found in a Pueblo I room group (Rooms 11–13, 54, and 84) that was added onto two previously constructed room groups (Rooms 1–2, 4–6, 8–10, 35–38, and 61). These dates suggest that Pueblo Bonito's north-

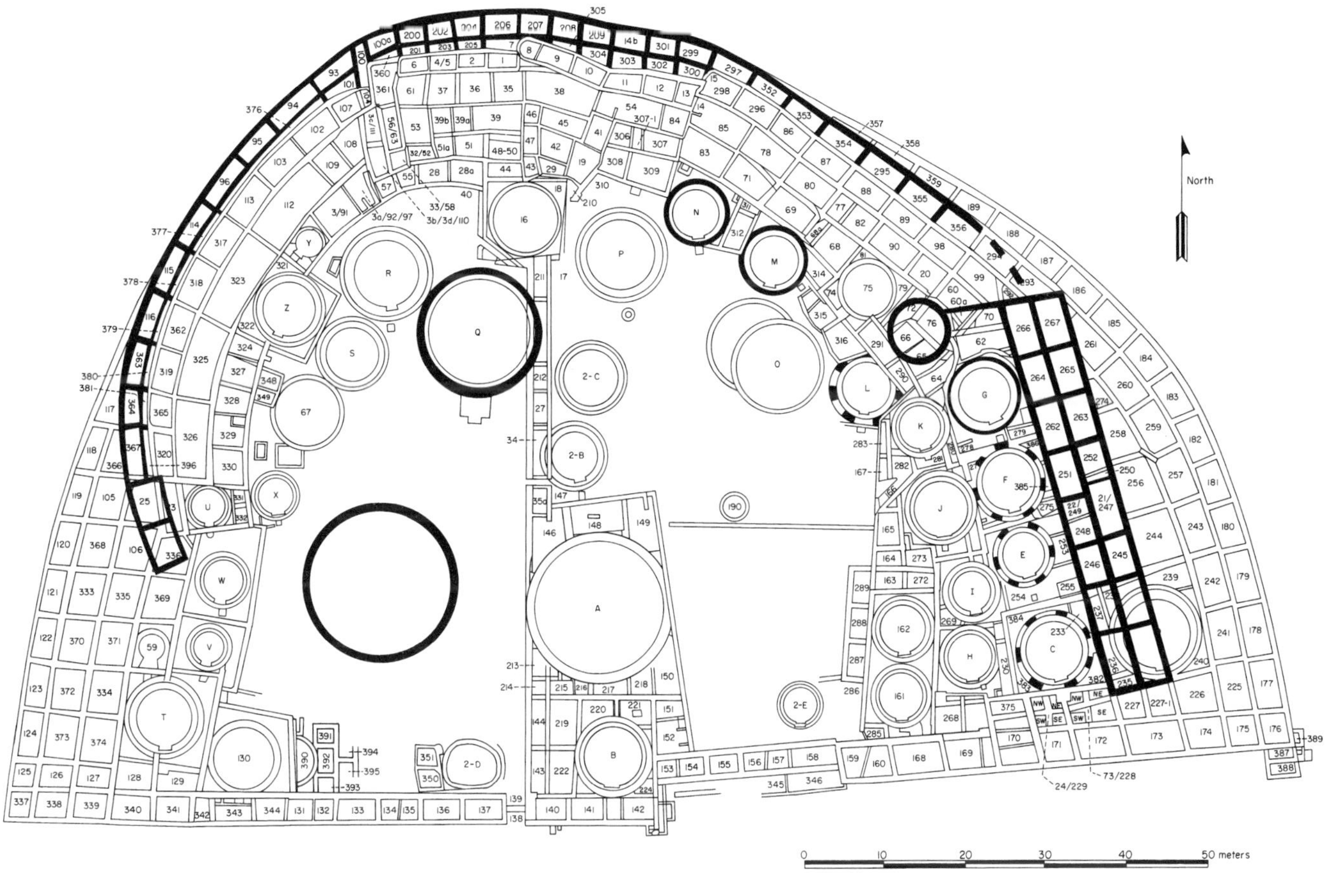

Figure 3.5. Additions to Pueblo Bonito in the A.D. 1040s. Dashed units are probable additions or mask probable buried units.

central area, which was once thought to date to 920–935 (Lekson 1986:27, 131), may be the earliest part of the site. Room 6, the westernmost storage room in one of the earlier room groups, still contains the original first-story roof vigas, or primary beams, and doorway lintels, but they cannot be dated because of the dominance of cottonwood. Room 6's location suggests that it is in the site's earliest structure (Rooms 1–2, 4–6, 35–37, and 61), dating to 860 or probably much earlier. Unfortunately, excavation notes are inadequate to determine whether or not these early Pueblo I units served as habitation suites, as would be expected in a normal Pueblo I house.

Judd (1964:Fig. 1) found early pit structures that were probably associated with these early above-ground constructions, but he did not explore them extensively. Other early pit structures undoubtedly exist—specifically just south of the early roomblocks (Windes and Ford 1992:Fig. 7-3)—but have been buried under later buildings.

The A.D. 900s

Our understanding of the rise of the Bonito phase and Chacoan great houses once rested heavily on a single well-dated roof in Room 320 on Pueblo Bonito's west side. From

its date of 919 and a few similar dates from nearby, archaeologists dated the initial construction of big-room suites, the basic units of Chacoan great houses (see Lekson 1986:131–132; Windes 1987a:356–362). New samples from lintels and roofing in the same construction unit, however, indicate that the earliest great-house construction at Pueblo Bonito occurred in the mid-860s, not in the 900s. A scattering of dates in the early 900s occurs elsewhere at the site but provides little insight into tenth-century construction. Abutments, house form, and new dates make it clear that the proposed early-900s construction in Pueblo Bonito's north center (Lekson's Stages IB and IC) is really a Pueblo I unit of three room groups built in the 800s. These room groups were extensively remodeled and continued in use for centuries. Further additions directly south of these buildings probably took place in the 900s, but overall there are very few construction dates from the 900s.

The Room 3 series of rooms (3a, 3b, 3c, and 3d), which overlaps the western big-room complex at its northern end (adjacent to Room 57 in Fig. 3.4, where the letter E overlies room numbers 3b and 3d), illustrates the interpretive difficulties at Pueblo Bonito. This series contains two intact roofs and several doorways. No visible piece escaped our Chaco Wood Project sampling of the 95 wood elements. Masonry style and the use of local wood species mark these rooms as early (e.g., 800s or 900s). Stratigraphically, the rooms overlie the big-room complex, which places the Room 3 construction later. The tree-ring dates range from the 800s to the late 1000s. Deric O'Bryan sampled these same rooms in 1940 for Gila Pueblo and, incredibly, selected only the few timbers that dated in the 1000s, thus suggesting an initial use of the rooms in the 1000s.

The Room 3 roofs are a hodgepodge of structural elements and closing materials. Yet the lack of uniformity of the roofs belies construction in the 1000s or even the need for repairs of roofs that have lasted a millennium. These rooms must have been built in the late 800s or early 900s. A photograph by Pepper shows that crews reroofed these rooms at least partially during his work there, and their reuse of later wood probably accounts for the late dates. Lekson's (1986:132) description of these rooms as a "warren" and "one of the most confusing areas" of the site is apt. Nevertheless, the special importance of this section of the site, with its wealth of unusual materials, cannot be overstated (see Neitzel, Chapter 9; Mathien, Chapter 10). Unfortunately, unraveling its complex architectural history is frustratingly inconclusive because it is unclear when these rooms were first constructed.

Cutting dates for Lekson's proposed Stage ID (section D in Fig. 3.4) range between 851 and 977. This unit, which is partially overlain by later construction, abuts on the west against the initial Pueblo I room groups dated at 891. Thus, dates, stratigraphy, and masonry style all suggest that Stage ID construction took place between 891 and 977. This area, which seems to have been used for habitation, was the only part of Pueblo Bonito where major building and renovations took place in the 900s. Parts of even later construction blend irregularly with the early construction, as if these early rooms were left unmaintained and then partly collapsed before new construction in the 1040s.

The A.D. 1000s

Several extensive construction events took place in the 1000s. They are apparent from date clusters that are much clearer than those for earlier events. Two building episodes, one in the 1040s and the other around 1080, stand out because of their strong date clusters, broad extent, close association with specific masonry styles, and identifiable construction units. Even though parts of Pueblo Bonito were of considerable age by the 900s and 1000s, their use is still evident. It cannot, of course, be determined whether this use was continuous. Ceramic data suggest that by the 1000s, many of Pueblo Bonito's older sections were no longer used as formal, bounded spaces or as floors for living and storage activities.

The A.D. 1040s

The long row of rooms appended to Pueblo Bonito's back arc (Fig. 3.5), reaching three stories in height and supporting an exterior balcony that later burned, is well dated between 1040 and 1049 (Lekson's Stage II). These rooms were attached as separate units to earlier roomblocks of the 800s and 900s, had doorway access almost exclusively to the outside or within the unit, and lay close, if not adjacent, to prehispanic roads. The best preserved pairs (Rooms 14b and 303 and Rooms 299 and 300; see Judd 1964:Pl. 12) were intact and had roof beams that spanned each two-room unit. Among the 44 dated timbers, 16 cutting dates cluster at 1029 and 10 cutting dates cluster at 1047. Adjacent rooms yielded smaller clusters at 1040 and 1047. A whole roof in Room 100a, shipped to the American Museum of Natural History in the 1890s and uncrated in the 1980s, yielded 22 timbers with 18 cutting dates between 1031 and 1049. The north doorway lintels of Room 100a date at 1049.

It could be argued that construction of these rooms began in 1029 and that later beams were replacements—but replacements would hardly seem to have been in order for roofs that have now survived for a millennium. Instead, a flurry of tree-felling activity at 1029, followed by sporadic cutting afterward, seems to herald years of stockpiling until more massive cutting in the 1040s and final construction in 1049 or slightly later. The widespread agreement of dates throughout this construction complex (23 multistory rooms and 42 features yielded cutting dates) and their association with Type II masonry mark this construction as a tight temporal unit.

A number of kivas yielded dates in the 1029–1049 period (Fig. 3.5), although most also revealed later remodeling. Three tree-ring samples cut between 1043 and 1048 were taken from Great Kiva Q during the Judd excavations. Their exact provenience is unknown, but they suggest that some construction or renovation took place in the kiva coeval with the addition of the road-associated rooms. The unnumbered great kiva in the West Court may also have been built at this time, if not a decade or so later. A date of 1039 on a wainscotting pole from Kiva M and the masonry style of Kiva N, along with a noncutting date of 973 from a pilaster log, indicate that these two kivas were built as a pair in front of the 900s living rooms. Although Kiva L yielded a number of later pilaster dates, one pilaster with a cutting date of 1047 suggests that the kiva might have been constructed or remodeled in the 1040s.

A north-south block of 12 to 16 rooms built in the southeastern part of the site may date earlier than Lekson's proposed 1050–1060 Stage IIIA (Lekson 1986:Fig. 4.20). This block yielded a scattering of cutting dates between 1027 and 1048 that suggests construction coeval with the road-related units. It is unclear how these two additions articulate, although foundations noted by Judd (1964:Figs. 4, 5) suggest physical linkage.

Several kivas built in a row fronting the southeastern rooms suggest a planned unit of kiva and room construction. The best data come from Kiva G, which revealed some Type II masonry and two 1029 cutting dates, one each from an intramural log and a wainscotting pole. Kivas C, E, and F are aligned in front of the north-south rooms and, unlike Kiva G, are elevated. Sometime about 1080, pit structures in great houses were built for the first time into the roomblocks, such that these nominally subterranean rooms were actually elevated above the ground surface. Thus, earlier kivas contemporaneous with Kiva G probably exist in the same alignment at plaza level under Kivas C, E, and F. Nearby elevated Kiva J yielded noncutting pilaster dates of 964, 978, and 1044, along with a cutting date of 1035 and later noncutting dates of 1080 and 1084. Either Kiva J was constructed at about 1035 or 1044 and later remodeled or it was built about 1084 and incorporated reused pilaster logs.

The A.D. 1050s and 1060s

Clear construction episodes during the 1050s and 1060s are not evident, although some remodeling of the north-south roomblock in the southeastern part of the site, or the addition of upper stories to it, may have taken place. A number of other units must have been built around this time (Lekson's [1986] Stage III, west side, and Stage IV), but dates and meaningful ceramic tallies are absent. A number of wood specimens dating in the 1050s and 1060s were found scattered in rooms buttressing the southern ends of Kivas C and D. Small date clusters suggest that parts of the earlier unit underlie or were incorporated into these later rooms or were salvaged from earlier units nearby when the later construction began. For example, Kiva C is architecturally suggestive of the late 1000s. It has one pilaster tree-ring date of 1120, but the remaining pilasters yielded three noncutting dates at or after 1064. Some of the date clusters are demonstrably earlier than the architecture in which they were found. This and other site examples suggest that wood reuse was localized within Pueblo Bonito, perhaps marking areas controlled by different social or political groups (see Ahlstrom et al. 1991:640 for an analogous example at Walpi Pueblo). It was also during the 1050s and 1060s that the lone ponderosa pine tree in the West Court died, surely an ominous event.

Dates from kivas rise dramatically during this period and shortly afterward. Kiva pilaster logs yielded a number of dates in the 1000s. Few were cutting dates, but overall most of the kivas visible at the site today can be said to have received at least some use in the last half of the 1000s or later. It appears that kivas built during this period and later were those used until much of the site was abandoned. Many of the earlier pit structures remain buried in the plaza and under later construction, where they are less accessible for investigation. Unfortunately for archaeologists, many kivas were built inside earlier ones and were later remodeled using salvaged stone, so that their occupational history as described by Judd, even with tree-ring dates, cannot be reliably deciphered.

A.D. 1071–1073

Dates from the early 1070s are rare at Pueblo Bonito but seem to indicate repair or remodeling of the 800s and 900s units in the northwestern sector. Dates from this period come primarily from 11 features (vigas and doorway and ventilator lintels) in 11 rooms. At least two of the outer doorways of the 1040s road-related units had their outermost lintels replaced at this time, presumably because of weathering. A few dated doorway lintels in the southwestern wing suggest either construction at this time or doorway repairs (Fig. 3.6A). This southwestern part of the site has few remaining wood specimens. The masonry style, however, suggests that much of it was built at this time (see Lekson 1986).

A.D. 1077–1082

Pueblo Bonito's last major construction event that is well-dated involved woodcutting between 1077 and 1082 (Fig. 3.6B). The wood samples that produced this cluster of dates were widely distributed, representing the most widespread building and renovation ever to take place at the site—an unprecedented event during Pueblo Bonito's long life. It was during this period that the procurement and treatment of construction wood became highly standardized (Windes and McKenna 2001). Cutting dates from this interval were obtained from 55 different features in 28 rooms, some of them three stories, and from Kivas C, F, G, J, L, Q, and X. A fourth story of limited extent was added to earlier rooms in the north-central area. The room dates suggest that first-story vigas and doorway lintels were cut mostly in 1076–1078, whereas latillas, or secondary roofing members, were harvested around 1080–1082. This latter interval probably represents the period of construction.

Renovations between 1077 and 1082, which previously went unnoticed by archaeologists because of a lack of dates and distinct masonry changes, took place throughout the site. New roofs were constructed and wall repairs were made in the very old rooms in the northern part of the site and in eastern areas built in the 1040s. Kiva X may have been built at this time. Many of the site's southeastern kivas, which had been built by the 1060s, yielded dates in the 1080s and were probably remodeled at this time.

Repairs were also widespread in the oldest western sections—those built in the 800s and 900s—particularly in doorways and ventilators. Oddly, it was the exposed lintels in room interiors that were replaced. A number of reasons might be suggested for this practice, including interpretations in the aesthetic and social realms. But practical considerations seem to have been paramount historically and probably were so in the past. Wood exposed to the elements in the Southwest deteriorates quickly and needs constant repair. But how is it that exposed lintels *inside* rooms would decay? This puzzling ques-

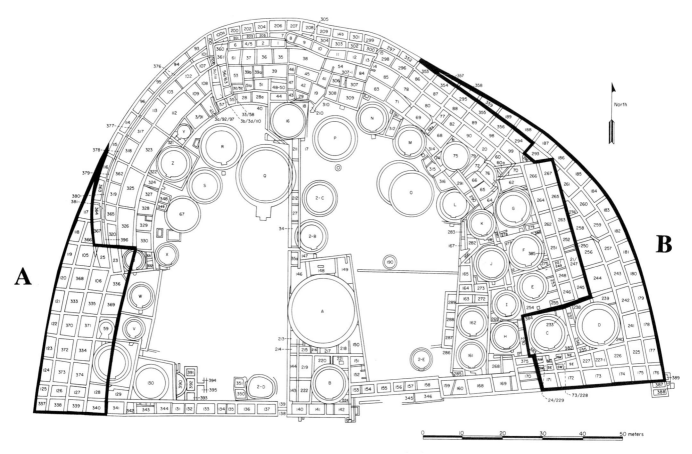

Figure 3.6. Additions to Pueblo Bonito in A.D. 1071–1073 *(A)* and in 1077–1082 *(B)*.

tion is difficult to answer if it is believed that Pueblo Bonito was kept continually in repair. If we envision the historic pueblos of Old Oraibi and Walpi (Ahlstrom et al. 1991), however, then we have a more realistic image of the site through time—one with newer buildings adjacent to those falling into decay. If the roofs of old rooms were salvaged for use elsewhere, then some inside lintels might have been exposed to the elements for long periods. Eventually, several of the older western rooms were renovated and used as mortuaries—four of them were deep in human remains (Judd 1964; and see Akins, Chapter 8)—and perhaps as an overall elevated platform (see Stein et al., Chapter 4).

A.D. 1082–1100

There is little evidence in the tree-ring record for major construction events after 1082, although extensive renovations continued. Dated lintels reveal that at least a few new doorways were added. A corner doorway in Rooms 242/244 was punched through the A.D. 1081 walls in 1089 (see Reyman 1976), and another doorway was added to Room 62 in 1090. A beam in Room 357 was cut in 1086, and finally, in 1097 a small room (Room 255) was sunk against Kiva C's outer retaining wall in the elevated east courtyard.

Disuse and Abandonment in the A.D. 1000s

Even while remodeling and new construction were under way at Pueblo Bonito, portions of the site had fallen into disrepair, something that can be seen in refuse deposition, mortuaries, and burned architecture. For this study I consider abandonment to have occurred when the architectural space no longer served as a formal enclosure with a formal floor. This definition disregards larger issues of ideology or cosmology. Furthermore, for purposes of this study I do not consider intermittent use of the architecture over the centuries for shelter, resources, and other activities to represent a continuum of Puebloan cultural use.

Interpretations of disuse and abandonment at Pueblo Bonito are greatly hampered by the poor quality of the data. This poor quality is attributable to early field methods, which dealt with complex postoccupational events as barely worthy of mention and treated fill as a mass of material to be disposed of quickly. In addition, relatively few of Pueblo Bonito's hundreds of lower floors and buried structures were extensively investigated. Finally, the record of events that does exist, as poor as it is, deals primarily with Pueblo Bonito's first story and offers only rare insights into upper-story use.

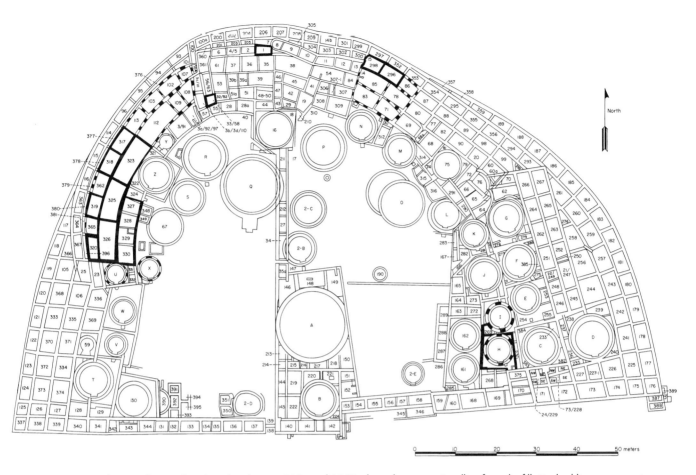

Figure 3.7. Architectural units abandoned in the A.D. 900s and 1000s, based on ceramic tallies from the fill. Dashed lines represent rooms primarily excavated by Pepper with poor ceramic information, along with subfloor deposits under kivas.

Despite these problems, a number of indicators allow appraisals of the last activities at the site and, importantly, when they occurred. These indicators include, among other things, the dwindling and eventual disappearance of later tree-ring datable timbers from the site; the deposition of pottery, including many whole vessels; the deposition of refuse on floors; and evidence of fires. Altogether, the data indicate that Pueblo Bonito underwent many of the same changes observed in historic pueblos—sections falling into disrepair and a continuous cycle of repairing, renovating, and abandoning enclosed spaces (see Ahlstrom et al. 1991).

Ceramic tallies by Roberts (n.d.) reveal that by the 1000s, many of Pueblo Bonito's western rooms were being used for refuse (Fig. 3.7) and burial. Overwhelmingly, whole vessels from these rooms are painted vessels of the 900s and 1000s. Room 326, for instance, yielded 75 identifiable vessels, the vast majority of them Red Mesa (22), Puerco (11), and Gallup or Chaco (32) Black-on-white, indicative of deposition beginning in the early 1000s, if not earlier, and then continuing. A similar pattern was observed for the 62 vessels collected from

nearby Rooms 320, 323, 329, and 330. The majority of the vessels dating to the 800s and early 900s unearthed at the site (13 of 16) were found in these rooms. Eleven late (post-1100) vessels also occurred in these and adjacent rooms, presumably in overlying deposits or fallen from upper floors.

Some of the old northern rooms, too, were filled with vessels. The vast majority of Pueblo Bonito's unique cylinder jars (Fig. 3.8) came from adjacent Rooms 28, 32/52, and 39B. As a group, these vessels were probably produced in the late 1000s and cached shortly afterward. Although Chaco-McElmo Black-on-white (3?), Chuskan Nava Black-on-white (1), and White Mountain Red Ware (1) cylinder jars were present (Toll 1990), vessels produced in the 1100s were rare in the cylinder jar caches overall. Considering the widespread use of Chaco-McElmo pottery in the early 1100s and its near absence in cylinder jar form, these forms may have been deposited by the late 1000s and seldom produced again.

The roomblock on Pueblo Bonito's eastern side built in the 1040s also seems to have accumulated refuse by the late 1000s, even though considerable use of the architectural spaces con-

Figure 3.8. Cylinder jars from Pueblo Bonito. Courtesy American Museum of Natural History Library, neg. no. 2A13697, photograph by P. Hollembeak and J. Beckett.

tinued. Room 266, for instance, yielded upper-floor cists packed with crushed vessels, suggesting ritual deposition similar to that of the crushed Gallup Black-on-white vessels found in the Pueblo Alto trash mound (Toll and McKenna 1987:178, 181; Windes 1987b:602). Cist 1 in Room 266 yielded 20 bowls of Red Mesa, Puerco, Gallup, and Chaco Black-on-white out of 22 identifiable bowls. Six Chaco-McElmo and two McElmo Black-on-white bowls from the twelfth century, as well as the majority of late painted sherds, were taken from trash deposits above the floor of Room 266 (Judd 1954:194), dating room abandonment no later than the late 1000s.

Overall, it appears that by the late 1000s, many of the older kivas and rooms, at the first-story level at least, had fallen into disuse. Ceramic tallies from under the uppermost floors of some rooms and kivas in the southeastern roomblock suggest a pattern of short use followed by refuse accumulation, then by a reflooring and presumably short reuse in the early 1100s, and finally by refuse accumulation again. This pattern is also seen in several kivas (Kivas H, I, U, V, X). Deposits under their upper floors were generally refuse and marked abandonment of the kivas or the earlier space underneath prior to the 1100s. This was followed by later renovation of the kiva or the construction of a new kiva in the earlier, rectangular enclosed space.

The Early A.D. 1100s

Pueblo Bonito continued to be occupied and used into the early 1100s (Fig. 3.9). The structure remained very much intact, with continuous construction, repair, and renovation. Its occupants, however, were treating it differently now: modi-

fying access, using much of the space for refuse deposition, and literally dismantling parts of it for building stone and timber. Similar behavior was taking place simultaneously at nearby Pueblo Alto (Toll 1985; Windes 1987b). The evidence that such activities were widespread at Pueblo Bonito consists of a smattering of late tree-ring dates, new and renovated structures, and abundant ceramic deposits dominated by Chaco-McElmo Black-on-white and red wares that appeared in the very late 1000s or early 1100s.

The widespread distribution of Chaco-McElmo Black-on-white ceramics indicates a substantial occupation or use of Pueblo Bonito in the early 1100s. Whole vessels of this type were prevalent throughout the area where Judd and Pepper excavated (60 vessels in the sample of 325 from 25 rooms and 1 kiva), along with White Mountain Red Ware vessels (11 vessels in 9 rooms and 2 kivas). Although we cannot be sure of primary deposition or redeposition of ceramics in many cases, it is clear that activities in the early 1100s occurred almost everywhere except, perhaps, in some of the site's older sections.

Construction at Pueblo Bonito during the early 1100s involved limited new building and extensive renovations. The evidence for this construction consists of a few tree-ring dates and the appearance of McElmo-style architecture. The general scarcity of tree-ring dates can be attributed to the poor preservation of McElmo-style construction, which was crudely done using soft mortar, soft sandstone, and salvaged beams. It should be noted, however, that substantial dendrochronological evidence exists for widespread construction of small and great houses at this time, both in the immediate vicinity of Pueblo Bonito and elsewhere in Chaco Canyon (Lekson 1986; Windes 1987a).

New building at Pueblo Bonito included rooms, kivas, and large firepits. Several types of rooms date to this period or later. Generally, they are smaller and less standardized in size than previously. First, there are some roomblocks (e.g., Rooms 287–289 and Kivas 161–162) appended to earlier architecture and appearing as a distinct small-house block. Second, there are small, single-story suites of rooms (e.g., Rooms 391–395 and Kiva 390) that were built adjacent to the plaza and mirror contemporaneous domestic architecture at nearby small sites. A cluster of rooms bordering the plaza's northeastern side (Rooms 65–66, 290–291, 315–316) contained firepits and suggests a warren of living rooms. Finally, there are semisubterranean habitation suites scattered about the plaza's periphery (e.g., Rooms 350 and 351 and Kiva 2-D; Windes 1987a:Pl. 10.13). Because of the paucity of tree-ring dates, it is impossible to say whether or not the different forms were coeval. Either way, they evidence a social change involving where and in what kinds of rooms Pueblo Bonito's residents were living or conducting rituals (many structures have ventilators and firepits).

Social changes are also indicated by Pueblo Bonito's new kiva construction during the early 1100s. This construction

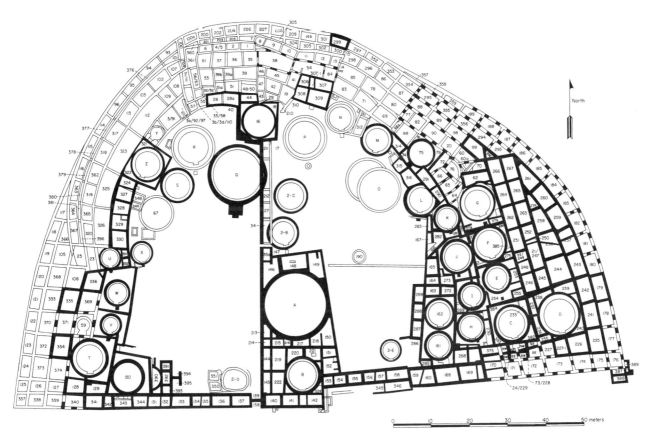

Figure 3.9. Construction and use of architectural space between A.D. 1100 and 1150, based on masonry style, ceramics, and tree-ring dates. Dashed units are probable use areas.

might indicate increased ritual activity. More likely, the shift to smaller, more dispersed kivas throughout the site, particularly in the plazas, signifies the return of small domestic units and corresponding small-house architecture at the site. Sometimes Judd (1964:184, Pl. 60) noted "Chacoan" kivas overlying non-Chacoan ones (e.g., Kiva 162), suggesting a reversal of architectural styles and plans, although this mixture of traits may be common to architecture of the 1100s.

The social significance of large firepits, which first appeared in Pueblo Bonito's plaza in the early 1100s, is unclear. These features have produced some of the site's latest dates, including the 1127 tree-ring date from a West Court firepit, just as they did at Pueblo Alto and Chetro Ketl. Almost all of the charcoal analyzed from these features at Pueblo Bonito was pinyon and juniper, indicating that the wood probably came from local trees. This procurement pattern differs from that documented for Pueblo Alto, whose large firepits were supplied with wood mainly scavenged from nearby roofs.

In addition to new construction, extensive repairs and renovations occurred at Pueblo Bonito during the early 1100s. This work involved major architectural refurbishing of structures that had fallen into disrepair as well as remodeling of existing structures. Delineating these repairs and renovations is

frustrating because building materials were scavenged, disrupting the reliability of masonry styles as temporal indicators. In addition, in some places it appears that the former masonry veneer had fallen away irregularly and had been replaced by later materials. As a result, many walls constructed or repaired in the early 1100s reflect a diversity of unclassifiable veneer styles.

The few tree-ring dates of the era indicate changes in access to space (i.e., doorways); this may also have been the time when many wall openings (doorways and ventilators) were sealed with the crude, blocky stone masonry typical of the period. New floors were added in older rooms and kivas, sealing beneath them refuse deposits that suggest a period of abandonment prior to the reflooring.

Renovations in Pueblo Bonito's older sections (Fig. 3.9) reveal that use of these rooms was still widespread during the early 1100s, although much decay is evident. For example, in the old northern section, beams cut after 1090 to 1116 were placed in Rooms 3d, 18, 44, 62/64, and 71. Some older rooms were subdivided by post-and-wattle walls (e.g., Rooms 256, 257, and 327–328) whose dates indicate construction in the 1120s or later. The exterior doorway in Room 299, one of the road-associated units of the 1040s, contains lintels cut in 1102, although, oddly, the doorway itself appears not to have been remodeled.

Some renovations also occurred in Pueblo Bonito's south-eastern areas. Changes made in and around Kiva D are perhaps most illustrative of renovations during this period. Kiva D was built by the late 1080s, if we are to believe the pilaster tree-ring dates, masonry style, and secondary placement of Kiva D within former rooms of the 1080s. Later, a narrow, ventilator-like tunnel was built extending east from an opening under Kiva D's bench to steps leading up to a doorway in Room 241. This tunnel would have cut into the first-story roof of Room 241 if it had been present, suggesting that the first story had been mostly filled in.

Kiva D and its enclosing wall were originally constructed of Type IV masonry. Sometime prior to the tunnel construction, portions of these walls either collapsed or were dismantled. When the kiva was subsequently remodeled and the tunnel built, the new walls consisted of large, McElmo-style stone blocks. The tunnel was roofed with planks that were covered with logs 12 cm in diameter; the latter date the tunnel construction to 1127 or shortly afterward. Sometime after this date, Room 241, Kiva D, and the southeastern wing burned.

More repairs and renovations are evidenced in kivas and rooms near Kiva D in the southeastern part of the site. Kivas C and 161 yielded pilaster-log dates of 1120 and 1109, respectively. Nearby, where Room 170 opened west into newly built rooms, the secondary doorway lintels were cut at 1107. Species use in the new rooms was dominated by spruce-fir and Douglas fir, revealing another shift in wood harvesting strategies. Tentative tree-ring dates also mark remodeling at 1102 of a doorway between Rooms 173 and 227.

Pueblo Bonito's latest construction tree-ring date of 1129 comes from a diagonal jacal wall that subdivides Room 256 in the southeastern wing. A similar post wall was built in adjacent Room 257. Both of these rooms were constructed in about 1081 or 1082, and the diagonal post walls were added roughly 50 years later to create access corridors through the rooms. During this 50-year interval, walls were repaired, ventilators were plugged, and doorways into some of the adjacent rooms and the outer rooms in the wing were blocked (Judd 1964:162). All of these renovations were done with crude masonry. The dates of the post walls place their construction with that of the Kiva D tunnel; Judd (1964:162) classified these walls as similar to late Pueblo III Kayenta architecture of the 1100s and 1200s.

The purpose of the post walls was to retain encroaching piles of trash. Refuse in the rooms is marked by quantities of the late ceramic type Chaco-McElmo Black-on-white. McElmo and Mesa Verde ceramics appear to be absent, suggesting that the space was abandoned by the 1130s or 1140s. Considerable windblown sand (46–69 cm) accumulated in the rooms after their abandonment (Judd 1964:32, 168), and the

rooms' collapsed roofs were subsequently burned (Judd 1964:32). This pattern is repeated elsewhere throughout the site, and it suggests that the general cessation of activities at Pueblo Bonito can be assigned to near the end of the 1100–1150 period.

The Mid- to Late A.D. 1100s and the A.D. 1200s

The site-use behaviors that characterized Pueblo Bonito in the early 1100s—modifying access, using much of the space for refuse deposition, and dismantling parts of the site for building stone, timbers, and perhaps artifacts—continued on a much reduced scale during the mid-1100s and into the next century (Fig. 3.10). Although the evidence for continuity is sketchy, it indicates limited use of a massive structure that resisted natural deterioration. When the structure was subsequently reoccupied in the late 1800s by Richard Wetherill and other new residents (see Levine 1989), their use of the site was similar to that of the 1100s and 1200s.

A paucity of recognizable cultural remains deposited between about 1150 and 1200 is not unique to Pueblo Bonito. It also characterizes both Salmon and Aztec Ruins, two other excavated Chacoan great houses located to the north near the San Juan River. The data from all these sites are problematical in two ways. First, distinctive masonry for the post-1150 period is an enigma, probably because so much stone was salvaged and reused and because earlier structures were often reoccupied. Second, no reliable tree-ring dates from either Chaco Canyon or the surrounding San Juan Basin exist for the 1200s. Because the post-1150 period is difficult to assess at sites other than Pueblo Bonito, it was probably a time of greatly diminished great-house activities throughout the San Juan Basin, with few residents and limited site use (see Brown et al. 2002).

The evidence for few residents and limited use at Pueblo Bonito after 1150 is both architectural and ceramic. The latest room masonry occurs in Rooms 28B, 55, and 57 and in the unusual "shrine" structures built at the site's southeastern corner (Judd 1964:173, 176). All of these rooms lie close together in the site's north-central area in front of the very earliest architecture, where a number of very late vessels were found. The rooms may represent a Mesa Verdean residential suite or special use area. Although similar room areas may exist elsewhere at the site, the evidence suggests that they are extremely rare. Judd (1964:173) noted that Kivas 16 and Z exhibited the latest masonry at the site and that some kivas exhibited Mesa Verdean plans (e.g., Kivas 59 and Y).

Late sherds and whole vessels were rare at Pueblo Bonito. The contexts in which they were found include abandoned rooms with substantial earlier deposition and structures with minimal refuse, suggesting that they were materials from last use. Either way, some activity is likely to have occurred nearby. That this late activity was primarily ritual is indicated by the

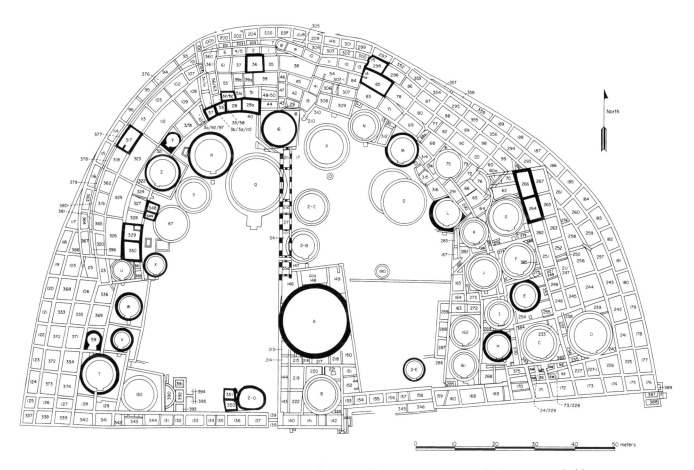

Figure 3.10. Architectural space used between A.D. 1150 and 1250, including upper stories. Dashed units are probable use spaces.

extremely limited evidence for habitation and the more plentiful evidence for the use of both kivas and uninhabitable rooms. The latter evidence takes two forms. First, late ceramics occurred most frequently in and around kivas. Second, many kivas were filled with natural sand (e.g., Kivas A, B, C, E, G, S, 2-B, 2-C), indicating that they remained in use until the end of the site's primary occupation (see Montgomery 1993:158), after which many were burned (Judd 1964:177). If few people were living at Pueblo Bonito after 1150, but many of the site's kivas continued to be used, then the kivas must have been serving people who lived elsewhere.

Determining how late particular kivas were used can be difficult, because of the complicated patterns of rebuilding and trash deposition. Great Kiva A, which was constructed of Type III masonry composed of "salvaged materials," yielded Mesa Verde sherds under the uppermost of its 17 floors and its latest bench, although the poor excavation records are not informative about the 16 earlier floors. It is likely that this great kiva, like others at Aztec and Salmon Ruins and probably Casa Rinconada and Chetro Ketl, experienced remodeling and reuse in the 1200s. Multiple floors (10–20) in several rooms at Pueblo Alto (Windes 1987b) were laid down in as few as 50

years, so those in Great Kiva A may not indicate particularly long, continuous use of the structure. Adjacent rooms, architecturally of the same construction, yielded firepit archaeomagnetic dates that could be interpreted as use in the 1100s or later, especially those from Rooms 215 and 220 (Table 3.1). Three shelf poles from Great Kiva A, recently tree-ring dated to 1113, may mark its initial construction.

Judd (1964:183–185, 196–197) was aware that in form and construction many late kivas (e.g., Kivas E, I, X, Y, 2-E, and 59) were "imports from beyond the San Juan River," although some may have been started much earlier. Much of their masonry was of scavenged stone. These were all associated with proto–Mesa Verde and Mesa Verde Black-on-white ceramics, although Judd may well have labeled Chaco-McElmo Black-on-white as McElmo (proto–Mesa Verde), as Vivian and Mathews (1965) did for the Kin Kletso ceramics. Either way, these kivas were clearly built late in Pueblo Bonito's use-life, although ceramics from them are largely missing from Roberts's (n.d.) tallies.

Other kivas with late ceramics are Kivas 2-B, H, and M. Kiva 2-B had been built in the early 1100s and was then abandoned and filled with naturally sterile sand for 1.5 m. Then, nearly a

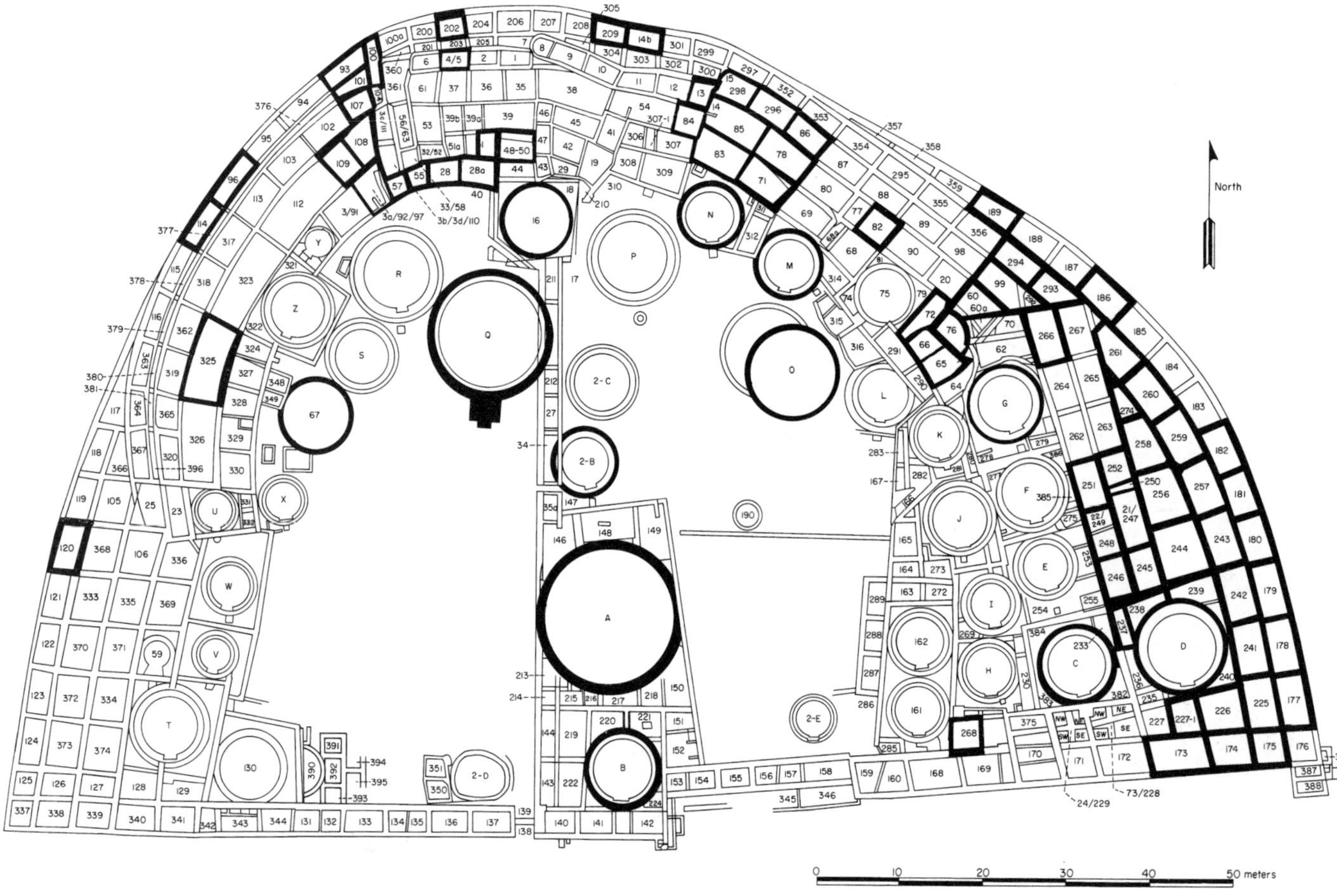

Figure 3.11. Architectural units burned in the A.D. 1100s, 1200s, or later.

meter of refuse associated with Mesa Verde Black-on-white sherds filled more of the kiva, until the remaining kiva roofing burned. Thus, the row of rooms subdividing the plazas and overlying Kiva 2-B (Fig. 3.10) must also be late. Kiva M contained a few McElmo Black-on-white vessels in its upper fill. The presence of a highly polished, pearly gray-brown (Mesa Verde White Ware) ceramic *paho* holder on Kiva L's bench and a McElmo Black-on-white bowl suggest the kiva's very late use.

Apart from kiva contexts, late ceramics also occur in rooms, some of which suggest ritual use. The most notable is Room 32, located in Pueblo Bonito's old north-central section. This part of the site contained numerous rare and valuable items (Pepper 1920; Neitzel, Chapter 9; Mathien, Chapter 10). Its contents included many ceramic containers of earlier periods as well as eight McElmo and Mesa Verde Black-on-white vessels, several of which were the diagnostic late mugs (see Pepper 1920:Figs. 47a, 48b, 49). The late vessels likely were additions to earlier caches, or perhaps the earlier materials were scavenged or curated. Either way, the late vessels suggest the perpetuation of ritual, although it might not have been temporally or culturally continuous.

Other rooms with late ceramics often occur in clusters. In

the old north-central section, McElmo–Mesa Verde Black-on-white bowls were found in adjacent Rooms 78, 14/85, and 298. Those in Room 14/85 were burned with the room contents, providing support for an archaeomagnetic date of the early to mid-1200s for the fire (Table 3.1). McElmo Black-on-white vessels were also collected in adjacent Rooms 264 and 266 and in a cluster of kivas (2-E, 161, and H) in Pueblo Bonito's eastern section. They also came from a cluster of rooms (323, 325, 327, and 330) and Kiva 67 in the site's old western section, as did a Tularosa Black-on-white vessel from Room 329. Room 317, in the same cluster, yielded two Mesa Verde Black-on-white jars. There is much earlier material in the room, however, which suggests it was abandoned long before the whole jars were left.

Pueblo Bonito's final Puebloan manifestation during the mid-1100s and into the 1200s suggests an opportunistic strategy of site use without full occupancy. The site's ultimate abandonment was marked by widespread fires (Fig. 3.11), which might have been simple vandalism or, more likely, ritual closure (e.g., Montgomery 1993:161; Wilshusen 1988; also see Stein et al., Chapter 4). Some of the people who used Pueblo Bonito in its final years and eventually burned parts of it possibly lived in the adjacent structure known as Hillside Ruin and

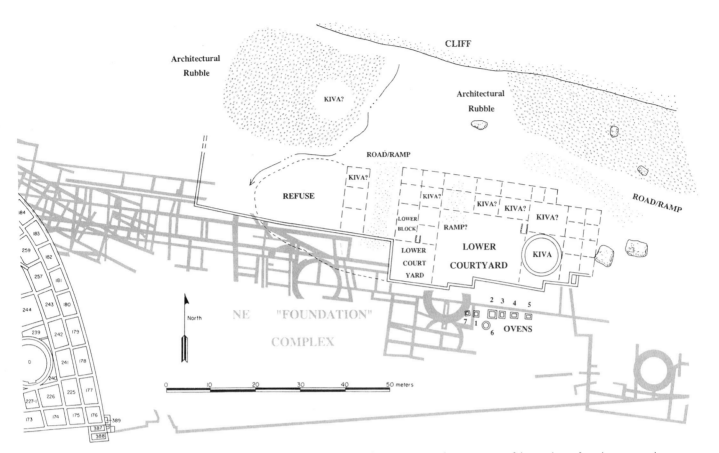

Figure 3.12. Plan of Hillside Ruin (A.D. 1100–1250), adjacent to Pueblo Bonito. Gray lines are part of the northeast foundation complex.

in the new post-1100 small houses that line the cliff base to either side of Pueblo Bonito and Chetro Ketl. Hillside Ruin is located a few meters east of Pueblo Bonito's standing walls and approximately 1.5 m above Pueblo Bonito's northeast foundation complex (Fig. 3.12), which was built in the mid-1000s. Hillside Ruin contains 20–30 rooms and kivas, courtyards, and perhaps platforms and ramps (see Stein et al., Chapter 4). It is constructed of "dressed block" masonry (Judd 1964:Pl. 47) of the 1100s McElmo style. When Judd (n.d., 1964:146–147) tested one of the site's kivas, he found proto–Mesa Verde sherds. He also noted that its construction was "decidedly non-Bonitian" and "later than Pueblo Bonito," although Stein et al. (Chapter 4) consider it an integral part of the architectural plan of downtown Chaco.

Similar settlements of the late 1100s and the 1200s appear adjacent to Chacoan great houses elsewhere. At Aztec's West Ruin, small hamlets were built just outside the great-house walls (Morris 1924). Their inhabitants used the great house for myriad activities, the most important of which were kiva rituals, storage, and burial (McKenna 1990). Limited stabilization excavations at Pueblo Pintado uncovered clear evidence of room reuse in the 1200s, with occupancy probably occurring in a late house built in the central plaza. At Pueblo Alto, a number of potential residential suites were built in the cor-

ners of the central plaza after the older roomblocks were abandoned (Windes 1987, vols. 1 and 2). A different pattern is evident at Salmon Ruin, which was practically dismantled and rebuilt by occupants during the 1200s (Irwin-Williams and Shelley 1980). These various patterns suggest a break in continuity between Chacoan and later use of the structures. Symbolic continuity not withstanding (e.g., Stein et al., Chapter 4; Stein and Lekson 1992), there seems to have been a distinct shift in site use and cultural continuity between the 1000s and the late 1100s.

CONCLUSION

Pueblo Bonito reveals a long, complex history of construction, remodeling, and deterioration. Our overall understanding of its construction events is probably good, but concurrent deterioration, dismantling, rebuilding, and abandonment episodes have been difficult to decipher. It is clear, however, that Pueblo Bonito does not represent an orderly, planned use of the entire site until an abrupt, final abandonment. Instead, it shares the complex stages of use and deterioration seen in historic Pueblo towns (e.g., Rothschild et al. 1993).

Pueblo Bonito's history, as outlined in this chapter, has implications for questions about how many people lived at the site and what its function was. The structure did serve as a residence, although architectural evidence for large numbers of inhabitants is lacking (cf. Vivian 1990:447). Unquestionably, occupation was widespread in the early 1100s. Exactly how many people lived at Pueblo Bonito and how their numbers changed through time is difficult to estimate, owing in large part to questions about how many of the structure's rooms (or kivas: Lekson 1988a, 1988b) were occupied at any one time. Attempting to answer this last question raises the issue of architectural abandonment, which has been a major theme of this chapter.

Keeping these difficulties in mind, the chronological reconstruction of Pueblo Bonito suggests that the site's resident population never exceeded 100 people (see Bernardini 1999; Windes 1984; Bustard, Chapter 7) and that it reached its peak either early (in the 800s or 900s) or in the early 1100s. Both periods seem to have generated much household refuse, especially firepit contents, which was relatively rare in the 1000s (Windes 1987, vols. 1 and 2). Although the relative lack of room habitation in the 1000s, marked by a paucity of domestic furniture, could be explained by a shift to kiva habitation (Lekson 1988b:128), kivas, too, lack the range of furniture associated with habitation space. After 1120 or 1130, residential population declined as widespread use of the site ceased.

Occupation of the site after 1150 was restricted in location and limited to just a handful of people until final Puebloan activities ended in the 1200s. Although the evidence is inconclusive, three or four areas adjacent to the plaza may have served for scattered residency of a few habitation groups each in the late 1100s and 1200s. The latest vessels collected from the site (McElmo and Mesa Verde Black-on-white) were scattered in rooms within and around the two mortuary areas and probably were associated with the small rooms with firepits that border the plaza. These places are typical for habitation because of plaza access and solar exposure and are concentrated in areas similar to those of residential small-site occupations.

Throughout its history, Pueblo Bonito was not just a residence. It also served other functions that changed in kind and relative importance through time. From the mid- to the late 1000s, ritual was an important, if not the premier, site activity, marked by the proliferation of large new kivas and great kiva construction, rare and unusual artifacts, and caches of status goods. Not only were construction events larger by the 1070s, but the harvesting of construction wood was intensified and more standardized, suggesting increased managerial control (Windes and McKenna 2001). Among specialized ceramics, cylinder vessel production flourished briefly, after which the jars were cached.

The site's ritual role may have shifted again in the 1100s, when many newly constructed kivas were small and bordered the plaza. New kivas and remodeled ones often reflected changes in architectural form in the construction of ventilators, roof-support pilasters, broad recesses, and, in one instance, a tunnel entrance to an adjacent room. By this time, orchestrated construction events seem to have been greatly weakened, and people returned to more diversified behavior in construction, habitation, and refuse deposition. Undoubtedly, links with previous events were embedded in ritualized behavior (see Stein et al., Chapter 4), but overall the kind of centralized effort that had characterized the earlier period was lacking (see Brown et al. 2002 on a similar shift in behavior at Aztec Ruins).

Another of Pueblo Bonito's functions, undoubtedly related to its role as a ritual center, was as a mausoleum, a role duplicated at Aztec's West Ruin. Sometime in the 1000s, at least, bodies began to be interred in two areas of the site's oldest sections (see Akins, Chapter 9). This practice, along with ritual deposition of artifacts, continued in these locations until about 1100, but surprisingly, later burials seem to be absent at Pueblo Bonito.

Besides addressing questions about the nature, timing, and intensity of Pueblo Bonito's various functions, I have tried to highlight the issue of continuity. Much of our sense of cultural continuity in great houses such as Pueblo Bonito arises from our interpretation of activities on the basis of material culture from a common architectural space. But this use of space, whether it reflects continuity or discontinuity in time and culture, masks activities, possible temporal breaks, and differences in cultural orientation by inhabitants adapting to an already present, massively built architectural environment resistant to normal deterioration. This study supports the possibility that Pueblo Bonito's cultural remains, perhaps by the early 1100s and certainly by the late 1100s, represent a non-Chacoan use of the site, that is, a break in cultural continuity. If so, then this break marks the cessation of Pueblo Bonito's role as the center of a complex polity that influenced events far beyond its local area.

ACKNOWLEDGMENTS

Analysis of tree-ring specimens from Pueblo Bonito has been funded by the Southwestern Parks and Monuments Association and the National Park Service, for which I am deeply grateful. My special thanks to Rachel Anderson for her computer skills and document research, Mary Jo Windes and Jill Neitzel for their very helpful editing, Cheryl Ford for greatly assisting with the computerized database, and John Stein, Dabney Ford, Anna Sofaer, and Gwinn Vivian for their lively discussions over what Pueblo Bonito was all about. John Stein and Richard Friedman also provided new insights into the form and possible use of Hillside Ruin.

4
Reconstructing Pueblo Bonito

John R. Stein, Dabney Ford, and Richard Friedman

From the onset of archaeological investigations in what is now the southwestern United States, Pueblo Bonito has been recognized as unique and important. As a consequence of the interest focused on this structure, it was extensively exposed and carefully mapped for purposes of exhibition and interpretation. Published plan views and cross sections of the site are exceptionally detailed (Judd 1964; Pepper 1920) and provide an excellent basis for reconstructing its architecture. Significant disparities exist, however, between popular reconstructions of Pueblo Bonito and the ground truth of the architectural remains. We use the term "ground truth" to include the physical remains as we experience them firsthand today as well as the primary archival documentation that describes the ruins at the time of their exposure.

In this chapter we present three popular reconstructions of Pueblo Bonito that picture the building as it might have appeared in the early twelfth century. Temporarily laying these images aside, we then assemble a comprehensive plan view of the building, dismantle it into construction periods, and model these periods in three dimensions. Finally, we offer some thoughts on Pueblo Bonito's design and purpose.

IMAGINING PUEBLO BONITO: A SHORT HISTORY

Credit for the first systematic description of Chaco Canyon's ruins goes to First Lieutenant James H. Simpson. In 1849, the Army Corps of Topographical Engineers commissioned Simpson to conduct a military reconnaissance of the Navajo country (Simpson 1850). The mapping effort was of very high quality, owing to the skill of Lieutenant Simpson and the talent of two artists, the brothers Richard and Edward Kern, who accompanied the expedition. At Chaco Canyon, maps, sketches, and descriptions were prepared for seven of the major ruins, including Pueblo Bonito (Fig. 4.1). Two of the expedition's guides—Hosta, of Jemez Pueblo, and Car-

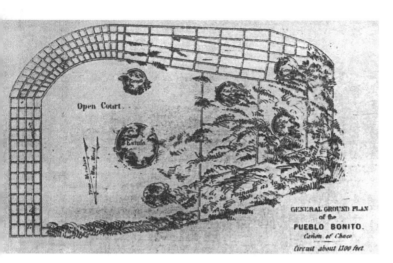

Figure 4.1. Plan of Pueblo Bonito by Richard or Edward Kern, 1849.

raval, of San Ysidro—are credited with naming many of the ruins. Simpson interpreted the buildings as the work of Aztecs, a common belief at the time.

In 1877, with Hosta as his guide, William Henry Jackson, a

photographer attached to the Geological and Geographical Survey of the Territories, visited Chaco Canyon with the intention of mapping, photographing, and describing the ruins. He mapped Pueblo Bonito (Fig. 4.2), produced an artist's reconstruction (Fig. 4.3), and cast several plaster models of the building (Jackson 1878). In the brewing controversy about whether Chaco Canyon's massive buildings had been built by indigenous people or by Aztecs, Jackson took the indigenous side. While en route to Chaco, he had visited Jemez Pueblo and the Hopi mesas. The influence of his familiarity with Pueblo culture can be seen clearly in his reconstruction of Pueblo Bonito. This image was, and continues to be, very influential. For example, the representation of Pueblo Bonito that currently hangs in the museum at Aztec Ruins National Monument (Fig. 4.4) is based on Jackson's reconstruction.

In 1888, Victor Mindeleff of the Bureau of American Ethnology, together with his brother Cosmos, spent six weeks surveying and photographing the central Chaco Canyon sites as part of a larger survey of Tusayan and Cíbola architecture (Mindeleff 1891:14). Like Jackson, the Mindeleff brothers were of the indigenous school. The Mindeleffs' major contribution

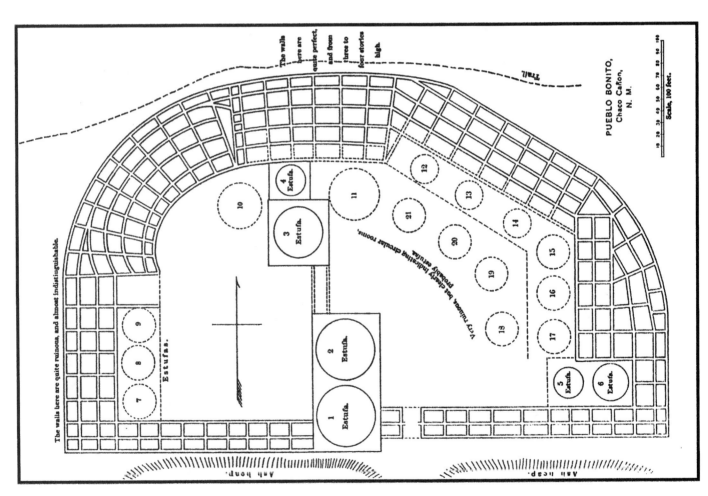

Figure 4.2. William Henry Jackson's plan of Pueblo Bonito, 1878.

is their photographs. Unfortunately, their maps and drawings of the Chaco ruins were never published and apparently have been lost.

In May 1896, the Hyde Exploring Expedition began excavations at Pueblo Bonito under the direction of F. W. Putnam of Harvard University and the American Museum of Natural History. Putnam was assisted in the field by George H. Pepper and Richard Wetherill. Between 1896 and 1899, their crews excavated 198 rooms and kivas, mostly in the building's north-central section, known as Old Bonito. In 1920, Pepper published what were essentially his excavation notes. They included a plan view of Pueblo Bonito showing the locations of excavated rooms (Fig. 4.5; Pepper 1920:Fig. 155). Pepper (1920:23) attributed this plan to Richard E. Dodge of Columbia University, N. C. Nelson, assistant curator of the American Museum of Natural History, and B. T. B. Hyde. In Pepper's book, N. C. Nelson described his role in making this map (Pepper 1920:387–388):

> Never having seen a satisfactory plot or ground plan of Bonito, I took occasion for my own satisfaction to make one, devoting some three days to the task. My only means were a table, a compass, a steel tape and some stakes; but I venture to hope that the general outline of the ruin as a whole, and also the really visible details of it along the southern and eastern sides, may be found to be tolerably correct. For although not made with this publication in mind, the plot has served, at least in part, as the basis for the appended ground plan, Mr. B. T. B. Hyde having, I believe, made some slight modifications as well as some additions based on Mr. Pepper's photographs, in that way making the ground plan exhibit features that are not now exposed to view. However, as the appended ground plan differs in several minor particulars from mine, e.g., in the vicinity of Room 76, I do not wish to be held entirely responsible for notable errors that may be discovered.

In his report on later excavations at the site, Neil Judd (1964:7) commented: "As explained in the 1920 publication, its accompanying ground plan was prepared by B. T. B. Hyde from Pepper's original memoranda and photographs, a preliminary survey made in 1900 or 1901 by Prof. R. E. Dodge, and a 1916 sketch by N. C. Nelson. That such a composite might include several inaccuracies was anticipated by Mr. Nelson . . . and those we have discovered have been corrected on our own plan . . . and so reported in text and tables."

Taking these disclaimers and criticisms into consideration, we georeferenced the Pepper (1920) plan view and the Judd (1964) plan view and then overlaid the two. We noted some minor oddities in the Pepper plan, such as the obvious addition of the mounds as an afterthought and the omission of detail in areas covered by backdirt or not yet excavated. However, the building's footprint and the outlines of excavated

Figure 4.3. William Henry Jackson's reconstruction of Pueblo Bonito, 1878.

Figure 4.4. Illustration of Pueblo Bonito at Aztec Ruins National Monument. Artist unknown. Courtesy Aztec Ruins National Monument, National Park Service; photograph by Taft Blackhorse.

features and rooms were essentially accurate. This should come as no surprise, considering that Dodge and Nelson were familiar with both field mapping techniques and Pueblo Bonito's architecture. If the Hyde Exploring Expedition produced a complete plan or reconstruction of Pueblo Bonito, we have no knowledge of it. We note, however, that despite Judd's claims to the contrary (Judd 1954:ix, 1964:v), Pepper's plan view was clearly the basis for later National Geographic Society reconstructions.

From 1921 to 1927, the National Geographic Society and the Smithsonian Institution conducted further excavations at Pueblo Bonito, under Judd's direction. Twenty years had

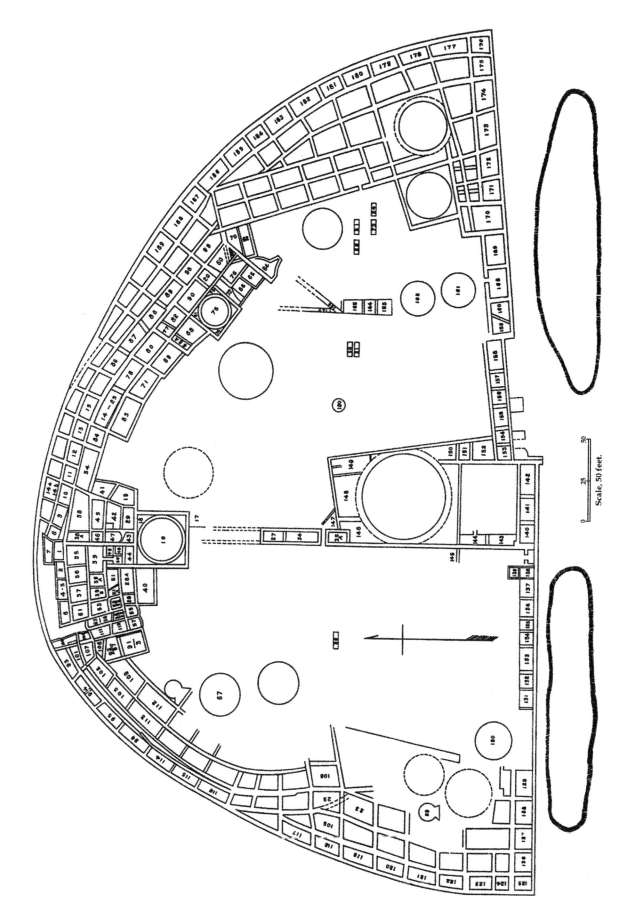

Figure 4.5. George Pepper's plan of Pueblo Bonito, 1920. Courtesy Anthropological Papers of the American Museum of Natural History.

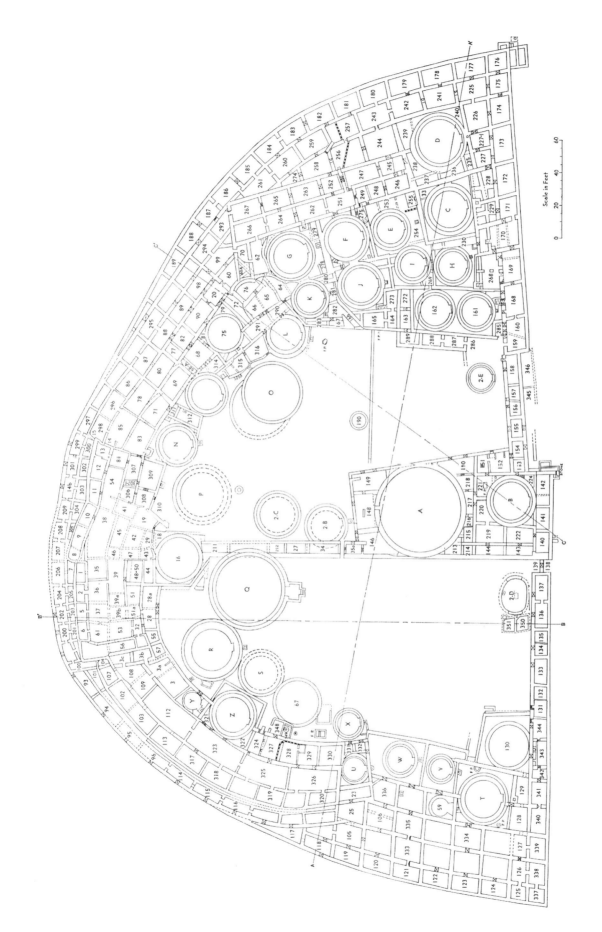

Figure 4.6. Plan of Pueblo Bonito by Oscar B. Walsh, 1925. Adapted from Judd 1964:Figs. 2–6. Lines labeled A, B, and C are cross sections illustrated in Judd.

Scale in Feet

0   20   40   60

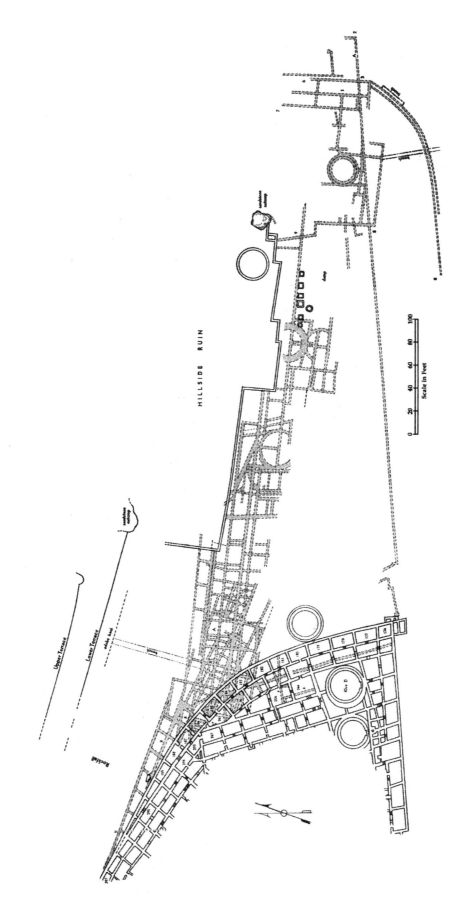

Figure 4.7. Plan of Pueblo Bonito's northeast foundation complex and Hillside Ruin, by Oscar B. Walsh, 1925. Adapted from Judd 1964:Fig. 11.

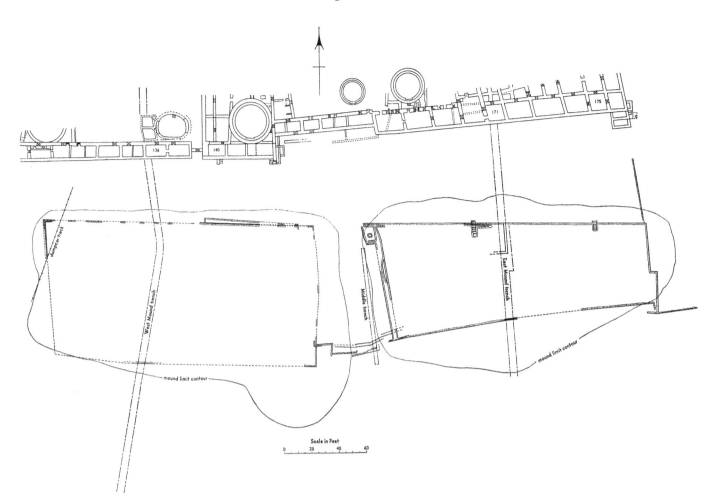

Figure 4.8. Plan of the mounds to the south of Pueblo Bonito, by Oscar B. Walsh, 1925. Adapted from Judd 1964:Fig. 23.

elapsed since the Hyde expedition, but its results had only recently been published (Pepper 1920). The objective of the National Geographic Society Expedition was to excavate Pueblo Bonito in its entirety and preserve it as an in-situ architectural exhibit. Judd's excavations balanced artifact collecting with architectural documentation and preservation (Judd 1954:17–18). As the ruin was exposed during the 1925 and 1926 seasons, Oscar B. Walsh of the U.S. General Land Office prepared ground plans and cross sections.

The complexity of Walsh's plan (Figs. 4.6–4.8) is apparent in the difficulty of illustrating it. In Judd's report (1964), it is presented in three components: the plan of the architecture within Pueblo Bonito's crescentic envelope (Judd 1964:Figs. 2–6), the plan of the foundation complex (Judd 1964:Fig. 11), and the plan of the mounds (Judd 1964:Fig. 23). The evolution of the structure is illustrated in four figures (Judd 1964:Figs. 3–6) supplemented by detailed cross sections (Judd 1964:Figs. 7, 13–15, 24). In order for these maps to be readable, they were reproduced in the volume at a scale that required an unwieldy, foldout format. These detailed plan views and cross sections were unavailable in published form until 1964, 35 years after

the close of the National Geographic Society Expedition and only 5 years before the initiation of the Chaco Research Center by the National Park Service and the University of New Mexico.

In 1926, Kenneth J. Conant of Harvard University's School of Architecture produced four reconstructions of Pueblo Bonito. Three of them are included here: the East Court (Fig. 4.9), an overview of the building looking south from the cliff edge (Fig. 4.10), and an overview of the building looking north from the south side of the canyon (Fig. 4.11). According to Judd (1954:ix, 1964:v), the Conant renderings were prepared especially for the National Geographic Society Expedition and were based solely on Walsh's plan views and cross sections. In reality, Conant's reconstructions were based on the plan produced by Dodge, Nelson, and Hyde and published in part by Pepper (1920). Evidence for the influence of Pepper's plan view includes, but is not limited to, the portrayal of the mounds without retaining walls, the depiction of a sunken square court where Kiva B should be located, and the omission of the northeast foundation complex and Hillside Ruin. Other details, such as the pine tree in the West Court, a fea-

Figure 4.9. Reconstruction of Pueblo Bonito's East Court by Kenneth J. Conant, 1926. Courtesy National Geographic Society, National Geographic Image Collection.

Figure 4.10. Reconstruction of Pueblo Bonito looking south from the cliff edge, by Kenneth J. Conant, 1926. Courtesy National Geographic Society, National Geographic Image Collection.

ture not discovered until 1924, suggest that Conant also communicated with Judd.[1]

It is curious that conspicuous features of the earlier, incomplete, and much maligned Pepper plan view survived Judd's scrutiny. One possible explanation is that Conant originally produced his renderings for fellow Harvard professor F. W. Putnam. If so, they may have been based on a more complete draft version of Pepper's published plan, produced by either Dodge or Nelson or by both. Renderings based on such

a plan could have been altered, or copied and altered, at a later date to reflect newly discovered features such as the pine tree. Another possibility is that Judd commissioned the renderings based on a more complete draft plan—the National Geographic Society Expedition did have access to the notes and photographs produced by the Hyde expedition for the American Museum of Natural History.

A closer look at both Conant's renderings and Judd's interpretations of Pueblo Bonito's architecture is warranted, given

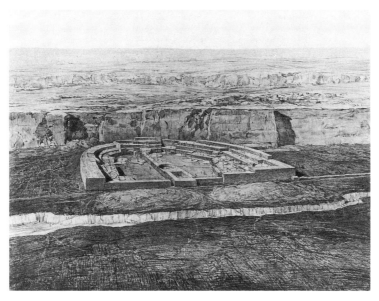

Figure 4.11. Reconstruction of Pueblo Bonito looking north, by Kenneth J. Conant, 1926. Courtesy National Geographic Society, National Geographic Image Collection.

our recognition that the Conant drawings were not based on Walsh's plan views, that we do not know who Conant's archaeological consultants were, and that disparities do exist between image and text. Judd believed that Pueblo Bonito was a village built and occupied by two distinct cultures, which he referred to as the "Old Bonitians" and the "New Bonitians." Judd saw the Old Bonitians as the occupants of Old Bonito for the building's entire use history. In his view, the New Bonitians arrived with their distinct masonry during what we call Stage II, completed Pueblo Bonito's construction, and then abandoned the structure to the custody of its first occupants.

Suffice it to say that Judd's view of Pueblo Bonito as village architecture is not entirely in agreement with the building portrayed in Conant's renderings, and conversely, important areas of formalization illustrated and discussed by Judd (which are also unvillagelike) were omitted by Conant. Conant illustrated a massive, highly integrated building with limited and controlled access. Broad open platforms form terraces four stories high on the east side of the crescent and two (three if one considers that the ground story of Old Bonito is buried) on the west side. Conant's treatment of Old Bonito shows the second story from grade in the north-center section as an open platform with narrow terraces of three- and four-story rooms occupying much of the northeast corner. Adjacent and to the east of this structure, Conant shows the north half of Old Bonito's east building as a single-story platform surrounded on three sides by three- and four-story massing, a configuration that again seems to derive from Pepper's plan view. In our reconstruction of this area, we show Old Bonito's

east building as standing three stories high, one story higher than the platform of the center wedge. Conant placed five stories in the center section of the back row of rooms. Were his model of Old Bonito's north-center section to be lowered by one story (because one full story lies below plaza level), such that the second-story roof is on the same level as Kiva 16's roof, our interpretations of this area would be in essential agreement. Overall, Conant's images of Pueblo Bonito are reasoned and generally faithful to the ground truth. Whoever coached these reconstructions was concerned with accuracy and was very familiar with Pueblo Bonito.

The most recent and perhaps best known reconstruction of Pueblo Bonito is an image painted by Lloyd K. Townsend for *Reader's Digest* (Fig. 4.12; Townsend 1986). It is reproduced on the cover page of the guidebook *Chaco Culture: Official Map and Guide* (National Park Service 1987) and also appears in the park's interpretive exhibit. The Townsend reconstruction appears to be based on the plan views published in Judd 1964 and is reminiscent of the Conant renderings, again suggesting that the artist relied on Judd (1954, 1964). Townsend also had access to expertise at the Chaco Research Center, and Stephen H. Lekson's influence may be inferred from the presence of the mounds (Lekson, personal communication 2000).

Having briefly discussed the dialogue (or lack thereof) between Judd and Conant, we now turn to that between Townsend and the Chaco Center. From our collective personal experience with both artists and archaeologists, we note that an information gap often exists where, in the interest of science, an archaeologist is clear and insistent on details of ar-

Figure 4.12. Reconstruction of Pueblo Bonito by Lloyd K. Townsend, 1986. Reproduced with permission from *Mysteries of the Ancient Americas,* © 1986 by the Reader's Digest Association, Inc., Pleasantville, New York, *www.rd.com.*

chaeological interest but vague or noncommittal about details the artist needs in order to paint a picture. In the interest of art (and to a great extent, practicality), an artist will fill this gap with material from his or her own background, experience, and belief. Townsend painted an appealing and powerful image of Pueblo Bonito, relying more, it appears, on his instinct as an artist than on the opinions of archaeologists.

The impact of this image owes much to technique—a stark contrast between the natural and the built landscape is emphasized by Pueblo Bonito's symmetrical and carefully balanced massing. The roof level on both the east and west wings is stepped uniformly from three stories on the south to five stories in Old Bonito's north-central building. The east and west halves of the crescentic form are portrayed as almost mirror images in both the horizontal and vertical planes. In short, Townsend masses Pueblo Bonito like a classical arch, emphasizing the keystone. In order to do this, he added three stories of fictional fabric to the footprint of Old Bonito's center wedge and one additional story to Old Bonito's east and west buildings. Although Townsend's reconstruction is striking and, we believe, successfully captures Pueblo Bonito's essence, it is not faithful to ground truth.

MODELING PUEBLO BONITO

Our approach to reconstructing Pueblo Bonito is that of reverse engineering. The term in its broadest sense describes the analytical process of dismantling a mechanical device in order to study its component assemblies and how they function together. This definition presupposes that we are already famil-

iar with the device's purpose. Here we use reverse engineering to analyze a foreign technology—a mechanical device constructed of unfamiliar parts, by unfamiliar hands, under unfamiliar circumstances, for unfamiliar purposes. We believe this approach is appropriate for the study of Pueblo Bonito because we view the structure as an assemblage of components arranged in ordered spatial and temporal relationships to accomplish a specific purpose (see Stein et al. 1997).

For this analysis, we are interested in visualizing in both two and three dimensions the spatial relationships among Pueblo Bonito's principal components through time. This goal requires that we be as accurate in three dimensions as we are in two. A tool used by architects to enable them to envision relationships between volumes is a "massing concept model." Such models allow architects to analyze and experiment with structural form as massing relationships among a building's primary volumes. At larger scales, massing models allow the architect to envision how the building will relate to context, such as adjacent buildings, a neighborhood, or features in the natural landscape.

Because massing concept models are intended to elucidate "pure form," they eschew unnecessary, distracting detail. Artists' reconstructions of pre-Columbian buildings often attempt the opposite—draping a veil of imaginative detail (children, turkeys, dogs, ladders, priests) over the form such that the structure becomes a prop for an interpretive message about daily life and ritual. We caution that the artist's reconstruction, and the message it conveys, is a powerful form of communication and should be used responsibly.

Building massing concept models of Pueblo Bonito involved four essential steps: combining Judd's two-dimensional plans into one comprehensive plan; identifying the boundaries and sequencing of the primary construction episodes; dismantling the plan and filling in gaps where necessary; and modeling the construction episodes.

Building the Comprehensive Plan

Our reconstruction of Pueblo Bonito is based on the detailed plan views produced for the National Geographic Society Expedition by Oscar Walsh in 1925–1926 (Judd 1964). The first stage of our analysis involved making a comprehensive site plan from Walsh's component plans. To accomplish this, we photocopied the published drawings and pieced them together using scissors and tape. We made multiple copies of the composite for use in the next stage of our analysis.

Identifying Construction Episodes

The second stage involved defining the boundaries of the principal construction episodes on the comprehensive plan. To accomplish this task, we had to rely on multiple lines of evidence—the results of previous analyses of Pueblo Bonito's tree-ring dates, masonry styles, and architectural relationships (Judd 1964; Lekson 1986; Windes and Ford 1996; Windes, Chapter 3).

In delineating Pueblo Bonito's primary construction episodes, we generally followed the sequence outlined by Lekson (1986). This sequence was derived from published dendrochronological dates that were available at the time of his study. Lekson also considered masonry style and architectural relationships. Our few deviations from Lekson's reconstruction are identified in our individual stage descriptions.

Recent dendrochronological analyses by Windes and Ford (1996) have led to several modifications of Lekson's sequence. The most significant changes are the revised dates for the initial construction, which is now conservatively placed at A.D. 860, and for the final construction, now placed at 1129 (Windes and Ford 1996:297). This span does not include the eighth-century pit structures discovered beneath the West Court, isolated dates in the 820s, or the possibility that the building was used well into the 1200s. Our version of Pueblo Bonito's closing hours (Stage V) follows Windes's (Chapter 3) analysis of the site's last construction and use as documented by ceramic, tree-ring, and architectural evidence.

Filling in the Gaps

Although previous researchers have produced a detailed picture of Pueblo Bonito's primary construction episodes, some gaps remain. They occur in several types of places: where the structure was razed for new construction, as in the case of Old Bonito's southeast room suite; where foundations disappear beneath construction that was not completely exposed by archaeologists, such as Great Kiva A and Hillside Ruin; and locations beyond the scope of archaeological excavations, such as the south half of the foundation complex. Filling these gaps was usually a simple matter of extending and connecting walls while taking into account proportion, measurement, geometry, symmetry, and pattern. We conducted this effort by hand, using trace overlays and colored pencils. It involved many layers of analysis and revealed a bewildering array of connections, patterns, and intriguing possibilities. These possibilities remind us that a great deal of Pueblo Bonito's architecture remains undiscovered or undocumented.

Two notable gaps, which we filled for this study, were the absences of plans for Hillside Ruin and the north platform. The National Geographic Society Expedition cleared the south outside wall and a kiva at Hillside Ruin; these features are shown on the published plan view of the foundation complex (Judd 1964:Fig. 11). Believing that Hillside Ruin was not related to Pueblo Bonito, Judd left it pretty much as he had found it—a reduced mound of adobe and masonry. We mapped the remains of the structure from visible wall alignments and mound contours (Stein et al. n.d.), then layered our interpretation of the building's upper north section onto Judd's interpretation of the lower south section. The two maps fit together nicely.[2]

We also included in our analysis the massive terrace or platform built north of Pueblo Bonito against the cliff wall and at the base of Threatening Rock. We obtained information about this structure, which is now completely covered by rockfall, from several sources. The terrace was described by both Judd (1959b:501–511, 1964:143–144, pl. 42, left) and Nelson (Pepper 1920:389–390). A topographic map drawn by A. D. Quackenbush (1934) shows the structure's shape and mass.[3] Quackenbush also showed the platform in his elevation and plan views of Threatening Rock. Details of this architecture may be seen in early photographs as well. At the time of the National Geographic Society excavations (1921–1927) and Quackenbush's mapping, only the platform's central portion was buried by rockfall. When Threatening Rock fell in 1941, it destroyed or concealed much of the platform's eastern end. A less spectacular but massive collapse occurred in 1987, dumping tons of debris onto the platform's western end.

Building the Models

The final stage in our analysis was building three-dimensional massing concept models for each of Pueblo Bonito's primary construction episodes. We began with a hands-on mechanical process. Plan views of Pueblo Bonito's progressive stages were copied, color-coded, and glued to a 5-cm-thick sheet of stiff Styrofoam insulation. A hot-wire device, designed to make finely controlled cuts on large sections of the Styrofoam, was

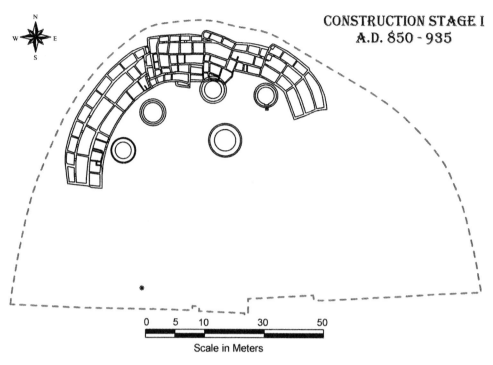

CONSTRUCTION STAGE I
A.D. 850 - 935

0   5   10   30   50

Scale in Meters

＊ Approximate Location of Ponderosa Pine

Figure 4.13. Stage I (Old Bonito) plan view (A.D. 860–935).

then used to cut along the construction episode boundaries and the elevation changes. A separate model was produced for each stage. We then took the models into Pueblo Bonito's ruins, where we determined basic massing relationships by direct observation. When questions arose, we resorted to excavation notes and archival photographs that illustrated the heights of standing walls or the contours of the rubble mound.

In addition to the three-dimensional Styrofoam models, we produced computer-generated models for each major construction stage. The computer modeling was accomplished in a Geographic Information System environment. Considerable time and effort were required to build spatially accurate, three-dimensional computer models. These costs, however, were offset by the need for spatially accurate data for future research in central Chaco Canyon, the dimensional accuracy of the models, and the savings achieved in manipulating and reproducing the images.

To produce the computer-generated models, we returned to the original published plan views (Judd 1964). These were scanned and digitized. Lines were converted to polygons, and individual components were assigned a feature type and a height. Height was determined initially by reference to the Styrofoam models and was subsequently cross-checked using 1:3000 and 1:6000 stereo aerial photographs acquired in 1973. At this step, we received a generous return on the effort invested in the solid models, because decisions about construc-

tion episode boundaries and massing relationships had already been made. Occasionally it was necessary to physically return to Pueblo Bonito for a reality check.

For our analysis of Pueblo Bonito's architecture to be as accurate as possible, we felt that our standards of positional accuracy should be equal to or better than the tolerances built into the structure by its original architect(s). This was no small challenge, considering that we were attempting to produce an as-built drawing of a large and complex building that was constructed of stone and adobe over a period of almost half a millennium, that was left open to the elements for another half millennium, and that has since been subjected to more than a century of treasure hunting, vandalism, "scientific" excavation, park development, and preservation work. Sources of error include, but are not limited to, concealed wall abutments; nonoriginal features in nonoriginal fabric; settling, twisting, and buckling of the masonry walls; errors introduced in the original survey through, for example, the stylizing of kiva form and general artistic license; and the effects of parallax on horizontal measurements.

Error is a possibility at every step and with every observation in every mapping effort, including that done at Pueblo Bonito. An example of error introduced by a survey mistake during the georeferencing process is the locational offset of Pueblo Bonito by more than 15 m to the northeast on the USGS topographic quadrangle. Error is often introduced dur-

Friedman, Stein, & Ford 2001

CONSTRUCTION STAGE I
A.D. 850 - 935

Figure 4.14. Stage I (Old Bonito) perspective view.

ing the drafting process—for example, in the use of uniform stylized wall widths, modification of awkward forms, and the arbitrary deletion or modification of significant detail. Distortion is also inevitably introduced in the printing process. An example of the perpetuation of this type of error is a widely published base map of Pueblo Bonito commissioned by the National Park Service, in which the draftsman copied distortion at the building's southwest corner (the corner closest to the book binding) that had been introduced in photocopying.

We used georeferencing to locate Pueblo Bonito's plan as accurately as possible. Ground coordinates were acquired for point locations that were stable and visible on both the ground and the plan view (e.g., the building's outside corners). Point data were collected over the course of many field sessions using a global positioning system (GPS) and a total station. Both of these technologies work to tolerances smaller than the radius of the range rod. After collecting sufficient georeferencing data, we translated Judd's published plan of Pueblo Bonito into real-world coordinates using an Afine Transformation Matrix to prevent uncontrolled warping of the original map data. We performed a number of tests for map accuracy, with the result that the maximum error in Pueblo Bonito proper was 0.5 m. Because most of the population of points analyzed was accurate, error in the occasional outlier could have been introduced in a variety of ways. The largest positional error occurs in the eastern end of the foundation complex. It was introduced by a poor match between

the original drawings at the foundation complex's western end (probably a drafting problem) and was exacerbated by the fact that most of the architecture in this area is buried and inaccessible as a landmark for georeferencing. Overall, a maximum positional error of 1.0 m (3%) in an area the length of three football fields is quite respectable and more than adequate for the purposes of this study.

STAGE DESCRIPTIONS

In this section we present our reconstructions of Pueblo Bonito's five major construction stages with a verbal description, a plan view, and a perspective view for each stage.

Stage I: Old Bonito (A.D. 860–935)

Old Bonito is a crescent of multistory surface rooms focused on a grouping of below-grade circular structures of the type Southwestern archaeologists call "kivas" (Figs. 4.13–4.14). One of these kivas exhibits the attributes of an early "great kiva" (Lekson 1986:143). Overall, Old Bonito's form resembles that of other houses of the period, but on a much larger scale (see Bustard, Chapter 7). Old Bonito's "big rooms" measure from 7.5 by 3.5 m to 10 by 4 m. This is some four to six times larger than the analogous rooms of contemporaneous households in Chaco Canyon (also see Windes and Ford 1996:300). Tree-ring dates for Old Bonito are few, but they suggest a construction history beginning perhaps in the A.D. 820s—certainly by the mid-800s—and concluding in the last quarter of the 900s (Windes and Ford 1996:301).

Old Bonito's boundaries are clearly delineated by the uniform use of Type I wall masonry (Fig. 3.1) and a characteristic room arrangement. Type I masonry encompasses a distinct structural technology, appearance, and texture. Walls of this type are characterized by limited stone-to-stone contact and wide mortar joints. The typical Type I wall is of simple or double simple construction (see Lekson 1986:20), with the width of the primary masonry slab elements determining the wall's thickness. Flakes were struck from the primary masonry elements in a treatment called scabbling, and the rather wide spaces between these elements were veneered with tightly packed, tabular spalls. Today, few Type I walls retain the original spall veneer. Without it, the narrowness of the wall and the exaggerated ratio of exposed mortar to masonry is a formula for structural failure.

From an engineering perspective, the Type I wall was clearly experimental—it could not bear the load or provide the loft required of later core-and-veneer masonry. According to Judd (1964:26), Old Bonito's ceilings averaged 2 m in height, with little variation, whereas ceiling height in the eleventh and twelfth centuries averaged 2.5 m and ranged to more than 4 m. Much of Old Bonito was three stories in height. However, keeping the foregoing figures in mind, the height of the building would have been less, possibly much less, than that of three stories of later construction. Even taking the low ceiling heights into consideration, three stories of Type I wall would have posed significant stability problems. In Stage II, the issue of stability may have been the impetus for the placement of fill around the old structure to a depth of one story.

As illustrated in Figure 4.13, Pueblo Bonito's two most notable characteristics—its arched back wall and its cardinal north-south central axis—are artifacts of Old Bonito. A closer examination of Old Bonito reveals three separate wedge-shaped buildings that in plan resemble the keystone and flanking voussoirs of a semicircular arch. Although the buildings are contiguous and share a common wall where they abut, this wall is like a firewall in that internal passage between the three units appears to have been restricted. In plan view, the individual buildings exhibit radial symmetry. However, the projected alignments of the internal architecture do not share a common focus. The central building establishes Pueblo Bonito's cardinal north-south central axis and is focused on this axis at its intersection with what would ultimately become Pueblo Bonito's front, cardinal east-west wall. This is also the gate into the West Court. The western building is focused on a large kiva in the West Court and also addresses the central gate in the north-south spine wall that connects the East and West Courts. The eastern building is focused on the center of the early great kiva.

Virtually all of Pueblo Bonito's high-status goods and

human remains came from Old Bonito, especially the center building (see Akins, Chapter 8; Neitzel, Chapter 9; Mathien, Chapter 10). Included in the long list of items is a cache of cylinder jars, including early as well as late ceramic types (Pepper 1909, 1920; Judd 1964:58). The central wedge is set apart from Old Bonito's east and west sections by the small size and apparent asymmetry of its interior rooms. Lekson (1986:132) described this area as a "warren of rooms." Judd described Old Bonito generally as a "haphazard agglomeration" with no recognizable "point of beginning," and he guessed that the "cluster of small, crowded structures at the top of the crescent" represented Old Bonito's nucleus (Judd 1964:58).

Of interest concerning Pueblo Bonito's earliest construction is Judd's (1964:22) discovery of the remains of two eighth-century pit rooms beneath the West Court. He illustrated the stratigraphic position of these pit structures in cross section (Judd 1964:Fig. 14), showing surface features at a depth of 2 m and the pit structures' floors at a depth of 3.5–4.0 m below the west plaza's surface. Judd (1964:21–22) described the eighth-century surface as deeply buried by natural overburden and speculated that the remains of this earlier construction were unknown to Old Bonito's builders. Contradicting this view is the cross section, which shows Old Bonito to have been constructed directly on the eighth-century surface. The floor of Great Kiva Q, a Stage II construction, lies at the same level as the older pit structures' floors—a coincidence perhaps, but suspicious.

Judd (1954:143, 154, 225–226) also described numerous examples of layered clay pavements. Many appear to have been localized, but one pavement below the northeast foundation complex, abutting the lower terrace of the braced-up cliff, was quite extensive. Its depth corresponds closely to the eighth-century surface, suggesting the possibility of significant site development (razing, leveling, sculpting, and paving) prior to or coeval with the establishment of Old Bonito. There are other possibilities. In the second generation of his notes (essentially the first draft of *The Architecture of Pueblo Bonito*), Judd mentions that the adobe pavement by the braced-up cliff was "piled up against" a massive retaining wall of Type III masonry. This places construction of the retaining wall and adobe embankment in Stage III or later. Nevertheless, we believe that the large-scale use of adobe originated in Stage I and continued throughout Pueblo Bonito's construction history.

Stage II (A.D. 1040–1050)

Our Stage II (Figs. 4.15–4.16) closely follows Lekson's (1986:132) Stage II, Judd's (1964:78–124) Second Bonito Addition, and Windes and Ford's (1996:301–302) dendrochronological sequence. From a technological perspective, Stage II features fully developed core-and-veneer masonry, Judd's Type II. Stage II appears to have had four primary objectives. One was the

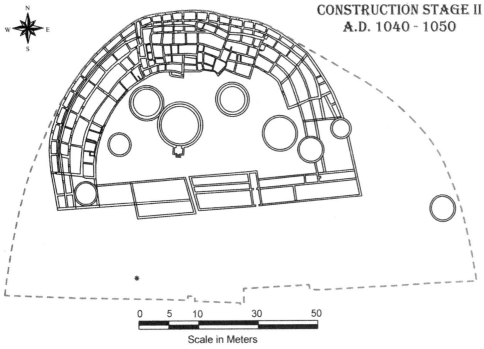

CONSTRUCTION STAGE II
A.D. 1040 - 1050

0   5   10   30   50
Scale in Meters

* Approximate Location of Ponderosa Pine

Figure 4.15. Stage II plan view (A.D. 1040–1050).

Friedman, Stein, & Ford 2001

CONSTRUCTION STAGE II
A.D. 1040-1050

Figure 4.16. Stage II perspective view.

construction of a massive structure wrapped around Old Bonito's back wall. This structure was one room or cell in width, 30-plus rooms in length, and up to four stories in height. This Stage II addition enlarged Old Bonito while being faithful to the building's original form. It also provided much-needed buttressing for the unstable fabric of Old Bonito, now approximately two centuries old.

A significant aspect of Stage II construction is the location

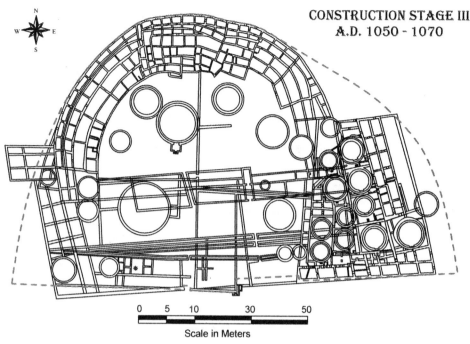

CONSTRUCTION STAGE III
A.D. 1050 - 1070

Figure 4.17. Stage III plan view
(A.D. 1050–1070).

0   5   10   30   50

Scale in Meters

＊ Approximate Location of Ponderosa Pine

of grade. By the time Stage II construction was initiated, the level of the West Court had been raised approximately 2 m. Outside Old Bonito's arc, grade had been raised 1.5 m or more. As a result, Old Bonito's first-floor rooms had become fully subterranean (Judd 1964:10). Thus, the foundations of the new Stage II (above-grade) construction correspond to the second-story floor level of the now partially buried Old Bonito. With its foundations at Old Bonito's second-story level and its ceiling heights of approximately 3 m, the Stage II addition would have stood considerably above the roof level of the earlier building, especially Old Bonito's center building, which was primarily of two-story construction.

In Figure 4.16, we show the Stage II addition as continuous across the back of the center building. However, after comparing the high massing on the ends of this building with the absence of standing wall and the minimal rubble in the intervening area (from examination of early photographs), we wonder whether Old Bonito's center building might have been open to the north to accommodate the central north-south axis. We can only guess at the nature of this opening; it appears to have been a wide notch in the Stage II addition and may have terraced outward and upward from the roof level of Old Bonito.

A second objective of the Stage II construction was to connect the ends of Old Bonito's crescent with low walls and what appear to have been raised platforms to formally delineate the space inside the arc. Although it is much larger and more complex, Pueblo Bonito's final enclosed form can be seen in the Stage II plan (Fig. 4.15). As Pueblo Bonito expanded

to the south, old construction appears to have been razed to foundation level, then filled, and finally paved over or concealed by new construction. There is also the possibility that some of these walls were never more than foundations. In our reconstruction (Fig. 4.16) we took the middle ground between full height superstructure and foundations at grade by showing the south, or front, enclosing wall as approximating the height of a high foundation or low stub wall (approximately 1 m). We then elevated the platform enclosures an additional 1 m, assuming that these structures were functional, filled platforms. The "foundations" are enigmatic structures created by means of pouring a rubble and clay slurry into trenches (Peter McKenna, personal communication 2000). Because they are below-grade structures, they could easily have been paved over.

A third objective of Stage II construction was the building of Great Kiva Q tangent to and west of the north-south center axis. We wonder to what extent the fill material utilized to raise the surface of the West Court was derived from the excavation of the great kiva.

The final objective during Stage II was to shift Pueblo Bonito's overall axis from 360 degrees to 351 degrees (9 degrees west of north) on the north-south axis and from 90 degrees to 85.4 degrees (4.6 degrees north of east) on the east-west axis (see Farmer, Chapter 5). The previously established cardinal axes had been consistently perpendicular, whereas these new axes were about 4.4 degrees from perpendicular. Up close, however, the intersections of wall alignments in the new orientation scheme appear to be perpendicular.

Figure 4.18. Stage III perspective view.

Stage III (A.D. 1050–1070)

In Stage III, Pueblo Bonito's plan became very complex, and many alternative interpretations are suggested by a labyrinth of foundation walls. In our Stage III scenario (Figs. 4.17–4.18), a building footprint emerges that articulates on its long axis with Old Bonito, preserves the axis bearing (85.4 degrees) established in Stage II, and pushes the closing wall farther south to accommodate the construction of a large great kiva in the West Court. The Stage III footprint is an elongated parallelogram with a block of elevated kivas on the eastern end facing a newly constructed great kiva on the western end. While this layout logically extends the theme established in Stage II, it also creates an independent great house–great kiva relationship with an orientation rotated to an axis roughly perpendicular to the orientation of the Old Bonito crescent. Thus, the placement of the great kiva in the West Court addresses the architecture of Old Bonito as well as the new Stage III addition, which is both independent from and integrated with Pueblo Bonito's emerging form.

Our Stage III generally agrees with the reconstructions proposed by Lekson (1986:134–135) and Windes and Ford (1996:302). At this point we depart radically from Judd (1964). His Second Late Bonito Addition (see Judd 1964:Figs. 4–5) includes sections of our Stages III and IV but only pieces of the massive eastern block of kivas, which is a critical component of our Stage III. We are confident that this block was built as a unit. Windes (Chapter 3) also views the east block as a unit but places it later in time, from A.D. 1081 to 1130. He is correct: the east block certainly has the appearance of a stand-alone, late (McElmo period) building, and the tree-ring record tells the story. Our question is, Does this building predate the mass of four-story construction behind it? Was the construction essentially coeval? Or could the east block have been a late intrusion into an existing mass of architecture?

Recognizing the reality of the 1081–1082 dates, we still decided to place the east block in our Stage III on the basis of the building's lower northeast corner, which had been plastered and partially razed and which abuts the northeast foundation complex (Judd 1964:145). From Judd's description of this corner, we postulate that a structure occupied all or portions of the east block's footprint during Stage III but was razed to foundation level (as was Old Bonito's southeastern corner) and replaced by part of the massive construction effort that finished Pueblo Bonito's east side. Thus, although we are reasonably certain that a building of proportions similar to the east block existed at that location in Stage III, the building in our illustration (Fig. 4.18) is probably a Stage IV replacement.

As a final note for Stage III, we decided, somewhat arbitrarily, to place the formalization of the north terrace—the platform at the base of Threatening Rock—in this construction stage. Our reasoning is not entirely logical, but no single

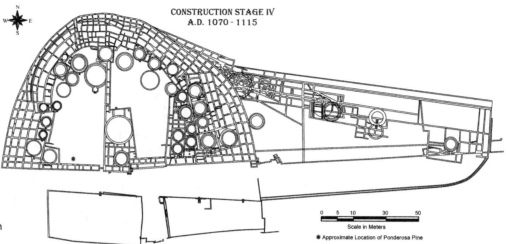

CONSTRUCTION STAGE IV
A.D. 1070 - 1115

0 5 10   30   50
Scale in Meters
✻ Approximate Location of Ponderosa Pine

Figure 4.19. Stage IV plan view (A.D. 1070–1115).

scenario is faithful to all of the facts as we know them. Our story is that the extensive clay pavement described by Judd (1964:20, 143) is essentially a Stage I surface. The foundations for Stage II construction behind Old Bonito were approximately 1.5 m above the level of the clay pavement (the floor level) of the earlier building. Judd (1964) described the fill underlying Stage II construction as natural accumulation. We wonder, however, whether it might have been intentionally placed there. Judd, in his notes, described the adobe embankment below the "Braced-up Cliff" as piled up against a masonry retaining wall of Type III veneer. We interpret his statement to mean that this masonry wall was behind the embankment and therefore must have preceded it in time. The massive adobe embankment, then, must postdate both the clay pavement and the masonry retaining wall. How did the adobe embankment come to be beneath Stage II fill? We do not have the answer, but we do know that in Pueblo Bonito's final form, the space between the back wall and the north terrace is a section of a formalized "roadway." We believe that this roadway is as old as Old Bonito.

Stage IV (A.D. 1070–1115)

Stage IV (Figs. 4.19–4.21) involved major construction throughout Pueblo Bonito, including razing the southern half of Old Bonito's east building and joining Old Bonito and the east block with new construction; laying the northeast foundation complex; formalizing the mounds; completing the crescent with the east and west additions; formalizing the site axes with construction of single-story room rows; and razing the great kiva in the West Court's southern half and constructing Great Kiva A. Our Stage IV incorporates Lekson's (1986:135–144) Stages IV–VII and Judd's (1964:Figs. 2, 5) Third and Fourth Late Bonito additions.

Old Bonito and the East Block

Stage IV began with a major construction event dated at A.D. 1077–1082, possibly the single most ambitious undertaking in Pueblo Bonito's construction history (see Metcalf, Chapter 7; Windes and Ford 1996:303). This event involved the razing of Pueblo Bonito's eastern section, specifically the southeast end of the Old Bonito crescent, to make way for a roomblock that articulated the east block with Old Bonito. This construction is essentially Lekson's (1986:135) Stage IVA and is included in Judd's (1964:Fig. 5) Second Late Bonito addition. As discussed previously, the east block may have been razed to its foundations and the superstructure replaced in a late eleventh-century form.

The Northeast Foundation Complex

The northeast foundation complex as described by Judd (1964:143–153) consisted of a network of low walls extending east from Pueblo Bonito (Figs. 4.19, 4.21). Lekson (1986:136) placed the complex in his Stage V and dated its construction at A.D. 1070–1075. We include the foundation complex in our Stage IV for convenience but entertain other possibilities in our conclusion.

The east-west alignments are 0.56–0.97 m wide and 1.35–1.47 m high and appear to have been built directly upon the Stage I clay pavement. The north-south alignments are 0.36–0.51 m wide and 0.15–0.51 m high. They were constructed upon 0.51–0.61 m of sand that rested in turn upon the clay pavement. Everywhere in this sand were construction waste, adobe droppings, and early and late potsherds. Judd (1964:149) explained that what he had formerly thought to be constructed "pavements" he now believed to be overbank sediment. Cultural or natural, Old Bonito and the foundation complex's major east-west alignments appear to rest on this surface.

Figure 4.20. Stage IV perspective view of Pueblo Bonito proper.

Figure 4.21. Stage IV perspective view of all of Pueblo Bonito.

Judd (1964) described the walls of the northeast foundation complex as consisting of friable sandstone rubble and copious amounts of clay mortar. He also indicated that these foundations were identical to those found elsewhere beneath Pueblo Bonito. Judd puzzled over the maze of alignments and concluded that they were plans for expanding Pueblo Bonito that were abandoned in favor of the building's present configuration.

Lekson (1981) suggested that the northeast foundation complex functioned as a construction blueprint at a one-to-one scale. He later observed that in great-house construction, the plan would have been formalized by completing the building's foundations before initiating work on the superstructure (Lekson 1986:15). Thus, the foundation functioned both as a necessary structural part of a wall and as a design tool (Lekson 1986:15, 136–137). In instances where a foundation was not built upon, it was left in place. Lekson (1986:136) noted limited evidence of razed superstructures on the foundations but generally agreed with Judd (1964:153) that they were never built upon.

In our reconstruction (Fig. 4.21), we show the northeast foundation complex with approximately 1 m of relief, as if the area of the foundations was filled and leveled. This may or may not be correct—the foundation walls pass beneath Pueblo Bonito's outside east wall at the same level as the foundations beneath the building. Judd (1964:Fig. 13), however, shows grade at approximately 0.75 m above the top of the outside east wall's foundation. This returns us to the question of whether the principal east-west foundation walls were constructed on the level of the clay pavement, with the space between walls subsequently filled, or whether the area was filled, leveled, and trenched to the clay surface and the walls then cast of clay slurry and rubble. Judd's mention of the foundation walls' bulk component being friable sandstone rubble is interesting, because it could explain the missing talus between Pueblo del Arroyo and Chetro Ketl (Fig. 1.4).

We suggest that Judd's (1964:125–142, 154–176) Second and Third Late Bonito additions should be considered part of the northeast foundation complex. Our reasoning is based on the continuity, on both the horizontal and vertical planes, between Pueblo Bonito proper and the northeast foundation complex. We also think it is no coincidence that Pueblo Bonito and the northeast foundation complex are exactly the same length (155.9 m). Given this continuity and balance, we conclude that the foundation complex plan also included what later became superstructure in other parts of the site: Pueblo Bonito's southeast and southwest corners (Lekson's Stage VI), Great Kiva A, the room row–causeway on the north-south axis, the closing walls of the East and West Courts, and the low platforms with banks of kivas at the outside corners of the East and West Courts (Lekson's Stage VII). Thus, we argue that superstructure construction at these various locations was preceded by a comprehensive building plan in the form of a foun-

dation complex that incorporated several distinct alignment and expansion themes. To design and build such a complex would have been a major construction effort requiring an impressive amount of time and labor (see Metcalf, Chapter 7).

The Mounds

Various interpretations have been made of Pueblo Bonito's two mounds (Fig. 4.20). Judd (1964:125–176, 212–222) thought they were refuse middens, although he found no stratigraphy during his extensive trenching of these features. He speculated that a large percentage of the west mound's mass was material displaced by the construction of the Stage III great kiva in the West Court (Judd 1964:130). He mapped retaining walls and steps that contained and gave access to the mounds, including a 1.5-m-high adobe embankment underlying the east mound's south retaining wall. This embankment is similar to the feature described earlier that abuts the north terrace's retaining wall. Following Lekson (1986:143–144) and Stein and Lekson (1992:93–95), we interpret Pueblo Bonito's mounds as architecture and not as trash dumps. The "mounds" are in fact paved platforms.

On the basis of ceramic assemblages, Windes (1987b:667) dated the mounds to A.D. 1050–1100. Lekson (1986:144) placed the construction of the retaining walls during his Stage VI or later (1075–1105). He noted that deposition continued above the pavement level of the platform mounds. From contour maps, photographs, and cross sections (Judd 1964:Figs. 7, 24), it appears that 0.6–1.2 m of deposition overlies the pavement.

Assuming that the mounded material postdates the use of the platform mounds for their intended purpose, we offer three possible explanations for the post-pavement deposits. One is that they are domestic trash, indicating a late reuse of Pueblo Bonito for either ritual or domestic purposes or both. A second possibility is that the platforms were intentionally buried as part of a termination ritual. A third is that the large quantity of material indicates the presence of secondary elevated platforms.

For our reconstruction (Fig. 4.20), we consolidated the mysterious overburden into second-level, adobe-walled platforms. We were primarily interested in the effect such features would have on Pueblo Bonito's image. We are certain, however, that adobe-walled, filled structures, once reduced and then disturbed by a mind-boggling number of trenches dug in the search for stratigraphy, could pass for unconsolidated, unstructured fill. We admit that the placement, shape, orientation, and mass of the adobe-walled platforms in our reconstruction are matters of conjecture, based on the apparent massing of the mounds.

The East and West Additions

These major additions to Pueblo Bonito's east and west sides completed the building's crescent shape (Fig. 4.20). As discussed earlier, we believe this construction effort involved rais-ing superstructures on existing foundations. These additions make up much of Judd's (1964:78–144, Figs. 5–6) Second and Third Late Bonito Additions. Lekson (1986:137–139) assigned them to his Stage VI, dated at A.D. 1075–1085. Windes and Ford (1996:296, 303) revised Lekson's dates to 1077–1082.

Despite the accessibility and visibility of these two addi-tions, our reconstructions differ significantly from those pre-sented previously. With the exception of the vertical place-ment of Kiva C, Judd (1964:Fig. 13) and Lekson (1986:117) are in essential agreement. We disagree with them, however, on some key points.

For the west addition, we follow Lekson (1986:117) in mass-ing the outer three-room rows to two stories. This places the roof level on the same plane as that of Old Bonito's west building. Lekson shows this early building to be two stories terraced to three. In our reconstruction, we show Old Bonito's west building as uniformly massed to three stories. (Remem-ber that the level of the roof is a combination of story height and the relative location of grade.)

The east addition comprises Pueblo Bonito's highest mass-ing. Elevation data indicate a level, unbroken rim of the back room row from slightly east of the north-south center line to the southeast corner. From there the rim extends west for five rooms or so along the front or south wall so as to enclose Kivas C and D. This massing measures 7.5–9 m above present exterior grade and roughly 12 m from the lowest excavation levels inside the building (as measured in 1934).

The number of stories required to achieve the consistent height of the east addition's back room row varied. In the northeast quadrant there were four stories, and in the south-east quadrant, three. The reasons for these different story counts are most likely to be found in the building's lowermost levels, now buried beneath tons of debris from the fall of Threatening Rock. We show Kivas C and D as second-story constructions. This agrees with Judd (1964:Fig. 13) but not with Lekson (1984:Fig. 4.20), who placed Kiva D at the third, or highest, level of this part of the east addition.

Formalization of Site Axes and Construction of Great Kiva A

This part of our Stage IV construction is Lekson's (1986) Stage VIIE, which he dated at A.D. 1085–1100+ and which occurred in two parts. One was the formalization of Pueblo Bonito's north-south and east-west axes with single-story room rows (Fig. 4.20). The room row that formalized Pueblo Bonito's north-south axis may have functioned as a causeway con-necting, on the same horizontal plane, the site's oldest section with its newest (Stein et al. 1997). The room row that formal-ized Pueblo Bonito's east-west axis enclosed the site's courts.

The other part of this construction effort was the building of Great Kiva A. Lekson (1986:142) compared Great Kiva A with the great kiva at Aztec West, finding the two structures

to be remarkably similar. Both stand a full story above grade and open into above-grade peripheral rooms. The configura-tion is circular at Aztec Ruins and rectangular at Pueblo Bonito. The Aztec great kiva is dated to 1115. Lekson (1986) suggested that this was a reasonable date for Pueblo Bonito's Great Kiva A as well, given the presence of McElmo and Mesa Verde Black-on-white ceramics.

Razing a Great Kiva

The final Stage IV construction event was the razing of the Stage III great kiva located in the West Court's southern half. The destruction of the West Court great kiva and the con-struction of Great Kiva A were probably related. After the West Court great kiva was razed to the bench, the resulting void was filled with 3 m of packed clay to the level of the West Court surface (Judd 1964:211). This required a massive amount of material. Because Great Kiva A is partially an above-grade structure, its construction would have contributed little to the backfilling effort.

Stage V (A.D. 1115–1250)

No consensus exists among archaeologists about how long downtown Chaco remained in use after the last dated con-struction efforts in the early 1100s. Nor is there any consen-sus about the nature of this use. Chronological indicators for construction and other activity during this period are pri-marily ceramics, architectural form, and masonry style (see Windes, Chapter 3). There is no evidence for construction re-quiring large quantities of newly cut, nonlocal timber after 1130. Wooden structural elements needed for new construc-tion were salvaged. It is possible, however, that some post-1130 construction remains undetected by archaeologists, especially if it involved uniform lots of salvaged wood or, for that mat-ter, no wood at all.

Documented construction and evidence of structured use during this period include remodeling in Kivas C and D; the addition of multiple floor levels, associated with Mesa Verde Black-on-white ceramics, in Great Kiva A; construction of small keyhole-style kivas flanking the courts; and construction of Hillside Ruin (Figs. 4.22–4.24). Examples of intentional burning, erasure, burial, and concealment suggest a period of termination ritual and possibly iconoclasm (see Windes, Chapter 3). On the basis of available evidence, we believe that Hillside Ruin was constructed in the first two decades of the twelfth century and that closure of Pueblo Bonito might have been as early as 1130, give or take a year or so. We are open, however, to the possibility that downtown Chaco, particularly Pueblo Bonito, was used, possibly even for its intended pur-pose, until well into the thirteenth century and perhaps even to the turn of the fourteenth. Mesa Verde Black-on-white is commonly found in Pueblo Bonito, including the areas of Old

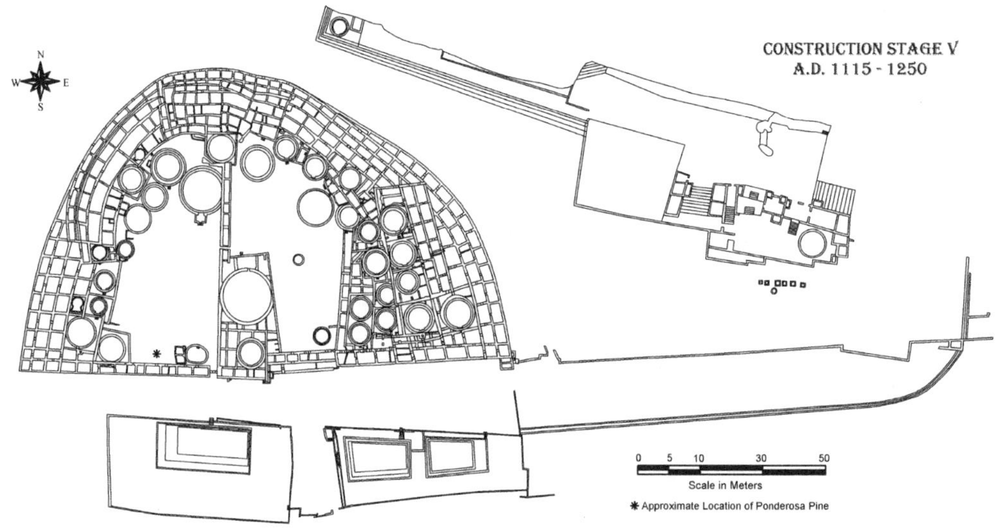

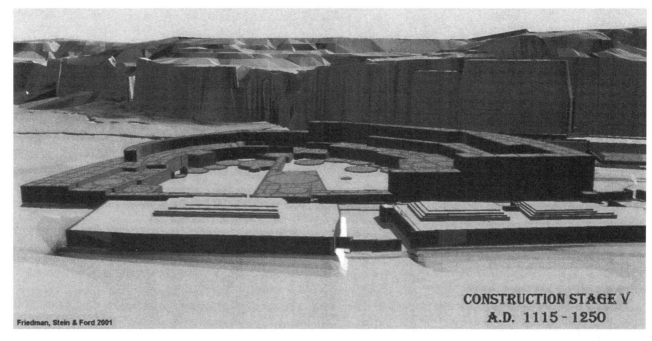

CONSTRUCTION STAGE V
A.D. 1115 - 1250

Figure 4.22. Stage V plan view (A.D. 1115–1250).

Friedman, Stein & Ford 2001

**CONSTRUCTION STAGE V
A.D. 1115 - 1250**

Figure 4.23. Stage V perspective view of Pueblo Bonito proper.

Bonito used for storage of ritual objects and high-status human remains (see Windes, Chapter 3; Akins, Chapter 8).

Kivas C and D and Great Kiva A

Evidence of the latest construction and remodeling within Pueblo Bonito can be found in Great Kiva A and elevated Kivas C and D. This evidence includes a passage constructed between Kiva D and Room 241 in A.D. 1127, a jacal dividing wall constructed in Room 257 in 1129, and a pilaster replaced in Kiva C in 1120 (Windes, Chapter 3; Windes and Ford 1996:303). In Great Kiva A, Judd (1964:203) noted 17 distinct layers of ash-darkened adobe or sand, which he interpreted as use surfaces.

If these levels represent an annual renewal ritual, and if we presume that Great Kiva A was built around 1115, then the most recent surface would date to approximately 1132.

Small Circular Rooms

Several small keyhole-style kivas were built around Pueblo Bonito's court perimeters in the early to mid-1100s and possibly later. These circular rooms are smaller than the smallest Chaco kivas. They were built of salvaged timbers and occur as both subterranean structures in the courts and above grade structures in already existing square or rectangular rooms. We agree with Lekson (1986:60–61) that these small circular rooms

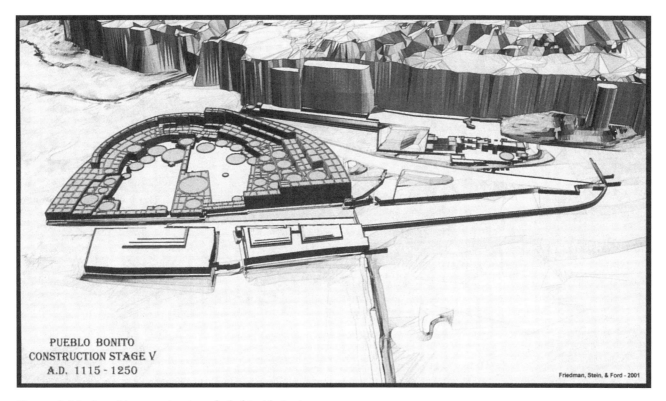

PUEBLO BONITO
CONSTRUCTION STAGE V
A.D. 1115 - 1250

Friedman, Stein, & Ford - 2001

Figure 4.24. Stage V perspective view of all of Pueblo Bonito.

are not foreign but rather a late expression of the Chacoan building tradition.

Hillside Ruin

We place the construction of Hillside Ruin in the first two decades of the twelfth century. Jackson (1879:442) described Hillside Ruin as a mass of ruins measuring 41 by 23 m with two circular rooms in the middle and a low retaining wall about 91 m long. In his investigation of Hillside Ruin's rubble mound, Judd (1964:146–147) observed only one kiva. When partially excavated, it revealed an above-bench diameter of 7.5 m and masonry somewhat similar to Judd's Type III. Judd also excavated three narrow exploratory trenches at the mound's west end, exposing the long front wall. This wall rests on an 18-cm-high adobe foundation that overlies part of the northeast foundation complex. Below the elevated court, which housed the kiva, and parallel to the retaining wall, Judd (1964:148) found a series of seven formalized fireboxes that are associated with Hillside Ruin. On the basis of what he called Hillside Ruin's "decidedly non-Bonitian" masonry and the presence of proto-Mesa Verde ceramics, Judd (1964:146–147) concluded that the ruin was "later than Pueblo Bonito," implying that it was not culturally or architecturally related.

Hillside Ruin's rubble mound is unusual—sufficiently so to have discouraged mapping for a century. Judd (1964) attributed its odd appearance to its having been robbed of building stone. But why rob from this site when Pueblo Bonito, the canyon's single largest source of building stone, was right next door? And who did the robbing, if Pueblo Bonito is presumed to have been abandoned before Hillside Ruin was constructed?

Judd gives the impression in both text and plan that Hillside Ruin is a building 91 m in length. Field investigations, however, reveal that it is actually a 58-m-long building with an additional 33 m or so of retaining wall. This extra 33 m of wall contains a culturally modified slope and not a building. Hillside Ruin itself is a glorified retaining wall for the north terrace's eastern extension. Below the retaining wall is a raised court containing the now partially excavated kiva. Integrated into the wall are two steps and landings that lead to the surface of the north terrace. These steps and landings are oriented perpendicular to the retaining wall and are flanked by terraced sets of low-walled open rooms and masonry boxes, the types of features often associated with Chacoan roads. The surface of the filled platform created by Hillside Ruin is also a wide avenue and ramps in a configuration resembling a circular drive.

Hillside Ruin, therefore, is essentially a massive stepped retaining wall that forms the south face of a platform or avenue. The lower level is an elevated, walled court that houses a single kiva. From the court rise steps to the upper platform. Attached to the retaining wall on the platform's surface are low-walled open rooms, masonry boxes, and elevated fireboxes or altars. There may be two or three roofed rooms in

Hillside Ruin; if so, they are located north and east of the excavated kiva.

Closure and Termination Ritual

Three lines of evidence suggest an organized closure of Pueblo Bonito and downtown Chaco. One is the widespread burning at Pueblo Bonito (see Windes, Chapter 3). Another is the systematic erasure of specific sets of glyphs from the canyon wall. The glyphs were deeply scoured and then scored. Because of the scoring, these locations have previously been interpreted as ax sharpening areas. Further evidence for termination and closure ritual is the mysterious rubble veneer applied over the benches of Pueblo Bonito's Great Kiva A, Chetro Ketl's Great Sanctuary, and possibly Casa Rinconada. This rubble veneer has previously been interpreted as sloppy (read non-Chacoan) workmanship by a late group of "refugees" who appropriated Chaco Canyon's great houses and great kivas as defendable places of residence. This model does not explain why such a group would intentionally cover sound, usable fabric with rubble glued on with adobe. We believe that like the other masonry types, this last rubble veneer was symbolic and that its rough character was exaggerated to project a high sign value (Fowler and Stein 1992:105). It is no accident that the most significant features of the core area, the great kivas, were treated in this manner. This intentional rubble veneer leads us to wonder, again, whether the overburden on the south platforms' surfaces could be the result of termination ritual.

PUEBLO BONITO'S DESIGN AND PURPOSE

The value of our stage-by-stage models lies in more than just providing archaeologists and visitors with images of what Pueblo Bonito looked like through time. Constructing the models yielded information on spatial and temporal relationships that in turn provides insights into Pueblo Bonito's design and purpose.

Pueblo Bonito's Design

Volumes can be written on aspects of Pueblo Bonito's design. Here, we touch on issues of chronology, boundaries, treatment of the north-central section, and symmetrical relationships between primary architectural forms.

Chronology

On the basis of our analysis, we disagree with Judd (1964) that Old Bonito's builders were unaware of the remains of the eighth-century pit structures that underlie the building. Old Bonito rests directly on the eighth-century surface. If, as current information suggests, construction of Old Bonito had begun by the mid-ninth century, then the ruins of the earlier

structures would have been quite conspicuous. The close correlation between the floor levels of the earlier structures and Great Kiva Q is suspicious, especially considering that the depth of Great Kiva Q was attained in part by raising the surface of the West Court by approximately 2 m.

Our primary evidence for defining each of Pueblo Bonito's stages has been wooden ceilings, which can be dated with dendrochronology, and associated masonry styles. Further evidence for relative position in the construction sequence may be determined from wall abutments, superimposed features, and artifact associations. Altogether, these various data sources enable us to reconstruct only part of Pueblo Bonito's architecture. A significant amount of labor was expended for construction that is difficult to recognize, interpret, and date. This type of building was coincident with Old Bonito's construction and continued throughout the rest of the construction sequence. It involved extensive leveling, filling, sculpting, and adobe paving of the landscape. A notable example of landscape modification is the complete removal of the talus against the cliff wall between Chetro Ketl and Pueblo del Arroyo.

Construction at Pueblo Bonito that used primarily adobe or fill is difficult to date. In addition to the clay required for mortar, floors, and plaster, clay-adobe was used extensively in primary structural contexts such as foundation walls, stub walls, cap walls, retaining walls, load-bearing walls, buttressing, and pavements. Massive amounts of fill material were required for elevating the courts and raising the terraces and platforms. With each construction stage, some of this material had to be removed and relocated. The substantial labor that would have been required for all of this is impossible to quantify. Landscape modification and adobe and fill building may explain the apparent 100-year gap in building activity between Stage I and Stage II that is suggested by the paucity of tree-ring dates for that span (see Windes, Chapter 3). Furthermore, it is unrealistic to separate construction at Pueblo Bonito from construction of other components of the Chaco complex. Construction at this larger scale may have been essentially continuous.

Expanding Pueblo Bonito's Boundaries

An important aspect of Pueblo Bonito's design is that Pueblo Bonito consists of much more than just the familiar crescentic envelope (Figs. 4.22, 4.24). It also includes "foundations," platforms, "roads," and Hillside Ruin.

Lekson (1986) described Pueblo Bonito's foundations as permanent features independent of superstructure. A building may exist as foundations only, or superstructure may be built, pulled down, and rebuilt on the same footprint. Alternatively, foundations that appear never to have been built upon may once have carried superstructure. We agree with Lekson (1981, 1986) that Pueblo Bonito's foundation functioned in part as a design tool, composing an analog of the site at a scale of one to one. We argue that the extensive clay pavement described by Judd, whether natural or cultural, served as a scratchpad on which foundations were used to lay out the future Pueblo Bonito in full scale.

The northeast foundation complex is of interest for several reasons. First, it exactly doubles the width of Pueblo Bonito. Second, the alignments are overlapping themes laid out in one plane. Finally, unlike Pueblo Bonito proper, the northeast foundation complex consists of foundations only, with no superstructure present. We disagree with Judd (1964) that the northeast foundation complex represents abandoned alternatives to Pueblo Bonito's final addition. Instead, we see it as a massive construction effort that was carefully designed and executed and served both as a full-scale schematic to guide future construction and as a proxy for structure. We view the foundations beneath Pueblo Bonito and those making up the northeast foundation complex as one architectural composition, comprising an integrated, unbroken network. Most notably, the foundations beneath Pueblo Bonito's east half are on the same plane as the northeast foundation complex and thus are clearly part of that complex. Of further interest is that some foundations in the northeast foundation complex, such as the long east-west trending alignments, are more massive than others, apparently to facilitate the planned height of the superstructure they were ultimately intended to support.

On the basis of this evidence, we think that prior to Stage II construction, the complete Pueblo Bonito was manifested in the form of marked alignments and formalized foundations. Consequently, we argue that Pueblo Bonito's massive building episodes were not designed and implemented on an episode by episode basis by generations of individual architects following their interpretation of established rules. Rather, we propose that Pueblo Bonito may have had a single architect and that succeeding generations needed only to follow the instructions encoded in the tangible foundation alignments, as well as those carried forward by a few individuals as intangible esoteric knowledge. Perhaps Pueblo Bonito was the vision of one man, made tangible and set in motion in a single lifetime.

Another component in our expanded definition of Pueblo Bonito's boundaries is the platforms that flank the north and south sides of the building. These platforms are elevated, earth-and-debris-filled structures. Some have rounded contours. Others are contained by masonry and adobe retaining walls, forming hard-edged, paved, elevated surfaces. Secondary mounds may have stood on the two southern platforms, as indicated by the mass of material present above the level of the retaining walls. Without a masonry armor, a low mound of adobe and fill would soon become indistinguishable from the fill beneath it.

The two northern platforms have been largely ignored by archaeologists, in part because the western platform is covered with rockfall and in part because the eastern platform was once the location of a historic material yard and National Park Service water tank. The northern platforms include masonry terracing, adobe embankments, multiple hearths, offering boxes, altars, and roads. A section of the northwest platform's massive retaining wall can still be seen beneath the remains of Threatening Rock. This wall has been popularly interpreted as a futile attempt to shore up the once imposing monolith (see Marshall, Chapter 2).

The final component in our expanded definition of Pueblo Bonito is Hillside Ruin. It has long been interpreted as a late Mesa Verde period "pueblo." To our surprise, we found that this long-ignored structure was built during the preceding McElmo period and was not a pueblo at all. Instead, it was a massive wall and fill structure that functioned both as a retaining wall for the northeast platform, with ramp access to the platform, and as part of an east-west avenue that passes between Pueblo Bonito and the north platforms.

Old Bonito

From our reconstructions, it is evident that Stage I construction, particularly the central section, was carefully maintained and curated throughout the use history of Pueblo Bonito. As the primary repository for exotic goods and high-status human remains (see Akins, Chapter 8; Neitzel, Chapter 9; Mathien, Chapter 10), Old Bonito's central section clearly served an esoteric purpose. Certain features of its architecture reinforce this interpretation: the symmetrical configuration of the building on greater Pueblo Bonito's cardinal north-south axis, its location at the northern extent of the crescent, and the focus of its outside walls at the intersection of the cardinal axes that would define Pueblo Bonito's final extent three centuries in the future.

In our reconstruction, Old Bonito's central building is a sunken court rather than a towering mass. This appearance began in Stage I when Old Bonito's east and west buildings were built 2 m higher than the central building. Then, in Stage II, two additions completed the screening of the now sunken court. One was the construction of the four-story-high room row around its north side (probably with an opening to accommodate the central north-south axis), and the other was a wall more than 2 m high across the western half of the court's south side and the north side of Kiva 16's housing. The eastern half of the court's south side appears to have been left open. With the completion of these Stage II additions, the wedge-shaped, sunken court has the feeling of an inner sanctum, a holy of holies.

In Stage IV, essentially the final formalization of Pueblo Bonito, the wedge-shaped form of the inner sanctum was recapitulated, in mirror image, as the housing of Great Kiva A. The two buildings, located at Pueblo Bonito's northern and southern extremes, respectively, were then connected by formalization of the north-south axis into an elevated causeway. We interpret this duplication and connection as a symbolic opposition signifying Pueblo Bonito's completion (Stein et al. 1997).

Old Bonito's east and west wings are also of interest because they are composed of spaces that satisfy the requirements for households. Household spaces are generally missing from Stages II through V (see Bustard, Chapter 7). In the east and west wings, these spaces are the "big-room suites." Four ground-floor suites are located in the west building, and arguably an equal number are in the east building. The roof level of the old crescent's east and west wings stands about 2 m (one low story) above the two-story construction of the center section. We imagine, therefore, that at approximately 6 m above grade, the suites would have been stacked three high.

Symmetry

A final aspect of Pueblo Bonito's design that is evident in our reconstructions is the importance of symmetrical spatial relationships in both the horizontal and vertical planes. These relationships are significant not only for what they reveal about the sophistication of Pueblo Bonito's builders but also for their symbolic meaning.

Doxtater (1984) and Washburn and Crowe (1988) have described symmetrical spatial relationships, particularly oppositions, as nondiscursive or nonlexical domains in which the ordering and meaning of space and time are communicated by symbolism and metaphor. Spatial relationships are a cultural and ritual means of organizing cognitive associations that are emotional and not easily communicated by means of language. Pueblo Bonito's symmetrical spatial relationships seem to encode information about motion, time, and sequencing, as well as symbolic and metaphorical meaning. Pueblo Bonito contains many examples of symmetry as a symbol for movement or as a syntax for the actual movement of a feature through ritual space. An example of motion by way of translation is the stage-by-stage expansion of Old Bonito's crescentic form. An example of reflection is the juxtaposition of Old Bonito's center building with the platform containing Great Kiva A (Stein et al. 1997). An example of rotation is the retirement and replacement of great kivas counterclockwise around a center point located on the north-south axis. This movement went full circle through the quadrants formed by the structure's cardinal alignment.

In the foundation complex, the plans for two buildings are clearly delineated. The plans were merged and constructed simultaneously in one plane. The same competing themes may be seen within Pueblo Bonito's crescentic envelope, where they appear to have been emphasized alternately from one construction stage to the next. The result is two Pueblo Bonitos within a common envelope exhibiting a reciprocating or oscillating motion with respect to one another. An artifact of this motion is frozen in the formalization of the south closing walls of the East and West Courts. The cardinal alignment of

the south wall of the West Court suggests a minimum periodicity of twice per year (at the equinoxes) when this alignment theme would have been recognized (see Farmer, Chapter 5). Obviously, the physical movement from construction stage to construction stage would have been a much longer cycle.

Pueblo Bonito's Purpose

Aspects of Pueblo Bonito's design can inform us about the site's purpose. A current and basic question is whether Pueblo Bonito functioned primarily as a residential or as a ritual structure. Whether or not the site was a residence may be addressed by looking at how it achieved its form. Two residential alternatives have been proposed: that Pueblo Bonito represents traditional village architecture—it was a pueblo—and that it was an apartment building. We will discuss why an apartment building is not like a pueblo. In what follows, we first review the idea that Pueblo Bonito was a residence, in the form of either a pueblo or an apartment. Then we present our view that Pueblo Bonito's primary function was ritual in nature.

The Idea of the Pueblo

As indicated by its colloquial name, Pueblo Bonito (Spanish for "beautiful town") was thought to have been a communal village or "pueblo," as such villages are called in the Southwest. Indeed, Pueblo Bonito is enshrined in the thought and literature of Southwestern archaeology as the archetype of the contemporary pueblo (Kidder 1924, 1927; Reed and Stein 1998).

The idea of the pueblo in the Southwest bears the mark of parsimony and is based largely on form. The quintessential pueblo is a multistory communal dwelling oriented around and terracing upward from a plaza or plazas. These buildings are rectangular, with rectangular cells, have flat roofs, and are constructed of adobe or stone and adobe with ceiling beams (vigas) extending through the walls and left exposed on the exterior for use in hanging strings of corn and chilies to dry. Rooms are often entered via a hatchway in the roof, and exterior ladders are used to reach upper-story rooms. The flat roofs function both as outdoor work areas and as platforms from which to observe activities in the plaza. Finally, large, circular (sometimes rectangular), subterranean (sometimes above-grade) chambers, or kivas, are located in the plazas and are identified with ceremonial activities.

This image of the pueblo is accurate in many respects. It is also an oversimplified composite. The idea of the pueblo was heavily romanticized and clichéd virtually from the onset of its use by Southwesternists. As conventional wisdom, the idea has been overused and underresearched. To use the term "pueblo" implies a traditional village architecture in which form is iconic and additive in nature. The form of a traditional village is determined primarily by biological, social, economic, ideational, and political forces as they affect the basic building unit—the household. Such processes include population increases and decreases and inheritance rules. As new households are added and existing households abandoned, villages change constantly. Through time, with growth and decline, traditional village architecture is an organic ordering of households. Pueblo Bonito does not match this characterization of a village. Its growth occurred in large blocks of mostly non-residential rooms (see Bustard, Chapter 7).

The Idea of the Apartment Building

In the literature of Southwestern archaeology, the primary buildings of the Chaco complex are variously called great pueblos, great towns, or great houses, and Pueblo Bonito itself has been referred to as an "apartment house." This nomenclature invokes two concepts: monumentality and residential function. In traditional societies, for the common people, these concepts would be contradictory. At the turn of the last century, however, they were in agreement with the emerging, uniquely American tradition of the skyscraper, an architectural form with an envelope enclosing many redundant, stacked spaces. The result is a stark, geometric, featureless structure with an exaggerated mass and a small footprint. Referencing the sheer facade and ratio of mass to footprint of the Pueblo Bonito envelope, it comes as no surprise that the building was viewed as an engineering artifact of a "high civilization" and was considered by some to be the first essentially modern commercial apartment building.

Pueblo Bonito as a Ceremonial Center

On the basis of our analysis of Pueblo Bonito's evolving form, we reject the view that the building's primary function was residential. Instead, we support the idea that Pueblo Bonito and the Chaco complex generally were intended to function in the esoteric realm. We use the term "ceremonial center" as a means of providing contrast to the idea of residential architecture, but we caution that "ceremonial center" has ambiguous meaning in the context of Southwestern archaeology. Old Bonito is composed of cells configured like living rooms, but they are many times the size of equivalent rooms in common households of the period. This, in conjunction with its cardinal orientation, symmetry of layout, and multistory construction, suggests that Old Bonito was intended as a special place and possibly as a residence for special occupants. In subsequent construction of Pueblo Bonito, however, few rooms or suites of rooms, if any, were configured like households. Architectural remains discovered beneath Old Bonito indicate continuity of use for this location, and unique features of the site such as its central location in Chaco Canyon, the towering mass of Threatening Rock, and the apparent existence of a unique living pine tree in the West Court reinforce the possibility that the site of Pueblo Bonito had long been considered a special place.

CONCLUSION

Reconstructions send powerful messages that are, ideally, a balance of fact and reasoned fantasy. The model of Pueblo Bonito that we have presented differs in significant respects from popular reconstructions. Our model is as accurate as we can make it given the time and quality of information available, but detailed documentation of the interior architecture of Pueblo Bonito has not yet been undertaken. Once this information is collected, our vision of Pueblo Bonito, too, may require rethinking.

Having completed the exercise of ripping Pueblo Bonito asunder and piecing it back together again, we find that a significant aspect of this architectural puzzle is the so-called foundations and the clay pavement they rest on. We believe Pueblo Bonito could have been conceived and calibrated as sticks and scratch lines on this unobstructed level pavement prior to the construction of Old Bonito. Were this the case, Pueblo Bonito could have been the brainchild of a single individual; the schematic proxy of the future building could have been developed and calibrated in an individual's lifetime.

The foundations, as a successive formalization of the original ephemeral schematic, ultimately form a complex composition that integrates at least two orientational modes for Pueblo Bonito. They also anticipate the evolution and expansion of the envelope, the movement of architectural forms within the evolving envelope, and the final form of the building, in which the two orientational modes are essentially frozen on a common footprint.

A remarkable aspect of Pueblo Bonito's design, then, is that it is four-dimensional: it incorporates motion, and consequently it incorporates time. The mechanical aspects of Pueblo Bonito bring us a bit closer to guessing its purpose. The reciprocating motion created by the alternating orientational themes suggests an escapement regulating the movement of a clockworks—but it is unlikely that Pueblo Bonito was a passive instrument created strictly for the benign purpose of marking time. Rather, Pueblo Bonito was an occult engine powered by the cycles of the cosmos.

Finally, the complex evolution of Pueblo Bonito's form and the encoding of this form into the foundations evokes an image of the predetermined life stages of an organism. The biological analogy seems more appropriate than the mechanical. Measured movement becomes a pulse, and the engine becomes a beating heart at the center of the larger "organism" that we are coming to know as Chaco.

ACKNOWLEDGMENTS

This study has been a long time in the making, and we have been assisted along the way by many people. Thanks to Taft Blackhorse, Tom Windes, Rachel Anderson, Scott Andrae, Bill

Phillips, Richard Loose, Jay Williams, Andrea Carpenter, Dorothy Washburn, Terry Nichols, Steve Lekson, Anna Sofaer, Rory Gauthier, G. B. Cornucopia, Dick Duman, Chris Hardaker, Peter McKenna, Phillip Tuwaletstiwa, Bill Stone, and Samir Wahid. We are indebted to Bret Blosser and the field school of the University of Southern California at Santa Cruz for their invaluable assistance in geophysical studies conducted in 1998 and 1999. We would like to recognize the invaluable assistance of Superintendent Butch Wilson, the staff of Chaco Culture National Historical Park, and especially the members of the Chaco Preservation Unit for sharing their technical knowledge about Chaco architecture. We also thank Emily Sollie of the Smithsonian Books for obtaining permissions to reproduce Figures 4.9–4.12 and Beth Richardson of the National Geographic Society for locating the images shown in Figures 4.9–4.11. Finally, we owe a special thanks to Jill Neitzel for her faith in us and her perseverance in squeezing this manuscript out of us.

NOTES

1. Figure 4.10 is apparently an original drawing by Kenneth J. Conant. In Judd 1964:Pl. 1, the drawing is altered to show a pine tree in the West Court.
2. A plan view of Hillside Ruin was also drawn by Tom Windes for this volume (Fig. 3.9). For the record, we shared information and ideas and even spent time on site together.
3. The shape and mass of this structure is captured on topographical sheets 69–70 of NM/CHAC-4940, a 1-foot contour map assembled by A. D. Quackenbush in July–August 1934 for DOI-NPS, Chaco Canyon National Monument, Office of the Engineer, San Francisco, California.

5

Astronomy and Ritual
in Chaco Canyon

James D. Farmer

In 1978, rock art specialists in Chaco Canyon, New Mexico, discovered that sunlight penetrating crevices between stone slabs atop Fajada Butte created distinctive "sun daggers" of light against the adjacent cliff wall (Sofaer and Sinclair 1987; see Fig. 1.5 for the location of Fajada Butte). At some point in the past, ancestral Puebloans had pecked spirals on the wall so that on annual solstices and equinoxes, daggers of sunlight either pierce or bracket the spirals. The most spectacular effect is the summer solstice sun dagger, which pierces the center of the larger of the two spirals at midday (Fig. 5.1). A similar, smaller spiral is also pierced by a dagger on the equinoxes, and the large spiral is bracketed by daggers on the winter solstice.

A substantial amount of scholarship has dealt with possible interpretations for the Fajada Butte sun daggers (Carlson and Judge 1987; Sofaer and Sinclair 1987; Zeilik 1987). Initially, it was suggested that the site served a calendrical function for regulating the agricultural year. Another opinion held that the site was a shrine for ancestral Puebloan sun watchers and priests, an opinion supported by historic Pueblo ethnography and informants. Other interpretations have linked the daggers with lunar events, particularly the 19-year lunar cycle.

In this chapter I elaborate on the idea that the Fajada Butte sun dagger site is a sacred shrine. My thesis is that the site's primary importance lay not in its particular calendrical or astronomical function but in its specific symbolic form or imagery and its visual interplay with sunlight. I suggest that the form and action of the sun daggers reflected an ancestral Puebloan paradigm for structuring the universe and articulating other forms of artistic expression.

After considering the history and iconographic significance of ancestral Puebloan spirals, I describe Pueblo Bonito's solar orientation and its possible connection to the sun dagger phenomenon. Then I examine how the idea of spiral directionality and celestial alignments might have been incorporated into the design of Chacoan great kivas. Finally, I explore the linkage between solar events, possible Chacoan rituals, and questions of gender.

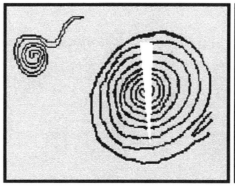 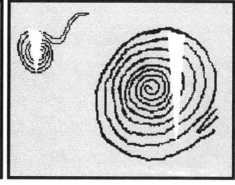

MIDDAY
SUMMER SOLSTICE

MIDDAY
EQUINOXES

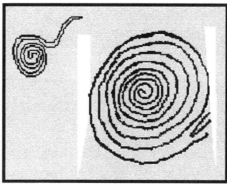 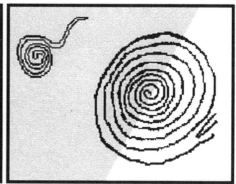

Figure 5.1. Solar and lunar light on the Fajada Butte spirals at the solstices and equinoxes.

MIDDAY
WINTER SOLSTICE

SUNRISE
MINOR STANDSTILL
OF THE MOON

ANCESTRAL PUEBLOAN SPIRALS

Since its discovery, interpreters have treated the Fajada Butte sun dagger phenomenon as a flat, two-dimensional event. If one views it as a three-dimensional event, however—a shaft piercing the center of a hemispherical spiral dome at a perpendicular angle—then its form suggests a structural relationship to certain other ancestral Puebloan forms and ideas.

Spirals embody a complex set of powerful, universal meanings for historic Pueblo people, variously symbolizing water, earth, migration, serpents, the sun's heat, wind, and the symbolic "center" of the universe (Ortiz 1969; Waters 1963). Rays of sunlight share a parallel set of related meanings, including lightning, serpents, arrows or spears, digging sticks, the sun's light (as distinguished from its heat), impregnation, and the sky. Both spirals and rays of sunlight are subsumed within the larger concept of fertility and creation—spirals are generally equated with female or mother earth symbolism, and rays or

daggers with male or father sky associations. Thus, the image of a sun dagger penetrating a spiral can be understood metaphorically as an abstract model of essential, dual, opposing yet unifying universal forces. Add to this the primary importance placed on solstices and equinoxes as demarcators of the sun's seasonal journey through the sky, which symbolically defines the limits of the sacred Puebloan landscape. The product is perhaps the most important organizing set of beliefs underlying the traditional Puebloan worldview. Presumably the ancestral Puebloans of Chaco Canyon shared similar beliefs.

At least a thousand years before the rise of Chaco Canyon, ancestral Puebloans of the earliest Basketmaker period (circa 1500–300 B.C.) placed large basket trays of woven yucca fiber over the heads of their buried dead. In 1991, while researching Basketmaker burial material from Utah, I noticed that most of the baskets and large burial trays had holes punched in their centers—some large and obvious, others subtler, but all apparently intentional (Nusbaum 1922:pl. 15). It struck me at the time that these holes were reminiscent of the so-called kill holes in the centers of ceramic bowls found in Mogollon Mimbres burials in southern New Mexico, which were generally contemporaneous with the Chaco phenomenon (Brody 1977). Though obviously of different material, the Mimbres bowls were constructed of coils of clay spiraling from the center outward, an ancestral and historic Pueblo technique of vessel construction that mimics the construction process of baskets and trays.

In addition, long, pointed digging sticks used for planting are occasionally depicted in Mimbres scenes, sometimes in direct association with images of copulating humans, probably referencing the fertility symbolism of the stick and perhaps the bowl itself (Moulard 1984:pl. 9). The sticks may in fact have been used to punch the holes in the bowls, and similar sticks have been found at Chaco Canyon, though not in Basketmaker contexts (Judd 1954:241). Because the Basketmakers practiced maize agriculture, they likely employed some similar planting device. Historic Pueblo Indians continued to use similar planting sticks as well.

The Mimbres kill holes probably symbolized spirit portals to the supernatural realm. Moulard (1984:xviii) argued that passage of the spirit through these holes in the bowls, commonly inverted over the heads of Mimbres deceased, symbolically replicated the mythological opening of the fourth world in Pueblo creation myths. The sacred hole, or *sipapu*, in later kiva floors is the symbolic architectural analog of this opening, as is the hole in kiva roofs. The holes of the large pierced trays in Basketmaker burials might have served a similar iconographic function as the spirit opening placed above the head of the deceased. Two basic premises are therefore suggested for further consideration: that spirals and related forms incorporating spirals have a substantial history in ancestral Puebloan art prior to and long after Chaco Canyon's florescence, and that the motif of spirals pierced in the center by shafts of some type held great iconographic or symbolic importance in both the ancestral and the historic Pueblo periods.

Swentzell (1992) has linked both the form and construction process of kivas to Pueblo conceptions of universal order, suggesting that the roofs symbolize giant inverted sky baskets, penetrated at the center to permit cosmic energy flow, germination, and emergence. Basketmaker pithouses, the architectural ancestors of kivas, reflect the same symbolic roof form (Roberts 1929:12). Indeed, it is possible that this iconography directly influenced the development of pithouse and later kiva form.

Analogous symbolism may be reflected in ceramic form as well. The circular or oval shape of ancestral Puebloan kiva jars replicates the general shape of kivas and pithouses (Breternitz et. al. 1974:47). Beginning in the Pueblo I period, about A.D. 700, the top halves of kiva jars were painted with abstract geo-metric designs resembling basket patterns, whereas the bottom halves were generally left plain. These jars probably served as ritual vessels partially submerged in the kiva floor. With a constricted opening in the top center, the vessel clearly resembles and repeats Swentzell's (1992) universal model in reduced scale. Accessing the interior of a kiva jar through a central opening at its apex replicates the piercing of the pithouse or kiva roof by sunlight. Following the implications of Swentzell's model, the top half of the kiva jar and the kiva roof serve similar symbolic functions: woven spiral hemispheres punctured by sacred shafts. This imagery reflects that of the earlier Basketmaker burial trays. The roofs of the Pueblo II great kivas replicated this form on a grand scale, and the spirals and daggers of Fajada Butte appear to reflect the same iconography.

The two Fajada Butte spirals curl in opposite directions (Fig. 5.1). Images of paired opposing spirals have analogs in other ancestral Puebloan forms. A late Pueblo II or Pueblo III kiva from Grand Gulch, Utah, exhibits the remains of paired adobe medallions or discs along its interior wall. (The same site also contained examples of earlier Basketmaker burials with large, pierced, spiral trays.) One well-preserved pair of medallions clearly displays opposed spirals (Hoge 1994:124). The placement and appearance of these medallions in turn recalls similar depictions in later Pueblo IV kiva murals from Pottery Mound, New Mexico (Hibben 1975:128–129). Medallions representing baskets or bowls are displayed in rows by members of the Lakón society, a Hopi women's ceremonial society charged with ritual performances each autumn at harvest. Similar paired spirals appear as opposed serpents, warrior shields, and star patterns throughout the Pottery Mound murals, strengthening the iconographic connections among these images.

The opposed directions of the spirals serve specific symbolic purposes. In an analysis of ancestral Puebloan pottery construction, Snow (1983) summarized the significance of clockwise versus counterclockwise circuitry, associating counterclockwise rotation with creativity, the sky, and positive life force, and clockwise rotation with the underworld, darkness, and negativity. Together, the two directions conceptually encompass the entire universal process, an idea reflected in Pueblo architectural design and ritual space.

Ortiz (1969:18–19) discussed the application of opposed spirals as organizing principles of Pueblo ritual procession and architectural space, principles apparently reflected in the plans of Pueblo II great houses such as Pueblo Bonito. In modern rituals, dancers and performers proceed through the pueblos in a highly regulated fashion. Variations can occur, depending on the specific ritual and pueblo, but the traditional pattern is for performers to emerge from a designated kiva into the surrounding plaza and then move around the pueblo and sometimes into the surrounding countryside in a uniform direction. Upon returning to the kiva, performers circumambulate its interior in the reverse direction, symbolically balancing the two processes and emphasizing the emergence from and descent into the symbolic world of the kiva. This belief system associated with opposing spirals is probably very old in ancestral Puebloan culture. The overriding preference for spiral construction of baskets, trays, and pottery suggests at least an early Basketmaker origin for the symbolism.

Although the focus of this study is on solar phenomena, the Fajada Butte spirals may be linked with lunar phenomena as well. For example, the light of both rising sun and moon on the day of the minor lunar standstill bisects the center of the large spiral, momentarily turning it into two semicircles, one in shadow and the other illuminated (Fig. 5.1). In effect, the double spirals appear to converge and coordinate specific points in the celestial calendar, manifesting a conceptually complete cosmic model, or cosmogram, of opposing yet balanced universal forces: day versus night, sun versus moon, spring/summer versus fall/winter, birth versus death.

PUEBLO BONITO

Solar orientations are apparent in Pueblo Bonito's final plan (Williamson 1987a, 1987b), but the plan was not preconceived in its entirety (cf. Stein et al., Chapter 4). Instead, it evolved through a series of major construction episodes over a span of more than 300 years. Near the end of this span, at roughly A.D. 1085, two significant changes occurred (Lekson 1986:139; see Figs. 3.6, 4.17, 4.18). The first was the addition of a series of roomblocks along the rear of the building, creating its final, semicircular form. This addition appears to have been less utilitarian than aesthetic in purpose, because many of the rooms apparently lacked direct access and are of such irregular proportions and dimensions that any reasonable use would have been difficult or impossible.

The second change was the addition of a long southern roomblock connecting the east and west ends of the semicircular plan. This south wall enclosed the inner plaza and created both a physical and a visual boundary between the plaza and the area south of the building. Henceforth, direct access was gained through a single doorway at the center of the south wall. This change might reflect a significant shift in the plaza's function, from that of an open, freely accessed, public space to that of a less public, more restricted space. The addition of the southern roomblock apparently had less to do with accommodating growth than with formalizing Pueblo Bonito's plan according to aesthetic considerations. In front of the south wall outside the plaza, two mounds were enclosed within masonry retaining walls. A passageway between the two mounds was aligned with the central doorway of the south wall.

Although the south wall is oriented almost perfectly east

west, it is not consistent, and this inconsistency may be significant. The eastern half of the south wall angles north of true east between 3 and 4 degrees, and a seemingly superfluous exterior platform was added to the southeast corner of the building (Fig. 5.2). Williamson (1987a:145) noted no apparent astronomical reason for this angle, and Judd originally noted no specific purpose for the platform, suggesting that it might have been a shrine (Lekson 1986:143).

The western half of the south wall, however, aligns due east-west. Hypothetically, if one sighted along this wall to the true western horizon at sunset on the fall equinox, one would see the sun setting at the point where the south wall visually intersected the horizon at the western end of the canyon (view A, Figs. 5.2 and 5.3). At this point, sunlight would parallel the south wall's western section. If the Pueblo Bonito plan is conceptually extended to a full circle, then the single doorway in the south wall falls at the center of the circle and at the point where the south wall bends. Hypothetically, the rays of setting sunlight at the equinox would pierce this center, matching the effect of the large Fajada Butte sun dagger at summer solstice (Fig. 5.4).

In fact, this phenomenon does not actually occur at equinox sunset. Sighting west along this section of the south wall, it is impossible to observe the true horizon at sunset because the distant canyon wall rises approximately 6 degrees above the horizon line, obscuring true sunset. On the fall equinox, however, if one sights west along the south wall's eastern half from the protruding southeast platform, the sun does set at the point where the reconstructed wall would visually intersect the elevated horizon (view B, Figs. 5.2 and 5.3). Conversely, when sighting due west along the wall's western section, the sun appears to set at the point where the western wall intersects the mesa-top horizon approximately eight to nine days before the true fall equinox (view A, Figs. 5.2 and 5.3). This process would occur in reverse for the spring equinox—that is, eight to nine days afterward.

On the basis of analogous modern Pueblo practices, Zeilik (1987) suggested that many such ancestral Puebloan sightings served as predictive devices for anticipating important astronomical events, rather than for noting specific current events. It is possible that the ancestral Puebloans used Pueblo Bonito's south wall for such purposes. Sunset, viewed from the south wall's true east-west line, would predict the pending fall equinox sunset eight to nine days later, and the equinox sunset itself could be viewed from the angled eastern wall section. It is also possible that the sight lines signaled commencement of rituals nine days before the fall equinox. This offers a possible explanation for the nine-day duration of many historic Pueblo rituals. It should also be noted that when sighting east along the south wall's western half from the far southwest corner of the pueblo, a true equinox sunrise can be observed at the far horizon (view A reversed, Figs. 5.2 and 5.3).

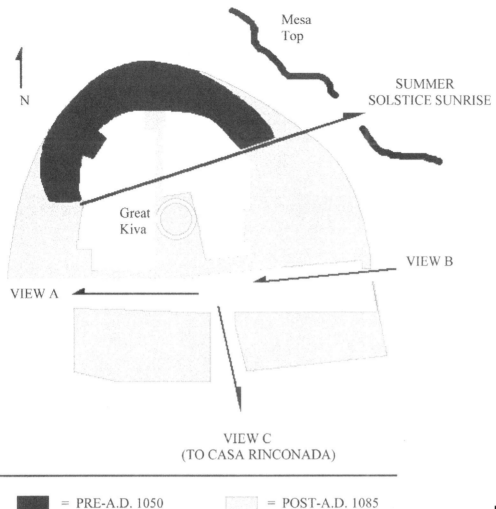

Figure 5.2. Pueblo Bonito plan and view angles.

The Chacoans may have had a relatively simple problem at Pueblo Bonito. They wanted a true east-west orientation with a line of sight for equinox sunsets (and probably sunrises), but because of Pueblo Bonito's location, this was impossible with a perfectly straight wall. The size, developmental history, and original reasons for the siting of Pueblo Bonito probably precluded relocating the structure itself, so an accommodation was necessary. The bent south wall provides a solution for both sight lines, though at the expense of formal or aesthetic harmony in the overall plan.

The effect at sunset near the fall equinox is conceptually bidirectional. Observers at the proper stations would look outward toward the setting sun while the sun's rays penetrated inward toward Pueblo Bonito. This inward penetration conceptually mirrors the Fajada Butte sun dagger phenomenon in three-dimensional architectural space, albeit horizontally. Sacred shafts of sunlight would pierce the center of a form designed to generate and accommodate symbolically laden, ritually produced spirals. An apparent inconsistency with this

symbolism, which I will return to later, is the implication that some ritual processions began not in Pueblo Bonito's kivas but at the doorway in the south wall. A possible explanation for this inconsistency lies in the ritual role of the great kiva of Casa Rinconada located across the canyon (Fig. 1.5).

The angle in the south wall may also relate Pueblo Bonito's ground plan to the large Fajada Butte sun dagger. If the ground plan is juxtaposed over the large spiral at its center and is penetrated by the solstice sun dagger, the angle of the sun dagger shaft matches the angle of the eastern half of the south wall (Fig. 5.4). It simultaneously mirrors the imaginary dagger created by the two different equinox sunset sight lines along the south wall. The symbolic meeting of these two daggers at Pueblo Bonito's center (by analogy a great architectural circle or spiral) is similar to another well-known sun dagger phenomenon at Hovenweep in eastern Utah. Near Holly House ruin, opposing sun daggers bisect spirals and concentric circles at summer solstice sunrise, eventually meeting each other and forming a single band of sunlight (Williamson 1987b).

Figure 5.3. Equinox sunset views from Pueblo Bonito.

The effects of sunlight at equinox sunrise and sunset would also have touched Pueblo Bonito in a related but subtler manner. For only the briefest of moments at each event, just as the sun is at the horizon point, the building itself is covered in shadow while the area immediately south of the east-west wall (the conceptual bottom half of the "circle") is bathed in raking sunlight. This effect mirrors the sunrise shadows cast along the large Fajada Butte spiral at the minor lunar stand-still (Fig. 5.1).

The sun dagger atop Fajada Butte is not a perfectly articulated image, so its juxtaposition against the Pueblo Bonito plan is admittedly inexact. But it is close enough to suggest the possibility that the large spiral and Pueblo Bonito's final plan were metaphorically related. This possibility is intriguing because Fajada Butte's spirals and daggers would then seem to mimic architectural forms while inverting the symbolism of the relative astronomical associations. In effect, a complete, conceptually dynamic model of universal process would have been created. Rituals enacted at these locations at coordinated times would have energized this model in the most profound sense.

GREAT KIVAS

My original inspiration for reconsidering the sun dagger arose out of a fascination with three seemingly innocuous, apparently minor, yet persistently bothersome details concerning the plans of Pueblo Bonito and Chaco Canyon's great kivas. These were the overall semicircular or crescent shape of Pueblo Bonito's final form, its peculiar broken or bent south wall, and the offset fireboxes in the various great kivas. Each of these apparent anomalies might be merely a random exception to the highly formalized nature of Chacoan architecture, occurring perhaps in response to practical or logistical concerns met during construction. But closer scrutiny suggests that a more sophisticated motivation underlies their appearance.

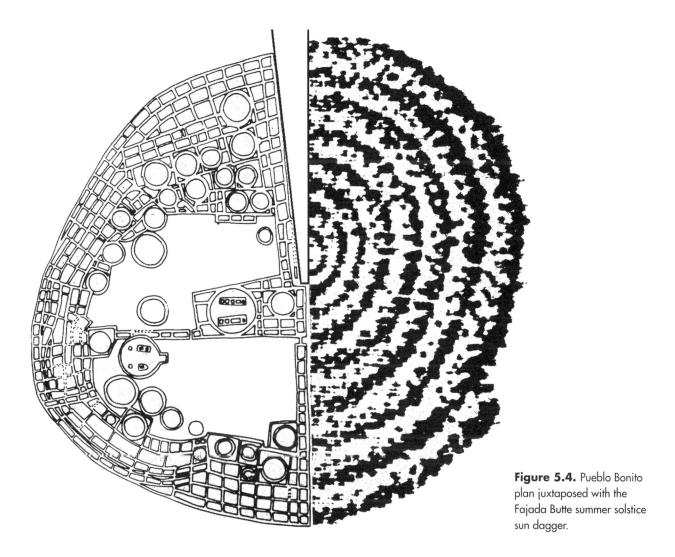

Figure 5.4. Pueblo Bonito plan juxtaposed with the Fajada Butte summer solstice sun dagger.

Ancestral Puebloan architects may have incorporated the idea of spiral directionality and celestial phenomena into the great kivas. Six great kivas have been fully mapped in Chaco Canyon; two align almost precisely north-south, and four are oriented approximately 10 degrees west of north. The latter group includes Casa Rinconada, the isolated great kiva located approximately 2 km directly south of Pueblo Bonito on the canyon's south side (Vivian and Reiter 1960).

Casa Rinconada clearly demonstrates the visual association of celestial counterclockwise rotation with architectural planning. When one views the north star, Polaris, above the horizon across the kiva's north-south alignment, the rest of the celestial bodies in the night sky appear to rotate from right to left, or counterclockwise, aligning the kiva with the conceptual center of the universe (Carlson 1990). For the other great kivas along the canyon's north side, such alignment is impossible, because the canyon wall obscures Polaris. The celestial rotation, however, is still visible.

Williamson (1987a, 1987b) and Zeilik (1987) have discussed certain solar alignments at Casa Rinconada and their possible significance. At the equinoxes, rays from the rising and possibly the setting sun strike the kiva at right angles. Sunlight at summer solstice sunrise might also have penetrated Casa Rinconada in an articulated fashion through a portal in the eastern wall (Fig. 5.5), striking a precisely located niche in the opposite western wall, although Zeilik (1987) has debated the accuracy of this conclusion. A similar event might have occurred at sunset on the summer solstice, although the appropriate portal is now missing, and another, similar event occurs between the south doorway and a west wall niche at winter solstice sunrise. There are also potential midday solar events. At midday summer solstice, sunlight would certainly have penetrated the interior of Casa Rinconada and other kivas vertically through their rooftop openings (Fig. 5.5), simultaneously with the appearance of the large Fajada Butte sun dagger.

These roof openings, in conjunction with the great kivas'

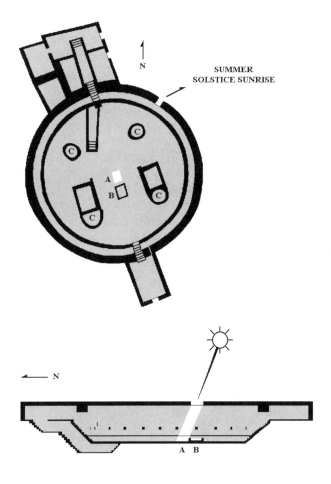

Figure 5.5. Reconstructed Casa Rinconada plan and cross section on the summer solstice. *A,* sun patch at midday; *B,* firebox; *C,* pillars.

offset fireboxes, might have served a sophisticated symbolic purpose. Unfortunately for archaeologists, the roofs of the four excavated Chaco Canyon great kivas have not preserved well enough to permit accurate reconstruction. The roof of the great kiva at Aztec Ruins, however, a Chacoan great house located approximately 150 km to the north, serves as a possible model for other great kiva roofs. In each of the Chaco Canyon great kiva floor plans, the large firebox is not located in the center of the structure. Instead, the north edge of the firebox lies approximately 12 degrees south of true center. At Casa Rinconada, this is approximately 1.5 m from the center point of the kiva floor (Fig. 5.5). The actual distance varies with the overall sizes of different kivas, but the relative distance (i.e., the degree of offset) is consistent.

The exact sizes and locations of the original roof openings in the Chacoan great kivas are impossible to ascertain with certainty, yet they may have been critical to any symbolic function of the opening. In his reconstruction of the Aztec Ruins great kiva, Morris (1921) located the roof opening directly

above the offset firebox. One might logically expect the large fireboxes to be located directly below the roof openings for ease of smoke ventilation. At the scale of the great kivas, the roof openings were probably used not for access but solely as ventilators and light portals.

Considering the offset fireboxes in conjunction with the Fajada Butte sun daggers reveals some intriguing concordances. If Swentzell's (1992) model of kiva symbolism is applied, then the great kiva roofs must be understood metaphorically as great sky baskets. A roof's opening would then symbolize the sky opening and primary axis of cosmic energy flow. Sunlight penetrating the opening would have carried great symbolic import, especially at summer solstice when the large Fajada Butte sun dagger event was taking place.

Because Chaco Canyon lies north of the Tropic of Capricorn, the sun never reaches true zenith there. On the summer solstice—when the sun reaches its highest daily point during the year—it rises 78 degrees above the southern horizon, or 12 degrees south of a true vertical point overhead at noon. This angle matches the offset angle of the fireboxes. By winter solstice the sun has receded south approximately 47 degrees, rising only to a point approximately 31 degrees above the southern horizon.

When the Fajada Butte sun dagger phenomenon is compared with the hypothetical play of light across Casa Rinconada's floor, a remarkable set of visual concurrences appears. Sunlight entering the kiva's rooftop opening at any time of year would have created a "sun patch" on the floor, reflecting the (presumed) rectilinear shape of the opening and mimicking the shape of the firebox. This sun patch would have appeared first near the base of the west wall between the western roof pillars and moved gradually across the kiva floor during the sun's daily progress, finally disappearing near the east wall at sunset. Depending on the exact size and location of the roof opening and firebox, a specific type of visual interplay would have been created between the firebox, the sun patch, and the kiva plan.

On the summer solstice, as the Fajada Butte sun dagger pierced the large spiral, a beam of sunlight would simultaneously have entered Casa Rinconada's roof opening. At noon, the resulting sun patch would have illuminated the kiva's center point, adjacent to the firebox's north edge (Fig. 5.5). This would have been the closest the sun patch came to the firebox; each subsequent appearance during the year would have been farther away. As the sun's ecliptic progressed farther south into winter, the midday sun patch would have receded farther north along the kiva floor, away from the firebox. By winter solstice, when the sun's angle is lowest, the patch may have completely disappeared, as it does at the Aztec great kiva.

If the location of the sun patch were noted at midday each day between the winter and summer solstices, it would appear to progress in a daggerlike motion from the kiva's north edge toward its firebox, mimicking the action of the Fajada Butte dagger. This "great kiva sun dagger" would have appeared regardless of the location of the rooftop opening (so long as it was located along the plan's central north-south axis), but its most spectacular effect would have occurred as described if the opening was located above the offset firebox. This phenomenon can indeed be observed at the reconstructed Aztec Ruins great kiva.

Beginning around the spring equinox, the midday location of the sun patch would have progressed from approximately 6 m north of the kiva's center point to just south of the center point, near and possibly just touching the firebox's north edge at summer solstice (again, at the same moment the large Fajada Butte sun dagger bisects the large spiral). A ritual performer or priest standing at the kiva's center, immediately north of the firebox, would have been spotlighted by the most sacred and dramatic sunlight at a most sacred time of year, the point at which the great kiva sun dagger pierced the kiva's center and neared (symbolically ignited?) the firebox.

THE GENDER OF RITUAL

This patterned semiotic recurrence of the spiral and dagger image further suggests that Fajada Butte, Casa Rinconada, and Pueblo Bonito might have been used together at certain times of the year in a coordinated program of rituals. The iconographic evidence suggests a specific mechanism for Casa Rinconada's role in the social integration of the canyon's south and north sides. It also suggests a method for understanding the spatial relationships among the different structures and forms within a greater Chacoan cosmogram.

Stein and Lekson (1992) characterized architectural space at Chaco Canyon as reflective of a unified and coordinated use of the landscape that created a cosmogram of the ancestral Puebloan worldview on a universal or macro scale. In this view, each aspect of ancestral Puebloan material culture and art is conceptually linked to the others by a fundamental, universal organizing principle. The cosmogram is reflected in the organization and use of space within a given room, within a given building, externally between different buildings, and between buildings and the greater landscape.

Stein and Lekson (1992) pointed out one such relationship between Casa Rinconada and Pueblo Bonito that is especially relevant to this study. The walkway between Pueblo Bonito's two southern mounds appears to align the structure's single southern doorway, the wall of its great kiva, and its central axis with Casa Rinconada (Fig. 5.2). This alignment creates a direct visual link between the two structures (a formal road or avenue might also have existed). Perhaps not coincidentally, the visual link is aligned approximately 10 degrees west of north, so that on the summer solstice, the angle of sunlight parallels it approximately 30 minutes before the sun's midday

high point, the Fajada Butte sun dagger event, and the appearance of the great kiva sun patches. Observation of the noonday shadows and the sun's location relative to Casa Rinconada, from between the Pueblo Bonito mounds and the angle in the south wall, suggest that rituals involving both structures could have either begun or concluded at Pueblo Bonito's single south doorway rather than in its interior. This relationship between Pueblo Bonito and Casa Rinconada offers a possible justification for conceiving of Pueblo Bonito as half of a great ritual spiral.

If the astronomical orientations built into Casa Rinconada, Pueblo Bonito, and Fajada Butte were intentional, then these orientations might have been connected through a series of interlocked symbolic and ritual activities. The addition of three-dimensional, spiral and dagger astronomical orientations to the list of previously documented astronomical orientations for Chaco Canyon provides a complex yet coordinated set of features for Chacoan architecture. On the solstices and equinoxes, coordinated sunrise, midday, and sunset observations and associated rituals could have taken place almost simultaneously at Pueblo Bonito and Casa Rinconada, in conjunction with relevant sun dagger events at Fajada Butte. It requires no great imagination to envision the intensity of activity that must have surrounded the sites on these particular days and times.

At summer solstice sunrise, sunlight first penetrates Casa Rinconada from an angle of approximately 23 degrees north. Because Casa Rinconada is situated atop a knoll along the south canyon floor, it receives a nearly true horizon sunrise at summer solstice. The same is not true for Pueblo Bonito. There, across the canyon next to the north canyon wall, the northeast horizon is obscured and the line of sight to true sunrise on the summer solstice is blocked. Because of this, summer solstice sunrise actually occurs about an hour later at Pueblo Bonito than at Casa Rinconada. No significant summer solstice sunrise orientations are currently evident in Pueblo Bonito's final plan, but Williamson (1987a:149) noted that in its original (pre-A.D. 1050) plan, Pueblo Bonito was apparently oriented to the solstice (Fig. 5.2). Summer solstice sunrise would have been visible from the old plan's western end, viewed directly across its eastern end. The visual effect would have mirrored the equinox sunrise profile shadows at Fajada Butte—a semicircle highlighted along its flat side by sunlight or, more conceptually, the full circle again pierced at the center. The same effect would have applied to sunset at winter solstice. Apparently, sometime after about 1050, the Chacoans reoriented Pueblo Bonito's plan in order to shift emphasis from solstice to equinox activities. Perhaps not coincidentally, at about the same time a change in burial patterns took place in the structure (see Akins, Chapter 8).

Pueblo Bonito and Casa Rinconada lie approximately 0.7 km apart. In a direct line, Pueblo Bonito is approximately 5 km west of Fajada Butte, although the walking distance following canyon trails is 6–7 km. Casa Rinconada is only some 100 m closer to Fajada Butte. These distances mean that Pueblo Bonito is only about 10 minutes' normal walking time one way from Casa Rinconada, and both structures are 1.5 to 2 hours' walking time one way from Fajada Butte. A round-trip walk beginning at Casa Rinconada at dawn could easily encompass Pueblo Bonito and Fajada Butte and return to Casa Rinconada at sunset (and would probably include stops at the other canyon-bottom great houses located along the way).

Beginning at Casa Rinconada on the summer solstice, one could observe the sunrise event through the northeast portal and then walk to Pueblo Bonito in time to observe sunrise there. One could then proceed up canyon to Fajada Butte, arriving in time to observe the midday sun dagger event. Variations in this pattern could be expected to have occurred as well. About 30 minutes before midday, for example, the angle of the sun between Casa Rinconada and Pueblo Bonito might have signaled commencement of a procession from one structure to the other, which would have arrived in time to witness the appropriate midday event.

Further evidence suggests the possibility that during the eleventh century, Chaco Canyon evolved into a center of specifically female-oriented rituals, possibly the ancestors of modern Pueblo rituals. For Pueblo Bonito after A.D. 1030, Akins (1986) has documented a shift in burial patterns from predominantly male to predominantly female bodies. This shift appears just before the 1050 reorientation of the building's plan previously noted by Williamson (1987a) and the 1085 construction project that produced the distinctive bent south wall and the plan's final overall crescent shape.

This timing suggests a symbolic purpose to Pueblo Bonito's final crescent shape. Both crescents and spirals are primary iconographic elements of certain Hopi women's ceremonies held each autumn (Hoge 1994), specifically the Lakón and Márawu ceremonies (spelling of the names of these ceremonies varies considerably; I use the spellings in Waters 1963). Two aspects of these ceremonies are of note here. First, although the major rituals for both ceremonies are conducted in autumn, preliminary rituals are conducted in early summer. Second, both are held in direct association with the fall equinox. Lakón is held in mid-September, prior to the equinox, and Márawu takes place in late September, immediately after the equinox (the two ceremonies temporally "bracket" the equinox). Historically, summer solstice marks the traditional end of the six-month katsina dances and the beginning of the plaza dances, and fall equinox marks the midpoint of the plaza dances. Although it is a bit simplistic, the obvious question is, Do Pueblo Bonito's mortuary and architectural changes somehow reflect a heightened emphasis on gender-based rituals in Chaco Canyon?

In *Book of the Hopi*, Waters (1963) documented the Hopi Lakón ceremony as it was performed early in the twentieth century. Lakón is traditionally a nine-day women's ceremony held just before the fall equinox, coincidentally near the same time the small equinox sun dagger appears atop Fajada Butte. Most significantly, Waters (1963:231) noted that "preliminary [Lakón] rituals are held at corn planting time in late May and early June, when four women members of the society, accompanied by . . . the Lakón mongwi [chief], enter the kiva for eight days." Although this appears to be too early to coincide with summer solstice, the suggestion of an early summer ritual linked to the autumn Lakón ceremonies is nevertheless provocative.

At first light on the seventh day, Lakón participants emerge from the kiva and proceed through the village, stopping periodically at shrines to leave offerings and prayers. At sunrise, they proceed down a trail from the village to the Lakón shrine beyond the mesa. They form a line around the shrine, which is described as "a huge black volcanic boulder out of whose flat top protrudes a complex of small brown nodules surrounded by curious whorls" (Waters 1963:232). In order to become adept at weaving plaques and baskets, the women must leave offerings and prayers and rub their hands in circular motions over the whorls. The whorls are said to symbolize the mother's womb. Hence, the entire ritual is a symbolic appeal for fertility. The spiral process of basket weaving is a metaphor for general fecundity and creation.

Waters (1963) did not illustrate the spiral whorls, but he cited frequent examples of women running their hands over sacred shrine markings in a circular motion during the women's ceremonies. Fewkes (1892:20) documented rock art at shrines around the Hopi mesas, including a carved spiral from "an isolated rock at the south base of the mesa under Hual-pi." This fits Waters's description of a Lakón shrine and underscores both the actual and symbolic importance of the petroglyph spiral to Lakón ritual. At the conclusion of Lakón, participants arrange themselves in a circle in the plaza, displaying their basket trays or plaques in a scene replicating Pueblo IV kiva murals. The baskets are subsequently distributed to onlookers, and the performers retreat back into the appropriate kiva. Lakón ceremonies are the primary women's ceremony conducted during the entire yearly cycle of Hopi ritual.

The evidence presented in this study suggests that similar rituals on a much grander scale might have been conducted at Chaco Canyon nearly a thousand years earlier. An account by Fewkes and Owens (1892) remains the most detailed historical description of the Hopi Lakón ceremony, and a remarkable number of similarities can be cited between this account and the events under consideration here for Chaco Canyon. Following is a selective list of key Lakón activities that might have had precedents in Chaco Canyon.

1. The most significant times for key daily Lakón rituals were sunrise, noon, and sunset.

2. At sunrise on each day of ritual, a Lakón priestess placed "standards or *na'-tci* at the kib-va entrance to indicate . . . that the kib-va was occupied by those who were celebrating the La'-la-kon-ta" (Fewkes and Owens 1892:108). Fewkes's illustration of a *na'-tci* is of a round bundle of corn meal supporting an ear of corn and feathers pierced through a hole in the top (Fewkes and Owens 1892:Pl. I-4).

3. At noon each day, Lakón participants made *ba'-hos,* sacred corn bundles placed as offerings at shrines. On the first day, "when the sunlight through the kib-va entrance fell in a certain place on the floor and indicated noontime, each of the four priestesses made a single *ba'-ho*" (Fewkes and Owens 1892:109–110).

4. "The early dawn of the second day . . . was ushered in by the departure of the novices to a shrine half way between Wal'-pi and Si-tcum'-o-vi [east of Walpi]. . . . As she placed the feather on the shrine she threw a pinch of meal toward the sun, the light of which was just beginning to redden the east. . . . This or a similar ceremony was repeated on the following mornings" (Fewkes and Owens 1892:111). The shrine east of Walpi was also revisited on the fifth and eighth days. The eastern location of Fajada Butte in Chaco Canyon could easily have accommodated a similar sunrise ceremony for most of the Chaco Canyon structures.

5. On the eighth day, preparations were begun for the concluding rituals the following day. "At about six PM a procession of women proceeded down the south trail to the spring Da-wa'-pa" (Fewkes and Owens 1892:122). "The members then passed on to the shrine among the foothills to the south of the spring, where they formed a semicircle, facing the south" (Fewkes and Owens 1892:123). Compare this procession with Pueblo Bonito's south-facing semicircular plan with its south doorway and associated south view and route to Casa Rinconada.

6. On the ninth and last day, "the women who performed the public dance formed in a line just outside of the kib-va at sunrise" (Fewkes and Owens 1892:126).

These points highlight major structural or symbolic similarities between historic Hopi use of ritual space and apparent features and orientations documented for Chaco Canyon. A close reading of Fewkes and Owens (1892) and Waters (1963) reveals other points of comparison as well.

CONCLUSION

Numerous deficiencies can be cited in an argument of this nature. Many apparent solar alignments might actually have been unintentional. Pecked spirals occur throughout Chaco Canyon's rock art; the Fajada Butte examples are only the best documented and most famous. Other buildings and rock art sites in the canyon might have served related ritual functions. Moreover, in making this argument, I have considered the apparent significance only of major points in the solar calendar; lunar and other astronomical events might also have played significant roles (Fewkes and Owens 1892:117).

Nevertheless, I believe that the implication of this argument for interpreting the ritual function of Pueblo Bonito and other canyon sites is profound. By A.D. 1100, Pueblo Bonito may have been the center of rituals dominated and dictated by women's societies. The site's central canyon location and long developmental period suggest some symbolic primacy over other Chaco Canyon structures. Given this apparent primacy, the role of women's rituals linked with astronomical events centered on Pueblo Bonito but coordinated with other sites throughout the canyon takes on a deeper significance than previously believed. Although such rituals might have originated during Basketmaker times, they were highly formalized at Chaco Canyon through the integration of older symbolic motifs (i.e., spirals) with sophisticated architectural forms (great houses and great kivas), providing a model and subsequent tradition for modern ritual. In this context, Pueblo Bonito and the Fajada Butte sun daggers articulate complex, powerful metaphors of ancient Pueblo worldview and ritual process.

6

Construction Labor at Pueblo Bonito

Mary P. Metcalf

The question of how much labor was required to construct Pueblo Bonito relates directly to the issue of how the people who built and used the site were organized. In Chapter 4, Stein, Ford, and Friedman outlined the massive construction that took place during each of the site's major stages. The question I consider in this chapter is how much effort was invested in each of those building episodes. I document how Pueblo Bonito's labor requirements varied through time, as well as which aspects of the site were the focus of construction at each stage. For some stages, the labor invested was substantial. I conclude that Pueblo Bonito can, in fact, be considered an example of monumental architecture.

This study expands on a previous labor study by Lekson (1986), who calculated the aggregate construction labor for all of Chaco Canyon's great houses. I use Lekson's construction stages and effort estimates to calculate stage-by-stage construction effort for Pueblo Bonito alone. In addition, I discuss variations between civic and noncivic construction at Pueblo Bonito. I consider the relationship between construction effort and political organization, review issues involved in estimating the labor requirements of prehistoric structures, present labor estimates for each of Pueblo Bonito's major construction stages, and consider the implications of these estimates for the people who built and used the site.

LINKING POLITICAL ORGANIZATION TO ARCHITECTURE

The literature that combines architecture and anthropology often focuses on the relationship between architecture and meaning, or thought. Can architecture be read as a text? Or perhaps as a grammar of social relations and cultural interconnections? Is the relationship between the size or location of one room and that of its neighbors based on the mental template of the builders or users? If so, then the messages are literally carved in stone—they are texts created when a structure was built. Additions and renovations might be analogous to revisions of a written text, though perhaps even more revealing of meaning, because both the initial structure and the later revisions might be discerned. Or is the relationship between structure and meaning a dynamic interchange? Once built, do architectural structures actively influence their builders or users, shaping their thoughts or at least encouraging some thoughts and discouraging others?

One kind of meaning that can be encoded in architecture is the relationship between architecture and political organization. Underlying my labor estimates is the view that the relationship between meaning and architecture is mutual and dynamic. Just as thought determines a structure's form, that form in turn affects thought (see Donley-Reid 1990; Hillier and Hanson 1984). This view has been characterized as symbolic and thus not amenable to labor studies (see Moore 1992 for this critique of the limitations of energetic studies, particularly as used by archaeologists). Yet the amount of labor and time involved in the construction of a building is an essential component of the structure's "message." It is not merely the great size, number of rooms, and elaborate decoration of a palace that convey the power of its residents; it is also the visitor's awareness that this structure required more resources to build than the average residence. These resources might have involved not only labor but also the skills necessary to employ specialized masonry techniques or produce certain decorative elements. A large labor investment indicates that the builders felt it was appropriate to expend a great deal of energy on the structure. That knowledge is a powerful aid when one interprets the meanings of a structure such as Pueblo Bonito, whether those meanings are economic, social, or symbolic.

One well-documented relationship between meaning and architecture concerns labor investment and political organization (e.g., Erasmus 1965; Kolb 1994; Quilter and Vargas 1995). In general, previous research has focused on monumental architecture in stratified political systems such as chiefdoms and states (for an overview see Haas 1982; Trigger 1990). Such studies have frequently been flawed by the absence of a definition of the term "monumental." Both Quilter and Vargas (1995) and Trigger (1990), however, offered clear definitions of "monumentality." According to Quilter and Vargas (1995:209), monumental architecture is "human constructions that require significantly greater energy investments to build than quotidian structures. . . . [It] entails the labors of more than the minimal social unit to build, takes up significantly more space than other constructions, and is commonly elaborated by features, such as decorations, that distinguish it from non-monumental works." Trigger (1990:119) similarly defined monumental architecture as having scale and elaboration in excess of that necessary for the practical function that "a building is intended to perform." This definition embraces large houses, public buildings, and special-purpose structures.

These authors agree that monumental architecture involves more labor expenditure than nonmonumental architecture, that the finished product is large, and that it frequently has elaborate nonutilitarian features. Of these criteria, labor input is the most straightforward to measure, and it is linked to the criterion of large size. Quilter and Vargas (1995) emphasize that the "non-quotidian" or noncommonplace nature of the structure is particularly useful as a criterion because it requires comparison not just with other monuments but with other contemporaneous and culturally related structures. Not only must monumental architecture be large on an absolute scale (as determined by comparison with accepted examples), but it must also be large in comparison with contemporaneous examples.

Studies of the relationship between monumental architecture and political organization have focused on the prerequisites for erecting large structures. They include management (implying a status of manager), people to provide the labor (and whose basic needs must be provided for during the period of labor), and possibly construction specialists. In addition, the laborers and specialists must be willing to provide the labor, indicating that the managers have the ability to induce or coerce cooperation for the project (see Erasmus 1965). Together, these requirements imply that monumental construction projects generally require complex political organization.

Complex political organizations in turn imply the presence of elites, and the link between architecture and wealthy or elite individuals and institutions has proven fruitful for archaeological study. Architecture is an area in which elite individuals or institutions express their power—from palaces and pyramids to roads and temples. This is done in two ways: either through the sheer "impressiveness" of the finished product or through the impressiveness of the amount of labor required to construct the finished product.

Webster (1991) discussed in detail the role of labor control in the rise of stratification in prehistoric Europe. He asserted that differential control over labor was the fundamental first step toward stratification, preceding even differential access to material wealth. He believed control over labor would be visible in the archaeological record as settlement hierarchies and variation in domestic structures. The implication is that in architecture, one can distinguish levels of wealth and prestige that are much subtler than the distinction between elites and nonelites in state-level societies (Gilman 1981; Hodder 1992; Horne 199; Peebles and Kus 1977).

Some scholars have argued that monumental architecture plays a crucial role in maintaining unequal political systems—that the impressiveness of the construction serves to reify, to embody, and to assert by association the impressiveness of the elites. Johnson (1982:376) suggested that much monumental architecture exists merely as a result of the elites' attempts to keep the nonelites busy. Elites are owed, or have the use of, a certain amount of nonelite labor, but the system is one of "use it or lose it." Therefore, elites invent projects to use nonelite labor (Johnson called this "piling behavior"). A cycle is created that reinforces the elites' right to control labor while simultaneously creating more, and more impressive, monuments associated with the elites.

Apart from political organization and social differentiation, architecture can carry other meanings. It can indicate a society's priorities, for example. The relative amount of labor involved in constructing civic structures is directly related to the significance of the civic structure for the builders' society. Civic space is any space that has relevance for the community as a whole, as opposed to domestic (or noncivic) space. An example was presented by Hodder (1992:232–233), who argued that competitive building projects were a medium of social competition during the Neolithic in Britain.

Architecture can also reflect or promote ideology (Bourdieu 1973; Fritz 1978, 1987; Littlejohn 1967; Montmollin 1989; Rappoport 1969; Schele and Friedel 1990; Smith and David 1995). For example, Kolb (1994) examined changes in the labor investment in *heiau,* Hawaiian religious shrines, through time. He correlated changes in island social and political organization with architectural changes and the rise of an islandwide political entity over the course of 500 years. Architectural construction can thus reflect several aspects of culture, including community organization, social stratification, and ideology.

ESTIMATING LABOR

Underlying all of the arguments about monumental and other kinds of public architecture is the concept of labor. Labor investment is an aspect of architecture that can be quantified, which may be one reason why labor studies have been used since the beginnings of archaeology as a science. Another reason is that one of the first questions that comes to mind when one looks at well-known prehistoric structures such as the Egyptian pyramids is, How did they build that?—usually followed by, How long did it take them? For archaeologists, these sorts of questions are equally intriguing when asked about less dramatic structures. In this section I consider previous efforts to quantify labor investment in prehistoric architecture. After identifying relevant variables for performing the calculations, I review the results of previous labor estimations for Chaco Canyon.

Relevant Variables

For the Egyptian pyramids or Stonehenge, the basic technological aspects of construction have provoked numerous theories, ranging from alien intervention to the simple "lots of sweat" theory. In contrast, the technical aspects of construction in the prehispanic northern Southwest are considered to be understood. Although the details of how some structures were placed in some out-of-the-way locations remain perplexing, a consensus exists on the general way in which the

masonry walls were built. One topic that still provokes debate and that will be addressed later is the construction of kiva roofs. Readers interested in the details of construction techniques are referred to Lekson's *Great Pueblo Architecture of Chaco Canyon* (1986). Additional details may be found in publications by the National Park Service (1981) and Durand (1992).

Quantifying architectural construction labor is less straightforward, and various methods for doing so have been proposed. Because visual appraisal may not be an adequate method for evaluating labor investment (see Arnold and Ford 1980), a more concrete approach is necessary. Studies in which researchers have attempted to determine construction rates fall into two categories, ethnoarchaeology and experimental archaeology. In the first, the archaeologist observes others performing similar construction tasks and determines the time or energy involved (e.g., Erasmus 1965; Lekson 1986). In the second, the archaeologist is involved in the construction itself (e.g., Lindsey, reported in Bradley 1988).

Generalizing from the results of these two kinds of studies can be difficult. It may be impossible to determine whether multistory construction was the result of many people working for a short period of time (a situation that would be more likely to require management) or of a few people working over a long period. Ethnographic studies have suggested some answers but cannot be definitive (see Ford 1972 for a discussion of how the hours worked in a person day vary). How people work today does not necessarily reflect how they worked in the past, whether in terms of hours per day, days per week, or some other organizational variable. Consequently, archaeological studies have tried to focus on the total number of hours worked, not on how that labor was distributed.

The focus of most labor studies has been on the labor involved in constructing large monuments, although a few researchers (e.g., Abrams 1994) have considered the effort required to build domestic structures. Considering both large monuments and smaller structures allows each type of building to be seen in comparison with the other, providing a more comprehensive view of construction labor within a society. Large monuments might not seem so massive when compared with the total volume of domestic construction or even with an individual domestic structure. Thus, it is not necessarily the total amount of labor involved in a construction that is of interest, but how that total compares with the amount of labor invested in other structures built by people of the same society. Both the absolute labor estimates for structures and the variation among structures should be considered (see Quilter and Vargas 1995).

Chaco Canyon Studies

Efforts to quantify the labor requirements for Chaco Canyon's prehispanic architecture began with research by Shimada

(1978). He asked several Navajo workmen employed in ruins stabilization and reconstruction to agree to wear cumbersome devices that measured their oxygen intake. He then used oxygen consumption and time to calculate the work rates of different men for tasks such as quarrying stone, shaping stone, transporting building materials, filling a rubble core, and constructing a limestone veneer. He documented the degree of variation among workers as well as the efficiency of different construction methods. Interestingly, for the construction workers whom Shimada studied, efficiency was not a major consideration (but see Durand 1992 for an opposite view).

A later study by Lekson (1986) focused on the aggregate labor requirements for constructing Chaco Canyon's great houses through time. Lekson relied on work rates published by Erasmus (1965) as well as rates provided by Steve Adams for the National Park Service (Lekson 1986:277) for the construction of flat roofs, dome roofs, and Type III masonry walls. Multiplying these work rates by the sizes of the relevant greathouse components, Lekson calculated the approximate person hours (PH) required for construction during each stage. His results indicated that labor requirements for great-house construction peaked in the years around A.D. 1050, remained high, and then peaked again in the early 1100s.

Lekson's calculations also indicated that the sizes of these peaks were relatively modest. The 1095–1100 peak was 55,645 PH per year, a figure that could have been produced by 16 industrious people working 10-hour days, 365 days a year. Lekson concluded that none of Chaco Canyon's great houses could be considered monumental, although he did suggest that they might be considered "modestly monumental." He interpreted the great-house structures, the increasing formalization in architectural style during the eleventh century, and the presence of other built forms such as roads as evidence of a chiefdom level of sociopolitical complexity.

In another study, Durand (1992) focused on architecture both in Chaco Canyon and at Salmon Ruin, a great house located outside the canyon. He interpreted the great houses' core-and-veneer wall style as the "most efficient" for walls intended to be several stories high. Durand (1992) concluded that the core-and-veneer architectural style was not truly a stylistic choice but rather an engineering one. His work is intriguing because it implies that Chacoan builders sought to minimize the time and effort expended in construction.

Nelson (1995) compared labor investment in architecture between two "sites," Chaco Canyon and La Quemada in Mexico, using Lekson's (1986) figures for Chaco and his own for La Quemada. Nelson emphasized that labor investment studies reveal two aspects of a society's organization: scale and hierarchy. Scale is indicated by labor investment; hierarchy is indicated through consideration of scale in relation to population size. Nelson argued that whereas Chaco Canyon represents a larger-scale society in terms of labor investment, La

Quemada represents a more hierarchical society. Because La Quemada had a smaller estimated population, each individual or household would have been required to contribute more construction labor to build the site than would have been the case at Chaco Canyon. This would have required more political control than Chaco Canyon's construction, indicating to Nelson a more hierarchical society. Nelson's distinction between scale and hierarchy is useful for labor investment studies because it emphasizes that concentrating only on construction products obscures important information about the construction process. In order to distinguish hierarchy from scale using Nelson's criteria, however, one must have a firm understanding of population, something that is lacking for Chaco Canyon.

CONSTRUCTION LABOR AT PUEBLO BONITO

In this section I calculate how many person hours were required to build Pueblo Bonito. I first consider methodological issues that affected my calculations and then present labor estimates for each of Pueblo Bonito's major construction stages. Last, I compare Pueblo Bonito's labor requirements with those of other Chaco Canyon great houses.

Methodological Issues

Two methodological issues must be addressed in order to calculate the labor requirements of Pueblo Bonito's construction. One is chronology. For my analysis, I relied primarily on the seven-stage construction sequence outlined by Lekson (1986). I did make two modifications to this sequence. First, following Windes and Ford (1996; also see Windes, Chapter 3), I used an earlier date than Lekson's for the beginning of Stage I building. Second, because my analysis focused on completed masonry architecture, I did not include the incomplete Stage V foundation complex or the two large rubble-and-trash-filled mounds located in front of Pueblo Bonito (see Stein et al., Chapter 4, for further discussion of these features). Moreover, I considered only initial construction labor, not labor required for repair or renovation.

The other methodological issue affecting calculations of Pueblo Bonito's labor requirements is what unit of measurement to use. I calculated labor in terms of person hours (PH) required to build walls and roofs, which is a rough measure of the scale of construction. A person hour denotes the quantity of work done by one person in one hour. I did not convert my person hour estimates into weeks, months, or years, because the amount of time required for construction is affected by many indeterminate factors such as workday length, workforce size, and the efficiency of the builders. In calculating the person hours required for each of Pueblo Bonito's building episodes, I broke the construction effort into two categories: that required to build domestic (rectangular) rooms and that required to build civic (circular) rooms. The purpose of this division was to investigate how the Chacoans chose to invest their time, labor, and resources in different components of Pueblo Bonito during each of its construction stages.

The person hour estimates were derived from analyses of completed masonry architecture, specifically walls and roofs. To calculate cubic meters of wall, I used the formula *volume = length × height × width*. On the basis of Lekson's work (1986), I considered great-house walls to be 0.6 m wide and 2.4 m high unless published data gave specific information on width and height. I converted wall volume to person hours using Lekson's (1986) "PH per cubic meter of wall" rates for compound walls.

To estimate the person hours required for roof construction, I analyzed flat and cribbed roofs separately. Smaller kivas probably had flat roofs similar to those of habitation and storage rooms. Kivas with four pilasters may have had either flat or cribbed roofs. Kivas with six or more pilasters had cribbed, or corbeled, roofs (see Rohn 1977:251). These divisions are not always clear; the vagaries of preservation can make it difficult to determine the number of pilasters. For flat roofs, I multiplied roof area by Lekson's (1986) figure of 30 PH per 5 m² of roof. This figure includes the costs of procuring, shaping, and transporting timbers as well as the cost of the roof construction itself.

Construction of a cribbed roof is a much more laborious undertaking than is that of a flat roof, particularly in terms of the volume and size of the timber required (e.g., Betancourt et al. 1986; Hovezak 1992). Dean and Warren (1983) estimated that a single beam for a cribbed roof might have weighed as much as 275 kg and that transport of beams to the canyon would have required six times the labor needed for cutting and processing alone. To estimate the person hours required for cribbed roof construction, I multiplied Lekson's (1986:283) cribbed roof shaping and transport figure of 128 PH per 5 m³ by 110%. The additional 10% was derived from Lekson's estimate that construction labor for flat roofs represented roughly 10% of the total labor. I believe my person hour estimate for cribbed roof construction is probably low, because it does not account for the procurement and placing of the nontimber fill used to flatten out the tops of cribbed roofs. It does, however, account for the fact that the increased timber volume in cribbed roof construction increases the amount of time involved in procuring, shaping, and transporting timbers. Consequently, using the 110% figure succeeds in giving cribbed roofs a much higher person hour construction estimate than that for flat roofs.

Total Labor Invested in Pueblo Bonito

My calculations indicate that approximately 805,000 person hours were required to build Pueblo Bonito (Table 6.1). This

Table 6.1

Construction Labor Estimates for Pueblo Bonito

Stage and Date A.D.	Person Hours	% of Total	Person Hours/Year
I (860?–935)	205,192	25.5	2,736
II (1040–1050)	108,381	13.5	10,838
III (1050–1060)	89,200	11.1	8,920
IV (1060–1075)	69,248	8.6	4,617
VI (1075–1085)	234,281	29.1	23,428
VII (1085–1100?)	98,810	12.3	6,600[a]
Total	805,112	100	

Note: These estimates do not include labor required for the structures dating to Lekson's (1986) Stage V—the foundation complex and the two platform mounds—or for renovations and repairs. Stage I dates are from Windes and Ford 1996; all other stage dates are from Lekson 1986.
[a]The labor-per-year figure for this stage is approximate, because the length of the stage is unknown.

estimate does not include construction of the Stage V foundation complex, the two southern platform mounds, or remodeling and maintenance efforts. Thus, the total labor expended on Pueblo Bonito would have been even higher than the figure presented here.

The amount of labor required for each construction stage varied tremendously, ranging from a low of 69,248 person hours in Stage IV to a high of 234,281 person hours in Stage VI.[1] In terms of percentages, Stage VI was again the highest, with 29% of the total construction effort.

The construction episode with the second greatest labor requirement was Stage I, which required approximately 205,192 person hours, or roughly 26% of Pueblo Bonito's total construction effort. The Stage I figures may be inflated, because Stage I (Type I) masonry is less complicated than that used during successive time periods (see Fig. 3.1). The Stage I labor figures may also be somewhat misleading because the time interval associated with this stage is at least 10 times longer than any of the succeeding stages. When the total person hour estimates for each stage are standardized to account for varying stage lengths, Stage I construction ranks last in terms of person hours required for construction per year.

Two other observations can be made with the standardized (per year) labor estimates. One is that Stage VI retains its position as the construction episode that required the most labor. Indeed, Stage VI building required more than twice as much labor per year as the second-ranked Stage II. The other observation concerns the considerable amount of labor invested in a relatively short interval after A.D. 1040. Stage I required 26% of the site's labor costs. After a roughly 175-year lull, the remaining 75% of the site's labor costs were incurred in Stages II–VII, during a span of roughly 60–75 years (see Windes, Chapter 3, and Stein et al., Chapter 4, for discussions of when Stage VII ended). During this interval, between 1040 and 1100,

Table 6.2

Noncivic versus Civic Construction Labor Estimates for Pueblo Bonito

Stage	Total Noncivic Labor (Person Hours)	Total Civic Labor (Person Hours)	Noncivic Construction as % of PH	Civic Construction as % of PH	Civic Construction Effort as % of Total Construction Effort[a]
I	195,097	10,095	95.1	4.9	1.3
II	88,428	19,953	81.6	18.4	2.5
III	54,017	35,183	60.6	39.4	4.4
IV	56,089	13,159	81.0	19.0	1.6
VI	205,662	28,619	87.8	12.2	3.6
VII	58,954	39,856	59.7	40.3	5.0
Total	658,247	146,865	81.8	18.2	18.2

[a]Total construction effort is the sum of civic and noncivic construction labor for Pueblo Bonito, or an estimated 805,112 person hours.

Table 6.3

Construction Labor at Several Chaco Canyon Great Houses

Great House	Estimated Construction Labor in Person Hours	Estimated Civic Construction Effort in Person Hours	Civic Construction Effort as % of Total Construction Effort
Pueblo Bonito	805,112	148,865	18
Chetro Ketl, Stages II–XV	544,038	54,404	10
Pueblo del Arroyo, Stages I–IV	321,000	70,620	22
Pueblo Alto, Stages I–V	198,449	53,581	27
Wijiji	147,863	3,000	2
Kin Kletso	134,501	13,450	10
Average	358,494	57,313	15
Standard deviation	266,628	51,844	9.2
Coefficient of variation	74%	90%	62%

Note: Construction stages follow Lekson 1986.

approximately 10,000 person hours were invested in Pueblo Bonito's construction per year.

As part of my analysis, I compared the amount of labor invested in domestic rooms and in civic rooms. Because of disputes over Pueblo Bonito's function, I was particularly interested in the site's "civic construction effort" (CCE). My analysis indicated that the labor invested in civic construction varied through time (Table 6.2).

Pueblo Bonito was initially built with little effort expended on civic construction. During Stage I, civic construction was composed entirely of small kivas. Stage I kivas represent only 1.3% of the total construction effort over the lifetime of the site and just under 5% of Stage I construction effort alone. These figures would be even lower if they were standardized to account for the disproportionately long time interval associated with Stage I in comparison with subsequent periods. It is entirely possible that kivas from Stage I are not currently known or were destroyed by later building. The existence of such structures would raise the percentage of the civic construction effort. Still, a very large number of unknown kivas would have to be present in order to change the figures dramatically.

During the eleventh-century expansion, civic construction increased overall. Two building episodes, Stages III and VII, had particularly large percentages of civic architecture. Although the basic outline of Pueblo Bonito was altered little as a result of this eleventh-century construction (see Stein et al., Chapter 4), both the amount of civic space and the labor expended on it increased significantly.

Pueblo Bonito Versus other Chaco Canyon Sites

Comparisons with other Chaco Canyon sites can help put Pueblo Bonito's labor requirements in perspective. Com-

parisons are made here with other great houses, with small sites, and with civic construction effort at both types of sites (Table 6.3).

All of Chaco Canyon's great houses required huge numbers of person hours to build, and Pueblo Bonito required the most. Construction effort at the other great houses ranged from a low of just over 130,000 PH at Kin Kletso to well over 500,000 PH at Chetro Ketl (Table 6.3; Metcalf 1997). The large amount of construction labor required to build Pueblo Bonito and all of the other Chaco Canyon great houses reflects both the scale of construction and the length of the construction commitment made by the builders. This investment is made even more impressive by the fact that much of the great-house construction took place simultaneously.

In contrast to Pueblo Bonito and the other great houses, the construction effort made for the canyon's small sites was much less. Small-site construction during the eleventh and twelfth centuries ranged from 4,500 to 20,000 person hours, with the average small site requiring approximately 9,000 PH (Metcalf 1997). Thus, the average small site required one-ninth the effort of Pueblo Bonito's smallest construction episode (Stage IV) and only one-twenty-fifth the effort of its largest episode (Stage VI).

The amount of labor required for great-house civic construction varied from a high of nearly 149,000 PH at Pueblo Bonito to a low of approximately 3,000 PH at Wijiji. Two groups of great houses can be identified on the basis of civic construction effort as a percentage of total construction effort: those with an overall CCE of 10% or less and those with an overall CCE of 18% or more (ranging up to 27%). The high investment group includes Pueblo Alto, Pueblo del Arroyo, and Pueblo Bonito. For all but two of its construction episodes, Pueblo Bonito's civic construction percentages are higher than the Chaco Canyon average, falling in the group of high CCE percentages (Table 6.2). The exceptions are Stage I, which had a very small civic component, and Stage VI, which consisted almost entirely of noncivic construction. Interestingly, the CCE scores at small Chaco Canyon sites can also be grouped into two sets: those of 13% and below and those of 28% and greater (Metcalf 1997).

IS PUEBLO BONITO MONUMENTAL?

The idea that monumental architecture was present in the Southwest has been considered previously in varying contexts. Lightfoot (1988) noted that the construction of a Pueblo I great kiva roof alone required more than 5,000 person hours of labor, matching the labor required to build a long barrow or causeway in Neolithic Great Britain (see Bradley 1984). If the roof alone can be considered monumental, then certainly the entire structure can be designated so. Adler and Wilshusen (1990) designated Basketmaker III great kivas as monumental. Several types of Hohokam construction have been considered monumental, including irrigation canals, platform mounds, and ball courts (see Neitzel 1991; Wilcox and Sternberg 1983). The question of whether Chaco Canyon's great houses are monumental remains debated. Lekson (1986:271) used the term "modestly monumental," noting that there is "little Chacoan architecture that could seriously be considered monumental." But "modestly monumental" begs the question, because no definition of monumental architecture is offered.

I think Pueblo Bonito and other Chaco Canyon great houses can be considered monumental architecture without modifying the term. They were much larger, in both size and construction labor, than the immediately surrounding small sites. Indeed, they were larger than was "common" for the time period and the region overall. In addition, the great houses were characterized by decorative elaboration, which is usually associated with monumental architecture and which was absent at Chaco Canyon's small sites. This decorative elaboration took the form of highly patterned masonry (Fig. 3.1), which may not have been visible during use, because of plaster coating. In comparison with structures at other ancestral Puebloan towns, large and small, the rooms and civic structures at great houses were larger and more elaborate. The individual rooms were larger not only in area but also in height, although a great deal of variation existed (see Stein et al., Chapter 4; also Lekson 1986:39–50). Chacoan great kivas were also larger and more heavily decorated than typical ancestral Puebloan kivas. The great kivas often included many niches, some containing exotic materials, and had more numerous floor features than contemporaneous small kivas. The niches and other great kiva features are further examples of the architectural elaboration commonly associated with monumental architecture.

Pueblo Bonito's function has little bearing on the judgment that it was a monumental structure. General definitions of monumental architecture have included both special purpose buildings (Trigger 1990) and residences (Quilter and Vargas 1995). The keys to determining whether or not a building is monumental are size, elaboration, and labor investment, not function. Regardless of whether great houses are ultimately determined to have served as residences, as special use buildings, or as some combination of the two, they were clearly nonquotidian in comparison with other pueblos both in Chaco Canyon and in the Southwest as a whole. By this standard, Pueblo Bonito is monumental.

This conclusion does not need to be qualified by uncertainties about how much calendar time was invested in Pueblo Bonito's construction. To consider issues such as scheduling, work crew size, and workday and workweek length requires a number of assumptions. For example, Lekson (1986:262) estimated that the 190,000 person hours he thought were required for Pueblo Bonito's single largest construction episode, Stage VIA, could have been achieved by 30 people working 10 hours per day for only 21 months. Alternatively, I suggest that all of Pueblo Bonito's eleventh-century construction could have been completed by 30 people working 40 hours per week for 10 years (distributed over a 45-year period). At first glance, both sets of figures suggest that the burden of Pueblo Bonito's construction was not huge. But we have no way of knowing whether the builders worked eight hours per day, five days a week, or at a more leisurely pace. Furthermore, by focusing on Pueblo Bonito alone and, in the case of Lekson's estimate, on only one building episode, the figures, even if accurate, are somewhat misleading. Construction was occurring simultaneously at other great houses, making the total effort much greater.

The relevance of timing can perhaps best be evaluated by comparing Pueblo Bonito with other structures. My analysis indicated that 75% of Pueblo Bonito's construction took place in 60–75 years (Stages II–VII) and required approximately 10,000 person hours per year. Even if Pueblo Bonito was built by a small crew working throughout the entire time span, this interval is shorter than those for many Old World structures that required approximately the same number of person hours as Pueblo Bonito to build and that are generally identified as examples of monumental architecture (e.g., causeways, small henges, barrows).

CONCLUSION

Pueblo Bonito is clearly an example of monumental architecture according to at least two definitions of monumentality (Quilter and Vargas 1995; Trigger 1990). The structure required substantial labor to build—its total labor investment exceeded 800,000 person hours. This figure is undoubtedly low, because it does not include the labor required for the Stage V foundation complex, the two platform mounds fronting the site, and ongoing renovations and repairs. Pueblo Bonito's two most labor-intensive construction episodes were Stage I (A.D. 860–935) and Stage VI (1075–1085), each requiring more than 200,000 person hours. Of the two, the Stage VI building episode was the more intense, because it was conducted over just a decade as opposed to the first stage's 75-year span. The Stage VI building effort was preceded by 35 years of ongoing construction and followed by at least 15 more years of work. Altogether, Stages II–VI required an average investment of approximately 10,000 person hours per year. This figure is extremely impressive, but as an average it obscures variability in Pueblo Bonito's labor investment through time. The investment was greatest during Stage VI, which would have required more than 20,000 person hours per year over the span of a single decade.

Not only did the amount of labor invested in Pueblo Bonito's construction vary through time, but so did the investment in civic and noncivic building. During Stage III (1050–1060) and Stage VII (1085–1100), civic construction in the form of kivas approached half of the construction effort. During other building periods, noncivic construction (i.e., rectangular rooms) was by far the dominant aspect of the building effort. Presumably, Pueblo Bonito's building history reflects the changing needs of its builders and users. That more civic space was required at some times than at others suggests variation in sociopolitical organization through time.

This analysis of Pueblo Bonito's construction labor has two other implications that are significant for models of Chaco Canyon's political organization during the 900–1100 period. First, the conclusion that Pueblo Bonito was a monumental structure implies that its residents and users were involved in a stratified political system. Second, the evidence that Pueblo Bonito's total labor investment was much greater than the investments in other Chaco Canyon buildings highlights Pueblo Bonito's central role in the canyon's sociopolitical organization.

It is important to remember, however, that Pueblo Bonito was not alone. Other great houses, both inside and outside the canyon, also required significant construction effort, even a "monumental" amount of labor. Pueblo Bonito represents only one of a number of significant structures. All of these great houses must be considered together in order to understand the political system that was centered on Chaco Canyon and extended throughout the ancestral Puebloan world. Only by evaluating all aspects of Pueblo Bonito, including its construction labor, within the site's broader contexts will the significance of this structure be truly appreciated.

ACKNOWLEDGMENTS

This research was supported in part by a National Science Foundation dissertation improvement grant and by the Department of Anthropology at the University of Virginia. Special thanks go to Jill Neitzel for organizing the original Society for American Archaeology session and for her subsequent assistance with this chapter. Stephen Plog, Jeffrey Hantman, Rachel Most, and Brad Tanner all offered advice on various versions of the paper.

NOTE

1. Stage VIB is Lekson's (1986:262) famous "single largest construction episode in the history of Chaco Canyon." This is an interval for which my labor estimates for construction effort in Chaco Canyon differ noticeably from Lekson's. He estimated (1986:261) that Stage VIB construction required 192,862 person hours, whereas I estimate that it required somewhat more than half of my Stage VI total, that is, about 117,100 person hours. The difference between these estimates does not alter the value of either set of numbers for internal comparison. Different methods yield different results, and comparisons of the different results may be akin to comparisons of apples and oranges. These differing results should not obscure the more important conclusion, that Stage VIB was the largest single construction effort in Chaco Canyon.

7

Pueblo Bonito

When a House Is Not a Home

Wendy Bustard

After six years excavating Pueblo Bonito and twenty-seven years pondering the results, Neil Judd (1954:23) concluded that "Bonitian architecture is often bewildering." This bewildering complexity is a problem for archaeologists, because architecture defines the Chaco system. We know that tenth- to twelfth-century Chacoan architecture was large-scale and technologically complex, but we do not know why such complexity developed at this time and place. The great house is the trademark of Chacoan architectural complexity. And of all the great houses in Chaco Canyon, Pueblo Bonito stands out: it was the largest in number of rooms, the tallest, and the richest in material culture. Yet after 100 years of excavation, testing, and analyzing, we still do not know exactly what Pueblo Bonito was. Was it a residence of elites or of simple apartment dwellers? Was it a ceremonial center? A storage house? A temple? All of these uses have been proposed and challenged, but none has been completely discounted. In this chapter I look at the most basic distinction—whether or not Pueblo Bonito was a home.

The conceptual framework for this chapter is the study of architecture as the enclosure of space. Saile (1977:159) noted that "architecture deals with 'place.' Place implies spatial organization, that is, the ordering of qualities which distinguish certain places from others or from nebulous undifferentiated space." But how do we identify the "ordering of qualities" to distinguish one kind of place from another? In other words, how do we determine basic functions such as residential use?

Enclosed space has two components: form and function. Architects and archaeologists often study the two separately, but enclosed space can best be understood when form and function are considered as parts of a whole (Hillier et al. 1984). Anthropologically, form is often linked directly to social or symbolic meaning through ethnography (e.g., Eliade 1961; Lawrence 1983;

Rappoport 1969). It is most often explained, however, by reference to cultural preference (e.g., Hall 1966; Rapoport 1980). Generalizations about form, which is the identifying trait of the Chaco system, are rare, because morphologically similar house plans can (and do) have different cultural and/or functional origins. Architectural function is defined here as use, and it can be studied at two levels: that of the individual space or room and that of the complete structure.

In this chapter I examine the function of great houses at the level of the complete structure. The question of great-house function dominates Chacoan architectural studies, and the proposed answers have changed over the decades. Early research was based on the assumption inherent in the terminology: great houses were by definition residential (e.g., Judd 1964). More recently, increasing uncertainty about the function of Chacoan great houses has generated a series of different models reinterpreting them as redistribution or periodic centers (Judge 1984; Windes 1987a, 1987b), as storage facilities (Lekson 1986), and as ritual centers (Fowler and Stein 1992; Judge 1989, 1991; Stein and Lekson 1992; Toll 1985).

Functional differentiation in monumental architecture has been identified for other complex societies in the form of elite residences, temples, markets, administrative centers, tombs, and the like (Peebles and Kus 1977; Renfrew 1973). None of these complexity markers is unambiguously present in great houses. The challenge, then, is to develop a functional explanation for structures such as Pueblo Bonito without the usual architectural clues that help us distinguish temples from tombs.

To investigate the question of Pueblo Bonito's function, I use space syntax, a relatively new approach to spatial analysis. After summarizing space syntax—its theory and analytical techniques for describing and measuring space and space use—I use a subset of space syntax, access analysis, to describe Pueblo Bonito's built environment qualitatively and quantitatively. On the basis of this analysis of form, I then evaluate the idea of Pueblo Bonito's function as a home.

SPACE SYNTAX THEORY AND METHOD

Embedded in the social theory paradigm, the space syntax approach has been developed over the past two decades by architects at University College London (Hillier and Hanson 1984; Hillier et al. 1987). Social theories of space assume a fit, but not an equivalency, between social organization and the built environment (Lawrence and Low 1990) and so provide a framework for the study of prehistoric spatial form. Architecture, or built space, is seen as structuring social order and facilitating social integration (Lightfoot 1994; Lipe and Hegmon 1989). Often it is impossible to determine whether social order is a result of intentional spatial strategies or of the aggregate built environment that constrains or promotes social relations in some fashion. Social theory focuses instead on pos-

sible effects of the built environment on social organization. For instance, the built environment can control social interaction, serve as a mnemonic device to reinforce social relationships, and provide cues for appropriate social behavior (Rapoport 1979).

The premise of space syntax is that social relations and processes express themselves in space through spatial configuration (Hillier et al. 1987:363). Spatial configuration is specifically defined in space syntax as the relations between and among architectural spaces, taking into account all other spaces in the complex being studied and also the relation of interior spaces to the outside world. The built environment is seen not as a passive reflection of society but as the result of an active "set of strategies in relation to social form" (Hillier et al. 1978:375). Identifying spatial configurations and patterns provides a means of understanding social strategies that relate to spatial organization.

The lack of a grammar for standardized, nonimpressionistic descriptions of the built environment has long been an analytic stumbling block in architecture and archaeology. Complicating matters, the architectural description of built form does not necessarily address questions of spatial organization. Space syntax provides a means of describing and studying the patterns of organized relationships that exist among architecture, built-in room features, and spatial configuration. Its methodology is topological, employing spatial concepts of access, connectivity, adjacency, and permeability. A subset of space syntax, access analysis, deals with boundary controls or movement permeability. Permeability is defined as the degree to which closed cells, entrances, and spatial configurations encourage or discourage access to and movement through structures or settlements.

A growing number of archaeologists are using space syntax techniques to interpret spatial structure and patterning in the architectural record. Syntactic studies have been conducted throughout the world on sites of varying levels of cultural complexity. Examples include Neolithic Near East structures (Banning and Byrd 1989; Byrd and Banning 1988), Chalcolithic tells in Bulgaria (Chapman 1990), Maltese monuments (Bonanno et al. 1990), medieval buildings in England (Fairclough 1992), Iron Age structures in Scotland (Foster 1989a, 1989b), prehistoric Peruvian sites (Czwarno 1988; Moore 1992), Sudanese houses (Osman and Suliman 1994), Nile Delta houses (Plimpton and Hassan 1987), and ancestral Puebloan structures and settlements in the American Southwest (Bradley 1993; Bustard 1996, 1997; Cooper 1995, 1997; Ferguson 1993, 1996; Shapiro 1997a, 1997b).

Southwestern studies illustrate the method's usefulness. In a comprehensive study of Zuni settlement systems from the 1500s to the present, Ferguson (1993, 1996) demonstrated how space syntax can be used to identify and explain certain spatial patterns. His study shows how the architectural structure of modern Zuni Pueblo derives from the diachronic reproduction of Zuni society through social interaction and how changes in spatial structure relate to changes in social structure that can be tied to historical events.

Bradley (1993) used space syntax to investigate site planning and architectural functional differentiation at Sand Canyon Pueblo, a large site in southwestern Colorado occupied during the A.D. 1200s. The identification of clusters of specialized architecture led Bradley to conclude that Sand Canyon Pueblo was not simply an aggregation of unit pueblo households but a complex, functionally differentiated settlement.

In his study of fourteenth-century Arroyo Hondo Pueblo in the Rio Grande Valley of New Mexico, Shapiro (1997a, 1997b) used space syntax to document change over time in spatial arrangements, from a relatively integrated to a more segregated settlement. The shift through time was toward privately controlled interior space, with plazas serving as community-wide integrating social spaces. Shapiro (1997b) concluded that these changes suggested a period of experimentation in social organization during Arroyo Hondo Pueblo's occupation, which coincided with the widespread adoption of the katsina cult in the Rio Grande Valley.

Cooper (1995, 1997) used space syntax to evaluate competing interpretations of great-house function in Chaco Canyon, focusing on access and control features of spatial organization to draw inferences about social usage. The quantification of spatial relations allowed Cooper to show syntactic differences within and among great houses temporally and spatially.

In my work on Chaco Canyon, I have focused on the spatial and social relationships of small houses to great houses (Bustard 1996, 1997). Syntactical analyses have shown that the simplistic size dichotomy between the two types of sites is misleading. Spatial diversity is the hallmark of Chacoan buildings, great or small. Despite the diversity in form, the functional organization of space is strongly patterned in small houses. On average, small houses contain more domestic features than do great houses, and mealing rooms are highly integrating places, spatially and socially. Great houses, on the other hand, display wide-ranging spatial and functional diversity, making single-use models unpersuasive.

ACCESS ANALYSIS OF BUILDINGS

The space syntax program was developed, in part, in response to the need for a descriptive theory of building form with which to understand building function (Hillier et al. 1984). At the most general level, buildings organize enclosed space. At the most specific level, they organize space use through the structured, functionally determined movement of people through individual spaces in a building (Hillier and Hanson 1982). As building size increases, strong spatial structure tends

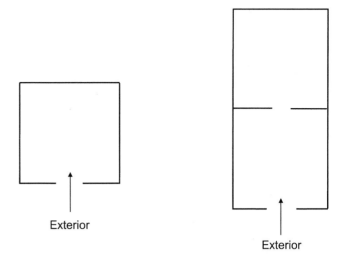

Figure 7.1. Bounded space. *Left,* enclosed cell; *right,* aggregated cells.

to decrease, and more complex patterns of spatial activity and movement develop (Hillier et al. 1984). That is, as building or settlement size increases, the potential for encounters between occupants and visitors becomes more probabilistic than deterministic (Hanson and Hillier 1987; Hillier et al. 1987).

Internal divisions of space vary according to perceived needs and, in the view presented here, according to the social relations among the building's inhabitants and visitors. The fundamental topological relation in the syntactical analysis of individual structures is access. The basal spatial unit is the enclosed cell, or bounded space (Fig. 7.1). Boundaries divide space; breaks in boundaries, such as doorways and gates, allow access to some and deny it to others, giving inhabitants control of their space (Steadman 1996). Walls are a special case of boundaries that relate to social rules regarding spatial territoriality, promoting inclusion or exclusion (Evans 1978). Each cell has at least one entrance and is therefore accessible via another cell or via exterior, unbounded space. Circulation patterns through a complex of cells create an "access structure" that can be graphed (Fig. 7.2). Access graphs are abstractions of spatial relations in which small circles or nodes represent individual spaces, and lines joining them represent their linkages. Adjacency does not determine the shape of the access graph; it is permeability between spaces that dictates how a graph is constructed.

Diagramming space or spatial relations is more than description; it is a research method in itself—a way of thinking and analyzing (Rapoport 1990). Although the architectural applications of graph theory are not new, Hillier and Hanson's (1984) contribution has been the idea of a "justified" access graph. On a justified access graph, the exterior is the "root"

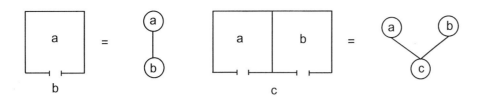

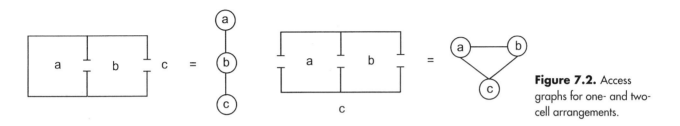

Figure 7.2. Access graphs for one- and two-cell arrangements.

or base level of the graph, and all spaces are arranged vertically above it according to their topological distance from the exterior (Fig. 7.2). Justified access graphs provide simple visual summaries of the topological structure of a building (Brown 1990). In space syntax methodology, constructing the access graph is the first step in the quantification of spatial relations.

The most useful measurement provided in space syntax is that of spatial integration, which quantifies the spatial relations observed in access graphs. Spatial integration refers to the degree to which an individual space in a building is shallow and accessible to inhabitants and visitors. The distinction between shallow and deep is central to interpreting syntactic measures. In space syntax, depth is defined as the topological distance, or number of steps or spaces, from an individual space to some other space, usually the exterior of the complex. Mean depth is the mean number of steps or spaces from an individual space to all other spaces in the complex (Hillier et al. 1984). The spatial concept of depth has a social component in that it is associated with privacy. On a public-private continuum, shallow spaces are more public, and deep spaces are more private.

Integration in space syntax is understood in the sense of "integration toward something," usually the exterior world (Teklenburg et al. 1993:349). A proxy measure for spatial accessibility, spatial integration is quantified by a formula comparing how deep each individual space is in relation to all other spaces in the building.[1] Integration is also a measure of linkage, or the number of spaces with which each individual space is directly linked. Access graphs with circulation rings linking multiple spaces (and thus offering at least two pathway choices to a particular space) exhibit high degrees of spatial integration (Fig. 7.3). Graphs with treelike, branching patterns have overall low degrees of integration, in that there is only one pathway from the exterior to any particular space.

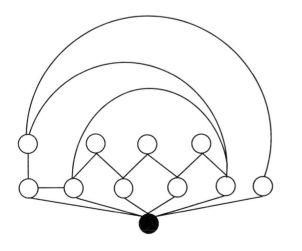

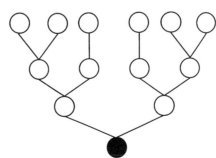

Figure 7.3. Examples of access graphs. *Left,* circulation rings; *right,* tree graph.

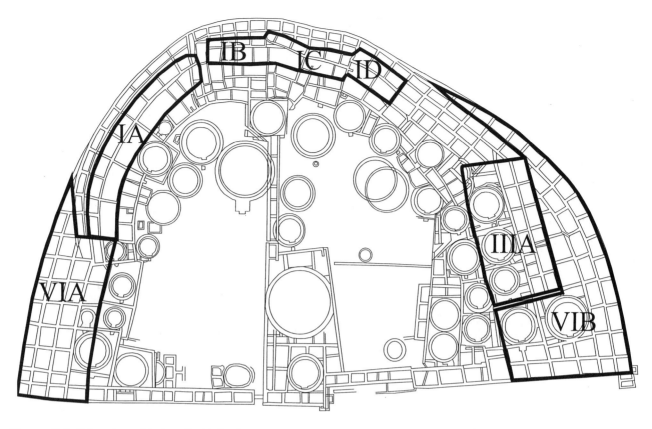

Figure 7.4. Selected roomblocks at Pueblo Bonito.

PUEBLO BONITO'S BUILT FORM

To construct access graphs of archaeological structures, one needs detailed information on spatial access and relations, which requires the excavation of entire structures or roomblocks. Pueblo Bonito, which has been almost completely excavated, is an excellent candidate for syntactical analysis of an archaeological site. Its excavation data provide an opportunity to look more closely at the spatial-functional organization of one of the most important great houses in the Chaco region. In what follows, I examine Pueblo Bonito's architectural space and interior spatial organization at three different moments in the structure's construction history.

Three Moments in Time

As described earlier, an access graph consists of spaces and linkages. In Chacoan great houses, enclosed rooms include rectangular surface rooms and both subsurface and ground-level rooms known as kivas, which are circular in plan. Unroofed built spaces, principally plazas and terraces, are also important. Linkages between Chacoan spaces may be doorways, hatchways, or exterior ladders. In ancestral Puebloan archaeology, the roomblock is an important architectural compo-

nent. Constructed as a unit, a roomblock contains at least two rooms, often more, and frequently incorporates kivas and terraces into its physical structure. Despite subsequent and often extensive remodeling, roomblocks maintain their structural integrity and are relatively easy to identify.

For large structures with long occupational histories, it is useful to look at individual construction stages. Most of Pueblo Bonito was built over the course of two centuries, from roughly A.D. 860 to the 1080s (cf. Windes, Chapter 3; Stein et al., Chapter 4). Extensive excavation and an ongoing project to obtain and date tree-ring samples (Windes, Chapter 3) have produced a temporal control over great-house construction that offers an opportunity to evaluate change through time. In a seminal study of Chacoan great-house architecture, Lekson (1986) divided the Pueblo Bonito construction sequence into seven stages, which I use here. I have selected five roomblocks from three construction stages (I, III, and VI) for analysis (Fig. 7.4).

New tree-ring dates suggest that Pueblo Bonito's earliest construction began around A.D. 860 (Windes, Chapter 3; Windes and Ford 1996), toward the end of the Pueblo I period. This period (700–900) was characterized by pit structures and associated small roomblocks scattered across the cultural landscape. Usually, the typical structure consisted of an arc of sur-

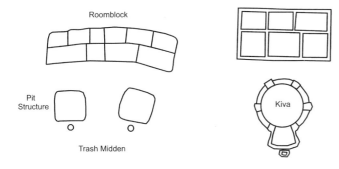

Figure 7.5. Pueblo I and II site plans. *Left,* Pueblo I unit house; *right,* Pueblo II Prudden unit.

face rooms, often two tiers deep, with jacal walls. The roomblock was fronted by an earth- and slab-lined pit structure for every five or six rooms, with a trash midden to the south (Fig. 7.5). Pueblo Bonito's earliest roomblocks followed this general architectural pattern, which continued through the Pueblo II period (ca. 900–1100). By the end of the Pueblo II period, the arrangement and construction of pit structures, or kivas, and roomblocks had become more formalized, with walls of coursed masonry. This suite of architectural units created the ubiquitous "unit pueblo" of the San Juan Basin (Gorman and Childs 1980). What distinguished Pueblo Bonito and the other early great houses from other Pueblo I and II struc-

tures were large, multistory rooms (see Windes and Ford 1992:Fig. 7.5).

Lekson divided Stage I construction at Pueblo Bonito into substages A, B, C, and D (see Lekson 1986:Fig. 4.20). Initially, Stage IA was an arc of five two-story front rooms, each paired with two three-story back rooms (Figs. 7.4, 7.6). The roomblock appears to have been constructed as a unit. Two pit structures sat in front of the arc, and a single-story ramada facing the plaza was later added over the pit structures. The access graph for the first floor of Stage IA is shallow, with three separate sets or suites of rooms (Fig. 7.6). Suites are bounded sets of rooms, each entered directly from the exterior, usually the plaza.

The Stage IB, IC, and ID roomblocks appear to have been constructed as individual, adjacent units (Figs. 7.4, 7.6). Together, they contain approximately the same number of rooms as the Stage IA roomblock, and I treat them as a single analytical unit. Extensive additions and remodelings have made the original construction record of these roomblocks less clear than that for Stage IA, but they have the same Pueblo I form. Recent tree-ring dates from Room 6 suggest that Stage IB was the first section built (Windes, Chapter 3). Originally, this section may have contained one large front room backed by four two-story rooms and fronted by a pit structure. Stages IC and ID were more irregular in floor plan: large, two-story

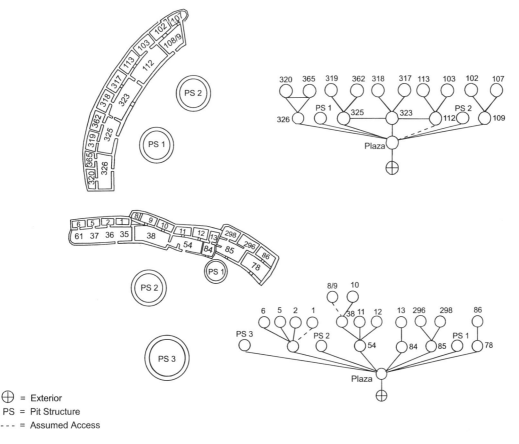

⊕ = Exterior
PS = Pit Structure
---- = Assumed Access

Figure 7.6. Pueblo Bonito plans and access graphs. *Top,* Stage IA; *bottom,* IB–D.

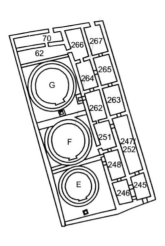

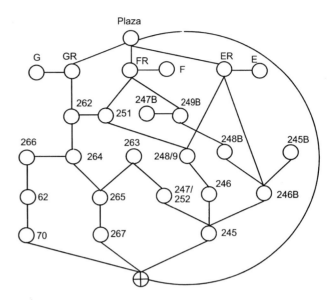

Figure 7.7. Pueblo Bonito plan and access graph, Stage IIIA.

⊕ = Exterior
B = Second Floor Room
R = Kiva Rooftop

front rooms backed by one or two three-story rooms and fronted by one to three pit structures (Judd 1964; Lekson 1986; Windes and Ford 1992). The access graph for Stages IB–D is one level deeper than the Stage IA graph and contains five separate room suites of varying sizes.

Pueblo Bonito's next major roomblock construction occurred 200 years later, in the mid-1000s. This Stage III building was remarkably different from its predecessors in form and interior circulation patterns. Large, rectangular roomblocks enclosed single or multistory kivas built on the ground surface or slightly subsurface. Originally, Stage IIIA, in Pueblo Bonito's east wing (Fig. 7.4), was a roomblock of 13 large, rectangular, ground-floor rooms and three kivas, dated to 1050–1060 (Lekson 1986; Windes and Ford 1996). Included in the access graph (Fig. 7.7) are second-story rooms in the roomblock's southern half. These rooms were linked to the first-floor rooms by an intramural stairway. The most striking aspect of this graph is its connectivity: there are many ways of getting from here to there, which is unusual in Puebloan architecture. Also, north and south doors in Rooms 70, 245, and 267 provided nonplaza entry, another unusual feature.

The site's next major roomblock construction began approximately 15 years later, between 1075 and 1085. Stage VI is divided into VIA and VIB (Lekson 1986). Stage VI construction completed Pueblo Bonito's final curved form by extending the east and west wings to enclose the hemispherical plaza. Despite the seeming symmetry of the two wings, their spatial organization differs. The Stage VIA roomblock abuts the south wall of Stage IA (Fig. 7.4). Stage VIA originally contained three north-south tiers of two-story rooms with a single-story tier of rooms on the east. These rooms were con-

structed on top of the razed Stage IIIB unit (Judd 1964; Lekson 1986). The access graph of Stage VIA (Fig. 7.8) presents an aspect of spatial organization distinct from that of Stage IIIA, with parallel room suites connected east-to-west and little north-to-south access.

Stage VIB construction defined Pueblo Bonito's final southeastern end (Fig. 7.4). This roomblock mirrors Stage VIA in placement but not in ground plan. Stage VIB abuts the east and south walls of Stages IIIA and IVA (Lekson 1986). It consisted of 39 ground-floor rectangular rooms, all of which were three stories except for Room 170, which was two stories. Kiva C was two stories, and Kiva D, three stories. I reconstructed first- and second-floor access patterns for this roomblock (Fig. 7.9). Characterized by excessive depth, both stories provided north-to-south and east-to-west access. The remarkable interconnection of rooms on the second floor was partly the result of a profusion of corner doorways. However, no interior connection between floors was discernible.

Change through Time

The access graphs for the three stages considered here differ widely. Those for the Stage I roomblocks are similar: shallow, with pairs of rooms branching off single front rooms. This is the typical Pueblo I–II small-house or unit pueblo spatial pattern. Stage IIIA's access graph is unique. Deep, complex, and characterized by extreme connectivity, this roomblock cannot be divided into room suites. Stage III represents the resumption of major construction at Pueblo Bonito after a long hiatus, and the access graph suggests that construction was initiated or accompanied by broad social changes. Stage VI, the

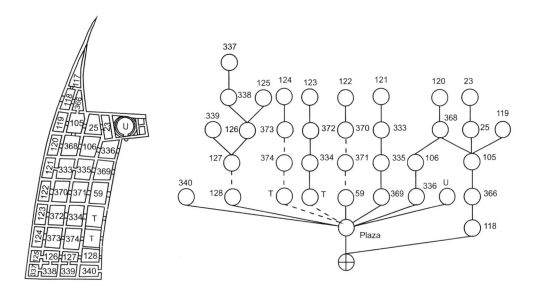

⊕ = Exterior
- - - - = Assumed Access

Figure 7.8. Pueblo Bonito plan and access graph, Stage VIA.

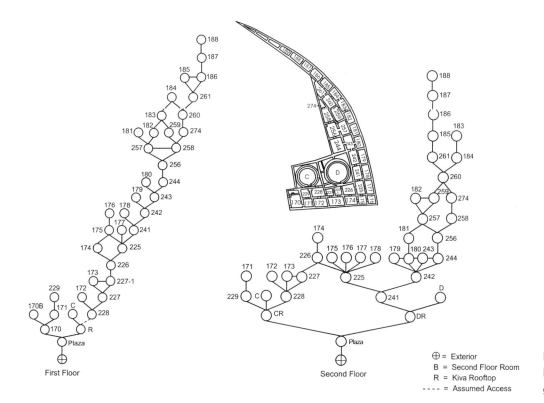

First Floor

Second Floor

⊕ = Exterior
B = Second Floor Room
R = Kiva Rooftop
- - - - = Assumed Access

Figure 7.9. Pueblo Bonito plan and access graphs, Stage VIB.

last stage in which large roomblocks were added to Pueblo Bonito, is characterized by asymmetry. The graph for the west wing, Stage VIA, is dominated by deep sequences of rooms—a mix of branching and nonbranching room suites, with the latter more common. In contrast, the graphs for the east wing's first and second floors, Stage VIB, are hyperdeep. The first-floor graph is continuously branching, usually from a single room,

which creates a lopsided spatial sequence. The second-floor graph is also deep but has a more balanced branching pattern with more connectivity. Of particular interest is that these two Stage VI wings were built essentially simultaneously yet exhibit markedly different spatial arrangements.

Pueblo Bonito's final ground plan was that of a massive, D-shaped structure formed by linking the east and west wings

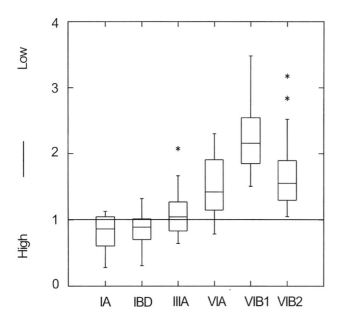

Figure 7.10. Box-and-whiskers plots of standardized integration values by roomblock. The superimposed line at level 1 is for visual clarity only.

with a line of rectangular rooms; a later series of circular rooms bisected the enclosed plaza (Fig. 7.4). An interesting aspect of the finished ground plan is that although the initial construction placed some restrictions on the direction and shape of growth, it was not until Lekson's Stage VI that Pueblo Bonito's form was finalized (cf. Stein et al., Chapter 4). The initial Stage I room arc was maintained and expanded, but it appears that Pueblo Bonito was characterized by more starts and stops in its ground plan than has usually been assumed (Cooper 1995). Lekson (1986) noted that constant remodeling was a hallmark of Chacoan small sites. Remodeling also characterized nearly every stage of Pueblo Bonito's construction, most notably the Stage V northeast foundation complex begun around 1070 and abandoned a few years later (see Windes, Chapter 3; Stein et al., Chapter 4). Midcourse corrections and modifications in the nearly constant flurry of construction at Pueblo Bonito in the 1000s were the norm rather than the exception, with symmetry more in the eye of the beholder than in that of the builder (cf. Stein et al., Chapter 4).

Spatial Integration within Roomblocks

The qualitative differences observed in the access graphs can be confirmed quantitatively. Calculating integration values using the formula published by Hillier and Hanson (1984:108–109) or, as in this case, computer software developed by the Space Syntax Laboratory at University College London creates data sets for each roomblock. These sets of integration values can then be standardized to eliminate sample size effects (Hillier and Hanson 1984:Table 3) and statistically compared across samples.

In cases where there are no explicit expectations, such as for data sets generated by space syntax, exploratory data analysis (EDA) is an appropriate place to begin. EDA places an emphasis on visual representations of data in order to evaluate assumptions regarding the normality of distributions. Box-and-whiskers plots, or box plots, are especially useful, illustrating the midrange, mean and/or median, and outliers of a distribution.

Box plots of the distribution of standardized integration values for Pueblo Bonito roomblocks reveal an interesting pattern (Fig. 7.10). Low values on the y-axis indicate high spatial integration, or spaces easily accessed from the exterior and other roomblock spaces. This plot suggests a steady progression through time at Pueblo Bonito from spatially integrated to segregated built space. Early Bonito Stage I space was more integrated than later Stage III–VI space. The first-floor rooms of Stage VIB were the least integrated. This inference can be confirmed using a standard statistical test, ANOVA, which measures the variance among sample means. Integration values for Stage VIB rooms are significantly different from those of all other rooms in this sample ($p = .0001$, $\alpha = .005$).

PUEBLO BONITO'S SPATIAL FUNCTION

What does Pueblo Bonito's architectural and spatial variation mean? Anthropologists originally interpreted Pueblo Bonito as a communal town. Early excavators referred to the Chaco ruins as "dwellings," "apartments," or "houses"—places where people lived. Today, archaeologists call Pueblo Bonito a "great house," to distinguish it from the small houses that also dot the Chaco Canyon and San Juan Basin landscapes. This descriptive terminology has reinforced the assumption that great-house Pueblo Bonito was also a home (Stein and Lekson 1992). Although this assumption has been challenged repeatedly during the past two decades (e.g., Fowler and Stein 1992; Neitzel 1989a; Stein and Lekson 1992; Toll 1985; Windes 1987a, 1987b; Windes and Ford 1992), the idea that house equals home has persisted (e.g., Sebastian 1988; Vivian 1990).

Was Pueblo Bonito ever a home? Households are interpreted as the archaeological expressions of domestic groups, or families. In the Southwest, as throughout the world, families are assumed to represent the basal social unit (Chang 1958; Dean 1989; Dohm 1988; Lowell 1991; Rohn 1965). The anthropological distinction between "family" and "household" was well summarized by Lightfoot (1994:145, emphasis in original): "Anthropologists since the 1950s have made a distinction between the *family*, as a kinship group, and the *household*, as a coresident group that shares in domestic and economic activities. In archaeology, the household is the preferred unit of analysis because it is defined behaviorally rather than structurally. That is, the household is a social group defined on the basis of the activities it performs rather than on the basis of the kin relations of its members."

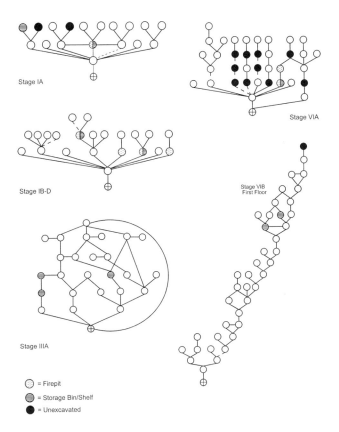

Stage IA

Stage IB–D

Stage IIIA

Stage VIA

Stage VIB
First Floor

◐ = Firepit
⊜ = Storage Bin/Shelf
● = Unexcavated

Figure 7.11. Locations of fixed features on graphs.

In his study of domestic groups, Goody (1972) suggested that households be broken down by function. Archaeologists have followed this suggestion, focusing on socioeconomic functions such as production, consumption, resource pooling, corporate ownership, reproduction, and coresidence (Ashmore and Wilk 1988; Blanton 1994; Gnivecki 1987; Manzanilla 1986). Socially, the family is the unit of reproduction. However, members of production, consumption, usufruct, and dwelling groups may vary. Lowell's (1991:3) recommendation that archaeologists focus on the "consumption unit" as the minimal definition of household is particularly apt for the Southwest, where "the material remains of the preparation of food for consumption are often preserved as hearths, grinding equipment, storage facilities, cooking and serving pots, and so on."

Here, I follow Lowell's definition of households as consumption units. I define a household architecturally as a limited set of interconnected rooms in which at least one is a domestic room with facilities for grinding, cooking, or storing food or for storing food-processing tools. At Pueblo Bonito, artifact provenience data are often not specified below the room level. As a result, I limit my criteria for domestic facilities to fixed features in nonkiva surface rooms: built-in mealing bins, firepits, and small storage facilities such as slab-lined bins, subfloor cists, and small shelves. Rooms with domestic features are assumed to be living, or habitation, rooms. Kivas

are not included because they have come to encompass a separate set of ceremonial assumptions whose supporting arguments are beyond the scope of this chapter.

For each of Pueblo Bonito's construction stages considered here, I coded the access graphs by fixed feature in order to illustrate the locations, types, and numbers of these features. Stage IA had one centrally located room that contained a firepit and a storage bin, and one back room with a built-in shelf (Fig. 7.11). None of the other Stage IA rooms had fixed features. Stages IB–D had three front rooms and one middle room with firepits; one front room and one middle room also contained storage bins. Stage IIIA had two rooms with subfloor cists and one room with a small built-in shelf. Stage VIA had two adjoining rooms with firepits, one of which also contained a storage bin. Neither the first- nor second-story Stage VIB rooms had floor features, but two first-story rooms had small shelves mounted above corner doorways. Interestingly, none of the roomblocks considered here had built-in mealing bins. In fact, only three of Pueblo Bonito's excavated rooms contained this type of fixed feature. Two mealing bin rooms were in the east Stage IV section, and one was in the final Stage VII construction.

Some of Pueblo Bonito's rooms contained fixed features unique to great houses—built-in platforms, usually made of wood. Platforms are distinguished from shelves by the following characteristics: they extend the width of the room, they are more than 1 m wide, and they are located more than 1 m above the floor. A masonry bench in Stage VIA Room 333 is also included in this category. Its length (> 1.25 m) is typical of other platforms, although its width (< 1 m) and especially its height (36 cm) are not.

Platforms may have made their first appearance at Pueblo Bonito during Stage IC in Room 38 (Fig. 7.12). Unfortunately, Pepper's (1920) description of this feature is confusing, and it may have been a shelf. Platforms reached their peak of popularity in Stage IIIA, when six first- and second-story rooms had such features. In Stage VIA there was only the masonry bench in Room 333; Stage VIB had one wooden platform. Evidence for these roomwide platforms also exists at Pueblo del Arroyo, Chetro Ketl, Pueblo Alto, and Peñasco Blanco (Lekson 1986). Their function is unknown, but they suggest storage of large quantities of goods. Only one platform at Pueblo Bonito was found in a room with a floor feature (a firepit)—the early Stage IC Room 38. This is a further indication that the Stage IC platform might not have been the same type that appeared in later Stage III–VI rooms.

Change over Time in Room Features

Altogether, the access graphs showing the locations of Pueblo Bonito's fixed features reveal how uncommon these features were (Fig. 7.13). Built-in mealing bins were nonexistent in the

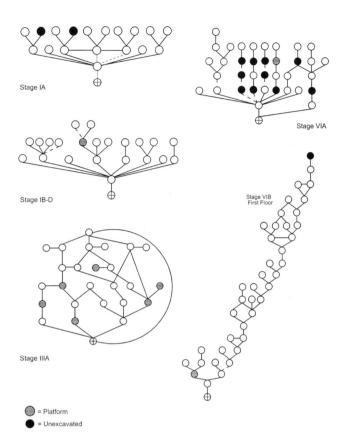

Figure 7.12. Locations of platforms on graphs.

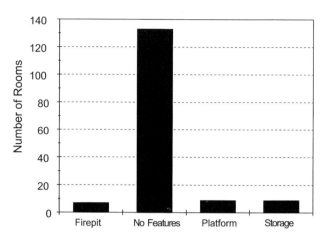

Figure 7.13. Frequency distribution of fixed features, entire sample of rooms.

sampled rooms; firepits, small storage facilities, and platforms were present but rare. Rooms with no floor features overwhelm the sample. When the distribution is broken down by roomblock, the proportional imbalance is greatest in Stage VIB (Fig. 7.14).

The perceived imbalance between rooms with and without fixed features can be tested statistically. Because of the small number of observations, I collapsed the firepit and storage bin categories into one "domestic feature" category. A chi-square test across the three construction stages (I, III, and VI) for rooms with domestic features, platforms, and no fixed features is highly significant (p = .000), meaning that the distribution of room features across time is not random. Fisher's Exact tests of homogeneity of proportions of paired comparisons (Table 7.1) reveal that this statistical significance is accounted for by the following: (1) the greater than expected number of domestic features and the near absence of platforms in Stage I rooms in relation to Stage III rooms; (2) the greater than expected number of domestic features and fewer than expected number of rooms with no fixed features in Stage I in relation to Stage VI; and (3) the greater than expected number of platforms and fewer than expected rooms with no fixed features in Stage III in relation to Stage VI rooms.

Space syntax provides an alternative means of identifying

differences in spatial organization, based on an analysis of differences in room access as quantified by the standardized integration value. Figure 7.15 shows the differences in standardized integration distributions among Stage I, III, and VI rooms with domestic features (firepits and/or storage facilities). The Stage I distribution for rooms with domestic features is distinct from the later Stage III and VI distributions. The Stage I rooms are spatially integrated, whereas the later ones are more segregated in terms of access. This suggests that in Pueblo Bonito's earliest occupation, rooms with domestic features were located such that they were easily accessible to inhabitants and visitors. Two centuries later, rooms with domestic features not only were few in number but also were placed in more private locations, distancing inhabitants from visitors and effectively restricting access.

Rooms with platforms show a different pattern (Fig. 7.15). The single, albeit questionable, platform in Stage I overlaps the Stage III distribution, but there is no overlap at all with the

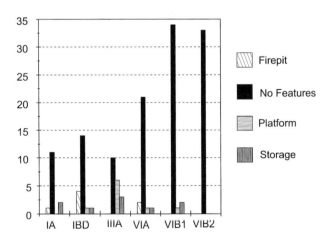

Figure 7.14. Frequency distribution of fixed features by roomblock.

Table 7.1

Tests of Homogeneity of Proportions

Construction Stages	Categories	Fisher's Exact Test p-Value
I and III	Domestic features	$p = .05$
	Platforms	
I and VI	Domestic features	$p = .00621$
	No fixed feature	
III and VI	No fixed features	$p = .000138$
	Platforms	

Stage VI distribution. Stage III rooms with platforms were located such that they were relatively easily accessible to users. It must be remembered that there are only two platforms in Stage VI; however, the box plot clearly shows that the standardized integration values for Stage VI belong to an entirely different population from the values for Stage III. Stage VI rooms with platforms are even more spatially segregated than Stage VI rooms with firepits and/or storage facilities.

Rooms with no fixed features (Fig. 7.15) are interesting. In Stage III, these rooms are more accessible than in either Stage I or Stage VI. This pattern is accentuated when room types are compared for each stage. In Stage I, domestic rooms are more accessible than featureless rooms. This agrees well with the widespread interpretation of ancestral Puebloan rooms suites during this time period: front rooms were living rooms while back rooms were used for storage. Storage areas, being more private spaces, were placed in less accessible locations than living rooms, where visitors would have been welcome.

Stage III rooms break with the long-established tradition of room placement. On a continuum, Stage III rooms with no features are more accessible than rooms with platforms, which are more accessible than rooms with domestic features. Knowing what to make of this spatial arrangement of functions is difficult, except to conclude that rooms with platforms were more private than featureless rooms, and that spatially segregated rooms with domestic features were not living rooms at all.

In contrast, the locational patterning in Stage VI is similar to that of Stage I: rooms with domestic features are more accessible than rooms with no features, and rooms with platforms are highly segregated spatially. In assessing these findings, however, it should be noted that out of 91 rooms in Stage VI, one room had a firepit, one had a firepit and storage bin, and two had shelves. These meager features are hardly evidence of domesticity. Nonetheless, it is noteworthy that the two rooms with firepits, the quintessential indicators of households (Windes 1984), are adjoining front and middle rooms, easily accessible to inhabitants and visitors.

Pueblo Bonito Households

How do these results accord with my definition of a household as a limited set of interconnected rooms that includes at least one domestic room containing a facility associated with food preparation? Using these criteria, domestic rooms (i.e., rooms with firepits and/or small storage facilities), and therefore households, are scarce at Pueblo Bonito, although large sets of interconnected rooms abound. Indeed, it is difficult to correlate the social unit of household with Pueblo Bonito's architectural units with any degree of confidence. The only convincing evidence for households is in the first roomblocks built.

Pueblo Bonito's early Stage I roomblocks appear, in form and interior spatial organization, to mirror small unit houses (Fig. 7.5), although at a larger scale. The original use of space has been obscured by later construction, but fixed features associated with the consumption of food are present. In particular, the Stage IB–D roomblock has five distinct suites of two to six rooms each. Four of these suites have firepits, and two also have storage facilities, suggesting that they housed consumption units. Stage I rooms with domestic facilities are more spatially integrated than similar rooms in later stages. As the pioneer of space syntax once remarked, "eating integrates" (B. Hillier, personal communication 1994). Using this measure, these small Stage I suites appear to represent households.

The Stage IIIA and VI roomblocks, which date to the great-

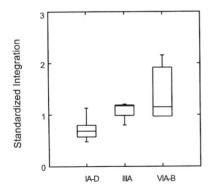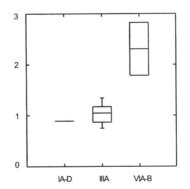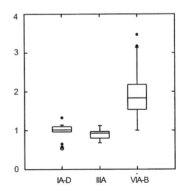

Figure 7.15. Box-and-whiskers plots of standardized integration values by construction stage for surface rooms with *(left)* domestic features (n = 16), *(center)* platforms (n = 9), and *(right)* no fixed features (n = 130).

house construction boom in the A.D. 1000s, appear distinctly different from earlier roomblocks and from each other, suggesting social units other than households and functions other than residential. The single, interconnected Stage IIIA unit has no reported firepits but does have three rooms with small storage facilities (subfloor cists and corner shelves). In terms of spatial integration, these rooms are the least accessible rooms in the Stage IIIA roomblock.

Stage VIA consists of six sequential units of rooms in the west wing. Of the four units for which adequate data exist, only one has domestic facilities. The Stage VIB east wing is a deep maze of interconnected rooms on both the first and second floors. There is nothing remotely domestic about either floor.

Complicating the identification of households are Pueblo Bonito's multiple stories. Historic and ethnographic reports of Acoma and Hopi architecture have shown that ground floors often consist of empty rooms used for storage, whereas living quarters are located in upper stories (Adams 1983; Nabokov 1986). Among the roomblocks considered here, no information (or inadequate information) exists for Stage I and VIA second-story rooms, but we do have sufficient information for Stage IIIA and VIB second-story rooms. Not only are the second stories of these two roomblocks empty of floor features, but no dividing walls mark individual household boundaries as they do at Acoma and Hopi. The exceedingly large number of interconnected rooms in Stages III through VI finds no parallel in historic Puebloan spatial organization.

CONCLUSION

By giving equal weight to form and function, space syntax provides a useful methodology for studying prehistoric architecture and spatial organization. Neil Judd (1954:23) was correct in characterizing Pueblo Bonito's architecture as bewildering. This architectural complexity is due to the structure's size and longevity, and it remains a stubborn problem for Chacoan archaeologists. Nonetheless, space syntax offers a way to break down this complexity into parts that can be more easily studied, compared, and understood. Spatial concepts of access, integration, and depth provide a means of quantifying social concepts of territoriality and privacy. Access graphs provide standardized visual representations and spatial information that supplement ground plans and descriptions.

Some general conclusions regarding Pueblo Bonito's spatial organization and function may be drawn from the available data. The analysis of spatial organization suggests that individual suites in the Stage IB–D roomblocks, the first built at Pueblo Bonito, may represent original dwellings, or households. Function, however, rarely stands still. During nearly 300 years of occupation, Stage I rooms acquired many artifacts generally described as "ceremonial" (see Neitzel, Chapter 9;

Mathien, Chapter 10), as well as most of Pueblo Bonito's burials (Akins, Chapter 8). Rooms that most likely began their use-lives as domestic quarters were converted to nondomestic space as Pueblo Bonito grew in size and complexity.

Not surprisingly, during the nearly 200 years that elapsed between the initial construction of Stage I and Stage III, social change occurred. By A.D. 1050, the architectural forms of roomblocks and their internal spatial organization were distinctly different. The functional nature of the Stage IIIA roomblock is difficult to assess. The hyperconnectivity of space, coupled with the profusion of roomwide platforms and the dearth of what could be identified as domestic fixed features, suggests specialized use by a large-scale corporate group.

By 1075, the Stage VI roomblocks presented yet another type of internal spatial organization, in which featureless rooms dominated. Spatial measures reveal the steady decrease in spatial accessibility, or integration, from Stage I through Stage VI. The accessible, integrated early domestic rooms gave way to highly segregated, featureless rooms with no interior access between floors.

The marked differences among the IIIA, VIA, and VIB roomblocks are puzzling. Only 25 years separate initial Stage III and Stage VI construction. Filling those years were the construction projects of Stage IV (a remodeling of the roomblock connecting Stages ID and IIIA) and Stage V (the soon-abandoned northeast extension). Constant construction over more than five decades suggests either a period of rapidly changing social needs, and perhaps social organization, or a period of intense social, and therefore spatial, experimentation. Confounding an already complicated picture is the recognition that Pueblo Bonito cannot be studied or understood in isolation. Located in downtown Chaco, it was surrounded by other great houses, each different from the next in form and perhaps function (Bustard 1996).

A century of excavation and documentation has not answered all our questions regarding Pueblo Bonito's architecture. Interest in form and function, and in change over time, continues. The analysis I have presented does not answer the big question: What was the function of the Chaco great houses? Another century of research may not provide an undisputed answer to that question. Nonetheless, it is evident that the question of great-house function must be addressed temporally and spatially. Change over time in spatial organization at Pueblo Bonito is clear. However it began, by the building boom of the 1000s, this great house was plainly not a home.

ACKNOWLEDGMENTS

I would like to thank Jill Neitzel for the invitation to participate in the Pueblo Bonito symposium at the 1996 annual meeting of the Society for American Archaeology. I would also like to thank Tom Windes and Cheryl Ford for sharing the most recent tree-ring dates for Stage I with me. The research for this chapter was done at the National Anthropological Archives of the Smithsonian Institution and in the Chaco Culture National Historical Park Museum Collection. I am indebted to the archivists at both institutions, Jim Glenn and Joyce Raab, respectively, for their assistance and guidance. I would also like to thank Bill Hillier and Mark David Major of the Space Syntax Laboratory, University College London, for their generous sharing of software and ideas. This research was supported by a Graduate Student Fellowship and a Pre-Doctoral Fellowship at the Smithsonian Institution and by a Challenge Assistantship from the University of New Mexico.

NOTE

1. Mean depth (MD) of a space *I* is expressed as

$$MD_i = \sum_{j=1}^{k} \frac{D(i,j)}{(k-1)}, j \neq i$$

where k = the number of spaces in a building (*B*), and $D(i,j)$ = the topological distance between spaces *I* and *j* in *B*, defined as the minimum number of linkages between the two spaces (Krüger 1989:9; Peponis 1985:389).

The integration of a space *I* is expressed as

$$I_i = \frac{2(MD_i - 1)}{(k-2)}$$

where k = the number of spaces in *B* (Hillier and Hanson 1984:108).

8

The Burials of Pueblo Bonito

Nancy J. Akins

Pueblo Bonito has produced some of the richest prehispanic burials excavated in the U.S. Southwest. The human remains and their associated grave goods have been studied separately, together, and with reference to burials excavated elsewhere in Chaco Canyon (e.g., Akins 1986; Nelson et al. 1994; Palkovich 1984; Stodder 1989). Perhaps the most significant interpretation resulting from this research is that the people who occupied Chaco Canyon a millennium ago were hierarchically organized—that is, their society was based on an ascribed status hierarchy.

In this chapter I begin with a detailed description of the burials and then summarize the inferences about Chacoan sociopolitical organization that have been derived from mortuary analyses. Finally, I consider questions about what Pueblo Bonito's human remains can tell us about the site's population and function.

THE BURIALS

The remains of at least 131 individuals have been excavated from Pueblo Bonito. Most were found in two room clusters located in the oldest part of the site, known as Old Bonito (Fig. 8.1). Probably the first documented human remains collected from the site are those cataloged by the American Museum of Natural History (AMNH catalog) as part of the First Richard Wetherill Collection. Two cataloged items, human finger bones from the surface and "human (?) bones," were collected on Wetherill's first visit to Chaco Canyon in the fall of 1895 (McNitt 1966:107–109). His was not the first expedition with an interest in human remains, however. Two years earlier, Earl Morris's father, Scott N. Morris, had searched Pueblo Bonito's trash mounds for burials (McNitt 1966:118).

In 1896, the Hyde Exploring Expedition uncovered the first significant number of human burials at Pueblo Bonito, in a room cluster in the site's northern section. They were described

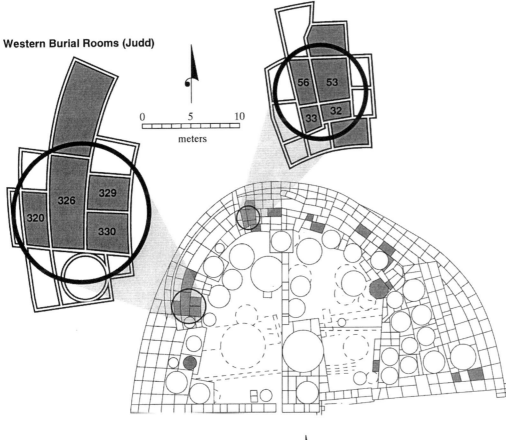

Northern Burial Rooms (Pepper)

Western Burial Rooms (Judd)

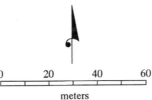

Figure 8.1. Locations of Pueblo Bonito's human remains. Gray shading indicates structures in which human bones have been found.

in an article by George Pepper (1909), the expedition's field director, and in his excavation report (Pepper 1920). During Pepper's excavations in the winter of 1897 and 1898, Warren K. Moorehead led a collecting expedition sponsored by Charles S. Peabody that worked in a few rooms in the northern room cluster. Moorehead (1906:34) excavated one burial and disturbed several others (Pepper 1920:216). Together, Pepper and Moorehead excavated a total of 24 to 28 burials (Table 8.1).

Extensive excavations sponsored by the National Geographic Society between 1921 and 1927 unearthed the largest number of burials from Pueblo Bonito (Judd 1954:vii–xii). About 95 burials were found in the western room cluster. Descriptions of them can be found in Judd's 1954 monograph on the site's material culture.

Descriptions and chronological placements of Pueblo Bonito's burials are often unclear in Pepper's (1909, 1920) and Judd's (1954) reports. Materials associated with a given indi-

vidual are not always included with the burial description, so provenience information often must be gleaned from text concerning ornaments, ceramics, and other artifact classes as well as from catalog records. Chronology is especially problematical, given the amount of disturbance, the long time spans associated with some ceramic wares, and the possibility that cu-

Table 8.1

Age and Sex Composition of Pueblo Bonito's Human Remains

Age and Sex	North Rooms	West Rooms[a]	Other Rooms
Female	7–8	43	1?
Male	11–12	23	1
Unknown adult	2	0	2+
Subadult	4–6	29	8
Total	24–28	95	12+

[a]From Palkovich 1984.

rated vessels were buried with individuals or placed in the rooms at later times. Pueblo Bonito's earliest burials are associated with Red Mesa Black-on-white vessels, dating between A.D. 900 and 1050. Other common wares are Gallup Black-on-white and Chaco Black-on-white, which cover a span from 1030 to 1150, and Chaco-McElmo Black-on-white, which dates between 1100 and 1175.

The Northern Burial Cluster

At least four and possibly five adjacent rooms in Pueblo Bonito's north-central section contained burials (Fig. 8.1). All are small interior rooms with no outside access. Estimates of how many burials were collected from the northern room cluster range from 24 to 28, depending on which body part is counted (Table 8.1). Pepper (1909, 1920) described objects in these rooms as they were encountered. Consequently, it is often difficult to determine associations and actual numbers of artifacts. Almost any reading of his report may result in different counts.

Room 32 has doorways in three walls, but the southern one was partially blocked when found. Removing the plug in this doorway, Pepper found Room 32 to be filled with drift sand. In the southeast corner were the disturbed partial remains of an adult (not found at AMNH or in the catalog) associated with fragments of wooden implements, a hematite bird with turquoise and shell inlay, cloth, cordage, two pitchers, and a nearby jar (Pepper 1920:134). Under the body was a piece of cactus stalk covered with cloth and resembling the badges of office carried by Hopi and Zuni priests and used on ceremonial altars (Pepper 1920:161). Also in the room were three pitchers, 10 bowls, a corrugated red-ware bowl, a water jar, three mugs, a dipper, three cylinder jars, six jar covers, nine turquoise beads and two shell beads in one of the cylinder jars, a circular jet object, well over 300 ceremonial sticks, unfinished wooden objects, a painted wooden slab, a quiver with more than 81 arrows, an elk antler club, at least three sandals, two baskets, galena, gypsum, a drilled piece of squash, reeds, and a metate (AMNH catalog; Pepper 1920:129–163).

The adjoining Room 28, to the south of Room 32, held no burials, but it did have a single human tooth, a cache of 114 cylinder vessels, eight bowls, 18 pitchers, 121 sandstone jar covers, a shell bracelet, pieces of worked and unworked turquoise, a piece of hammered copper, an obsidian projectile point, a jet object, fossils, sulfur, and ochre. Among the cylinder jars and bowls were 12 pendants, 109 beads, inlays, and bead fragments of turquoise, as well as 198 figure eight–shaped beads, 148 Olivella beads, nine bracelets, and 165 disc beads of shell (Pepper 1920:112–126).

Room 33, the smallest room in the northern burial cluster, is entered only from Room 32 (Fig. 8.1). Excavation revealed Room 33 to be filled with drift sand and to contain most of the northern burial group's burials. Above a floor constructed of hewn planks were as many as 16 disarticulated individuals and a large number of goods that could not be associated with a particular individual. The remains included seven males and seven females by fibula counts, six each by crania. All but two young females and a young male were middle-aged or older. An infant's femur and partial cranium and a child's cranium fragment were also found.

Room 33's artifacts included a corrugated and probably smudged bowl, 11 pitchers, 13 painted bowls, a partial corrugated jar, and two cylinder vessels. Turquoise pieces included 512 pendants, 24,932 beads, and 451 inlays, as well as 1,052 pieces of turquoise matrix. Shell items numbered 2,042 beads, 17 pendants, 89 bracelet fragments, 98 worked pieces, and 11 Haliotis discs, along with two Olivella beads and an inlaid pendant of shell. Other ornaments were 173 inlays of jet and stone, a jet ring, two iron pyrite inlays, and a turquoise-inlaid hematite cylinder. Also in the room were on the order of eight flageolets (large wooden flutes), 42 ceremonial sticks, four throwing sticks, a reed object, three jar covers, walnuts, pinyon nuts, seeds, textiles, quartz crystals, a chipped quartz crystal knife, minerals and pigments, six projectile points, gizzard stones, a circular yucca mat, and an awl fragment (Pepper 1909).

At least three of the Room 33 burials found above the plank floor were mostly intact. Two others had articulated vertebrae attached to the skull. An articulated foot and leg were found along a wall. Only one skull was crushed, and crania were spread fairly evenly throughout the room, many with adhering pieces of cotton cloth. Ceramic types include Red Mesa, Puerco, Gallup, Chaco, and McElmo Black-on-white, reflecting a time span of anywhere from 50 to 175 years. The association of one individual with a cylinder vessel, two bowls, a pitcher, and a jar cover (Pepper 1909:212–214) and the location of a group of four bowls and five pitchers just north of another skull (Pepper 1909:214–217) indicate that these were once intact burials.

Pepper (1909:210) attributed the mixing of human parts and burial goods to streams of water pouring through the doorway after heavy rains. Neither his description of the fill in Rooms 32 and 33 as drift sand nor the positions of the skeletons and crania are consistent with this interpretation. Water action would have concentrated the body parts away from where the water entered and would have left evidence of puddling. Instead, the crania and burial goods are described as having been dispersed throughout the room, and some were found above and others beneath the more or less intact individuals. The bones are generally complete, and some were found in anatomical units (e.g., crania with cervical vertebrae, legs), indicating varying degrees of disarticulation. Complete but rearranged bones, along with an abundance of burial goods, could indicate either some form of hasty secondary burial or the disturbance of secondary or primary burials by later occupants of the site or by looters. It is not what we would expect from violence, mutilation, or cannibalization (cf. Turner and Turner 1999).

Once the upper burials were removed, Pepper found a floor constructed of planks laid east-west. The eastern end of one board had a hole in it, 10 cm in diameter. Under the planks were two male burials associated with large numbers of ornaments and other objects. These two burials are by far the most lavish uncovered at Chaco Canyon (AMNH catalog; Pepper 1909:197–252, 1920:163–178).

Beneath the floor, offerings had been placed in all four corners of the room. Around a post in the northeast corner were 983 beads and pendants, 27 inlays, and 26 pieces of turquoise; six stone and jet inlays; a shell bead; and two fragmentary reed arrows with wooden foreshafts. In the northwest corner were 51 beads, five pendants, and five worked pieces of turquoise; a piece of malachite; a *Haliotis* shell disc; and two fragmentary reed arrows with wooden foreshafts. The southeast corner held 589 beads, 57 pendants, seven inlays, and 65 worked and unworked pieces of turquoise; a jet inlay; and a *Haliotis* shell pendant. The offering in the southwest corner consisted of 42 pieces of malachite, shell bracelet fragments, and a bone bracelet. A Red Mesa Black-on-white vessel and a smudged bowl rested against the north wall.

One of the two burials, Burial 13, was extended with his head on the right side and to the northeast. Scattered around his lower legs were 2,997 turquoise beads, with another 698 around his right ankle. His upper left arm was surrounded by 1,628 beads, a large pendant, and a small set of turquoise. Also in association were an additional 568 beads, nine pendants, three inlays, and a piece of matrix, all of turquoise, and three beads and a small piece of shell.

The other burial, Burial 14, was placed on a layer of clean sand covered with wood ash. He was probably on his back with his knees slightly flexed upward, head to the north, and feet resting against the south wall. He had chop marks on his left parietal and temporal, a gash in the right parietal, and cuts and chops on the distal left femur, suggesting a violent death. Burial 14 had more goods than the other individuals in the room. On his chest were one large and eight small turquoise pendants and a turquoise ornament composed of 1,980 beads. On his abdomen lay five jet inlays and a deposit of turquoise items: 2,642 small beads, 168 small pendants, three inlays, two rabbit-shaped pendants, a shoe-shaped pendant, and an unfinished pendant. Around his right wrist were 617 beads, 147 small pendants, and four inlays, all of turquoise; a shell bead; and two stone beads. The left wrist was surrounded by 2,384 disc beads, four cylindrical beads, 194 pendants, and five pendants shaped, respectively, as birds, a foot, a bifurcated form, and an irregular form, all of turquoise; and five irregularly shaped shell pendants.

Around his right ankle were 322 disc beads, two cylindrical

Figure 8.2. Turquoise-inlaid cylindrical basket from Burial 14 in Room 33. Courtesy American Museum of Natural History Library, neg. no. 2A13712, photograph by P. Hollembeak and J. Beckett.

beads, and five pendants of turquoise. The left ankle was surrounded by 434 beads and eight pendants of turquoise; eight small stone and shell beads; and a cylindrical shell bead. At his right knee were a shell trumpet, four complete *Haliotis* shells, 26 complete shell bracelets, and 15 shell bracelet fragments. Under one *Haliotis* shell were the remains of an 8-by-15-cm cylindrical basket covered with 1,214 pieces of turquoise mosaic (Fig. 8.2). The basket was filled with 2,150 beads, 152 small pendants, and 22 large pendants of turquoise; 3,317 beads and small pendants, 78 cylindrical beads, and 68 large pendants of shell; five shell pendants with turquoise inlay; and an animal form stone pendant with turquoise inlay. Near the body lay the remains of turquoise and shell mosaic on basketwork composed of rows of more than 500 turquoise beads alternating with double rows of thin, overlapping pieces of shell. Other objects in the area were a long inlay of red stone, shell ornament fragments, pieces of turquoise matrix, small turquoise inlays, and part of a bivalve shell. Pepper (1909:223, 225) deduced from the care bestowed on Burial 14 and the character and quantity of the objects found with him that he had been a person of high rank.

Room 53, immediately north of Room 32 (Fig. 8.1), can be entered from the north, south, and west. Room 53 was partially excavated by Moorehead, who entered the room by tearing down the north and east walls. Cleaning up after Moorehead, Pepper found two pitchers, a small bowl, and a cylinder jar fragment against the east wall and a child's cranium with a deposit of more than 4,000 turquoise beads and 30 shell beads and pendants nearby. A skeleton missing only the cranium (probably one of those collected by Moorehead) was found at the south end of the room. Pieces of feather cloth and portions of cradle boards, ceremonial and gaming sticks, vessel fragments, and turquoise beads were unearthed from the general debris (Pepper 1920:210–213). Human bone from this room, at the American Museum of Natural History, consists of tibiae from at least four adults and scapulae from six individuals, representing at least one adolescent male, a middle-aged male, and an older female. The child's cranium and the bones of a newborn infant are also present.

Room 56 is located west of Room 53, which provides its only entry. In Room 56 Moorehead (1906:34) found the "splendidly preserved skeleton of a young woman wrapped in a large feather robe." He noted that some pottery accompanied the burial. Pepper (1920:216–218), cleaning up after Moorehead, commented that there were two subfloor graves as well as bones scattered throughout the dirt piled in the room's northeastern and northwestern sections. One of the graves had a bottom formed by sticks and sides made of boards. It was also covered by boards or matting. Fragments of both were found in Room 53, and some of the human bone from this room is cataloged as "thrown from Room 56." The catalog for the Charles S. Peabody Museum of Archaeology at the prestigious Phillips Academy in Andover, Massachusetts, where Moorehead was curator, lists a reed mat and feather robe that covered a burial found in Pueblo Bonito's northwest corner. This individual, a male about 40 to 44 years of age, is probably one of the individuals from Room 56, possibly Moorehead's splendid young woman.

Room 61, just north of Room 53, may also have housed burials. The American Museum of Natural History catalog lists material from the room north of Rooms 63 and 53, probably Room 61, as having been purchased from O. H. Buck, whom Pepper hired for unspecified duties (McNitt 1966:141). Among the materials attributed to Room 61 are *Haliotis* shell pendants, shell beads, a turquoise bead fragment, and shell bracelets found with an adult male skull. Pepper (1920:222–223) found fragments of a burned human skull in the room's southeast corner as well as a few unburned bones. He did not mention prior disturbance except that the west wall had been demolished.

Pepper's (1909:247; 1920:376) overall conclusion was that Pueblo Bonito's northern rooms were used for burials and to store ceremonial materials. The presence of valuable ornaments and ceremonial paraphernalia with nearly all of the bodies suggested to him that the deceased were members of the priesthood and that they were buried in the pueblo as a sign of respect and to protect their graves.

The Western Burial Cluster

Four adjacent rooms in Pueblo Bonito's western section also contained burials, and a fifth room (Room 325) held a partial cranium (Fig. 8.1). Judd collected 95 burials from these rooms (Table 8.1), which are all interior rooms with no outside access. He estimated that almost 70% of the burials had been disturbed by prehispanic vandals who looted stores of corn and ornaments (Judd 1954:334, 340). Judd's accounts of the material found in these rooms are often incomplete. His sections on dress and adornment and on ceramics illustrate objects found with the disarticulated burials, but these are not mentioned in the burial section of his report. Additional information on associations is found in the U.S. National Museum catalog.

Room 320, a small storage room with a flagstone floor, was, when investigated, connected to Room 326 by a doorway. Plastered between two of the flagstones were a four-strand turquoise necklace and two pairs of pendants. According to Judd (1954:84, Pl. 9), these were found in a hollow deliberately put between two of the floor flagstones. The necklace was coiled and covered with mud that was packed down and stained with ashes to hide the cache. On the basis of crania, Judd (1954:325–326) reported that eight women and two girls had been buried in Room 320. By analyzing all elements, Palkovich (1984:106) determined that 21 individuals were represented in Room 320, including an infant, two children, two adolescents, two young adults of unknown sex, a young male, and 13 females ranging from young adult to over 50 years of age.

Room 320's burials and disturbed parts were covered with earthy debris, drift sand, a collapsed ceiling, and finally household trash. Judd did not always detail, and the catalog does not distinguish, which material from this room could have been associated with the individual burials. Two females were placed side by side on the same rush mat. They lay on their backs with heads to the east. Traces of feather cloth, yucca cordage, and cotton cloth were found on each. A Red Mesa Black-on-white pitcher, half a bowl, and two baskets were placed nearby (Judd 1954:325–326). An older woman who was fairly intact, missing only her cranium, was sprawled face down. Beneath her were two ring baskets and a mat of peeled willows (Judd 1954:326). In addition to the goods associated with the three intact burials, the room contained seven bowls, 14 pitchers, six Chaco Black-on-white cylinder vessels, a ladle, a pipe, turquoise ornaments (six rectangular beads, seven pendants, 126 disc beads), a handful of shell and stone beads and pendants, galena, malachite, azurite, sulfur, bone awls, a bone scraper, projectile points, a basket cup, a bifurcated basket with a painted design, a sandal and sandal fragments, other basket and matting fragments, two willow mats, two sets of four loom sticks, at least four ceremonial sticks, and a bow.

Room 326 (Judd 1954:326–331) was a habitation room located east of Room 320. Two doors in the east wall were wholly and partially closed, respectively, and two doors in the west wall were open. By Judd's count, Room 326 held the remains of 10 adults (one male and nine females) and an infant. Palkovich (1984:106) counted 14 adults (four males, 10 females), a young adult of undetermined sex, an adolescent, and two children. Her seven additional individuals are probably those cataloged as collected from in front of the doors in the west wall and as detached bones in the middle of the room.

The first individual interred in Room 326 was a 30- to 40-year-old female who may have died in the room. She was covered with mud and mortar with no offerings other than the bulrush mat on which she lay. Fill within the room was leveled before another female was laid on a bulrush mat with 11 bowls, two pitchers, an olla, an oval basket tray, a humerus scraper, a turquoise pendant, and a three-strand turquoise bracelet. This second female was so shallowly covered that another burial mat rested on the vessels. This mat was probably for the partially disarticulated female found between the mat and the wall (Judd 1954:327–328).

Like Room 320, Room 326 contained a dual burial, consisting of two females placed side by side on their backs with their heads to the east. A joint offering of four bowls, two sets each consisting of an oval tray and a humerus scraper, and a cylindrical basket lay between their heads. One female was accompanied by three additional bowls, a pitcher, two digging sticks, and two pendants, one of jet and the other of turquoise. The other female had a bowl, two pitchers, and a turquoise pendant (Judd 1954:328). Also in the room was an infant placed on its back with its head to the east. Parts of a cylindrical basket and a bifurcated basket were found just above the infant (Judd 1954:328).

Room 326 filled with trash and natural deposits before another three bodies were interred there, probably in fairly rapid succession. These undisturbed burials lay on their backs on mats, parallel to each other and with heads to the east. Each had offerings of pottery vessels just beyond the head. Three bowls and a pitcher were noted for one individual, along with a basketry pillow and a "napkin ring." Four bowls and two pitchers, an oval basket tray, and a deer humerus scraper were recorded for another. The third had traces of a twilled rush mat over the body (Judd 1954:329).

Just before the ceiling of Room 326 collapsed, two partially disarticulated skeletons were apparently dragged from their burial mats while some parts were still held together by flesh and ligaments (Judd 1954:330). Also in the room were at least 34 bowls, seven pitchers, six turquoise pendants, small turquoise pendants and pendant fragments, worked turquoise fragments, stone beads, a hematite bead, a quartz crystal, a fluorite crystal pendant, a green stone cylinder, hematite fragments, tubular bone beads, a bone button, eight projectile points, two cylindrical and two bifurcated baskets, wooden staves, and fragments of cotton cloth and baskets.

Room 329 lies east of Room 326 (Fig. 8.1), which provided its only access. A partially plugged doorway suggests that Room 329 might once have had a ceiling hatchway. Because Room 329 had only a ventilator and central fireplace, Judd (1954:331–333) surmised that it was a council or secret society chamber abandoned after Room 326 became a burial chamber. Judd counted 17 females, a male, and six children in this room. Palkovich (1984:106) counted 10 females, two males, and 12 children. Of these, only five children were undisturbed. An eight-year-old lay on his back on a bulrush mat, with three pitchers and a bowl near his head. A child under six years old had two pitchers, a small bowl, and a duck pot. Another child under six lay in the corner, partially flexed on the right side, with four bowls and two shell pendants. Another six-year-old and an infant less than two years old had no offerings. An unspecified child had a turquoise pendant. The intact burials were found on or near the floor and at the edges and corners of the room. One disturbed burial, that of a child about 12 years of age, was found on its back with head to the east. The head had been twisted off and left face down. The body lay on a willow screen. Just beyond the skull were a bowl and two pitchers.

The other individuals in Room 329 were scattered everywhere, with parts missing. Material that could have been associated with the disarticulated individuals included 17 to 19 bowls, three to eight pitchers, a Gallup Black-on-white effigy pitcher, a ceramic effigy in a bifurcate basket form, a reddish brown pitcher, six cylinder vessels, azurite and malachite pellets, a jet bead, cotton cloth fragments, 10 awls, and copper bell fragments. Turquoise objects included a duck effigy, beads, undrilled beads, mosaics, and fragments. Shell objects consisted of bracelet fragments, pendants, and beads.

Room 330, east of Room 326 and south of Room 329, was entered through a ceiling hatchway. It was square, with a central firepit, and Judd (1954:333–335) thought it might have been another council or ceremonial chamber. He counted 23 individuals in this room: 13 males, four females, and six children. Palkovich (1984:106) found 32 individuals: 16 males, nine females, two adolescents, and five children. Only four of the males and a child were undisturbed. Two of the undisturbed males were buried under the floor. One, a 25- to 28-year-old, is not described in Judd's report, but a photograph shows a burial on its back with knees up, associated with a bowl and a pitcher (Judd 1954:324). The text indicates that a shell necklace and paired pendants were found on the chest (Judd 1954:334). No information is given for the other subfloor burial other than to note that the individual was in his late twenties at the time of death. The child was placed on the floor in an adobe bin constructed for that purpose. The third intact adult was a warrior in his prime placed on his back in the middle of the room with head to the east. He had 28 projectile points arranged in a triangle between his knees, a bundle of reed-shafted arrows under his right hip, and a bowl. A fourth male, presumably undisturbed, is described only as arthritic; a pair of *Haliotis* shell disks were at his side.

Judd (1954:333) described Room 330's remaining individuals as "callously pulled and kicked about." Photographs indicate that the disturbance took place while many elements were still held in place by ligaments. Associations with parts of individuals include paired pendants of an unspecified material with a child, a lignite disc with an adult male, four jet rings with another male, eight projectile points with an adult male, a bulrush mat with an adolescent male, a fiber mat with another male, a shell necklace and two shell zoomorphic pendants with a male, and fragments of shell pendants with a child. Catalog cards and other text identify 16 bowls, 14 to 16 pitchers, a duck pot, a canteen, six cylinder vessels, a double stirrup canteen, a ladle, unfinished shale pendants, galena, a garnet, kaolin, pigment, azurite pellets, fragments of cotton cloth and willow mats, a cylindrical basket, basket fragments, and three bone awls. Also identified are a turquoise-on-shell mosaic, a jet effigy with turquoise inlay, and a few turquoise beads, mosaics, and fragments. Shell artifacts include a whole shell and bead necklace measuring 6.91 m, seven or so pendants, beads, and mosaic fragments. Other stone beads were also found, including 3.45 m of stone beads at the head of a skeleton.

Other Pueblo Bonito Human Remains

A small number of burials have been found outside of Pueblo Bonito's two burial clusters, mainly in the northern and eastern parts of the site (Fig. 8.1, Table 8.1). Judd excavated an infant from the fill of Room 287, an infant from a fireplace in Room 290, a fetus from the corner of Room 309, and a fetus from a hole in the floor of Room 306. He also reported single teeth from Rooms 226 and 227 and Kiva L, a partial femur from Kiva V, and an adolescent pelvis from the West Court (Judd 1954:336–337). Pepper found an infant beneath the floor of Room 90 (Akins 1986:163), a child beneath the floor of Room 79 (Pepper 1920:264), and burned and broken human bones in Room 80. He believed the last had fallen from an upper room and had been used for a ceremonial purpose, because it was not the custom to bury even portions of bodies in upper-story rooms (Pepper 1920:267). An unprovenienced partial mummy (female?) and a foot from Room 39 are also listed in the AMNH catalog.

Most isolated burials were of fetuses or infants with no discernible burial goods. Room 309, which Judd considered a ceremonial room, also held a macaw skeleton. Similarly, Room 306 contained three macaws buried in holes in the floor (Judd 1954:336).

PREVIOUS ANALYSES

My previous research on Pueblo Bonito's burials has been in the context of burials excavated from Chaco Canyon (Akins 1986). I have compared great-house and small-site burials in order to draw conclusions about how Chacoan society was organized. Almost all of the great-house burials are from Pueblo Bonito. Much of the burial information for the small sites is incomplete, and it has a significant bias toward room excavations. Midden burials are commonly disturbed or lack information on associated ceramics, making them difficult to place chronologically. As a result, our current knowledge of Chacoan burial practices may not represent the entire range. In this section, I consider the published biological and paleopathological studies of Pueblo Bonito's burials, summarize mortuary practices, and offer interpretations of sociopolitical organization.

Biological Analyses

No comprehensive study of Pueblo Bonito's skeletons has been reported, although several researchers have looked at the collections for various purposes (e.g., Akins 1986 for demography, craniometrics, basic inventory, and stature; Barnes 1994 for developmental defects; Palkovich 1984 for demography and pathologies related to nutritional stress). This rather sparse information is the basis for assessing health at Pueblo Bonito.

When a segment of a population is healthier and more robust than others, it can be an indication of access to more or higher-quality resources (Wason 1994:73). Perhaps the best evidence of better health over a number of generations is attained growth, or stature, because this is one of the more sensitive indicators of nutritional status (Nelson et al. 1994:97). It is particularly significant for Pueblo Bonito, where both the males and the females from the northern room cluster are the tallest reported for Southwestern populations (e.g., Stodder 1989:184–185). Femur lengths for the northern cluster burials average 44.5 cm for males and 41.6 cm for females. Western cluster males have a mean of 43.6 cm, and females, 41.3 cm. The averages for small-site males are 42.8 cm, and for females, 39.1 cm (Akins 1986:136).

Palkovich (1984:107, 111) argued that the age profile for Judd's Pueblo Bonito burials and their rates of nutritional and infectious disease indicated that these individuals were not buffered from the effects of dietary inadequacy characteristic of ancestral Puebloan groups. However, this view does not stand up to scrutiny (Nelson et al. 1994:89; Stodder 1989:179). In addition to greater stature, the rate for porotic hyperostosis—indicative of iron deficiency anemia—at Pueblo Bonito (25% for infants and children) is among the lowest reported for Southwestern populations and far lower than the figure for the Chacoan small-site population (83%). Furthermore, nutritional deficiency is not the only cause of anemia. Coprolites from Pueblo Bonito indicate a high rate of helminth parasitism (Reinhard and Clary 1986:184), a consequence of communal living, poor sanitation, and contamination of food and drinking water. One of these parasites causes anemia and may well have been the source of some or all of it at Pueblo Bonito (Stodder 1989:182). Similarly, the life table for Judd's Pueblo Bonito population indicates that this group had a relatively high mean age of death, higher than others reported from the Southwest (Martin et al. 2001:63; Stodder 1989:176). The longer life span suggests that these individuals might have enjoyed preferential access to resources (Nelson et al. 1994:90).

Other studies have focused on assessing the degree of relatedness among and between the Pueblo Bonito burials and other populations. Discriminant analysis of craniometric data from Pueblo Bonito, Pueblo del Arroyo, and small sites around Fajada Butte indicates that the two Pueblo Bonito burial clusters are distinct populations, but they are more closely related to each other than to other Chaco Canyon groups (Akins 1986:75). On a broader scale, when compared with crania from Mesa Verde, Aztec Ruins, Pecos, Grasshopper, and Point of Pines, Pueblo Bonito's crania are the most isolated, whereas those from Mesa Verde, Aztec Ruins, and Pecos are relatively closely related (Lumpkin 1976:91). The homogeneity of Pueblo Bonito crania with respect to those from other sites in Chaco Canyon and the relative separation of Chaco crania from Aztec Ruins and Mesa Verde specimens supports the proposition that the Pueblo Bonito burials represent closely related groups rather than accumulations from a wider region brought together on ceremonial occasions.

Mortuary Practices

The following summary of burial location, position, and grave goods is based on the better documented and dated burials from great houses and small sites in Chaco Canyon.

No change in burial location through time is evident at Pueblo Bonito—all of the site's burials were found in rooms. Burial location at small sites seems to have changed through time. Placement in middens at small sites slowly decreased in favor of burial in rooms (Akins 1986:108), although some of this trend may be due to excavation bias in favor of rooms in the later sites.

Extended burial was frequent at Pueblo Bonito but relatively rare at small sites. Placement of the body on the back, face, left side, or right side shows no clear chronological trends. Proportions of extended burials increase with time at Pueblo Bonito while decreasing and then increasing again at small sites. Overall, Pueblo Bonito has the more regular pattern, with most individuals buried on their backs. No one position dominates in the small-site population.

Great-house burials also differ in orientation. The great-house burials (from Pueblo Bonito and Kin Kletso) show higher proportions of individuals oriented in a single direction (to the east) throughout the time span. In contrast, the predominant small-site orientation changes over time from west

Figure 8.3. Turquoise bead and pendant necklace from Room 33 at Pueblo Bonito. Catalog no. H/9235. Courtesy Digital Imaging, Division of Anthropology, American Museum of Natural History.

to east. Like position, orientation was more consistent at great houses, regardless of time period, indicating a more formal mortuary program than that found at small sites.

Significant differences characterize the grave good assemblages from the great-house and small-site burials. Pueblo Bonito's burials have greater quantities of all kinds of grave goods as well as items that are unique to the site. Unique goods found with or in the same rooms as the burials include ceramic cylinder vessels, copper bells, shell trumpets, inlaid pendants, *Haliotis* shell discs, and a turquoise encrusted basket.

The more common grave goods—ornaments and ceramic vessels—occur at both great houses and small sites. Ornaments, however, especially those of turquoise (Fig. 8.3) and shell, are found more frequently and in greater quantities with great-house burials, at least with those from Pueblo Bonito. There, both turquoise and shell decreased over time (Akins 1986:108). At small sites, the proportion of burials with shell increased while that with turquoise decreased over time.

Turquoise, shell, and other ornaments entered the archaeological record through different means at the two types of sites. Ceremonial deposition, in which objects were sealed in niches or boxes in kivas, and deposition with burials are the more frequent contexts for ornaments at great houses. At small sites, these materials represent predominantly debris from workshops, discard of broken items, loss, and, on rare occasion, placement with a burial (Akins 1986; Mathien 1984).

Ornaments were available to the small-site population, but such objects were passed on rather than retired from the system by inclusion with a burial. Few Chaco small-site burials have more than a few beads. Yet at one small site, a woman who was buried accidentally wore a necklace of almost 4,000 shale beads (McKenna 1984:357), far more than have been found with anyone intentionally interred at a small site. The only comparable find with a burial was the grave goods accompanying an adult, probably a female, at Bc 59, who had a necklace of 103 jet and 52 shell beads as well as a McElmo Black-on-white pitcher, a smudged bowl, quartz crystals, and stone cylinders (Akins 1986:157). Ellis (1968:67) observed that contemporary Keresans removed a few beads from a necklace the family wished to keep and placed them with burial offerings of food and other personal possessions. The same might have been true at Chacoan small sites.

The other frequent offering found with Chacoan burials is ceramics. Overall, the Pueblo Bonito burials have more pottery than the small-site burials. The largest difference is in burials associated with Gallup Black-on-white or similarly dated vessels. These Pueblo Bonito adults were buried with more than four times as many ceramic containers as adults from small sites. At both site types subadults usually had fewer vessels than adults. But on average, subadults with pottery at great houses had more vessels than adults with pottery at small sites (Akins 1986:111).

Several temporal trends are evident in the occurrence of ceramic vessels with burials. For example, culinary and corrugated vessels were never numerous as mortuary offerings at either great houses or small sites, but at the small sites they tended first to increase though time and then decline. At small sites, too, burials with no vessels decreased through time while the number of vessels per person increased for adults up until the latest period.

Although no studies have been done comparing the quality of vessels found at the two types of sites, certain vessel forms, such as cylinder vessels, may have been at least somewhat exclusive. Almost all of those collected are from Pueblo Bonito, and a good many of those came from Room 28, which is slightly offset from Pepper's Room 33. This form was found with both Pepper's and Judd's Pueblo Bonito burials but with no small-site burials. Apart from special forms such as cylinder vessels, ceramics appear to have been relatively nonvalued utilitarian offerings that, when included with a burial, at least in small numbers, were no great loss to the household.

Organizational Inferences

Mortuary analyses have contributed significantly to our thinking about how the prehispanic occupants of Chaco Canyon were organized. Early researchers focused on the architectural differences between the great houses and small sites and interpreted them as representing distinct cultural groups. Kluckhohn (1939:158–159), for example, found it unlikely that the people living in great houses such as Pueblo Bonito were of the same cultural tradition as those living in small sites on the canyon's south side. He thought the two groups might even have spoken different languages. Kluckhohn viewed the southsiders as poor relations who migrated to Chaco Canyon from another region, drawn by the canyon's prosperity, the mag-

nificence and power of its ceremonialism, or the protection afforded by the populous towns.

This view was later adopted in a modified form by Judd (1954), who interpreted Pueblo Bonito's architectural differences as indicating two distinct groups of inhabitants. In his reconstruction, the Old Bonitians were the community's founders, who built the site's original section. In the eleventh century they were joined by the Late Bonitians, who, after moving into Pueblo Bonito, usurped village leadership and added to the pueblo with superior building skills. Judd (1954:36) viewed the Old Bonitians as ultraconservatives clinging to their old ways and the Late Bonitians as the creators of classic Chaco culture. He identified the Pueblo Bonito burials as those of Old Bonitians who continued to occupy the pueblo after the Late Bonitians migrated elsewhere. Judd (1954:340) thought the diminished population had been unable to defend the pueblo and had become victims of a small band of raiders who took the Old Bonitian's stored corn, women, and jewels from the shallowly buried dead.

More recent analyses have shifted the focus away from Pueblo Bonito and back toward a canyonwide perspective (Akins 1986). Instead of viewing great houses and small sites as representing different cultures, researchers view the two site types as having interacted to form a single social group. From this perspective, Pueblo Bonito's burials must be evaluated within the context of all of Chaco Canyon's burials rather than as a population in and of itself.

One conclusion that can be drawn from a canyonwide perspective is that the canyon population was hierarchically organized into at least three tiers. The lowest tier is represented by small-site burials. These typically were placed in midden and room locations and were interred primarily with readily available items. Ceramic vessels were the most common offerings, averaging fewer than two per individual. Occasionally, an ornament was also included. When the demographic characteristics of age and sex are examined, there is little to indicate differentiation within the small-site sample. Small-site adult burials are more likely to have vessels and to have more vessels than subadults, suggesting distinctions based on age. Some individuals have more grave goods than others, but those goods seem to represent nothing more than personal possessions and tokens of esteem. The distribution of grave goods among small-site burials is consistent with achieved status.

The two upper tiers in canyon hierarchy are represented by Pueblo Bonito's two burial clusters. Multiple lines of evidence support the conclusion that individuals buried in Pueblo Bonito had higher status than those buried at small sites. Individuals buried at Pueblo Bonito were taller and healthier, suggesting that they received preferential access to more and higher-quality resources. Their burial context was more formal, and they were placed in interconnected rooms rather than in the midden and room locations typical of small sites.

Perhaps the most convincing evidence for their high status is the distribution of grave goods. In comparison with small-site burials, Pueblo Bonito's burials have more grave goods and goods of greater value as indicated by raw material choice and extra workmanship. Furthermore, the differential distribution of valuable grave goods within Pueblo Bonito itself reveals status differences between the site's two burial clusters. One additional insight that can be gained from analyses of Pueblo Bonito's burials is that the high status of these individuals was ascribed rather than achieved.

The middle level of the canyon hierarchy is represented by Pueblo Bonito's western burial cluster. It is distinguished from small-site burials by burial location—individuals were placed in four adjacent interior rooms that had no outside access. In the western cluster, trash dumping followed a period of accumulation of windblown sand and usually roof collapse (Judd 1954:326), suggesting either that access was not exclusive or that these rooms eventually lost their exclusivity. Grave goods for these burials are intermediate in quantity and quality. The average number of vessels and ornaments per individual is greater than that for small sites, and each individual has some form of ornamentation. It is difficult to say how much more, because basic data on the number of individuals and the quantities of artifacts are unclear in Judd's report and are not always enumerated in the catalog. Burials in this cluster do have items that are absent or rare in small-site burials, such as cylinder vessels, exotic minerals, baskets, ceremonial sticks, inlaid humerus scrapers, and a variety of beads and pendants.

The uppermost tier in the canyon's hierarchy is represented by Pueblo Bonito's northern burial cluster. Rooms in this cluster are distinguished by their location in what may be the site's oldest section (see Windes, Chapter 3). Access to these rooms, deep within the roomblock, was more limited than to those in the western cluster (see Stein et al., Chapter 4). Sealed and empty of fill or filled with drift sand, they were not subject to trash dumping. Rather, Pueblo Bonito's entire north-central section seems to have served as a repository for ceremonial paraphernalia, including large quantities of ceremonial sticks, cylinder vessels, and pipes (Akins 1986:133; see also Neitzel, Chapter 9; Mathien, Chapter 10). Further evidence that the northern burial cluster is a population distinct from the western cluster is found in craniometric studies, which indicate that the two groups represent distinct populations.

The northern cluster includes the two individuals who exhibited the greatest energy investment in terms of facility preparation (the layer of clean sand, ashes, and plank covering) and quantity and quality of goods. Other individuals in this group typically have more of the kinds of objects that were highly valued than do those buried in the western cluster. Exclusive to the northern cluster, but not necessarily to burial contexts, are large quantities of ceremonial sticks, rare minerals, beads, bracelets, and pendants, as well as exclusive forms of shell inlay and the turquoise-covered cylindrical basket.

Thus, evidence for two different hereditary status groups at Pueblo Bonito is found in the presence of two clusters of burial rooms, the demographic composition of the two clusters, and their biological dimensions. Communal or clustered burials representing several burial events are almost always associated with social groupings of considerable importance and unambiguous membership, most likely kin groups. Cross-culturally, the status of individuals within such clusters is generally ranked, but high status and leadership positions can still be achieved within a rank (Wason 1994:89–92).

At Pueblo Bonito, the evidence suggests that status was ascribed. Although the proportions of males, females, and children differ between the burial clusters (Table 8.1), some children were buried with quantities of turquoise, indicating that ranking was hereditary rather than achieved (e.g., Brown 1981:29; Wason 1994:98). Materials, artifact types, and quality of workmanship in grave offerings indicate a high ascribed status for those buried in Pueblo Bonito's northern rooms, especially the two Room 33 subfloor burials. The northern burials include artifacts found nowhere else, such as the turquoise-covered cylindrical basket, shell trumpets, and inlaid shell pendants. Some of these items might have served as symbols of office rather than as prestige goods. Also exclusive to the northern cluster, but not necessarily to burial contents, are large quantities of ceremonial sticks, rare minerals, and turquoise and shell beads, bracelets, and pendants. The quantities of these goods certainly indicate greater access to such materials and higher, probably ascribed status. Unlike individuals buried at small sites, these people were sufficiently important to have merited the retiring of large amounts of valued, nonutilitarian goods from the system upon their deaths.

The Room 33 subfloor burials can be interpreted in at least two ways. Burial 14, the most elaborate in both burial treatment and burial goods, is a male with moderate dental wear who was around 40–45 years old at death (cf. Akins 1986:163). Although the care given to his burial suggests that he was the most important person buried at Pueblo Bonito, this need not have been the case. The unusual circumstances of his death, which was probably caused by his wounds, could have altered practices to the extent that his treatment represents his status in death rather than in life (e.g., Wason 1994:69–70). That is, his placement in the northern burial cluster indicates that he was a person of high status, but an inference that he was the highest-ranking individual may be unwarranted. Death in battle or in defending something of value might have altered the typical burial practice.

Burial 14's mortuary assemblage does not indicate that his primary role was that of a warrior or even a war leader (see McGregor 1943:273, 295; Morris 1924:192–194; Wilcox 1993:80).

Instead, the evidence suggests that he was a member of a closely related group that had already achieved its rank, not merely a big-man who commanded temporary control of resources. It is the presence of two groups, probably kin based, with indications of hereditary positions that is most significant, not the finding of one elaborately buried individual whose circumstances of death may have influenced his mortuary assemblage.

Decorated ceramics provide clues to when the ascribed status hierarchy evident in the two Pueblo Bonito burial clusters emerged. Ceramic types associated with the two room clusters indicate that both could have been used as burial facilities for at least 130 years. Late Red Mesa Black-on-white vessels dating to around A.D. 1020 were found in both room clusters, as were McElmo Black-on-white ceramics, suggesting that the rooms continued to be used as family burial facilities until about 1150.

ADDITIONAL INFERENCES

Pueblo Bonito's mortuary remains provide what are perhaps the most informative data for answering questions about how the people who built and used the pueblo, as well as the society of which it was a part, were organized. These data can also contribute to the other two themes of this volume, those of Pueblo Bonito's population and function.

Population

Few of Pueblo Bonito's early visitors and excavators doubted that the site was a large town or communal dwelling occupied for many years, if not centuries (e.g., Judd 1954:1; Pepper 1920:13–27, 375). To Judd (1954:22), Pueblo Bonito was more than a big, empty warehouse. Rather, trash heaps in abandoned rooms suggested to him the shifting of families or a reduction in population that left rooms open for dumping. In keeping with their interpretations of Pueblo Bonito as primarily a residential site, both Pepper (1920:376) and Judd (1954:340) were baffled by the paucity of burials. Rather than altering their interpretations of the site, both felt that a cemetery would eventually be found outside the pueblo, covered by silt and sand.

Calculating the number of expected deaths in a pueblo with a peak population of over 1,000, Judd (1954:325) estimated that between 4,700 and 5,400 deaths should have occurred at Pueblo Bonito. Current counts indicate that only about 135 burials and parts of individuals have been unearthed at Pueblo Bonito, representing more than 300 years of occupation (Table 8.1). This averages to fewer than one death every other year. Such a low number suggests that either Pueblo Bonito's resident population was very small or not all of its residents were buried at the site.

Bernardini (1999:457) recently calculated Pueblo Bonito's

population on the basis of the number of residential suites per construction stage. He estimated a peak population of 12 households, or 70 residents. Using Bernardini's figures and assuming a generation of about 45 years, a total of as few as 210 persons might have resided at Pueblo Bonito. If Pueblo Bonito's residential population was in fact this low, then the site's burials could represent nearly all who lived there.

Craniometric evidence for at least two families is not inconsistent with a low resident population. Beyond that, we can only speculate about whether other residents were buried elsewhere. Questions about the magnitude of the site's population simply cannot be answered from the burial data.

Site Function

Whatever its initial function, by A.D. 1020 to 1050 Pueblo Bonito was more than a common residence (see Bustard, Chapter 7). In addition to the two family burial facilities, which continued in use until at least 1100 to 1150, the northern rooms served as repositories for ceremonial paraphernalia, indicating a connection between the burials and some function involving ritual (see Neitzel, Chapter 9; Mathien, Chapter 10). Recently, Turner and Turner (1999:129) suggested that some of Pueblo Bonito's rituals involved human sacrifice and cannibalism. Their evidence for this claim is Pueblo Bonito's disturbed burials, especially those in Room 33. Specifically, the Turners cite the disarticulated skeletons and bones that they think were broken at the time of death. They reject grave robbing as the cause of disarticulation, because of this "perimortem" damage (Turner and Turner 1999:127–129). They argue that such damage is more likely to have been due to antemortem events than to postmortem grave robbing.

The argument that the disturbed burials at Pueblo Bonito, especially those in Room 33, represent sacrificial victims is unconvincing. Disarticulation is not enough to imply that these individuals were sacrificed. Yet Turner and Turner maintain that disarticulation, along with just about any breakage, provides such evidence. Although they insist that perimortem damage is easily distinguished from postmortem damage to bone (Turner and Turner 1999:316), others (e.g., Martin et al. 2001:21), including myself, disagree with their interpretations of some instances as perimortem damage and with their portrayal of many examples of violence as much more than that. Furthermore, many breaks that they identify as perimortem may in fact be postmortem. Human burials from sites along La Plata River in northwestern New Mexico exhibit numerous examples of archaeological damage to bones that, except for the freshness of the breaks, match many of Turner and Turner's (1999) photographs of bones with breaks interpreted as perimortem (Martin et al. 2001:156–159).

Burial 14 from Pueblo Bonito has unequivocal evidence of violence in the form of cuts and chops, but the Turners disingenuously include this evidence, from an undisturbed burial sealed beneath a plank floor, with the disturbed burials above the floor to conclude that "the cutting and breaking is not all easily blamed on turquoise-seeking grave robbers" and that "the Room 33 skeletons suggest human sacrifice with later carnivore disturbance" (Turner and Turner 1999:127). Whatever occurred with the Pueblo Bonito dead, it was definitely not the norm for the Southwest. However, it most likely represents no more than what LeBlanc (1999:163) calls "evidence of possible violence and the very careless handling of the remains of some individuals."

I am inclined to favor Judd's interpretation (1954:340) of plunderers causing the disturbance found in Pueblo Bonito's burial rooms. Some bodies remained intact, whereas others appear to have been pulled apart and tossed around. Some grave goods remained associated with some body parts, but others were scattered throughout the rooms. Looters may have selected special items and left much of what they encountered, or they might have lacked the time for a more thorough search. Mutilating the dead of an unrelated group is another possibility.

Secondary burial of important individuals brought to Pueblo Bonito for interment is another possible explanation for the burials' disturbed deposition (Saitta 1997:15). Reburial is not uncommon in the Southwest (see Morris 1939:90–96). The major flaw in the reburial explanation is that the craniometric data and demographic profile indicate that those who were buried at Pueblo Bonito represent closely related groups. The same flaw discredits another inference about Pueblo Bonito's rituals that has been derived from the site's burials—that the rituals involved pilgrims and that the burials represent individuals who were brought together "before or during periodic ceremonial aggregations and were accorded 'status' mortuary treatment in great houses because of the timing and/or circumstances of their death rather than strictly because of their social position" (Saitta 1997:15). The Pueblo Bonito burials do not speak directly to the idea that rituals at the site involved pilgrims from the surrounding region. But if there were pilgrims, and if any died while at Pueblo Bonito, the craniometric data indicate that they were not buried there.

CONCLUSION

Pueblo Bonito's burials reveal much about the organization of the site's residents and the society of which they were a part. Mortuary analyses confirm the conclusion drawn from settlement pattern studies—that a millennium ago, Chaco Canyon's residents were hierarchically organized. Mortuary analyses also provide insights into the nature of this hierarchy—status in the upper levels was ascribed. The presence of an ascribed hierarchy assumes further significance when integrated with other developments in Chaco Canyon. For ex-

ample, a beginning date of around A.D. 1020 for Pueblo Bonito's two burial clusters coincides with large-scale construction in the central canyon (e.g., Judge 1989:237–238) and the use of great kivas (Windes and Ford 1996:308). Furthermore, some individuals in these earliest burials, specifically Burial 13—the second largest of the Pueblo Bonito males as well as one of the two richest burials—had already lived for 50 years (cf. Akins 1986:163) under conditions that allowed for optimal growth. This implies that privileged access to resources and political centralization were in place no later than A.D. 970 and, perhaps, that from its initial construction in the late 800s, Pueblo Bonito was more than a residence for ordinary people.

A relatively early date for these burials and continued use of Pueblo Bonito as a family burial facility until at least 1100–1150 fits well with some reconstructions of Chacoan society's origin and duration. Dean (1992:38–39) credited a hydrologic transformation around 925 as benefiting floodplain farming, especially in Chaco Canyon. Enhanced predictability of rainfall between 900 and 1150 would have stimulated population growth. These climatic developments, combined with spatial variability in climate, would have reinforced any redistributive aspects of the Chacoan economy, promoting the accumulation of excess production from favored areas for redistribution to less favored locales. Prolonged and serious summer droughts between 1130 and 1180 would have severely affected farming that was dependent on rainfall, undermining the society's ability to sustain itself. This chronology fits well with the early date for Pueblo Bonito's burials and for the duration of burial at the site.

Recently, Brandt (1994:19–20) challenged the notion that the ethnographic pueblos were egalitarian. Her analyses indicate that all of the pueblos were hierarchically ranked, with relatively permanent positions and well-developed organizational and bureaucratic systems that must have developed to control much larger populations. Ranking within the pueblos could be effected through religious societies, clan groups, lineages, and households with either hereditary or appointed leaders. It was justified ideologically on the basis of the order of emergence, the order of arrival, or the importance of ceremonial property owned. Power arose from factors that included the importance of ceremonial property or objects symbolically identified with authority, group size, the timing of the particular ceremony controlled, the possession of important knowledge, or the quality of resources and land controlled by the group. Differential access to resources could be controlled through ceremonial knowledge and ceremonial property; control of knowledge important in regulating food production, such as an understanding of the lunar and solar calendrical systems; control of knowledge about and access to specific minerals, plants, and animals used for curing; access to shrines and to agriculture land; regulation of trade within and between communities; and guarantees of production exclusivity. Secrecy was essential for preserving the value of this "property," and public display of power and ideology served to solidify the positions of leaders. Leadership was considered an onerous burden. This, combined with tight control of information, discouraged others from seeking positions and kept the number of elites relatively small.

Brandt's conclusions about status differences and social inequalities in the ethnographic pueblos have implications for our understanding of the Chacoan sociopolitical hierarchy. Rather than being viewed as an aberration, Chacoan society, with Pueblo Bonito at its center, should be viewed as the progenitor and apex of long-overlooked patterns found in the ethnographic record. This organizational continuity between the prehispanic and the ethnographic pueblos strongly suggests that Pueblo Bonito was the seat of Chacoan power. The site was occupied by hereditary leaders who controlled access to ritual knowledge and paraphernalia, and it was the place where both nonpublic and public ceremonies were performed. The Chacoan hierarchy was maintained for at least 150 years by Pueblo Bonito's control of resources such as land, turquoise, and ritual knowledge. Then, evidence for disruption, including perhaps desecration of burial rooms, signifies a shift in authority and a less central role for Chaco Canyon and those who inhabited Pueblo Bonito.

ACKNOWLEDGMENTS

Thanks to Robert Schultz for drafting Figure 8.1 and to Lori Pendleton and Barry Landua for providing access to the digital image of Figure 8.3.

9
Artifact Distributions
at Pueblo Bonito

Jill E. Neitzel

Among the many reasons Pueblo Bonito is a remarkable site are the artifacts excavated from burial and nonburial rooms in its north-central section. These objects include Pueblo Bonito's two most frequently illustrated artifacts, a carved jet frog with inlaid turquoise (Fig. 9.1) and a cylinder-shaped basket inlaid with more than 1,000 pieces of turquoise mosaic and filled with turquoise and shell jewelry (Fig. 8.2). They also include artifact caches such as one with more than 100 ceramic cylinder vessels (Fig. 3.8) and another with more than 250 ceremonial sticks. The most numerous objects collected from this part of the site are those of shell, which number more than 7,000 pieces, and those of turquoise, which exceed 50,000 pieces (Fig. 8.3).

Not surprisingly, archaeologists have focused most of their attention on the artifacts from these north-central rooms. Materials from the rest of the site have received much less consideration, and the issue of artifact distributions has not been addressed in any systematic way. In this chapter I hope to remedy this gap in our understanding of Pueblo Bonito by offering an overview of the site's artifact patterning and by comparing the distributions of a series of both fancy goods and ordinary goods. First, however, I consider issues related to the task of linking Pueblo Bonito's artifact patterns to human behavior.

FACTORS AFFECTING ARTIFACT DISTRIBUTIONS

Using Pueblo Bonito's artifact distributions to draw inferences about past behavior requires a consideration of two issues—dating and cultural formation processes. Few of Pueblo Bonito's artifacts can be dated directly, and even decorated ceramics are problematical because of the lengths of their associated time spans (Toll 1985:110–117). For this discussion, the most useful chronological evidence is the site's architectural sequence (Windes, Chapter 3), which can be used to say whether certain artifacts were found primarily in older or more recent rooms.

Table 9.1

Analyzed Artifact Types, in Descending Order of Frequency

Artifact Type	Number	No. Rooms Where Found	Max. % from a Single Room
Turquoise	61,650	85	86
Shell	8,309	110	72
Jet	4,032	11	99
Fossil shell	1,246	19	80
Projectile points	1,028	90	33
Worked bone	997	138	4
Manos/metates	787	79	18
Whole bowls	395	72	15
Ceremonial sticks	365	30	73
Jar covers	324	50	38
Whole jars	320	73	17
Whole cylinder vessels	172	18	65
Pipes	53	18	38
Other stone jewelry	16	20	18
Crystals	14	7	41
Copper	11	11	9
Spindle whorls	4	4	25
Food/plants	Present	11	—
Cordage, etc.	Present	18	—

Figure 9.1. Jet frog with inlaid turquoise from Room 38, Pueblo Bonito. Courtesy American Museum of Natural History Library, neg. no. 2A6738, photograph by Rota.

Many cultural formation processes undoubtedly affected the quantities of different types of artifacts found throughout the site. These processes include the cleaning, reuse, and remodeling of rooms, accidental artifact loss, deliberate caching of artifacts, and trash disposal. Documenting spatial patterns is a necessary first step in distinguishing the various processes. For example, the occasional occurrence of an artifact might be the product of accidental loss or incomplete cleaning. But if a number of artifacts of a particular type are found together in a room, or if the artifact type evidences a consistent distribution across rooms, then that pattern might reflect deliberate behavior by the site's occupants.

Two of Pueblo Bonito's most important cultural formation processes are evident in the site's north-central section. One is human burial. Akins (Chapter 8) describes how the greatest quantities of the most valuable artifacts were excavated from four adjacent burial rooms located there. The other cultural formation process is the making of ceremonial offerings, as evidenced by the caching of large quantities of several types of artifacts in nonburial north-central rooms. A third important cultural formation process, trash dumping, is evident throughout the rest of the site. Windes (Chapter 3) notes that as new construction was undertaken at Pueblo Bonito, some

of the site's older portions fell into disrepair and were abandoned and then used for trash dumping. Trash began to accumulate in early west-side rooms by the early A.D. 1000s and in early east-side rooms by the late 1000s. Windes describes how trash deposition at Pueblo Bonito was not only widespread but also complicated. Initial use of older rooms and kivas was followed by refuse accumulation during the 1000s, by reflooring and short reuse in the 1100s, and finally by refuse accumulation again. By the early 1100s, refuse accumulation was so great in some parts of the site that walls had to be built to retain it. Clearly, trash deposition had a major effect on Pueblo Bonito's artifact distributions.

OVERALL PATTERNING

In an initial attempt to examine Pueblo Bonito's artifact patterns, I collected available data on the proveniences of 19 types of artifacts in the site's rectangular rooms (Table 9.1); artifacts in kivas and great kivas were not tabulated. I obtained this information from the site's excavation reports (Judd 1954; Pepper 1920); from catalogs and notes at the American Museum of Natural History, the National Museum of Natural History, and the Heye Foundation; and from my own examination of the collections at the three museums. The data gleaned from these sources were not always consistent.[1] As a result, I sometimes had to make judgments about which counts to use for particular artifact types. Other researchers might make

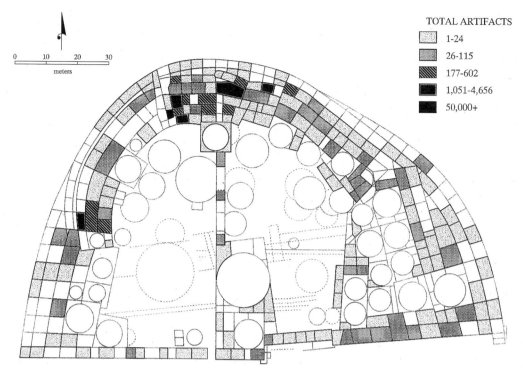

Figure 9.2. Total artifact counts per room.

different judgments and thus derive different totals for some types.

Once I felt that my inventory was as complete as possible, I totaled the artifact counts for each room and plotted the results (Fig. 9.2). The site contains one extremely prolific room, a burial room (Room 33) with more than 50,000 artifacts.[2] The artifact totals for the next most prolific rooms are an order of magnitude less than that for Room 33: five rooms each contained between 1,000 and 5,000 artifacts. Of this group, the two rooms with the most artifacts are located in the site's north-central section. One, with 4,656 artifacts, is Room 38, the largest room in Pueblo Bonito's north-central section. The other, with 4,040 artifacts, is Room 53, a burial room contiguous with the northeast corner of Room 33. Two of the remaining rooms in this group—Room 12, with 1,162 artifacts, and Room 28, with 1,051—are also located in the site's north-central section. The third—Room 320, with 2,684 artifacts—is part of the western burial room group. Although the contents of Room 33 are truly extraordinary, as the contents of the other five rooms would be at any other site, they do not together make up Pueblo Bonito's full artifact inventory. Artifacts were also found throughout the rest of the site, albeit in smaller quantities. It is the patterning for the entire site, not just the contents of the most prolific rooms, that is the subject here.

A comparison of the total counts of the different artifact types reveals a tremendous range, with a maximum of more than 60,000 pieces of turquoise and a minimum of four spindle whorls (Table 9.1). Considerable variation also exists in the numbers of rooms in which the various artifact types were found; the most widely distributed types were worked bone and shell. When total artifact frequency is compared with numbers of rooms in which the types were found, some interesting patterns emerge (Fig. 9.3). Not surprisingly, the most infrequently occurring artifact types (e.g., spindle whorls, crystals, copper, stone jewelry) have restricted distributions. However, some artifact types that occur in moderate quantities (e.g., fossil shell, ceremonial sticks, cylinder vessels) also have restricted distributions. The most frequently occurring artifact types exhibit the entire range of distributions from extremely restricted (jet) to moderately distributed (turquoise) and widely distributed (shell).

To examine these distributional patterns further, I compared, for each artifact type, the maximum percentage of the total count that was collected from a single room with the number of rooms in which the type was found (Fig. 9.4). Among the most frequently occurring and most widely distributed artifact types, turquoise and shell turned out to be almost as concentrated as jet. Among the artifact types that occurred in moderate frequencies with restricted distributions, fossil shell was more concentrated than ceremonial sticks, which were more concentrated than cylinder vessels.

DISTRIBUTIONS OF FANCY ARTIFACTS

In this section I document the distributions of ten kinds of fancy artifacts at Pueblo Bonito. In this category I include imported materials such as turquoise, shell, jet, and other stone, which

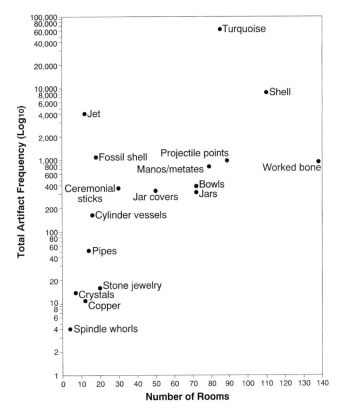

Figure 9.3. Comparison of total artifact count and number of rooms in which each artifact type was found.

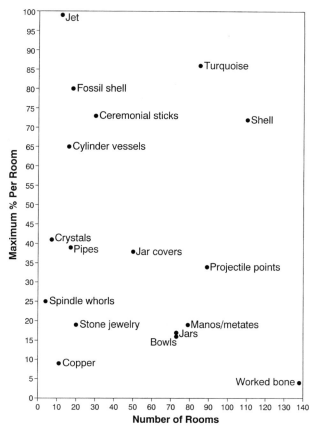

Figure 9.4. Comparison of maximum percentage per room and number of rooms where each type was found.

the Chacoans used for jewelry, and other artifacts such as ceremonial sticks, cylinder vessels, fossil shell, pipes, crystals, and copper, whose purpose seems to have been ceremonial. My distinction between fancy and ordinary goods is to a certain extent arbitrary and is intended for heuristic purposes only.

Turquoise

The most frequently occurring fancy artifact considered here is turquoise. Pueblo Bonito's turquoise comes in a variety of forms—jewelry such as beads and pendants (Fig. 8.3), mosaic inlays used to decorate other artifacts (Figs. 8.2, 9.1), debitage, and raw chunks or matrix. Turquoise was excavated from many rooms throughout the site (Fig. 9.5), but within this wide distribution, it was quite concentrated. Room 33 in the northern burial room group overwhelmed all others in its quantities. Indeed, the more than 50,000 pieces of turquoise from this one room represent 86% of all of the turquoise collected at the site. The room with the second greatest quantity—Room 53, with approximately 4,000 pieces—is also located in the northern burial room group. The room with the third greatest quantity of turquoise—Room 320, with more than 2,500 pieces—is situated in the western burial room

group. Thus, there is a strong correlation between large quantities of turquoise and rooms with multiple burials.

Shell

The second most frequently occurring fancy artifact considered here is shell, most of which was used as jewelry in the form of beads and pendants. The distribution of shell is similar to that of turquoise in several ways. First, shell was found in many rooms located throughout the site (Fig. 9.6). Second, within this wide distribution, shell was quite concentrated. Third, the same room in the northern burial room group, Room 33, overwhelmed all others in its quantities of shell—72% of the total. The major difference between the distributions of shell and turquoise is that the other rooms with large quantities of shell are not burial rooms. Instead, all are non-burial rooms located in the site's north-central section. The room with the second greatest quantity of shell—Room 28, with more than 500 pieces—is located adjacent to the northern burial room group. The next three rooms, which each contained 100–400 pieces, are located either in other parts of the north-central section or adjacent to it.

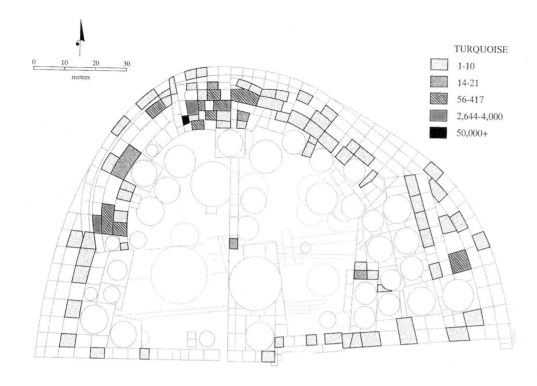

Figure 9.5. Frequency of turquoise per room.

Jet

The third most frequently occurring fancy artifact considered here is jet. It consists primarily of beads, along with some pendants, mosaic pieces, and the famous jet frog. The distribution of jet differs from that of turquoise and shell in that jet was uncovered in only a handful of rooms (Fig. 9.7). Within this limited distribution, jet was extremely concentrated. Room 38 contained 99% of all the site's jet, including the frog. This room is the nonburial room in the site's north-central section

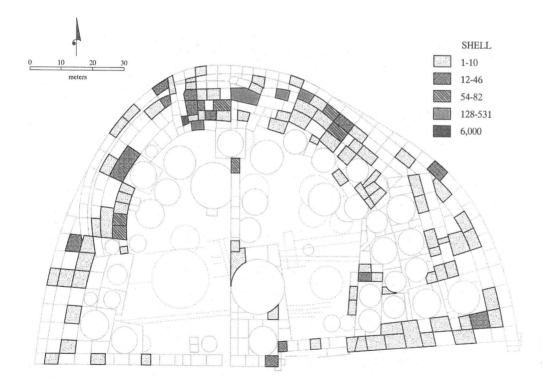

Figure 9.6. Frequency of shell per room.

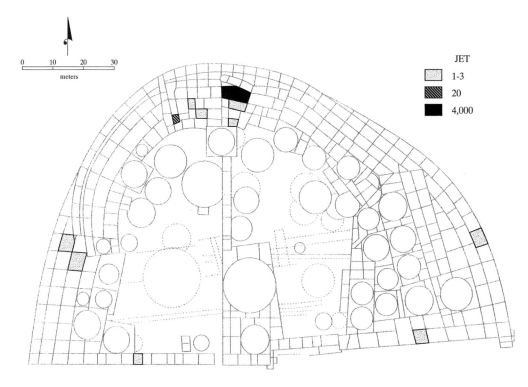

Figure 9.7. Frequency of jet per room.

that contained the third highest frequency of shell, as well as inlaid bone scrapers, a number of turquoise bird forms, and 14 macaw skeletons (Mathien, Chapter 10). The room with the second greatest quantity of jet—Room 33, with 20 pieces—is the room in the northern burial room group where the site's largest quantities of turquoise and shell were found.

Fossil Shell

The fourth most frequently occurring fancy artifact considered here is fossil shell. It occurs in its natural form and seems to have functioned as ritual offerings. Fossil shell was collected from only 19 rooms, 16 of which were located in the site's

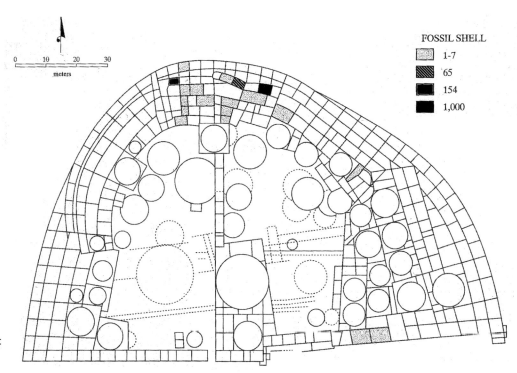

Figure 9.8. Frequency of fossil shell per room.

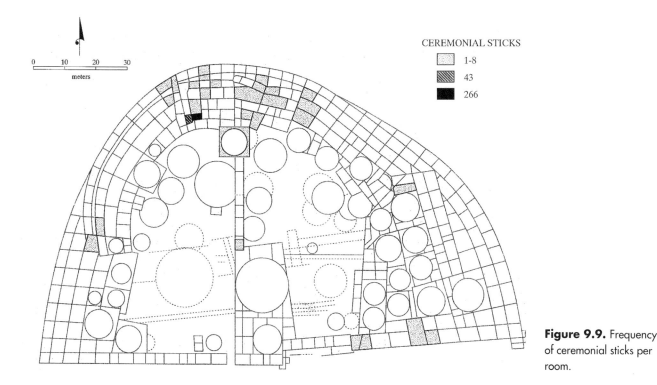

CEREMONIAL STICKS

1-8
43
266

Figure 9.9. Frequency of ceremonial sticks per room.

north-central section (Fig. 9.8). Within its limited distribution, fossil shell was extremely concentrated. One room in the north-central section, Room 12, contained 1,000 pieces, or 80% of the site's fossil shell. This room also produced a large quantity of regular shell (128 pieces).

Ceremonial Sticks

The fifth most frequently occurring fancy artifact considered here is ceremonial sticks. As their name implies, these objects are modified wooden sticks that are thought to have served a ritual function. Pueblo Bonito's ceremonial sticks are intermediate in both their overall frequency and the number of rooms in which they were found. Although rooms with ceremonial sticks are scattered throughout the site, most are located in the north-central section (Fig. 9.9). Within this section, ceremonial sticks were extremely concentrated. One room in the northern burial room group, Room 32, contained 73% of all of the site's sticks (see note 1).

Cylinder Vessels

Whole ceramic cylinder vessels are the next most frequently occurring fancy good considered here. These jars are thought to have had a ceremonial purpose (Washburn 1980). Among the 18 rooms where cylinder vessels were found, the containers were extremely concentrated (Fig. 9.10). Sixty-five percent of the site's cylinder vessels came from Room 28, which is adjacent to the northern burial room group (see note 1). The

room with the second greatest frequency of cylinder vessels—Room 39B, with 19 vessels—is also adjacent to the northern burial room group. In the western burial room group, the association of cylinder vessels and burial rooms is direct rather than neighborly. Each of the four rooms in this group contained cylinder vessels.

Pipes

The least frequently occurring fancy good whose distribution I mapped is pipes. Made primarily of clay, these pipes are thought to have been used during ceremonies. They were collected from only 18 rooms, 13 of which are located in the site's north-central section (Fig. 9.11). All but one of these rooms contained only a few pipes. The exception is Room 10, with 20 pipes. Room 10 is adjacent to Room 38, the room that yielded 99% of the excavated jet, relatively large quantities of regular shell, and 14 macaw skeletons.

Other Fancy Artifacts

I also collected data on three other fancy artifact types: other stone jewelry, crystals, and copper, each of which occurs in very small quantities at Pueblo Bonito (Table 9.1). The "other stone jewelry" category includes items of jewelry, primarily beads, made of stone other than turquoise or jet. Of the 39 known examples, 29 were found in nonburial north-central rooms. The largest quantity per room was seven items from Room 42, which also had 140 manos and metates, and six

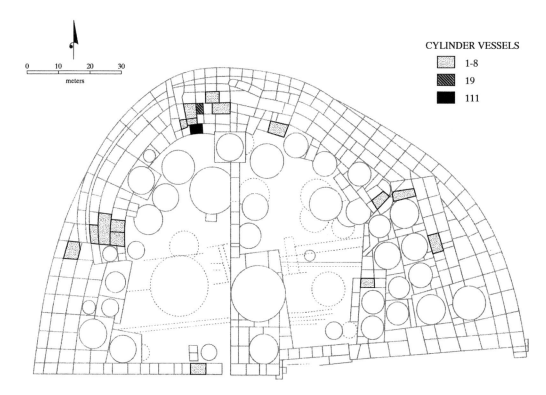

CYLINDER VESSELS

▨ 1-8
▩ 19
■ 111

Figure 9.10.
Frequency of cylinder
vessels per room.

items from Room 12, which also had 1,000 pieces of fossil shell.

A less frequently occurring fancy artifact is crystals, which are thought to have been used in religious rituals. Of the 14 recorded crystals, 12 came from nonburial north-central rooms. The largest quantity per room was seven crystals in Room 12, the room with the 1,000 pieces of fossil shell.

The least frequently occurring artifact type that I classified as a fancy good is copper. This material is relatively rare at prehispanic Southwestern sites and occurs primarily in the form of bells (Sprague and Signori 1963; Vargas 1995). Copper at Pueblo Bonito is infrequent and isolated; I was able to verify only 11 pieces in 11 rooms (see note 1). These rooms include one in the northern burial room group, two nonburial northern rooms, and eight miscellaneous rooms.

COMPARISON OF FANCY ARTIFACTS

The distributions of the fancy artifacts considered here can be compared in four sets of rooms: the northern burial room group, nonburial rooms in Pueblo Bonito's north-central section, the western burial room group, and miscellaneous, nonburial rooms in the rest of the site (Table 9.2).

North-Central Burial and Nonburial Rooms

The most striking pattern in the distributions of fancy artifacts is their strong association with rooms in Pueblo Bonito's north-central section. The artifact types vary greatly in the ex-

tensiveness of their distribution; some were found throughout the site, and others in only a handful of rooms. But regardless of the extent of their overall distributions, each of the seven most frequently occurring fancy types was extremely concentrated. With the exception of pipes, approximately two-thirds or more of each of these seven fancy artifact types was collected from a single room (Table 9.1). And without exception, each of the rooms containing the maximum percentage of one of the fancy artifact types was located in Pueblo Bonito's north-central section.

The kinds of fancy goods associated with the northern burial room group and with northern nonburial rooms differ (Table 9.2). The greatest quantities of turquoise, ceremonial sticks, and shell were excavated in the northern burial room group. In contrast, the largest quantities of fossil shell, jet, pipes, and cylinder vessels, as well as crystals and other stone jewelry, were taken from nonburial northern rooms.

The differential distributions of these two groups of fancy artifacts can be partially explained by their functions. Two of the three artifact types associated primarily with burials, turquoise and shell, consist mostly of jewelry. Burying items of personal adornment, notably those that function as status markers, is a common practice in intermediate-level societies (Binford 1971; Carr 1994; Tainter 1982). In contrast, four of the six artifact types found primarily in nonburial northern rooms (fossil shell, pipes, and cylinder vessels, as well as crystals) are generally assumed to have had a ceremonial function. Apparently, rituals involving the caching of these ceremonial objects were associated with these nonburial rooms.

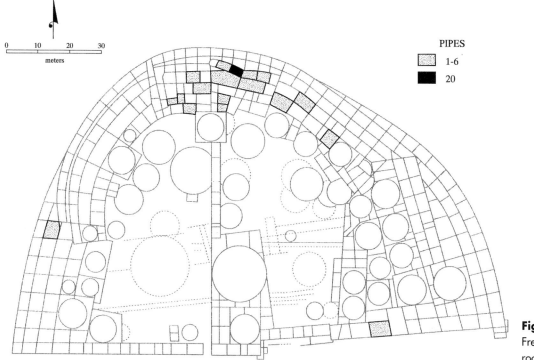

PIPES

1-6

20

Figure 9.11.
Frequency of pipes per
room.

Function alone, however, cannot completely account for the differential distribution of fancy artifacts in burial and non-burial rooms in Pueblo Bonito's north-central section. One reason is that jet, a material used primarily for jewelry, was found almost exclusively in one nonburial northern room, Room 38. Jewelry made of stone other than turquoise or jet was also found mostly in nonburial northern rooms. Perhaps turquoise and shell jewelry had different symbolic significance for the Chacoans than jet and other stone jewelry.

Turquoise, too, seems not to fall into one functional category. In addition to being used for jewelry signifying high status, turquoise in the form of both finished ornaments and

scrap, which occurred in large quantities in the northern burial rooms, apparently had a ritual function (Mathien 1992; Windes 1993a:394). The importance of turquoise in Chacoan ritual is suggested by its presence in nonburial ritual contexts such as shrines, kiva pilasters and niches, and great kiva roof support beams. Another fancy artifact type that may have had a dual function is cylinder vessels. Although they seem to have been used primarily as ritual offerings, they were also found in both burial room groups.

The presence of the richest burials and largest caches of ritual artifacts in Pueblo Bonito's north-central section strongly suggests that these rooms composed a sacred part of the site. Architectural evidence indicates that these north-central rooms are the site's oldest (Windes, Chapter 3). Ceramic data indicate that human remains and artifacts were deposited intermittently in the northern burial rooms over a span of at least 130 years (Akins, Chapter 8). Whether fancy goods were cached permanently in the nonburial northern rooms or were periodically retrieved for ceremonies is unknown. But their presence there was deliberate, and the act of their deposition must have been of great ceremonial significance. These nonburial rooms were not simply storage rooms. Otherwise, considering the value of their contents, they would have been emptied when the site was abandoned.

Western Burial Room Group

Other rooms where the deposition of fancy goods was deliberate are those in the western burial room group. These

Table 9.2
Percentage Distribution of Fancy Artifacts in Different Kinds of Rooms

Artifact Type	Northern Burial	Northern Nonburial	Western Burial	Miscellaneous
Turquoise	92.7	1.4	5.4	0.5
Ceremonial sticks	85.2	9.9	1.1	3.8
Shell	72.6	15.1	1.7	10.5
Fossil shell	0.0	97.7	0.0	0.3
Jet	0.5	99.4	0.0	0.2
Pipes	0.0	88.5	0.0	1.5
Crystals	0.0	85.7	0.0	14.3
Cylinder vessels	4.1	82.5	9.4	4.1
Other stone jewelry	7.7	74.4	0.0	18.0
Copper	9.1	18.2	0.0	72.7

rooms are similar to those in the northern burial group in three ways. First, they contain the same kinds of fancy goods—turquoise, shell, and ceremonial sticks. Second, rooms in both burial groups generally lack jet, fossil shell, and pipes. Third, both contain cylinder vessels. The absence of jet, fossil shell, and pipes in both burial room groups, along with their presence in nonburial rooms in the site's north-central section, suggests some kind of separation of burial rituals from rituals that produced artifact caches. The occurrence of cylinder vessels in both burial room groups in low percentages and in one nonburial northern room in a very high percentage might indicate a special role for this artifact in more than one kind of ritual.

Although rooms in the western burial room group contained the same kinds of artifacts as those in the northern burial room group, the percentages are, with one exception, dramatically lower (Table 9.2). The only artifact category found in greater quantities in the western burial group than in the northern group is cylinder vessels. Altogether, individuals interred in the northern burial room group had approximately 18 times more fancy artifacts than those in the western burial room group.

The reason the northern burial room group had such higher percentages of turquoise, shell, and ceremonial sticks than the western burial room group is probably related to the identities of those buried in the rooms (Akins, Chapter 8). Considering their location in Pueblo Bonito's oldest section, I think both room groups were in some way associated with prominent, founding families, perhaps serving initially as their residences. At some point in the early eleventh century, the residential function ceased as these rooms were transformed into mausoleums for their original occupants and their descendants. The relative ranking of these two elite families is evidenced not only by the larger quantities of turquoise, shell, and ceremonial sticks found with individuals in the northern burial room group but also by the location of these northern rooms in Pueblo Bonito's sacred precinct, where ritual artifacts were cached in nonburial rooms.

Miscellaneous Rooms

Determining whether the presence of fancy artifacts in other parts of the site was due to deliberate deposition or some other site formation process such as accidental loss or trash dumping is difficult. Given the ritual significance and economic value of these artifacts, it seems unlikely that they would, under normal circumstances, simply be thrown away with trash. A more likely possibility is that they were deliberately deposited as ritual offerings.

Several kinds of evidence support this hypothesis. The first is that a few miscellaneous rooms contained more turquoise and shell than one would expect as a result of trash dumping (Table 9.3). For example, Room 298 contained 258 pieces of shell,

Table 9.3

Fancy Artifacts in Miscellaneous Rooms

Artifact Type	Number of Rooms	Largest Quantity per Room	% Rooms Where Type Was Found with Another Fancy Artifact Type
Turquoise	55	56	84
Ceremonial sticks	27	8	37
Shell	82	258	60
Fossil shell	3	1	100
Jet	2	1	100
Pipes	6	2	100
Crystals	2	1	100
Cylinder vessels	4	1	100
Other stone jewelry	6	2	83
Copper	8	1	62

and six other rooms each contained more than 25 pieces. Rooms 80 and 244 each contained more than 50 pieces of turquoise. These frequencies pale in comparison with those associated with rooms in the northern burial room group, but they fall within the ranges seen in the western burial room group.

Another reason for thinking that fancy goods collected from miscellaneous rooms were deliberately deposited is the co-occurrence of different kinds of fancy artifacts. With the exception of ceremonial sticks, fancy artifacts rarely occurred alone in miscellaneous rooms (Table 9.3). For example, turquoise and shell often appeared together—84% of the miscellaneous rooms with turquoise also contained shell, and 56% of the miscellaneous rooms with shell also contained turquoise.

The fancy artifacts associated with large ritual caches in Pueblo Bonito's north-central section occurred in extremely low frequencies in miscellaneous rooms. At first glance this seems at least to suggest the possibility that the presence of one or two pieces of fossil shell or jet, or one or two pipes, crystals, or cylinder vessels, in a miscellaneous room was the result of their inclusion with trash. However, that none of these six types was found in a miscellaneous room without at least one other kind of fancy artifact suggests the opposite conclusion—that they were deliberately placed there (Table 9.3).

The distribution of copper presents an interesting problem. At first glance, its strong association with miscellaneous rooms (Table 9.2) might suggest that this material did not function as a ritual item after all. However, if some small quantities of fancy goods in Pueblo Bonito's miscellaneous rooms were ritual deposits, then the same might have been true for copper as well. If so, it would appear that copper's ritual role differed from that of other types of ritual artifacts that are more strongly associated with Pueblo Bonito's burial rooms and nonburial northern rooms. The finding of a single piece of copper in the northern burial room group and in each

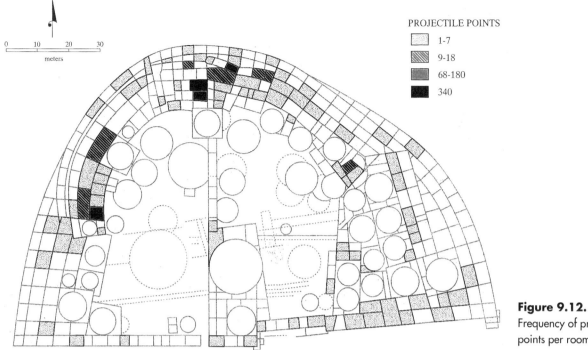

PROJECTILE POINTS

☐ 1-7
▨ 9-18
▦ 68-180
■ 340

Figure 9.12.
Frequency of projectile points per room.

of two nonburial northern rooms seems to support the view that this material did have some ritual significance.

A final reason for thinking that fancy goods found in miscellaneous rooms were deliberately placed there is the rooms' locations. Of the 19 miscellaneous rooms containing fancy goods, 10 lie either in the site's oldest section or directly adjacent to it. All but one of the remaining rooms are adjacent to or near a kiva, and four of these rooms occur in pairs. These locations suggest the deliberate, probably ritual, deposition of fancy artifacts.

All of this does not mean that fancy goods never found their way into trash. Given the site's extensive refuse deposition from a very early date (Windes, Chapter 3), it was probably inevitable that some fancy goods were mixed with trash. But there is no reason to assume that the sort of caching of ritual artifacts that took place in Pueblo Bonito's north-central section did not occur to a lesser degree elsewhere in the site. Even in rooms for which substantial trash dumping has been documented (see Windes, Chapter 3), fancy goods might have been deposited before or after the trash. Whether or not this is true cannot be determined from artifact counts alone. Rather, it requires detailed stratigraphic information on the contexts in which the fancy artifacts were found.

DISTRIBUTIONS OF ORDINARY ARTIFACTS

In this section I document the distribution of seven kinds of artifacts that served obvious utilitarian purposes for the Chacoans: worked bone, projectile points, ground stone, ceramic bowls, ceramic jars, sandstone jar covers, and spindle whorls. Again, my distinction between fancy and ordinary goods is to a certain extent arbitrary and is intended for heuristic purposes only.

Projectile Points

The most frequently occurring ordinary artifact considered here is projectile points. Although projectile points were found in rooms throughout Pueblo Bonito, their distribution was in fact fairly concentrated (Fig. 9.12). Three nonburial northern rooms contained two-thirds of the site's projectile points: Room 39, with 340 points; Room 10, with 180 points; and Room 48-50, with 154 points. The room with the fourth greatest quantity of points was Room 330 (68 points), which is part of the western burial group.

This distribution suggests that my classification of projectile points as ordinary may be incorrect. I originally identified them as ordinary artifacts because they can serve a practical function as hunting implements. The strong association between projectile points and nonburial northern rooms, as well as with a burial room, however, suggests that the site's projectile points had ritual significance and thus should have been classified as fancy artifacts. An unanswered question is whether the projectile points found in small quantities in miscellaneous rooms were also deliberately deposited ritual objects.

Worked Bone

Of the ordinary artifacts considered here, worked bone was the second most frequently occurring, the most widely

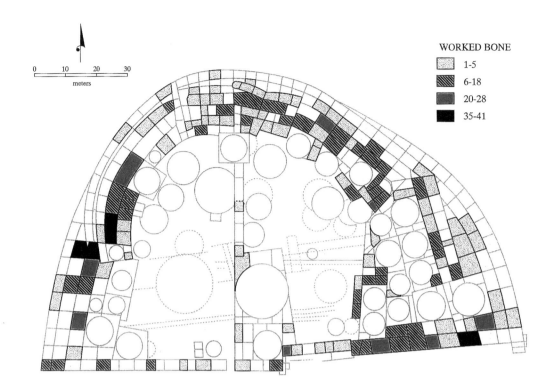

Figure 9.13.
Frequency of worked
bone per room.

WORKED BONE

- 1-5
- 6-18
- 20-28
- 35-41

distributed, and the least concentrated (Figs. 9.4, 9.13). Pueblo Bonito's bone artifacts take a variety of forms such as needles, awls, and beads. Rooms with the greatest quantities of worked bone (35–41 pieces) were Room 326 in the western burial room group, the nearby adjacent Rooms 25 and 105,

and Room 173 in the site's southeast corner. Each of these rooms contained only 4% of Pueblo Bonito's collected worked bone, reinforcing the conclusion that this artifact type occurred in small quantities throughout its wide distribution.

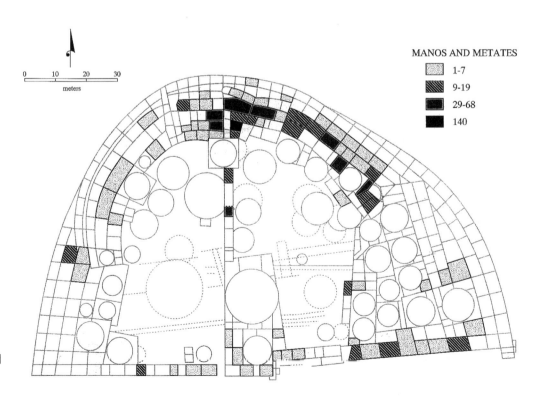

Figure 9.14.
Frequency of manos and
metates per room.

MANOS AND METATES

- 1-7
- 9-19
- 29-68
- 140

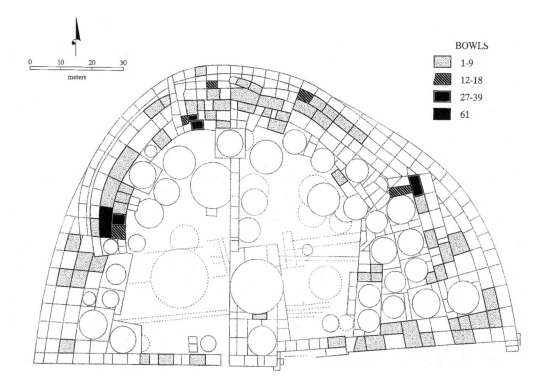

BOWLS

▨ 1-9

▨ 12-18

■ 27-39

■ 61

Figure 9.15.
Frequency of bowls
per room.

Manos and Metates

The third most frequently occurring ordinary artifact type considered here is manos and metates. These ground stone objects are fairly widely distributed throughout the site, but their relative frequency per room is uneven. The room with the most ground stone, Room 42, is located in the site's north-central section, as are four of the eight other rooms with more than 25 manos and metates (Fig. 9.14). One of these rooms, Room 38, also contained 4,000 pieces of jet, 400 pieces of shell, and 14 macaw skeletons. The relatively large number of manos and metates in this part of the site suggests that the artifacts were deposited as ritual caches. If so, then it may be that the more than 25 manos and metates in each of four miscellaneous rooms were also deliberately deposited ritual caches. This suggests that in certain contexts a normally ordinary good such as ground stone could have ritual significance.

As with Pueblo Bonito's projectile points, there may be a problem in classifying the site's manos and metates as ordinary goods. Certainly these artifacts are used for the mundane task of grinding corn and other seeds into flour. But at a ceremonial center such as Pueblo Bonito, the grinding of flour might have held special religious significance. Furthermore, some of Pueblo Bonito's manos and metates are not ordinary in their appearance. Made from a fine-grained raw material, some are well crafted into a formalized shape with a highly burnished finish (Windes and Mathien 1987, and

Windes, personal communication). Finally, some of the manos and metates in north-central caches may never have been used, being intended instead as ritual offerings. These should not be considered ordinary objects.

Bowls

The fourth most frequently occurring ordinary artifact considered here is whole ceramic bowls. Within their fairly wide distribution, Pueblo Bonito's bowls were somewhat concentrated (Fig. 9.15). Approximately one-half of all whole bowls were excavated from five rooms. Two of these rooms, including the one with the greatest number of specimens—Room 326, with 61 bowls—are part of the western burial room group (the other was adjacent Room 329, with 27 bowls). Two more are located in the site's north-central section, one in the northern burial room group (Room 32, with 28 bowls) and the other adjacent to it (Room 28, with 39 bowls). The latter room also held the cache of 111 cylinder vessels and more than 500 pieces of shell.

The large numbers of bowls found in these rooms suggest that bowls were deliberately deposited as part of burial and other ritual activities. The same is probably true for the room ranked third in numbers of bowls—Room 266, with 37 examples—which is located in the east-central part of the site, and perhaps for rooms with fewer bowls located elsewhere. Whether the bowls themselves were ritual objects (and thus a fancy good in my original definition) or simply ordinary ob-

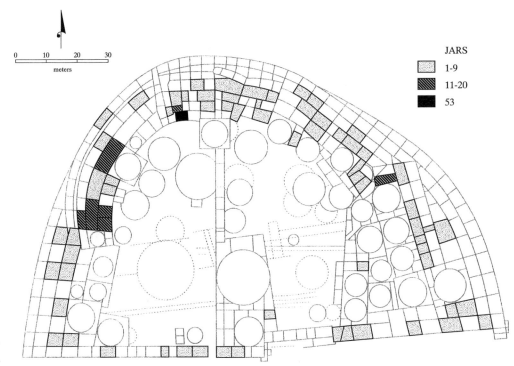

Figure 9.16. Frequency of jars per room.

jects included in ritual activities (e.g., to serve food) may be a moot question. Whether they were ritual or ordinary to begin with, their deposition in sacred contexts made them out-of-the-ordinary.

Jars

In the category of jars I include all jarlike ceramic containers, such as true jars, pitchers, canteens, and effigy vessels. Their practical function was to store foods, either dry or liquid, depending on the diameter of the vessel's mouth. Although whole jars were found much less frequently than whole bowls, both appeared in approximately the same number of rooms (Table 9.1), and both were somewhat concentrated (Fig. 9.16). One-half of Pueblo Bonito's jars derived from eight rooms, two of them located in the site's north-central section. The room with the most jars was a nonburial room—Room 28, with 53 jars—located adjacent to the northern burial room group. This is the same room that contained the cache of 111 cylinder vessels, the second highest number of bowls (39), and more than 500 pieces of shell. Of the seven rooms with 11–20 jars, four make up the western burial room group, and one is part of the northern burial room group.

As with bowls, the large numbers of jars found in these contexts suggest that they were deliberately deposited as part of burial and other ritual activities. This is probably also true for the jars collected from the two other rooms with relatively high frequencies, one near the western burial room group (Room 323, with 11 jars) and the other adjacent to a kiva in the

east-central part of the site (Room 62, with 20 jars), and it is perhaps true for other rooms with fewer jars. Whether it was the jars, their contents, or both that had ritual significance at their deposition is unknown.

Jar Covers

Although sandstone jar covers occurred in approximately the same quantities as jars, they were found in fewer rooms (Table 9.1). Six rooms in the north-central section contained more than two-thirds of all of Pueblo Bonito's recorded jar covers (Fig. 9.17). The room with the most was Room 28 (121 jar covers), which also contained the cache of 111 cylinder vessels, 53 jars, 39 bowls, and more than 500 pieces of shell. Two other rooms with lesser concentrations of jar covers were Room 39B, with 31 covers as well as 19 cylinder vessels, and Room 37, with 26 covers. All three rooms are adjacent or catercorner to the northern burial room group. The remaining three northern rooms with more than 10 jar covers include one burial room (Room 32, with 13 covers) and two nonburial rooms (Room 2, with 18 covers, and Room 54, with 15). Interestingly, even though rooms in the western burial room group contained relatively large numbers of jars and cylinder vessels, none held jar covers. The high frequency of jar covers in some nonburial rooms and one burial room in Pueblo Bonito's north-central section suggests that they were deliberately deposited as part of ritual activities. The same is probably true for smaller quantities in other northern rooms and may also be true for rooms elsewhere in the site.

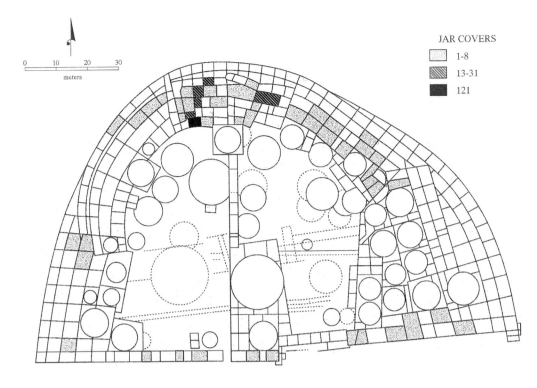

Figure 9.17.
Frequency of jar covers per room.

JAR COVERS
- 1-8
- 13-31
- 121

Spindle Whorls

Only four spindle whorls are recorded for Pueblo Bonito. These objects were used for spinning fibers into thread for cordage and woven cloth. Two of the spindle whorls were uncovered in separate rooms in the northern burial room group. If these objects were originally ordinary objects, they were transformed into ritual items when they were buried in the elite mausoleum. Pueblo Bonito's other two spindle whorls came from two adjacent rooms at the east end of the site's south or front wall.

COMPARISON OF ORDINARY ARTIFACTS

The distributions of artifacts classified here as ordinary can be compared for the four kinds of rooms considered in the earlier discussion of fancy artifacts (Table 9.4). Such comparisons reveal that ordinary goods occurred predominantly in two kinds of rooms—nonburial rooms in Pueblo Bonito's north-central section and miscellaneous, nonburial rooms in other parts of the site. They also show that the kinds of ordinary goods associated with these two types of rooms differed.

Nonburial North-Central Rooms

Two artifact types classified here as ordinary were most strongly associated with nonburial rooms in Pueblo Bonito's north-central section—projectile points and sandstone jar cov-

ers (Table 9.4). Approximately three-quarters of both artifact types were collected from this part of the site. Although each was found in varying quantities in rooms throughout this section, each was also characterized by one cache that was dramatically larger than the quantities appearing elsewhere. Of three notable projectile point caches, the largest was in Room 39, with 340 points; the others were in Rooms 10 and 48-50, with 180 and 154 points, respectively. Only one large cache of sandstone jar covers was found—the 121 covers in Room 28.

Other ordinary artifact types that occurred less frequently in northern nonburial rooms were also found in caches. Approximately one-half of all of Pueblo Bonito's manos and metates derived from this part of the site. The largest cache consisted of 140 pieces of ground stone in Room 42. Caches of 53 jars and 39 bowls were discovered in Room 28, which also

Table 9.4

Percentage Distribution of Ordinary Artifacts in Different Kinds of Rooms

Artifact Type	Northern Burial	Northern Nonburial	Western Burial	Miscellaneous
Projectile points	0.7	75.0	8.2	16.2
Jar covers	5.0	71.2	0.0	23.8
Manos/metates	0.1	50.7	0.0	49.2
Jars	7.8	24.7	19.7	47.8
Bowls	10.4	18.0	28.6	43.0
Worked bone	0.3	10.8	4.5	84.3
Spindle whorls	50.0	0.0	0.0	50.0

Table 9.5

Nonburial North-Central Rooms Producing the Maximum Percentage per Room of an Analyzed Artifact Type

Room	Quantity and Type	Comments
10	20 pipes	
12	1,000 pieces fossil shell	
28	111 whole cylinder vessels	Adjacent to northern burial room group
	121 jar covers	
	53 whole jars	
38	4,000 pieces jet	Includes jet frog; also 14 macaw skeletons
39	340 projectile points	
42	140 manos/metates	

Table 9.6

Ordinary Artifacts in Miscellaneous Rooms

Artifact Type	Number of Rooms	Largest Quantity per Room	% Rooms Where Type Was Found with a Fancy Artifact Type
Projectile points	62	9	93
Jar covers	32	8	91
Manos/metates	54	51	67
Jars	53	20	75
Bowls	49	37	84
Worked bone	103	41	77
Spindle whorls	2	1	100

contained III cylinder vessels, 121 jar covers, and more than 500 pieces of shell.

Several comparisons can be made between the occurrence of ordinary goods and fancy goods in nonburial rooms in Pueblo Bonito's north-central section (Tables 9.2, 9.4). First, for goods that were found most frequently in such rooms, the percentages are generally higher for fancy goods, and more artifact types are involved. Similarly, for individual rooms containing the highest percentage of an artifact type, the percentages are, with one exception, higher for fancy goods than for ordinary goods (Table 9.1). The exception is pipes, whose highest figure per room fits more closely with the range associated with ordinary goods.

Finally, there is a remarkable lack of overlap in the locations where the maximum percentages of individual artifact types per room occurred. Whereas numerous individual rooms contained variably sized caches of different artifact types considered here, only one room contained the maximum percentage per room of more than one artifact type (Table 9.5). The maximum percentages of jet, fossil shell, projectile points, manos/metates, and pipes all fall in separate rooms. The exception to this pattern is Room 28, adjacent to the northern burial room group. It produced the maximum percentages of three artifact types, which are either ceramics (cylinder vessels, jars) or ceramic related (sandstone jar covers). Room 38 is also notable, because in addition to its huge jet cache it contained Pueblo Bonito's largest concentration of macaw skeletons.

I think my conclusions concerning the deposition of fancy artifacts in Pueblo Bonito's north-central section also apply to the artifacts labeled here as ordinary, regardless of their percentage occurrence either overall (Table 9.4) or per room. If the fancy goods were deliberately deposited, most likely as part of ceremonies held in this sacred area, then ordinary goods found in these same rooms were probably deposited in the same way. If this is true, it casts doubt on my initial distinction between fancy and ordinary artifacts, not just for projectile points and manos/metates but for the other so-called ordinary artifacts as well. No matter how ordinary any of the

other ordinary goods might have been prior to deposition, once they were placed in Pueblo Bonito's north-central section, they, too, assumed ritual significance.

Miscellaneous Rooms

The other kind of room where artifacts classified here as ordinary occurred most frequently was nonburial rooms outside Pueblo Bonito's north-central section. Altogether, these miscellaneous rooms contained more than three-quarters of Pueblo Bonito's worked bone and approximately one-half of the site's manos and metates, jars, bowls, and spindle whorls (Table 9.4). Approximately one-quarter of Pueblo Bonito's jar covers came from miscellaneous rooms, and the percentage was even less for projectile points. However, even the low of approximately 16% associated with projectile points is much higher than the percentages associated with most of the fancy artifact types found in miscellaneous rooms (Table 9.2). Overall, ordinary artifacts were much more strongly associated with miscellaneous rooms than were fancy artifacts. This association is also evident in two other comparisons of fancy and ordinary artifact types: (1) between the numbers of miscellaneous rooms in which artifacts of the two categories were found and, to a lesser degree, (2) between the largest quantities of artifacts of the two categories found per miscellaneous room (Tables 9.3, 9.6).

Determining which depositional processes were responsible for the occurrence of various ordinary goods in particular rooms is difficult. Trash dumping is known to have occurred in many of these rooms. But just as I argued that fancy artifacts could have been deliberately deposited in miscellaneous rooms as part of ritual activities, the same could be true for ordinary goods. It can most easily be argued that deliberate deposition took place in miscellaneous rooms with significant quantities of fancy goods, particularly shell and turquoise. For example, considering in isolation the two projectile points in miscellaneous Room 298, it would seem reasonable to conclude that their presence was the result of trash dumping. However, that 12 bowls, 285 pieces of shell, one piece of turquoise, and two ceremonial sticks were also uncovered in this room raises the possibility that the points were deliberately placed there as part of ritual activities.

The co-occurrence of an ordinary artifact type with fancy artifacts can be seen in most miscellaneous rooms where ordinary artifacts were found (Table 9.6). For example, 93% of all miscellaneous rooms with projectile points also contained at least one example of a fancy artifact type. This strong association holds for all of the other ordinary artifact types collected from miscellaneous rooms.

The distributions of various ordinary goods raise some interesting questions about the dating of cultural processes that resulted in artifact deposition. The two burial room groups and the nonburial north-central rooms date to the site's initial construction stage, and thus artifact deposition there could potentially have occurred any time during the site's roughly 300-year occupation span. Ground stone and worked bone, however, were found in significant quantities in rooms dating to the site's last two decades of construction (Figs. 9.13, 9.14; Windes, Chapter 3) and so could not have been deposited until after that time.

Some miscellaneous rooms produced sufficient numbers of ordinary artifacts to raise the possibility that these artifacts represent ritual objects rather than merely trash. Seventeen miscellaneous rooms each contained more than 25 ordinary objects. In most cases these deposits comprised one artifact type, usually worked bone, which was accompanied by one to five examples of other kinds of ordinary artifacts. Given the distributional patterns documented for north-central rooms, this predominance of one artifact type is suggestive of ritual deposits.

This suggestion is further supported by the locations of some of the miscellaneous rooms containing more than 25 ordinary goods. They are located in close proximity either to each other, to other miscellaneous rooms with more than 10 fancy artifacts, or to kivas. This patterning suggests that these ordinary goods might have been deposited ritually. Whether this is also true for rooms containing just a few ordinary goods or whether these artifacts are simply trash is not known. Another possibility is that different kinds of depositional processes acted within individual miscellaneous rooms at different times (see Windes, Chapter 3). Ritual deposits could have preceded trash dumping or vice versa.

Burial Room Groups

Overall, ordinary artifacts occurred less frequently in the two burial room groups than in other types of rooms (Table 9.4). The ordinary artifacts that appeared with the greatest relative frequency in burial rooms were ceramic jars and bowls (discounting spindle whorls because of their small sample size). Comparing the two burial room groups, it can be seen that ordinary artifacts were generally more numerous in the western group than the northern one—a relationship inverse to that of fancy goods. The latter, with one exception, occurred in dramatically larger quantities in the northern burial room group. The exception is cylinder vessels, which occurred twice as often in the western burial room group, consistent with the pattern evidenced for bowls and jars. For some reason, ceramics were deposited more often in the western burial room group than in the northern burial room group. The association of ceramics with the western group does not apply, however, to sandstone jar covers, which occurred more frequently in the northern group.

Regardless of their frequency, most of the ordinary goods from the two burial room groups, if not all, were probably deposited there deliberately as parts of mortuary rituals. That some of the percentages for ordinary goods in the burial room groups are low has implications for understanding depositional processes elsewhere in the site—small numbers alone do not preclude an artifact, either fancy or ordinary, from being a ritual deposit.

ROOMS WITH FEW ARTIFACTS

Even though the prolific burial and nonburial rooms in Pueblo Bonito's north-central section tend to dominate archaeological attention, the distributional maps and comparisons presented here reveal intriguing patterns in other rooms as well. To investigate these patterns further, I used a multivariate statistical technique developed for analyses of cultural consensus (Kempton et al. 1995; Romney at al. 1986; Romney et al. 1987; Weller 1987). The purpose was to examine the degree of correspondence in the distributions of different artifact types in rooms where they occurred in low frequencies. The analysis compared the occurrence of all tabulated artifacts in the 71 rooms that each produced 10–100 specimens of the artifact types considered here. A minimum residual factor analysis was done of the correlations among individual artifact type loadings for rooms meeting the selection criteria. The results are displayed in a graph showing the first and second factor loadings on the horizontal and vertical axes, respectively (Fig. 9.18).

The horizontal axis in Figure 9.18 shows each artifact type's similarity to the distributional pattern of all artifact types combined in rooms meeting the selection criteria. Artifact types near 1.0 have a distributional pattern similar to that exhibited by all types combined. Artifact types near 0 have a distributional pattern with little similarity that of the overall group. Artifact types with negative values have a distributional pattern very different from that of the overall group. The vertical axis displays any remaining variation not shown on the

ARTIFACT COMPARISONS

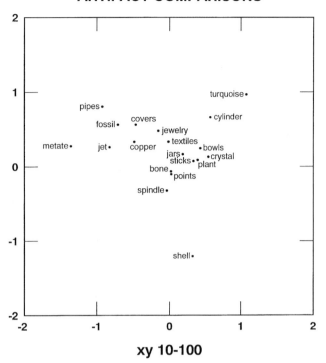

Figure 9.18. Graphical display of distributional similarities of different artifact types in rooms with 10–100 artifacts.

horizontal axis. No direct interpretation can be made of positive and negative values on the vertical axis.

The most evident pattern in Figure 9.18 is the spread across the horizontal dimension, indicating a lack of correspondence in the distributions of the different artifact types in rooms containing 10–100 artifacts. On the vertical dimension, all but one of the artifact types fall into a narrow range, indicating that most of the variation in the type distributions was captured on the x-axis (or the first factor loading). The one artifact type that does not fall into this horizontal band is shell.

The artifact type whose distribution most strongly corresponds to that of the overall group in rooms with 10–100 artifacts is turquoise. The different positions of turquoise and shell on the graph, as well as that of jet, which is one of the artifact types whose distribution is most different from that of the overall group, are among the most intriguing results revealed in Figure 9.18. All three materials were used primarily for jewelry and all may have been deposited during rituals. But for some unknown reason, when they were deposited in rooms with only small quantities of artifacts, they were deposited in different rooms. This patterning reinforces my earlier conclusion that my category of fancy goods may be lumping artifact types with quite different functions and associated depositional processes.

The artifact type whose distribution is most different from that of the overall group is manos/metates. The remaining

artifact types are spread out along the x-axis between the two extremes of turquoise and ground stone and can be arbitrarily divided into three indistinct groups. First, there are the artifact types with x values near 0, indicating that their distributional patterns in rooms with few artifacts bear little similarity to that exhibited by all types combined. The types in this first group include textiles, worked bone, projectile points, and spindle whorls. Jars and other stone jewelry could be included in this first group as well.

The second group includes artifact types with positive x values. Those with higher values have distributional patterns that correspond more closely to the pattern of all types combined. The types in this second group include, in order of increasing similarity to the overall pattern, ceremonial sticks, shell, plant remains, bowls, crystals, and cylinder vessels. The proximity of cylinder vessels and turquoise is interesting, because it may reflect similar ritual functions, at least in rooms with few artifacts.

The final group includes artifact types with negative x values. Those with lower values have distributional patterns that are quite different from the pattern of all types combined. The types in this third group include, in order of increasing dissimilarity to the overall pattern, sandstone jar covers, copper objects, fossil shell, jet, and pipes.

Perhaps the most important conclusion to be drawn from the graph is that interesting distributional patterns also characterize rooms in which relatively few artifacts were found. Efforts to investigate these patterns may produce useful insights into the functions of Pueblo Bonito's different artifact types and the behavioral processes that were responsible for their deposition.

CONCLUSION

This chapter should lay to rest the notion that with the exception of a few highly prolific burial and storage rooms, Pueblo Bonito was an empty site artifactually. Certainly Pueblo Bonito is characterized by several truly spectacular rooms in terms of the quantities and kinds of artifacts excavated from them. But a variety of artifacts was also found throughout the rest of the site. When the distributions of these artifacts are considered together with those from the more prolific rooms, several behaviorally meaningful patterns can be seen. These patterns distinguish both different sets of rooms and different kinds of artifacts.

Among the three types of rooms considered in this chapter—burial rooms, nonburial rooms in Pueblo Bonito's north-central section, and nonburial rooms elsewhere in the site—the northern and western burial room groups are distinguished from the rest of the site, as well as from each other, by their numbers and kinds of fancy artifacts. Some nonburial north-central rooms also contained large quantities of both fancy and ordinary goods. The kinds of fancy goods found in these rooms were different from those that dominated the two burial room groups. Some of the high totals in nonburial north-central rooms reflect the presence of just one kind of artifact, and some reflect the presence of several kinds. The behavioral significance of this variation deserves further investigation.

I argue that all the rooms in Pueblo Bonito's north-central section, both burial and nonburial, made up a sacred part of the site. Whether this sacredness was derived from the presence of the northern burial room group or whether the northern burial room group was located there because it was a sacred area is unclear. Either way, I think the nonburial north-central rooms were an integral part of this sacred precinct, and their contents, whether they occurred in large or small quantities, were ritual offerings.

The numbers of artifacts found in rooms throughout the rest of the site range from moderate to low. The moderate quantities are equal to those in some nonburial north-central rooms, and I think the possibility of ritual offerings should be considered for these miscellaneous rooms as well, especially when their artifacts include the same kinds as those from the nonburial north-central rooms. As in the nonburial north-central rooms, sometimes the moderate quantities of artifacts found elsewhere in the site reflect just one kind of artifact, and sometimes they reflect small numbers of a variety of goods. Again, the behavioral significance of this variation deserves further investigation.

Pueblo Bonito has many rooms in which only small quantities of artifacts were found. In some cases these artifacts might have been ritual offerings. Alternatively, they might represent activities undertaken in the rooms or be the products of accidental loss or trash disposal. Finally, at least 60 rooms at Pueblo Bonito contained none of the artifact types considered here (Fig. 9.2). These empty rooms date significantly more often to the site's later construction stages (Windes, Chapter 3), suggesting that different depositional processes affected older versus younger rooms. Younger rooms may have been more likely to be devoid of artifacts because they were occupied or used until the site's abandonment. This would have precluded trash dumping or ceremonial deposits. Moreover, later occupants might have removed their belongings at the time of abandonment.

In addition to comparisons among different kinds of rooms, comparisons can be made of different kinds of artifacts. Turquoise, ceremonial sticks, and shell occurred predominantly in the northern burial room group. Jet, cylinder vessels, fossil shell, pipes, projectile points, and jar covers occurred predominantly in nonburial north-central rooms. Ground stone was roughly evenly divided between nonburial north-central rooms and nonburial rooms in the rest of the site. Worked bone occurred predominantly in the miscellaneous rooms, as did approximately one-half of the bowls and jars.

This association of different kinds of artifacts with different kinds of rooms is significant for three reasons. First, it evidences functional differentiation among the various artifact types. Second, it suggests that this differentiation existed not just between fancy and ordinary goods but within these categories as well. For example, some so-called fancy goods occurred primarily with burials, and others, as ritual deposits. Finally, the association of different kinds of artifacts with different kinds of rooms reveals problems with the archaeological classification of some artifact types as fancy and others as ordinary. For example, manos and metates are usually considered to be utilitarian objects. Yet the presence of 140 manos and metates in a room located in Pueblo Bonito's sacred precinct suggests that these artifacts were not ordinary, at least at the time of their deposition. The same conclusion applies to small quantities of jars, bowls, and worked bone in nonburial north-central rooms that also contained large quantities of jet, fossil shell, pipes, projectile points, or jar covers.

Trying to draw behavioral inferences from Pueblo Bonito's artifact distributions raises the issue of equifinality, in which different depositional processes might have produced the same result. I argue that most, if not all, of the artifacts from Pueblo Bonito's nonburial north-central rooms represent ritual offerings. I then extend this argument to say that when the same artifacts are found elsewhere in the site, they may also represent ritual offerings, albeit on a much smaller scale. This view is easiest to defend when the quantities of artifacts are comparable to those seen in the northern rooms, but I think it also applies to rooms with small quantities.

Other depositional processes also need to be considered. Windes (Chapter 3) documents the widespread and substantial trash dumping that occurred at the site. Other possible site formation processes include activities that occurred in the rooms when they were in use, accidental loss, deliberate caching for nonritual reasons, and haphazard cleaning. Most likely, a variety of behaviors produced Pueblo Bonito's artifact distributions, and these behaviors may have varied in different parts of the site and at different points in time. I think that ritual deposits were made in north-central rooms throughout the site's occupation and that trash dumping did not occur there because of the sacredness of this part of the site (see Stein et al., Chapter 4; Akins, Chapter 8). Elsewhere, however, ritual deposits may have been made where trash dumping occurred, and vice versa.

My inferences about the behaviors that produced the distributional patterns documented here have implications for Pueblo Bonito's function. If the site's northern burial and nonburial rooms did in fact compose a sacred precinct where ritual offerings were made, and if such offerings were also made on a much reduced scale throughout the rest of the site, then Pueblo Bonito as a whole would have functioned as a kind of temple or center for religious ceremonies. This function does not preclude others, such as a residence for a priestly elite. But most, if not all, of the artifact types considered here were used to varying degrees in religious activities involving burial or ritual offerings.

Many unanswered questions remain about the nature of Pueblo Bonito's religious ceremonies. How public or private were they? How many people were involved? What did the participants do? How did ceremonies in different kinds of rooms—burial, northern nonburial, miscellaneous—vary? It seems likely that the most dramatic ceremonies occurred in the northern rooms, which make up Pueblo Bonito's oldest and most sacred precinct. A few of these rooms contained the site's richest burials, and others contained enormous quantities of artifacts, some of which were of great value. We know that bodies and artifacts were added intermittently to the northern burial room group. Each of these additions was probably a part of religious ceremonies. Ritual deposits of different sizes and types were probably also made intermittently in north-central nonburial rooms. Each of these deposits, too, would have been part of a religious ceremony. Thus, ceremonial activity in Pueblo Bonito's north-central section was probably ongoing, periodically punctuated by a major ritual event.

The primary lesson to be drawn from this chapter for future research is that in order to interpret the behavioral significance of Pueblo Bonito's artifact distributions, we cannot focus on just one subset of rooms or just one kind of artifact. Rather, we must compare the distributions of different kinds of artifacts in different kinds of rooms. Pueblo Bonito is indeed a rich site artifactually, not only in its contents but also in the behavioral inferences that can be drawn from its artifact distributions.

ACKNOWLEDGMENTS

This research was supported by a Weatherhead predoctoral fellowship at the School of American Research, a postdoctoral fellowship at the National Museum of Natural History of the Smithsonian Institution, a Boechenstein postdoctoral fellowship at the American Museum of Natural History, a National Endowment for the Humanities Travel to Collections grant, and a Richard Carley Hunt postdoctoral fellowship from the Wenner-Gren Foundation. James Boster performed the multivariate analyses. Robert Schultz drafted the figures. Tom Windes answered my questions about Pueblo Bonito's artifacts and depositional processes. Jane Kepp read an earlier version of this chapter and made many useful suggestions for improvement.

NOTES

1. Cylinder vessels offer a good example of how inconsistent Pueblo Bonito's various data sources can be. In his artifact summary table, Pepper (1920:359) recorded Room 52 (the upper story of Room 32) as containing 20 cylinder jars. In his text, however, he reported only an unspecified number of cylinder jar fragments (Pepper 1920:210). One whole cylinder jar from this room was located in the American Museum of Natural History collections, and that was the number used for this analysis. Moreover, for the cache of cylinder vessels in Room 28, my total count for whole vessels is 111, whereas Akins (Chapter 8) reports 114. Similarly, Akins (Chapter 8) reports more than 300 ceremonial sticks from Room 32, whereas my total is 266. Another discrepancy can be seen in the count for copper reported in this chapter (11 pieces) and by Mathien in Chapter 10 (29 pieces). In each of these examples, the disparities do not affect conclusions about the overall patterning of the artifacts' distributions.

2. Room numbers can be found on site maps in Chapter 3. Locations of burial rooms are shown in Figure 8.1.

10

Artifacts from Pueblo Bonito
One Hundred Years of Interpretation

Frances Joan Mathien

The 1896–1899 excavations at Pueblo Bonito uncovered the most spectacular artifacts recorded in Chaco Canyon to date. The majority came from the site's north-central section, part of which was used last as a burial chamber and storage area (see Akins, Chapter 8; Neitzel, Chapter 9). The artifacts included flageolets (flutes), ceremonial sticks and other wooden objects, copper bells, inlaid bone objects, macaw skeletons, cylindrically shaped jars, a painted stone mortar, shells including *Strombus, Olivella, Haliotis,* and *Murex,* and thousands of pieces of turquoise, especially with human burials in Room 33 (Pepper 1899, 1905, 1906, 1909, 1920). Although more than a century of archaeological research has greatly expanded our knowledge of the prehispanic Southwest, Pueblo Bonito continues to stand out for its unusual architecture and wealth of items. As Toll (1991:85–86) pointed out, the "Bonito factor"—this unusual wealth of artifacts at one site—is abnormal. To date, such numbers and variety of items have not been discovered at other large sites in Chaco Canyon or the surrounding Chacoan regional system, no matter how the latter is defined.

The wealth of imported and unusual objects at Pueblo Bonito has affected proposed explanations for the rise of Chacoan society, many of which depend on our understanding of the role of imported materials and the functions of trade networks. Pepper (1906, 1920) recognized that several objects were similar to those found in culture areas to the south. Nevertheless, he considered Pueblo Bonito's inhabitants to be ancestors of contemporary Pueblo Indians. He concluded that many of the objects were ceremonial in nature and indicative of the religious or clan positions held by the people using Pueblo Bonito's oldest rooms. Others have proposed that the artifacts support any one of several versions of a hypothesis that Chaco was the center of a regionally oriented, incipient stratified society (Akins 1986; Akins and Schelberg 1984;

Mathien 1993; Schelberg 1984), the center of a regional system that redistributed goods in order to even out resource shortfalls in a patchy and stressed environment (Judge 1979; Schelberg 1982), the head of a turquoise production and distribution center (Judge 1989), a center for groups who participated in regularly scheduled ceremonies (Judge 1989; Toll 1984a, 1985), and a response to Mesoamerican traders searching for exotic goods, specifically turquoise (e.g., Di Peso 1968a, 1968b, 1974; Frisbie 1980; Kelley and Kelley 1975).

In this chapter I review the available data on nonlocal materials, including their sources, their quantities and forms, and their distributions in Pueblo Bonito, in other great houses, and in small sites. I also draw inferences about how each material type might have functioned in Chacoan society. Finally, I use available data on nonlocal materials to evaluate proposed models of Chacoan social organization and of Pueblo Bonito's role in Chacoan society.

IMPORTED ITEMS AND THEIR POSSIBLE SOURCES

Long-distance trade networks linked Southwestern populations for hundreds of years before the rise of the Chaco phenomenon. These networks expanded and changed through time, especially during the Bonito phase (A.D. 900–1150). The imports reviewed here include copper bells, macaws, shell, turquoise, ceramics, lithics, and wood. Copper bells and macaws found to date are few in number and were imported from the south and southwest, particularly from Mesoamerica and what is now northern Mexico. Both are considered luxury items, and they appeared in limited numbers in the American Southwest at approximately 1050–1100. In contrast, the initial appearance of shell, turquoise, ceramics, and lithics was much earlier (A.D. 500–700), and during the Bonito phase these imports occurred in much greater quantities than copper bells and macaws. Sources of shell and turquoise and of some of the imported ceramics and lithics lay outside the San Juan Basin. During the Bonito phase, these items were obtained in greater numbers and were more abundant in great houses than in small sites. The relative importance of the various sources shifted through time, as did the overall proportion of imports. Sources for the large quantities of wood imported for construction timbers also shifted from nearby to distant areas.

Copper Bells

Archaeologists think that copper bells found at Southwestern sites originated to the south, primarily in northwest Mexico. Copper artifacts have been collected at earlier sites and in more forms there than at sites in the American Southwest (Sprague 1964; Sprague and Signori 1963; Vargas 1995).

To date, 41 copper bells or bell fragments have been found at Chaco Canyon. Most came from Pueblo Bonito (approximately 29 bells and/or fragments; Judd 1954). Seven other bells or fragments came from Pueblo del Arroyo (Judd 1959a; Smithsonian catalog),[1] three bell fragments were found in the great kiva of Casa Rinconada (Vivian 1932; Vivian and Reiter 1960:24), and two bells came from Pueblo Alto (Mathien 1987). No copper bells were reported from other excavated great houses (Chetro Ketl, Kin Kletso, Una Vida). One additional bell was found at a late small site, 29SJ633 (Mathien 1991:42). Proveniences for all of the copper bells are thought to date after 1050.

Because most copper bells were found in fill, only a few proveniences suggest who used them or how they might have been used. At Pueblo Bonito, Pepper (1920:Table 8) excavated one from the floor in the southwest corner of Room 83, and Judd (1954:86) excavated another from the northeast corner of Kiva J. At Casa Rinconada, Vivian (Vivian and Reiter 1960:24) found two in the upper floor level. In his discussion of copper bells from Pueblo Bonito and Pueblo del Arroyo, Judd (1954:109) wrote, "We have no reason to suppose ownership was restricted to the priesthood; no reason to believe the bells were in any way connected with rituals."

How copper items were obtained is also unclear. Judging from the numbers of bells found in Chaco Canyon, the Mimbres Valley, the Flagstaff area, and the Hohokam region, Vargas (1995) thought Chaco Canyon's bells were possibly traded through intermediaries in the Hohokam area and that the distribution pattern represented prestige goods exchange originating in western Mexico. Their appearance around 1050 indicates that copper bells were a new item reflecting acquisition of ideas and goods from the south.

Several attempts have been made to identify specific sources of the copper used in Chaco Canyon's bells. In 1928 Root (in Judd 1954:110–111) determined that 16 of Chaco Canyon's bells, including 8 from Pueblo Bonito, had been made using the lost-wax technique, probably from ores in New Mexico, Arizona, or Chihuahua. Because there was no evidence for prehispanic use of copper deposits in those areas and no proof of metalworking in the Southwest before 1540, Judd was uncomfortable with these suggested sources. He then submitted seven ore samples from sources in Mexico and New Mexico and eight copper bells from Pueblo Bonito and Pueblo del Arroyo for spectrochemical analysis. Although two bells from Pueblo del Arroyo were thought to come from the same ore source (Meggers in Judd 1954:112), none matched the seven analyzed ore samples (Judd 1954:109–115).

Recently, Palmer (1994; Palmer et al. 1998) reported on an analysis of copper-related materials from several Southwestern sites. The samples included five copper bells from Pueblo Bonito and one from Pueblo del Arroyo, all of which were included in the spectrographic analysis reported by Judd (1954). These six bells, along with two bells from the Sundown site in

Arizona, were compositionally similar to one another and different from those from Casas Grandes in west-central Chihuahua (Fig. 1.1) and several other sites throughout the Greater Southwest and western Mexico. This result is similar to that obtained by Root (in Judd 1954:110–111), who found that Chaco bells differed from Mesoamerican bells (see Hosler 1994:263–265). Palmer et al. (1998:379) suggested that the Chaco bells might represent an early period in bell-casting technology, which began around 1000. In Palmer's analysis (1994; Palmer et al. 1998), the remaining Southwestern bells fell into other composition groups that were manufactured at a later date. Although they were unable to locate the source of the Chaco bells, Palmer et al. (1998:380) suggested that several early copper workshops might have been located close to copper-cuprite sources in the Anasazi and Hakataya regions.

Macaws and Parrots

The prehispanic Chacoans imported colorful macaws and parrots from Mesoamerica. Hargrave (1970) identified all of Chaco Canyon's macaw remains that he examined as scarlet macaws (*Ara macaw*). This species has colorful red, yellow, and blue feathers and is native to the humid lowlands south of Tamaulipas, Mexico (Blake 1953). Previously, Pepper (1920) identified some of Pueblo Bonito's macaws as military macaws (*Ara militaris*), green macaws that live in oak and pine forests in semiarid southern Sonora and southern Chihuahua (Blake 1953). Una Vida's thick-billed parrot (*Rhynchopsitta pachyrhyncha*) is found in mountain forests of the Sierra Madre Occidental and has been seen occasionally in southern Arizona and New Mexico (Blake 1953).

On the basis of the ages of Chaco Canyon's macaws, particularly the fact that none was newborn, Hargrave (1970) concluded that all were imports. Where they came from is open to discussion. The sites of Wupatki and Point of Pines in Arizona also had clusters of macaws and parrots, but neither was a breeding site. Casas Grandes was a breeding site, but it dates too late to have been Chaco Canyon's supplier (Dean and Ravesloot 1993; Di Peso 1974; Minnis et al. 1993).

One possible candidate is the Mimbres area in southwestern New Mexico. Sites in this area were contemporaneous with the Chaco phenomenon, and Mimbres pottery shows birds being carried in burden baskets. Creel and McKusick (1994:517) found eggshells with an older macaw at the Old Town site. However, they questioned whether this was evidence of breeding, because older females often lay unfertilized eggs. Instead, Creel and McKusick (1994) proposed that the Galaz site was the intermediate node in the transport of macaws to Chaco Canyon from the south.

The exact number of macaws excavated in Chaco Canyon varies by report, but the total is small. Great houses with bird remains include Pueblo Bonito, with 37 macaw skeletons and

a number of bones; Pueblo del Arroyo, with 5 macaw skeletons; Kin Kletso, with 1 macaw skeleton; Una Vida, with 1 parrot skeleton; and Chetro Ketl, with several macaw feathers (Charmion McKusick, letter, 1971, CCNHP Museum Archive 2023-5). At the small site 29SJ1360, five macaw bones, probably from the same bird, have been found along with a possible bin for raising macaws and/or parrots (Akins 1985:328; McKenna 1984:50, 321, 387).

The distribution of macaws at Pueblo Bonito provides clues to their function. The largest repository was Room 38, located in the site's north-central section. It included 12 skeletons among bird droppings on the floor and 2 more in separate circular cavities in the floor on the room's south side (Pepper 1920:194). This association of birds with the south sides of rooms also appeared in Room 71, where one parrot and one macaw were found in the southeast corner, and in Room 78, where two macaws were buried in trash, again in the room's southeast corner (Pepper 1920). Another intriguing association exists between macaws and human infants (Judd 1954:97). Three macaws were buried in a pit with an infant in Room 306, and another with an infant on the floor between the ventilator and the deflector in Room 309. The other major repository of macaw remains was Room 249, which contained a cluster of four skeletons and parts of another bird (Judd 1954:108, 263–264).

The greater number of macaws excavated from Pueblo Bonito suggests that their function was most closely attached to this site, where imported birds were kept in captivity. However, the presence of parrot and macaw remains at other great houses and the possible bin for raising birds at one small site (29SJ1360) indicate that bird handling was not restricted to Pueblo Bonito. Judging from historic Zuni practices, both Pepper (1920:195) and Judd (1954:263) suggested the presence of a Macaw clan at Pueblo Bonito. Its members would have used macaw feathers in their ceremonies.

Shell

Thousands of shells and shell fragments have been uncovered at Chaco Canyon sites dating from the Basketmaker III period through Pueblo III. Specimens include marine shell, freshwater shell, and fossil shell (Judd 1954:89; Mathien 1997; Pepper 1920). Sources of the marine shell were the Pacific Coast, from California south into Mexico and perhaps as far as Panama, and the Gulf of California, from the mouth of the Colorado River south past the Baja California peninsula (Mathien 1997:Table 10.2). Sources of the freshwater shell include Texas, Arkansas, and perhaps California. Local fossil shell comes from Pennsylvanian and Cretaceous formations (Judd 1954:291).

The prehispanic Chacoans had a long history of shell collecting. Through time, the number of shells and species increased, reaching a peak in the Bonito phase. Around A.D. 500, Basketmaker III sites contained *Olivella dama* and *Glycymeris gigantea,* which indicate trade from the Gulf of California. The presence of *Haliotis cracherodii* in Pueblo I sites suggests the addition of sources along the California coast prior to the florescence of the Chaco culture. During the Bonito phase, 17 new genera appeared, including both snail species and bivalves. More than 20 species have been identified at Pueblo Bonito alone (Judd 1954:89), and more than 20 additional species at other canyon sites (Mathien 1997:Table 10.2). Some of the rarer shell species dating to the Bonito phase may have traveled through a prestige or elite trade network. The only shell that appears somewhat later is *Nassarius,* which was found in post-1100 proveniences.

Quantities of shell and diversity of species vary among Chaco Canyon's Bonito phase sites (Mathien 1984, 1997). Pueblo Bonito produced the most in both categories. Its shell came primarily from burials in the site's oldest section (see Akins, Chapter 8), and it was often found in the context of kiva offerings, especially those postdating 1050. Other canyon great houses have yielded less shell and fewer species. Small sites have the least in both categories. Although some species occur only at Pueblo Bonito and in limited numbers, the distribution of many species was not restricted. For example, the two species *Glycymeris* and *Olivella* occur most frequently at both Pueblo Bonito and small sites. Many of the other species also occur at both great houses and small sites.

Both unmodified shell and finished artifacts were imported to the canyon. A possible shell workshop was located in Pueblo Bonito's Room 40, which contained a large stone slab, a number of shell beads, and small turquoise fragments (Pepper 1920:199–200). Jewelry workshops existed in other great houses and small sites beginning around A.D. 900 and continuing through the 1100s (Mathien 1984). These workshops were identified by the presence of turquoise debris, partially finished items, and, in some cases, tools. Unfortunately, the identification of shell debris is difficult because of its light color, which is easily missed in sand.

One type of shell that was imported in its natural form and was seldom modified was fossil shell. The Chacoans' collection of fossil shell seems to have had a long history—both fossil shells and their impressions have been found at early canyon sites (Mathien 1997:Table 10.3). At Pueblo Bonito, large quantities of fossil shell were found in two north-central rooms (Rooms 6 and 12; Fig. 9.8). A few were also found in post-1050 kivas. Interestingly, many of the fossil shells excavated in Rooms 6 and 12 were covered with red and yellow ochre, as were some crinoid stems (Pepper 1920). Judd (1954:261) noted that "fossils, concretions and oddly shaped stones have a place on certain altars and in certain shrines of the present-day Pueblos," but he was uncertain of their significance.

Freshwater and marine shells were generally modified into jewelry and ritual objects. Jewelry included beads, pendants, bracelets, and mosaic inlay. Beads were strung together into necklaces, pendants, and anklets. Among several types, discoidal beads are most frequent, and cylindrical and figure-eight (or bi-lobed) beads are much rarer. The popularity of different bead forms as well as the appearance of certain bead types (e.g., *Olivella* beads) changed through time (Judd 1954:89). Different beads were also apparently used for different purposes (Pepper 1920:83–88). Large quantities of beads were found with Pueblo Bonito's richest burials, indicating that such jewelry was a status marker (see Akins, Chapter 8). Beads and other shell artifacts and fragments have also been found as ritual deposits, most notably in kiva pilasters.

Whereas some shell artifacts initially served as jewelry and later assumed ritual significance, at least one shell artifact—the shell trumpet—was intended for ritual use from the start. A number of trumpets made from *Strombus, Murex,* and *Phyllonatus nitidus* Broderip were uncovered at Pueblo Bonito. They were probably used originally in religious ceremonies (Judd 1954; Pepper 1920). Once broken, they were often reused for other purposes, which probably indicates that the costs of shell procurement and the value of shell artifacts were high.

Turquoise

Like shell, turquoise was an early import into Chaco Canyon. The amounts of turquoise found in Basketmaker III and Pueblo I sites have been small. Items include raw turquoise and finished forms such as beads, pendants, and inlay, all of which continued to appear through time. The quantities of turquoise at all sites increased dramatically during the Early Bonito phase, A.D. 920–1020 (Mathien 1997:Tables 10.6, 10.9, 10.11). Though almost every Early Bonito phase site has a turquoise object (some turquoise debris scattered over the area; a lost bead or pendant), there are three major proveniences for this material—turquoise jewelry workshops, burials, and kivas.

Jewelry workshops appear in both small sites and great houses dating to the Early Bonito phase. The most notable turquoise jewelry workshop was excavated at a small site, 29SJ629, where thousands of minuscule chips were found (Mathien 1984, 1992; Windes 1992). Another possible workshop is Pueblo Bonito's Room 40, where Pepper (1920:199–200) uncovered a large stone slab, a number of shell beads, and small turquoise fragments.

The greatest number of non-workshop-related turquoise objects were collected from Pueblo Bonito's burials (see Akins, Chapter 8). These burials proved to be the major repositories of turquoise, not just in sheer numbers of items but also in the variety of ways in which turquoise objects, particularly inlaid objects, were made and used. Consumption at Pueblo Bonito could account for the items made at other sites

Table 10.1

Possible Sources of Chacoan Turquoise

Source	Identifying Technique	Reference
Cerrillos, N.M.	Visual inspection	Zachary brothers, Albuquerque turquoise traders (personal communication 1976)
	Electron microprobe	Ruppert (1983)
	Neutron activation	Weigand and Harbottle (1993)
King Mine, Colo.	Visual inspection	Zachary brothers (personal communication 1976)
	Electron microprobe	Ruppert (1983)
Cripple Creek, Colo.	Emission spectrometry	Sigleo (1970)
Villa Grove, Colo.	Neutron activation	Weigand (1994:29)
		Harbottle and Weigand (1993:84)
	Visual inspection	Zachary brothers (personal communication 1976)
Mineral Park, Ariz.	Emission spectrometry	Sigleo (1970)
	Electron microprobe	Ruppert (1983)
Courtland-Gleeson area, Ariz.	Electron microprobe	Ruppert (1983)
Morenci, Ariz.	Visual inspection	Zachary brothers (personal communication 1976)
Crescent Peak, Nev.	Emission spectrometry	Sigleo (1970)
New Pass Range, Nev.	Neutron activation	Harbottle and Weigand (1993:84)
		Weigand (1994:29)
Old Blue Gem, Nev.	Visual inspection	Zachary brothers (personal communication 1976)
Blue Gem, Nev.	Visual inspection	Zachary brothers (personal communication 1976)
Royston Group, Nev.	Visual inspection	Zachary brothers (personal communication 1976)

in the canyon. The turquoise found with Pueblo Bonito's burials includes the turquoise-encrusted cylinder basket (Fig. 8.2), inlaid jet objects (Fig. 9.1) and bone tools, intact necklaces (Fig. 8.3), and thousands of loose beads. The greatest quantities of turquoise objects accompanied Pueblo Bonito's burials, especially the two beneath the floorboards of Room 33. The richest, Burial 14, had several strands of turquoise beads around his body.

Turquoise jewelry seems to have functioned as a status marker (Akins 1986, Chapter 8). Burials 13 and 14 had more turquoise than all 12 burials excavated above Room 33's floorboards together. These burials in turn had more turquoise than those in the western burial room group. Very few pieces of turquoise have been found with burials from other great houses or from small sites. However, the fact that after A.D. 1000 a few small-site inhabitants did have at least some turquoise suggests that the stone was significant to everyone within the Chaco system.

The third major context for Chaco Canyon's turquoise is kiva caches. As with shell, the practice of burying turquoise items during kiva construction has a long history. The great kiva at 29SJ423, which dates to the Basketmaker III period, had such an offering (Mathien 2001; Windes 1975). Similar offerings were found in later great kivas such as Casa Rinconada (Vivian and Reiter 1960) and those at Pueblo Bonito (Judd 1954; Pepper 1920:83–84) and other great houses (Chetro Ketl, Hewett 1936; Pueblo del Arroyo, Judd 1959a; Pueblo Alto, Mathien 1987, Windes 1987a, 1987b). In kivas constructed in the late 1000s, turquoise and shell offerings are often found with pi-

lasters (Judd 1954; Pepper 1899, 1920; Mathien 2001). The number of objects in each pilaster varies, and the turquoise offerings may consist of scraps or lesser-quality pieces (Judd 1954; Pepper 1920). It appears that turquoise, like shell, was used as a kiva construction offering that held some ritual meaning whose importance increased during the Classic Bonito phase (1020–1120).

The sources of Chacoan turquoise are not well delineated. The closest source is Cerrillos, New Mexico (Fig. 1.1), where evidence of prehispanic mining has been documented (Warren and Mathien 1984). However, numerous other turquoise mines have been detected throughout the Southwest and northern Mexico, and approximately 30 of these show evidence of prehispanic use (Weigand 1994:31). A variety of analytical techniques has been applied to Chaco Canyon's turquoise in order to determine its source or sources (Table 10.1). The combined results indicate that Chaco's turquoise came from numerous mines located in New Mexico, Colorado, Arizona, and Nevada.

On the basis of neutron activation analyses of turquoise from both sources and sites, Weigand and Harbottle (1993) identified two turquoise trade networks in which Chacoans might have participated between 900 and 1200. One linked a source in the Cerrillos area with artifacts from Chaco Canyon, the Tucson Basin, and La Quemada in Zacatecas. The other linked a second source in the Cerrillos area and artifacts from Chaco Canyon, the Tucson Basin, and Gusave in Sinaloa. That both of the Cerrillos sources linked Chacoan artifacts to Tucson Basin artifacts and then to artifacts in Mesoamerica sug-

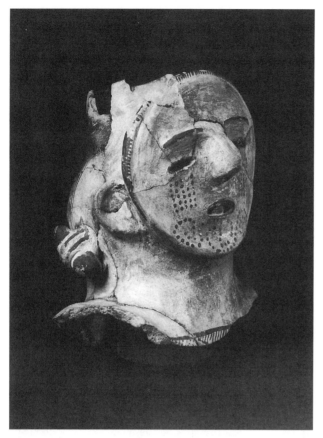

Figure 10.1. Human effigy on the handle of a ceramic pitcher. Courtesy American Museum of Natural History Library, neg. no. 2A13713, photograph by P. Hollembeak and J. Beckett.

gests that the Hohokam might have acted as intermediaries for turquoise moving south. Given the presence of turquoise artifacts in Chaco Canyon during the Basketmaker III period, it appears that turquoise trade networks were established early, and they undoubtedly changed through time as various cultures grew or the participants were reorganized.

Ceramics

The number of ceramic vessels imported into Chaco Canyon from the larger San Juan Basin and from greater distances varied over time and by type or ware. Using conservative estimates of nonlocal tempering materials from canyon sites studied during the National Park Service's Chaco Project, Toll and McKenna (1997) found that from the 800s through approximately 1100–1200, imports increased to 50.4 percent of all pottery and then decreased slightly to 45.7 percent. The lack of fuel in Chaco Canyon for firing ceramics is considered a major reason for the large number of imports, but there may have been other, social reasons as well (Toll and McKenna 1997:149) Although all major nonlocal temper types were found to be present through time, the relative importance of different

sources changed (Toll and McKenna 1997:Table 2.58). For example, San Juan tempering materials were relatively abundant during the early and later periods. Chalcedonic sandstone temper peaked during the 800s. Trachyte increased in the 800s and was the dominant imported tempering material from about 1040 to 1200. The sources of red wares also shifted through time.

Altogether, the temper data indicate that Chaco Canyon had trade relations with people living in all parts of the San Juan Basin and that these relationships shifted through time. The direction of heaviest importation changed from the Red Mesa Valley in the south during the 900s to the Chuska Mountains in the west during the middle and late 1000s; in the early 1100s it shifted again, to the San Juan River in the north (Fig. 1.1). Canyon residents also participated in ceramic trade over even greater distances. Toll (1985; Toll and McKenna 1997) documented a small number of imports from the Mogollon and Kayenta areas from the Basketmaker III through the Pueblo III period.

Pueblo Bonito's ceramic data are consistent with these canyonwide patterns. Shepard's temper analysis of Pueblo Bonito sherds indicated that up to 56 percent of the cooking pots contained sanidine basalt (trachyte), a material probably obtained in the Chuska Mountains to the west (Judd 1954:181–184, 234–235). This figure is close to the 60 percent that Toll (1984b:115; Toll and McKenna 1997:Table 2.58) recorded for trachyte-tempered wares during the Classic Bonito phase. Shepard's small but increasing percentages of andesite temper through time also match Toll's results (1984b, 1985; Toll and McKenna 1997).

Pueblo Bonito's ceramics do differ from those at other, contemporaneous large and small sites in the presence of unusual ceramic forms, including cylinder jars (Fig. 3.8) and effigy forms (Fig. 10.1). Among Southwestern sites, cylinder vessels come almost exclusively from Chaco Canyon, and within the canyon, almost entirely from Pueblo Bonito. Of the 210 known cylinder jars collected from Chaco Canyon, 192 came from Pueblo Bonito (Toll 1990:282–283). This form dates from sometime after 1050 until the early 1100s. Most cylinder vessels are white wares or gray wares of the Gallup Black-on-white and Chaco Black-on-white types (Toll 1990:289; Toll and McKenna 1997:70; Windes, Chapter 3). Three red-ware specimens were reported from Pueblo del Arroyo (Judd 1959a). Pueblo Bonito's cylinder vessels may have come from several sources (Neitzel and Bishop 1990). Some contain trachyte temper, indicating that they were imported from the Chuska area.

Within Pueblo Bonito, cylinder jars were found primarily in groups in northern rooms (Fig. 9.10). The largest cache came from Room 28, where five layers of such vessels were deposited along the room's western side in association with 18 pitchers and 8 bowls. Six other cylindrical jars were found in Room 52, just to the north (Pepper 1920:121). Room 39B contained 19 broken cylinder jars that Pepper (1920:199) thought were larger than those from Room 28. Additional fragments were found in Room 52; other isolated finds were reported in Rooms 32 and 33 and among Moorehead's material from adjoining rooms (Pepper 1920:210). Pepper (1920:377) considered cylinder jars to be ceremonial objects because of their presence in rooms that for other reasons were considered to have been ceremonial. Toll (1990, 2001) noted that the variability in their workmanship might indicate that these jars were special forms used during specific functions.

Human effigy forms also were concentrated in Pueblo Bonito (Fig. 10.1). Most are white wares. They have been collected from northern rooms (Rooms 15 and 38) as well as from other parts of the site (Judd 1954:217–223). No inferences about their use have been made.

Lithics

The percentages of different types of chipped stone imported into Chaco Canyon varied through time (Cameron 1997). Prior to the Classic Bonito phase, imports made up no more than 10 percent of all lithic materials. During the Classic (1020–1120) and Late (1120–1230) Bonito phases, they reached 30 percent or more. Imports then decreased to approximately 12 percent during the Mesa Verde phase (ca. 1220–1320) (Cameron 1997:Table 3.9). The amounts of each type of import also varied through time (Cameron 1997:Table 3.9). Before 920, the most frequent import was obsidian. Washington Pass chert was the most frequent import in the Early Bonito phase (920–1020) and the Classic Bonito phase, when it peaked at 21.1 percent of the canyon's chipped stone materials. Cameron (1997:533) determined that with one exception, imported or exotic lithics were more abundant in great houses. The exception was Washington Pass chert, for which differences between great houses and small sites were ambiguous (Cameron 1997:602).

For Pueblo Bonito, the lithic database is less well refined than that for the canyon as a whole. Pepper (1920) said very little about chipped stone, but he did mention several rooms in which he found unusual numbers of projectile points (Fig. 9.12). Of 17 points in Room 2, he identified 6 as obsidian and the rest as chalcedony. In Room 10, Pepper uncovered 180 points but did not identify their material. Sixteen of 18 points from Room 13 were obsidian. The 211 perfect points and 112 point fragments in Room 39 were made of obsidian, chalcedony, and jasper. In Room 48, most of the 102 complete arrow points and 52 broken ones were made from chalcedony or obsidian. The material type for a hafted knife on the floor of Room 107 was not given.

Judd (1954:253–257) reported more than 300 arrow points. In three instances, sets of arrow points were found with burials in Room 330 (see Akins, Chapter 8). Burial 9 had 8 points near the right knee. Burial 10 had a quiver with 16 arrows beneath

him, as well as an offering of 28 points placed in a triangular pattern between his knees. A fine-grained quartzite arrow point was taken from the third lumbar vertebra of another disarticulated skeleton buried in this room. Judd considered these burials, which were found in Pueblo Bonito's older, western section, to have been late.

Judd (1954) noted the presence of several other types of chipped stone tools, including knives, drills, and scrapers. Unfortunately, he did not provide specific material types. He did report that obsidian, a silicified dark limestone, and a quartzite were used to make knives (Judd 1954:128–129). Drills were made of flint and chalcedony (Judd 1954:132). Debris from the manufacture of blades and points consisted of spalls of flint, jasper, and obsidian (Judd 1954:130). The majority of hammers were of silicified wood, which could be found in the badlands north of Escavada Wash, an area that also could have been the source of quartz and jasper pebbles (Judd 1954:292).

In his review of the points, knives, and drills from the Chaco Project, Lekson (1997) examined some artifacts from Pueblo Bonito and made comparisons with other excavations. He found that Pueblo Bonito stood out for its unusual number of arrow points, the contexts in which those points were found, their raw materials (unusual cherts and chalcedonies), their unusual form, and the workmanship invested in their manufacture. This high-quality workmanship applied to other lithic artifacts as well, such as Pueblo Bonito's four large knives—three from a cache in Kiva Q and one fragment from a cache in Room 316. The disproportionately large number of projectile points excavated at Pueblo Bonito is unmatched by any other contemporaneous large Chacoan site, with the possible exception of nearby Pueblo Alto.

Cameron's (1984, 1997) chipped stone analysis indicated that exotic materials were procured from several directions. Like Toll (1991; Toll and McKenna 1997), Cameron saw a constant interaction between the Chacoans and people to the south, west, north, and east, but with different regions predominating at different times. Toll (1991) tried to correlate the ceramic and lithic source areas to determine whether control over exchange networks could be discerned. He concluded that despite some overall agreement, at times ceramic and lithic source areas differed. The Chuska Mountains, which provided Chaco Canyon's greatest percentage of lithic imports, are an example of agreement. Between 1050 and 1100, the Chuska Mountains were Chaco Canyon's major source area for both imported lithics and trachyte-tempered ceramics.

Wood

Only within the past few decades have archaeologists recognized the tremendous amount of wood that was imported into Chaco Canyon, probably from the Chuska area, for use as roofing timbers. As many as 200,000 trees would have been needed to provide ceiling beams for only 10 of Chaco Canyon's great houses. Dean and Warren (1983) estimated that five of the canyon's large great houses (Chetro Ketl, Pueblo Bonito, Peñasco Blanco, Pueblo Pintado, and Kin Bineola) required approximately 26,000 beams each, and five smaller ones (Pueblo Alto, Una Vida, Pueblo del Arroyo, Hungo Pavi, and Wijiji), some 15,000 beams each. More recently, Windes and Ford (1996:297) estimated that Pueblo Bonito required 50,000 beams.

In a recent review of the use of construction wood in the Chaco area, Windes and McKenna (2001) observed a predominance of pinyon, juniper, and cottonwood in both large and small sites during the 800s and early 900s. At this time, three early great houses (Pueblo Bonito, Una Vida, and Peñasco Blanco) also had limited ponderosa pine and a few spruce and fir logs among the beams. By the 1000s, ponderosa had become the predominant species, and spruce and fir increased through time. These trees probably came from the Chuska Mountains. The importation of wood was probably necessary because the local supply of long, straight logs had been depleted. Wood depletion in Chaco Canyon began around 700 and most certainly affected procurement strategies by the 1000s (Betancourt et al. 1986; Samuels and Betancourt 1982). During the 1000s, the percentage of imported wood varied at different great houses: at Pueblo Bonito, 92 percent of all construction wood was imported; at Chetro Ketl, 93 percent; at Hungo Pavi, 85 percent; at Una Vida, 71 percent; and at Pueblo Pintado, 20 percent. These data suggest that central canyon sites had differential access or need for imported construction timber. Pueblo Pintado, located close to remnant stands on Chacra Mesa, apparently needed the fewest imported roof beams.

Wood species represented at Pueblo Bonito were varied, and their percentages changed through time. Windes and Ford (1996) noted that during Pueblo Bonito's earliest construction phases, the majority of timbers were cottonwood, ponderosa pine, and some pinyon, all of which would have been locally obtainable. Only a small number of Douglas fir and juniper timbers were present. After about 900, however, the proportion of ponderosa pine increased. After 1050, builders at Pueblo Bonito continued to use ponderosa pine and pinyon, but unlike during earlier periods, when beams were obtained from older trees, younger trees now predominated.

The sources of Pueblo Bonito's wood artifacts differed from those of its roof beams. The site's numerous ceremonial sticks and flageolets, found predominantly in Rooms 32 and 33 (Fig. 9.9), were probably made from local material (Pepper 1909, 1920). When he reported on them, Pepper wrote that these items were made from cottonwood, greasewood, and mountain mahogany, all of which are found in Chaco Canyon. Apparently, the choice of wood species depended in part on the size and function of the object to be prepared. Ceremonial sticks and flageolets, which were probably used specifically for ceremonial purposes, were neither long nor thick and thus could be made of local materials.

Summary

Chaco Canyon's importation of both daily necessities and "exotic" or "luxury" items changed through time. For the first pithouses, constructed during the Basketmaker III period (A.D. 500–700), the presence of imported ceramics (Toll and McKenna 1997), lithic materials (Cameron 1997), a few species of shell from the Gulf of California, and turquoise (Mathien 1997) indicates trade from well beyond the perimeters of both Chaco Canyon and the San Juan Basin.

Between 900 and 1050, the quantities of these already established imports increased, as did the number of shell species from the Gulf of California and the Pacific Coast. For this period, jewelry workshops have been identified in the canyon. The predominance of the Red Mesa pottery style suggests closest ties to the south, but smaller amounts of other imported ceramic types indicate contact with the west and north. At this time, wood species used for roofing timbers changed somewhat; new species were obtained from higher elevations at some distance from the canyon. Reasons for this last shift include continued depletion of local wood resources as well as the need for longer beams to span the larger rooms being constructed in great houses. Depletion of wood also would have affected the Chacoans' ability to fire their pottery (Toll and McKenna 1997). Thus, more intense trading relationships might have been needed with those who could supply both wood and pottery.

After about 1050, copper bells, macaws, and additional shell species were introduced. Reliance on ceramic and lithic imports from the west (Gallup Black-on-white and Washington Pass chert) grew, and tremendous increases were seen in the number of roof timbers acquired from the perimeters of the San Juan Basin. Altogether, these changes indicate a greater investment in importing materials for both utilitarian and nonutilitarian purposes. It is difficult to assign specific dates to some of the changes in shell artifact form, but the presence of complete and broken shell beads and turquoise in kiva pilaster offerings during the late 1000s suggests increased use of these items in ritual. The importation of a limited number of copper bells and macaws indicates that contacts to the south and southwest probably expanded, but the nature of these contacts is not fully understood. Although the uses of copper bells are not obvious from the archaeological record, exotic birds were probably kept for their feathers.

By the twelfth century, only slight changes appear in the numbers of ceramic and lithic imports, but more ceramics were coming from the north. *Nassarius* shells were the only new exotic introduced at this time. The beginning of the thirteenth century was characterized by modest decreases in ceramic and lithic imports and dramatic decreases in exotic imports.

Because Pueblo Bonito is the great house with the largest numbers of all kinds of imports, including copper, turquoise, shell, unusual ceramic forms, and unusually well-made arrow points, it is difficult not to attribute a special meaning to the site. The only other completely excavated canyon great house, Kin Kletso (Vivian and Mathews 1965), dates to the later part of the Bonito period, and it has few exotic items characteristic of the earlier Bonito phases. The numbers of exotic goods from other, partially excavated great houses (e.g., Chetro Ketl, Pueblo Alto, Pueblo del Arroyo, Una Vida) do not match those from Pueblo Bonito. Hewett (1936) was disappointed with how little he found in Chetro Ketl's rooms—no burials, no copper bells, no great amounts of turquoise. Yet unique black-and-white stone bead necklaces were found in Chetro Ketl's great kiva (Hewett 1936), and an unusual cache of wooden objects came from one of its rooms in later salvage excavations (Vivian et al. 1978). These finds raise several questions: Does Pueblo Bonito's preeminent position in terms of imports reflect a sampling problem? If not, did the various great houses have different functions? Or did the people who used these structures hold different ranks within Chacoan society? The greatest archaeological attention has been directed toward this last question, resulting in a number of proposed models of Chacoan social organization.

MODELS OF CHACOAN SOCIAL ORGANIZATION

Most proposed models of Chacoan social organization attempt to account for the wealth discrepancies apparent in the differences between Pueblo Bonito's imported artifacts and those from other great houses and the canyon's small sites. These wealth discrepancies have been inferred from the kinds, quantities, sources, and distributions of imported items and materials. The initial model resulted from Pepper's work at Pueblo Bonito. Others have been proposed as excavations of other sites and surveys of Chaco Canyon and the surrounding region have been completed.

Pepper's Interpretations

Pepper (1899, 1905, 1906, 1909, 1920) made three contributions to models of Chacoan social organization. First, he recognized some of Pueblo Bonito's artifacts as long-distance imports. Second, he reasoned that despite these outside contacts, the society that arose in Chaco Canyon was an indigenous devel-

opment. Finally, he viewed this society as ancestral to contemporary Pueblo Indians.

Pepper recognized some of Pueblo Bonito's artifacts as evidence of possible trade or influence from Mesoamerica. For example, some of the site's macaw skeletons were initially identified as *Ara militaris.* Pepper (1920:195) noted that macaws were common in northern Mexico and possibly southern New Mexico and Arizona. Hargrave (1970) subsequently identified all of Pepper's macaws as *Ara macao,* which indicates a source even farther south.

Pepper (1909, 1920) also recognized Pueblo Bonito's copper bells, a sandstone cloisonné piece, and two iron pyrites as rare objects with possible Mesoamerican origins. He considered these objects representative of ceremonial items used by an intelligent, indigenous group. For Pepper the materials from Mexico and Central America were too few to enable him to attribute great significance to their origin. He realized that such imports implied some type of communication, but he did not discuss the organization of trade networks that moved them from various places in Mesoamerica to Chaco Canyon.

Pepper's analysis of human effigy ceramic figures (Fig. 10.1) exemplifies his interpretation of Pueblo Bonito's imported goods. He concluded that such vessels were common in Mexico (Pepper 1906:333), but he questioned how much influence Mexican cultures had on the Puebloans, because Chaco Canyon's effigy forms were different from those found at Casas Grandes, Chihuahua. He thought the idea might have been copied and modified from cultures to the south (Pepper 1920:377).

Pepper (1920) interpreted Pueblo Bonito's cylinder jars similarly. The cylindrical jar form resembled that found in Central America, particularly among the Cakchiquel Maya. The Mayan cylindrical vessels, however, were red wares, and the Southwestern forms were predominantly gray wares, which Pepper viewed as typical of the region. Pepper unearthed one red-ware cylindrical jar at Pueblo Bonito (Judd [1954] later found three more at Pueblo del Arroyo). The jar was darker than the usual red wares known from the ancestral Puebloan region, and Pepper (1920) suggested that it was a model used by potters making white wares. Overall, Pepper treated Pueblo Bonito's ceramics as part of a regional phenomenon.

In addition to artifacts with possible Mesoamerican origins, Pepper considered one import from a closer source—turquoise. He thought Pueblo Bonito's turquoise was obtained from the Cerrillos mines near present-day Santa Fe, New Mexico. Not only was there evidence for extensive prehispanic quarrying at these mines, but Pepper (1909, 1920:377) also noted similarities between thin veins in the Cerrillos mines and the trachyte matrix of some of Pueblo Bonito's turquoise artifacts. For Pepper (1905, 1920), Pueblo Bonito's turquoise artifacts represented the zenith in Pueblo arts. On the basis of the high-quality craftsmanship of some pieces, specifically those with inlaid turquoise mosaic, Pepper concluded that master workers had been present.

Pepper observed that many of Pueblo Bonito's artifacts were similar to ceremonial items used by Hopi and Zuni clans. As a result, he concluded that many of Pueblo Bonito's rooms had been used for ceremonial purposes and that ethnographic analogy with the historic Pueblos could be used to draw inferences about Pueblo Bonito's social organization. For example, he identified Room 38, which contained the remains of macaws and a platform holding objects encrusted with turquoise and other tesserae, as a ceremonial room (Pepper 1920:193). In addition, he thought the macaws suggested the presence of a macaw totem similar to the Zuni's Múla-kwe (People of Summer) (Pepper 1920:195; see Cushing 1896:384–386).

Many other examples exist of Pepper's reliance on ethnographic analogy with the historic Pueblos. He considered Room 67, a kiva under the West Court, to have been a council house (Pepper 1899:2, 1920:251–254), and he noted that the practice of placing offerings in kiva pilasters resembled the Hopi practice of inserting turquoise in the walls of new homes. Pepper (1906:334) compared the human effigy vases from Room 38 and the adjacent Room 46 with the He'he and He'he mana, modern Hopi katsinas. Some of the flageolets (flutes) collected from Room 33 were similar to those used by Hopi Flute priests, and Pepper (1909:250) suggested that the burials found above the floor of Room 33 were representative of an early Flute fraternity. Overall, he considered Pueblo Bonito's wealth of material, especially that found in Room 33 with Burials 13 and 14 and in nearby rooms, as the jewelry and ceremonial paraphernalia of a priesthood or leaders who held important positions in Chacoan society (Pepper 1909, 1920).

More Recent Models

As a result of numerous surveys and excavations carried out in the last century (e.g., Kantner and Mahoney 2000; Marshall et al. 1979; Powers et al. 1983), we now have a much broader view of Chacoan society than Pepper had. We know that between approximately 1050 and 1100, Pueblo Bonito was the center of a regional development that involved the construction of great houses, roads, and irrigation systems, widespread ceramic exchange, and the import of exotic goods (Judge 1989). We also know that the unusual artifacts Pepper excavated were not typical of other large or small sites in Chaco Canyon or the surrounding region.

This knowledge has generated new models of Chacoan social organization (see Vivian 1990:391–419). Proponents of some of these models argue that Mesoamerican influences caused the development of Chacoan society. Others adopt Pepper's view that Chacoan society was an indigenous development. These models differ regarding what kind of social or-

ganization developed, with proposals ranging from egalitarian organization to various degrees of ranking. Some of the indigenous models also suggest that Chacoan society was ancestral to that of the historic Pueblos.

External Influences on Chacoan Society

A number of investigators have proposed Mesoamerican influence as the cause for the development of Chacoan society. Contacts among people throughout the southwestern United States and northern Mexico were long-standing, extending at least as far back as the Archaic period, when Mesoamerican corn and other food crops were introduced into the Southwest. The evidence for Mesoamerican influence on Chacoan society includes the presence of copper bells and macaws, the increased use of turquoise and shell, and the construction of great houses, great kivas, and roads, which resemble manifestations farther south built between A.D. 900 and 1150.

Research in the southwestern U.S. and northern Mexico has produced several scenarios about interaction and trade that identify Chaco Canyon and Pueblo Bonito as the end nodes in a long-distance trade network headquartered in central Mexico. The best-defined models are those of Di Peso (1968a, 1968b, 1974) and Kelley (Kelley and Kelley 1975), which were formulated to explain how rare items moved great distances between these areas. Frisbie (1978) and Reyman (1978b) both proposed that Mesoamerican traders had been physically present in Chaco Canyon. Each suggested that the rich burials in Pueblo Bonito's Room 33 were the remains of Mesoamericans who managed the Chaco node of the long-distance trade network.

These models cannot be supported empirically. The artifacts imported into Chaco Canyon from Mesoamerica and northern Mexico are too few, and their appearance too late, to enable the conclusion that groups or individuals from their source areas were the moving force in Chacoan development. In addition, craniometric analyses by Akins (1986, and Chapter 8) and Schillaci et al. (2001) discredit the idea that Mesoamerican traders were buried at Pueblo Bonito. Their research indicates that Pueblo Bonito's two most elaborate burials are linked to ancestral and historic Puebloan populations, not to Mesoamericans.

The presence of a few objects from Mesoamerica and northern Mexico in Chaco Canyon, as well as similarities in the production of other artifacts, can best be explained by the importation of prestige goods or the existence of down-the-line trade networks (Mathien 1981a; McGuire 1980). Such networks could account for the transport of both the occasional rare item and new and useful information over long distances. Schaafsma (1999) has provided an interesting discussion of how, over a millennium, ideas, symbols, and some goods might have been passed among Mesoamerican and Southwestern cultures and adapted to local needs (see also Carpenter and Sanchez 1996; Schaafsma and Riley 1999).

Indigenous Growth

Early investigators (Hawley 1934; Hewett 1936; Judd 1954, 1964) assumed that the Chacoans were ancestral to the historic Pueblos. They derived their inferences about Chacoan social organization from ethnographic analogy with what they considered egalitarian Pueblo groups whose members participated in clan and/or sodality interactions. Seldom did they specify which historic tribes were related to Chaco Canyon, or how. During the 1960s and 1970s, reliance on ethnographic analogy fell into disfavor. The focus shifted to cultural ecology, which was the basis for much of the work carried out by the National Park Service's Chaco Project. With the detailed reconstruction of environmental shifts through time (Dean 1992; Robinson and Rose 1979), investigators recognized the limitations imposed by Chaco Canyon's semiarid environment. They tried to correlate perturbations in climatic variables, especially rainfall patterns, with cultural events (Judge 1979; Schelberg 1982; Sebastian 1992b; Vivian 1990).

Although these efforts focused primarily on the Bonito phase, the significance of earlier periods became evident as researchers recognized that the Bonito phase had developed from preexisting sociopolitical foundations. Schelberg (1982:229–242) suggested that low-level ranking developed during the Basketmaker III and Pueblo I periods when dependence on agricultural products tied people to local areas. The need to share information and products in order to buffer poor agricultural seasons in a semiarid environment provided the underpinnings for later Chacoan developments.

The movement of imported goods also contributed to later Chacoan developments. Many Bonito-phase imports (excluding copper bells, macaws, and some wood species) began to be traded into Chaco Canyon during Basketmaker III times. Wilcox (1996:248) thought that a regional tribal organization developed as early as Basketmaker II to move small quantities of shell through a trade network extending east from the Pacific coast to the upper San Juan River. According to Wilcox, this tribal organization became more firmly established during Pueblo I.

The possibility that later Chacoans had a ranked or stratified society was suggested first by Grebinger (1973, 1978). Altschul (1978) proposed that Chaco Canyon was part of a larger interaction sphere. He viewed this loose confederation as an attempt to sustain farmers throughout the larger region during dry periods. Similarly, Judge (1979) proposed a model of how a complex cultural ecosystem in such an environment could have been buffered through trade, initially in a reciprocal manner and later through a redistribution network centered in Chaco Canyon.

With the recognition that Chaco Canyon was part of a larger regional system from 900 to 1150 and that it might have been the system's center from 1050 to 1100, researchers carried out a number of studies to determine the system's complexity. Schelberg (1984:18), for example, judging from the sizes of great houses, suggested a three- or even four-level site hierarchy, which would have been a complex chiefdom or a simple state. Powers (1984), too, arrived at three size divisions for great houses. Akins (1986:129–132) and Schelberg (1982; Akins and Schelberg 1984) analyzed grave goods that accompanied human burials from Chaco sites. They concluded that evidence existed for at least two levels of social stratification: a subordinate level represented by burials from small sites and a superordinate level represented by those from great houses. The superordinate level could in turn be subdivided into two tiers, the lower one consisting of Pueblo Bonito's western burial room group and the higher one consisting of its northern burial room group.

In addition to determining the complexity of the Chacoan system, efforts were made to investigate the kinds of connections that held it together. Toll (1985:369–406) explored the ceremonial aspects of modern Pueblo life and noted that the exchange of goods was an integral part of many ceremonies. He recognized the difficulty of ranking large Puebloan gatherings along scales from sacred to profane, closed to open, or religious to economic. However, he proposed that several aspects of these events could be recognized, including the distribution of goods from various distances among participants, the lack of strong governmental control over the events (e.g., no coercion to attend, no taxation), the somewhat regular scheduling of events by ceremonial authorities, the relative safety for diverse participants, and the long-standing occurrence of such events. Toll suggested that similar events took place in the prehispanic period and provided the means to redistribute large quantities of food to dispersed and mobile populations.

By 1989, Judge had elaborated his previous reconstructions (e.g., Judge 1979) and proposed that Chaco Canyon was the focal point of a system organized around scheduled rituals during which many goods were consumed. In his new model, the system's initial operation during the 900s was funded through control of turquoise production. Although turquoise was heavily used in ritual practices, it also became a buffer that could be exchanged for subsistence goods when low rainfall led to poor crop production. By 1020–1050 the system was formalized, and between 1045 and 1080 a period of favorable summer precipitation allowed it to expand considerably. Judge (1989) proposed that environmental fluctuations during the 1080s and 1090s caused a number of participants to establish new centers to the north, in the San Juan River drainage. Competition from these centers eventually led to the downfall of Chaco Canyon as the system's central place, but the canyon did not succumb entirely until an extended downturn in precipitation between 1130 and 1180 brought abandonment.

Renfrew (2001) recently considered how a location of ceremonial importance such as Chaco Canyon might have operated. It would have needed leaders to coordinate ceremonial events, a local population to support the ceremonial headquarters, including the leaders and their families, and people who would come to the location at intervals to participate in the ceremonial events. Each group would have had specific tasks and roles within the system, and each would have needed to give and receive different items, foodstuffs, or labor to produce the whole.

Although one of the goods being exchanged might have been turquoise, it seems not to have played the key role assigned to it by Judge (1989). Turquoise objects from sites in both Chaco Canyon and the San Juan Basin do support Judge's (1989) proposition that the stone was closely associated with ritual (Mathien 1981a, 2001). That canyon inhabitants controlled turquoise production, however, is questionable (Earle 2001; Mathien 2001; Peregrine 2001). There is no evidence for turquoise stockpiling, which would be expected if this material was financing the system (Earle 2001).

Sebastian (1992b) argued that the Chaco system was financed by staple products, not turquoise, a view recently reiterated by Earle (2001). Like Schelberg (1982), Sebastian concluded that leaders were present in Chaco Canyon by the 900s, after which their power base grew and changed. She proposed that during periods of adequate to above-average rainfall, the system was able to expand. The construction of irrigation systems on the canyon's north side (Vivian 1974) would have enabled great-house residents to take better advantage of water running off the mesas by directing it to farm plots. The result might have been the emergence of local leadership, which subsequently evolved into stable leadership centered in Chaco Canyon and extending throughout the surrounding region.

Stuart (2000) suggested that the years between 1020 and 1130 might have been a time when leaders focused less on the subsistence farmers whose basic support made the system work and more on exhibitions of power through construction of great houses, roads, and other large structures. So long as these leaders retained sufficient energy (food, fuel, and resources) to maintain the system, including their leadership roles, the system functioned. When drought disturbed the regime around 1090 and then set in for a 50-year period around 1130, the system reorganized. During each drought episode, farmers headed to uplands where they could meet their subsistence needs. Continued adaptations to fluctuating rainfall regimes eventually led to the reorganization of their society into the forms seen among the Pueblo Indians today.

Wilcox (1993:84) has proposed greater Chacoan organizational complexity than any other scholar to date. He suggested that Chaco might have been a simple state with its administrative center at either Pueblo Bonito or Chetro Ketl. In Wilcox's model, territorial chiefs, located in outlying communities, provided tribute to Chaco Canyon's ruling families. Wilcox suggested that a force of 500 to 1,000 warriors would have been sufficient to enable such a state to exist. If the highest canyon population estimates of approximately 10,000 people are accurate, then one out of every 10 to 20 people would have been needed in this force. If the lower population estimates of approximately 2,500 people are accurate, then one out of every 2.5 to 5 people would have been needed. If we consider that half of the canyon's residents were probably female and others were children or elderly, then it seems that such a force could not have been fielded. Many factors have to be considered in estimating how many people lived in Chaco Canyon, but the low proposed estimates seem most likely (Windes, 1984, and Chapter 3; Neitzel, Chapter 11). Although population estimates and the level of social complexity continue to be debated, it is unlikely that Chaco Canyon was ever the center of a state-level society.

Relationship to Historic Pueblos

Pepper (1920) was the first to suggest that Chaco Canyon's prehispanic residents were ancestral to historic Pueblo Indians. Today these groups speak different languages yet share many similar customs. Several researchers have recently suggested that two or more of these groups can be traced back to Chaco Canyon. The idea that two or more cultural groups lived in Chaco Canyon has a long intellectual history. It was first proposed by Kluckhohn (1939) to explain the differences between contemporaneous great houses and small sites. Later, Vivian and Mathews (1965) suggested the presence of three groups to account for differences in architecture and ceramics at small sites and the Bonito-style and McElmo-style great houses. More recently, Vivian (1990) traced the San Juan Basin's prehispanic period from the Archaic through the Pueblo III period and suggested the early presence (Basketmaker III–Pueblo I) of four different groups. According to Vivian, the different settlement patterns and other cultural traits of these groups coexisted, intermingled, and changed through time. By the height of the Chaco phenomenon, Vivian suggested, southern Cíbolan and northern San Juan people were living side by side, one in great houses and the other in small-house sites. Using a Tewa-based model in which dual leadership is exercised through moieties that are each responsible for events during half the year, Vivian (1990) explained how egalitarian societies could have coordinated Chacoan regional developments.

On a smaller scale, Judd (1954, 1964) applied the two-group idea to Pueblo Bonito in order to explain the concentration of valuable artifacts and elaborate burials in the site's oldest section versus their absence in the newer sections. Craniometric analyses by Akins (1986, and Chapter 8) and Schillaci et al. (2001) support this view. Both analyses indicate that members of two different populations were interred in Pueblo Bonito's northern and western burial rooms, respectively. Akins (1986) found that individuals from each of Pueblo Bonito's two burial groups resembled individuals from canyon small sites more closely than they did each other. Those in the northern group were linked to burials from two small sites near Fajada Butte, several miles up the canyon. Those in the western group most closely resembled burials from Bc 59, a small site located near Casa Rinconada across the wash from Pueblo Bonito. These correspondences suggest that burial in either of Pueblo Bonito's two burial room groups might not have been restricted to the site's inhabitants.

In addition to their craniometric differences, Pueblo Bonito's two burial room groups differed in two other ways (Akins 1986:Table B.1; Judd 1954:325–334; Pepper 1909). First, the two sets of rooms apparently had different functions prior to their use as burial chambers. The small rooms in the northern group were probably storage rooms (Pepper 1920:163; cf. Stein et al. Chapter 4), whereas those in the western group might have been council chambers (Judd 1954). Second, among burials that could be tentatively assigned to the Red Mesa ceramic period (900–1040), those in the northern room group had greater quantities of turquoise, shell, ceremonial sticks, and flageolets. Based on the results of her mortuary analyses, Akins (1986:132, and Chapter 8) concluded that hereditary ranking was present among the Chacoans. She also noted, however, that Pueblo Bonito's northern burial group contained not only numerous highly valued grave goods but also many ceremonial objects. Both burial and nonburial rooms in Pueblo Bonito's northern area served as repositories for many objects that were similar to ethnohistorically documented religious paraphernalia (Akins 1986:129–133). Thus, Akins's data support Pepper's (1909, 1920) suggestion that the individuals in the northern burial group were priests or leaders who held important positions in Chacoan society.

Evidence exists for both continuity and discontinuity between Pueblo Bonito and the historic Pueblos. Biological continuity is suggested by the results of Schallaci et al.'s (2001) craniometric analyses. These results also provide support for the idea that Pueblo Bonito's burials represent two cultural groups. Schallaci et al. found that Pueblo Bonito's northern burial group was more closely related to populations from later sites in the modern Hopi-Zuni area, and its western burial group was more closely related to later sites in the northern Rio Grande area.

Some degree of organizational continuity is also evident between Pueblo Bonito and the historic Pueblos. Reyman's (1987b) review of Puebloan ethnographies reveals how historic Pueblo leaders had both power and authority. Ranking, however, was limited, and priests who served as leaders could be removed from office. The major discontinuity between Pueblo Bonito and the historic Pueblos lies in their burial practices. Reyman's (1987b:141) ethnographic review revealed historic Pueblo burial practices to be notably unelaborate, even for priests.

Together, these biological, organizational, and mortuary data provide a picture of continuity and change. Chaco Canyon's prehispanic residents were ancestral to several historic Pueblo groups, but organizational complexity, as evidenced by mortuary practices, was much greater among the prehispanic Chacoans than among any of their descendants.

Leadership at Pueblo Bonito

On the basis of Pueblo Bonito's size, its focus as the terminal point for the prehispanic road network, its wealth of objects not found at other sites, and the richness of its burials, many researchers believe that Pueblo Bonito was the central place for a well-organized society and that the society's important leaders were buried there. These leaders have been characterized in different ways. Akins (1986, Chapter 8; Akins and Schelberg 1984) interprets Pueblo Bonito's burials as elite sociopolitical leaders. Peregrine (2001) and Earle (2001) have proposed a somewhat different view based on a cross-cultural comparison of prehistoric chiefdoms. They identify Chaco as a corporate chiefdom whose leaders are invisible archaeologically. From this perspective, the rich Room 33 burials represent a unique event rather than typical Chacoan leadership practices. (For an alternative view, see Neitzel, Chapter 11.)

Another interpretation of Pueblo Bonito's leaders is that they were ritual or clan specialists (Gabriel 1991; Renfrew 2001; Stein and Lekson 1992; Toll 1984a, 1984b, 1985). Yoffee (2001) sees rituality serving as an integrating mechanism among competitive Chacoan groups. Ware (2001) has examined the interrelationships between kin and sodality organizations of the historic Rio Grande pueblos. He finds that such organizations facilitate the exchange of sacred knowledge and material goods among ceremonial elites. He concludes that similar types of organization might have operated in Chaco Canyon.

Who, then, was living in or buried at Pueblo Bonito? I see no reason why the two men in Room 33 could not represent religious leaders who participated in an unusual event (both had marks on their skulls that indicated trauma, possibly a battle). The disproportionately large quantities of ceramics, shell, and turquoise that accompanied these men might not tell us exactly what happened to them, but they do indicate that they held a unique position in Chacoan society. Possibly contemporaneous burials from Pueblo Bonito's western burial group include a warrior interred above the floor boards and two young men beneath the floor of a room that might originally have been a ceremonial structure. Perhaps the northern and western burial populations were leading members of clans who lived side by side at Pueblo Bonito. Could these clans have controlled two different sets of ceremonies throughout the year, as Vivian's (1990) model suggested? Or do they represent the honored leaders of kin-based ceremonial organizations who were struggling with tensions among kin and sodality-based ceremonial groups?

Using historic or ethnographic data to reconstruct behavior hundreds of years earlier is fraught with problems (Schelberg 1984). But knowing that the trajectory leads to modern Pueblo society (Ware 2001), we must consider various possibilities for historical change. Fewkes (1900:1007) discussed the differences between Hopi societies and clans in the ethnohistoric period. He believed that clans probably once controlled all of Hopi society. But it is well documented that people continually migrated into and out of historic Pueblo villages (Fewkes 1900; Parsons 1939), and the addition of new people into the sacerdotal societies would have introduced differences into ceremonial performances. We cannot assume that the present and the past were so different that such an ebb and flow of groups did not take place and ceremonies did not change.

With these problems in mind, I would like to return to Pepper's (1905, 1920) interpretations. How can we evaluate his suggestions about Pueblo Bonito's inhabitants and the functions of the site's northern section? Could it have been an area used by the ancestral Flute clan or Macaw clan? Were these two groups separate or related? Within the last century, ethnologists have reported the presence of the Flute clan mainly among the Hopi. Parsons (1939:Table 1) examined ceremonial organization at the Zuni, Hopi, Keres, Jemez, Tewa, Isleta, and Taos pueblos and listed the presence of the Flute society for Hopi and Jemez (Flute-Flower). Lowie (1929:342–343) noted that in 1916 the Blue Flute ceremony on Second Mesa was associated with the Parrot clan. There was another Flute fraternity on Second Mesa (Drab Flute fraternity), as well as other Flute fraternities on other mesas. Parsons (1939:Table 1) mentioned that the Big Parrot people were present in Taos.

Fewkes (1900:987–1011) reported that the Flute ceremony took place in five of the Hopi pueblos (Walpi, Shipaulovi, Oraibi, Shumopovi, and Mishongnovi) but not at Sichumovi or Hano. The nine-day ceremony was performed by two divisions of Flute priests, the Cakwaleña (Blue Flute) and Macileña (Drab Flute) societies in these villages, but not all of the ceremonial altars and paraphernalia were identical. The Flute ceremonies were performed not in kivas but in ancestral (living) rooms of the Flute clan. The ceremonies were marked by the stacking of stands of maize at the ends of these rooms. An altar was placed in front of the maize. This altar usually consisted of a wooden reredos, figurines of Flute youth and Flute maiden, bird effigies, mounds and sticks representing flowers, and other common ceremonial paraphernalia such as six-directional maize, rattles, medicine bowls, baskets containing sacred meal, and honey pots. Participants used pipes, whizzers or bull roarers, and feathers during parts of the ceremonies. Not all of these objects would have survived the centuries after Pueblo Bonito's abandonment, but they do provide an outline of the kinds of materials that might be expected in a Flute clan ceremonial room. The discovery of unusual wooden objects in Room 93 at Chetro Ketl (Vivian et al. 1978) suggests that ceremonial altars were present in Chacoan great houses. The material from Chetro Ketl also included bird figures (Vivian et al. 1978:Figs. 2.3, 2.4, 2.10).

If, as Lowie (1929) believed, the Hopi Blue Flute ceremony was associated with the Parrot clan, then perhaps there is some antiquity to this combination. Pueblo Bonito's Room 38 was a rectangular room, possibly a living room, built in the site's oldest section just east of the cluster of rooms used for burials and storage (Pepper 1920:184–195). A number of turquoise bird forms were found there, along with inlaid scrapers, macaws, and other materials. These data fit with Fewkes's description of the Flute ceremony and thus support the idea that some antiquity might exist for the use of the Flute ceremony by the Parrot clan.

Pepper (1909, 1920) suggested that Pueblo Bonito's richest burials were those of either caciques or members of a priesthood. Burials 13 and 14, from beneath the floor of Room 33, were males. Although they were accompanied by the greatest wealth of grave goods, one had severe head injuries, indicating a violent death. The burials above the floor in Room 33 included six adult males, five adult females, and one possibly female adult (Palkovich 1984). It is possible that these men and women were members of a Flute fraternity. Recent discussion with Louis Hieb (personal communication 1996) reveals that Hopi women do participate in the public aspects of the Blue and Gray Flute ceremonies. Hieb also said that one clan could maintain ownership of a ceremony.

Pueblo clan membership usually includes people from several families in the local area. For several Pueblo societies, Reyman (1987b) documented the hereditary passage of positions of power within lineages making up a clan. Akins (1986) documented a tie between burials in the two older sections of Pueblo Bonito and small sites in different areas of Chaco Canyon. Both small sites, Bc 59 and 29SJ1360, show evidence of turquoise processing. Bc 59 also had a burial with turquoise (Akins 1986; Mathien 1984:743–744). At 29SJ1360 we have the only macaw remains found to date at a canyon small site. Were the inhabitants of 29SJ1360 local clan members who supported the ceremonial leaders at Pueblo Bonito? Room 33's burials might represent the most important or powerful lineage in the clan that was responsible for a flute ceremony. Pepper's suggestion that these individuals were either members of a priesthood or caciques is reasonable and deserves further consideration.

CONCLUSION

Even though we now have greater knowledge about outlying communities, the road network, and the kinds and quantities of various materials used in Chaco Canyon, Pueblo Bonito's wealth remains an enigma awaiting full explanation. Pepper's (1920) concept of Pueblo Bonito as a center of trade and fine craftsmanship has been elaborated and supported. So too have his conclusions that Chacoan culture was an indigenous development ancestral to that of the historic Pueblos. Other than a few rare items such as copper bells and macaws, there is limited evidence for contact with people in central or western Mexico. The overall distribution of these items does not preclude the possibility that members of distant societies visited occasionally and brought items to give to their hosts, but neither does it support major Mesoamerican influences on Chacoan culture. Furthermore, similar objects found in two locations (e.g., Chaco Canyon and Mesoamerica) were not necessarily used in the same way. Finally, as Johnson (1989) suggested, the information exchanged with an item might have been more useful than the item itself. Such information might have included the availability of food supplies, who was controlling intermediate areas, whether or not these groups were friendly, new techniques for crafting objects, or even the presence of a new god who, if properly placated, could bring rain or assistance.

The long-distance contacts and exchange of the Classic Bonito phase had a long history, as is evidenced by the presence of shell and turquoise at Basketmaker III sites. The greater number of shell species after 950–1000 was not limited to Pueblo Bonito, suggesting that their acquisition was not controlled by only a few members of the society. Excavation of shell and turquoise placed as offerings in kivas and great kivas and with burials in Room 33 indicates a religious or ceremonial deposition of these items. We can ask whether the increased use of these materials during the Classic Bonito phase was a function of formalization of ritual during this period. The tradition of using shell and turquoise also continued on a diminished scale after the Classic Bonito phase, often in ritual contexts. For example, the prehispanic practice of making turquoise offerings during great kiva construction (e.g., at 29SJ423 and Chetro Ketl; Mathien 1997, 2001; Windes 1975) has its historic counterpart in Hopi and Zuni offerings made during the building of new houses.

Pepper's (1920) suggestions about the antiquity of certain clans or lineages, possibly dating back to the Chaco era, are difficult to evaluate. Not only do researchers have a limited range of surviving artifacts on which to base their inferences, but they also recognize that Puebloan ceremonies have changed through time (Ware 2001). Because they are unable to see exact matches between historic descriptions of clan ceremonies and related paraphernalia, they cannot be specific about the functions that might have taken place at Pueblo Bonito. But some of the items excavated by Pepper might have belonged to clans or religious groups as he suggested.

That Chaco was part of a regional system is definitely supported by recent research. Pepper did not spell his ideas out in great detail, but his comments fall within the explanatory frameworks current today. Toll's (1991:101,104) discussion of how modern Pueblo Indians deemphasize the individual's role and focus on the group offers avenues for additional research. Was the period between 1030 and 1120 an anomaly in the development of the Chacoan system when, for a brief period, leadership by clans was more visible than it is today (or visible insofar as can be determined from material culture remains)? Was it a period of peace (LeBlanc 1999) or an experiment during a time when the power of at least certain individuals was enlarged (Stuart 2000)? As Feinman (1992:179) has cautioned, Southwestern archaeologists may not be able to make distinctions "between horizontal versus vertical, kinship versus hierarchical, or sequential versus simultaneous organizational forms," a difficulty compounded by the possibility that these forms might have coexisted. Were a few groups or clans living in Pueblo Bonito responsible for the formalization of the prehispanic antecedents to the modern Blue Flute ceremony and the Parrot/Macaw clan? Was there tension between kin groups and sodalities (Ware 2001)? We may never fully comprehend the meaning of Pueblo Bonito using ethnographic analogy, but after 100 years Pepper's initial interpretations of Pueblo Bonito's burials and goods as being representative of ceremonial activities are still viable.

ACKNOWLEDGMENTS

A number of people contributed to this chapter. Jill Neitzel, who organized the centennial Society for American Archaeology symposium on Pueblo Bonito, allowed me to participate in this endeavor and was most patient as I reformulated my presentation into this chapter. The reviewers of the manuscript for this book suggested that its focus be reoriented toward the function of Pueblo Bonito and the social organization of its residents. Their suggestion inspired rethinking, especially after I had the privilege of attending a number of recent seminars on Chacoan research. C. T. Wilson and Dabney Ford recognized the need to synthesize data collected during the NPS Chaco Project and to reevaluate thoughts about the people who were responsible for Chacoan culture. They supported Stephen Lekson, who, with the assistance of Chacoan experts and outside scholars, organized a number of conferences that discussed specific topics to develop new perspectives on Chacoan organization. Finally, credit is due to the participants in several of the mini-seminars on Chaco that resulted in new ideas from "outside" archaeologists whose visions of Chaco were tempered by their experiences of other geographic areas and different theoretical perspectives. They pulled the Chacoan archaeologists up to new levels of thought. To all, I say thank you and forgive me for any misrepresentations of your ideas.

NOTE

1. A copy of the catalog cards from both the American Museum of Natural History and the United States National Museum pertaining to the collections of artifacts from Pueblo Bonito is on file at the Chaco Culture National Historical Museum Archive. Information from these cards was used to supplement published reports on excavations at Pueblo Bonito.

II

The Organization, Function, and Population of Pueblo Bonito

Jill E. Neitzel

After more than a century of research, archaeologists continue to grapple with basic questions about Pueblo Bonito. How were the people who built and used this enormous structure organized? What was the building used for? How many people lived there? The answers to these questions are critical for our efforts to see Pueblo Bonito not as the ruin it is today but rather as it was 1,000 years ago—a living place occupied and used by real people. The answers are also important for understanding how Pueblo Bonito was able to dominate the most complex society ever to develop in the northern U.S. Southwest in prehispanic times. This concluding chapter synthesizes the information presented in this volume about Pueblo Bonito's organization, function, and population.

ORGANIZATION

Pueblo Bonito's architecture, artifacts, and burials all support the view that Chacoan society was hierarchically organized with an intermediate degree of complexity. Archaeologists have applied a variety of labels to this kind of society. In Service's (1962) evolutionary typology, such societies are classified as chiefdoms. The lack of fit between Service's type definition and the characteristics of specific cases, however, has fueled vigorous discussions about the validity of the chiefdom category and the usefulness of the typological approach as a whole (Feinman and Neitzel 1984). One consequence of these discussions has been a general reluctance to apply the chiefdom label and, correspondingly, a tendency to use vaguer terms with less intellectual baggage. Alternative labels include middle-range societies, sedentary prestate societies, intermediate-level societies, and societies with moderately developed hierarchies. What all these labels refer to is societies that fit organizationally in between egalitarian societies and states.

Several aspects of Pueblo Bonito's architecture suggest that Chacoan society featured a moderately developed social hierarchy. The first line of evidence is the structure's monumental appearance. The second is the labor costs involved in its construction, which, according to Metcalf's calculations (Chapter 6), were quite high. The actual labor investment was probably even greater than Metcalf's figures indicate, because they do not include the effort invested in constructing the site's two platform mounds, building and rebuilding the northeast foundation complex, and renovating existing rooms.

Metcalf's figures fall within the range documented cross-culturally for monumental structures erected by intermediate-level societies (Castleden 1993; Earle 1997; Haas 1982; Kolb 1994; Milner 1998; Neitzel 1991; Quilter and Vargas 1995; Trigger 1990). Of course, given sufficient time, it would be possible for an egalitarian society to build a monumental structure, but this seems not to have been the case for Chacoan society. Building at Pueblo Bonito was not continuously incremental. Rather, it took place in discrete episodes, some of which were quite short. Furthermore, the timing of any construction tasks would have been constrained by various nonbuilding activities (Wills 2000). Perhaps the strongest architectural evidence that Pueblo Bonito was not built by an egalitarian society is that Pueblo Bonito was just one, albeit the largest, of a series of large-scale building projects undertaken concurrently in Chaco Canyon. Some kind of centralized leadership, combined with the political power necessary to mobilize and administer the necessary labor, must have been present for this massive, simultaneous construction to be completed.

Pueblo Bonito's artifacts also support the view that Chacoan society had a moderately developed social hierarchy. They include objects found only at this site, such as shell trumpets, a turquoise-encrusted basket (Fig. 8.2), inlaid pendants, and shell disks. Akins (Chapter 8) suggests that these unique items might have served as symbols of office rather than just as prestige goods. Pueblo Bonito's artifacts also include the greatest quantities of imported materials excavated from any Chacoan site (Mathien, Chapter 10; also see Neitzel 1989b). Some of the imported materials were transported over long distances (e.g., shell, copper), whereas others were obtained from closer sources (e.g., turquoise, ceramics, wood). Craft specialists might have been responsible for transforming some imports into finished artifacts, either at their point of origin, locally within Chaco Canyon, or somewhere in between.

The differential association of Pueblo Bonito's most valuable artifacts with burials provides convincing evidence that Chacoan society had a moderately developed organizational hierarchy. Akins's mortuary analysis (Chapter 8) reveals that Chacoan society consisted of three tiers—the upper tier represented by Pueblo Bonito's northern burial group, the middle tier by the site's western burial group, and the lower tier by small-site burials. Her analysis also indicates that whereas status among the small-site burials was achieved, status within Pueblo Bonito's two burial groups was ascribed.

Craniometric analyses indicate that Pueblo Bonito's two burial groups represent different populations, most likely families, and that these families more closely resemble individuals from different sets of small canyon sites than they do each other (Akins 1986; Schillaci et al. 2001). These correspondences could reflect biological relations among fellow clan members. They also suggest the possibility that burial at Pueblo Bonito was not restricted to the site's residents (Mathien, Chapter 10).

Together, Pueblo Bonito's architectural, artifactual, and mortuary data provide strong support for the conclusion that Chacoan society was hierarchically organized with an intermediate degree of complexity. In addition, these data offer insights into the nature of the hierarchy (Nelson 1995:614; Rautman 1998:326). Building on previous work by Renfrew (1974) and Drennan (1991), Blanton et al. (1996) recently distinguished two political-economic strategies characterizing hierarchical societies (also see Blanton 1998; Feinman 1995, 2000a, 2000b, 2000c, Feinman et al. 2000). The corporate mode, which corresponds to Renfrew's (1974) group-oriented chiefdom, emphasizes communal activities and group rituals. It is manifested in collective labor projects and monumental public architecture. The network mode, which corresponds to Renfrew's (1974) individualizing chiefdom, emphasizes differential access to personal wealth. It is manifested in the accumulation of prestige goods, which are often obtained through long-distance trade and produced by craft specialists, as well as in the construction of elaborate residences and tombs for rulers.

In applying this approach to understanding hierarchical social forms to the prehispanic Southwest, researchers have argued for the presence of the corporate political-economic strategy in Chacoan society (Earle 2001; Peregrine 2001) and elsewhere (Feinman 2000a, 2000b, Feinman et al. 2000; various other articles in Mills, ed., 2000). This characterization is strongly supported by Pueblo Bonito's massive architecture, which required a tremendous amount of labor to build and whose primary function, for much of its history, was as the setting for communal rituals (Stein et al., Chapter 4; Farmer, Chapter 5; also see Judge 1989; Renfrew 2001; Toll 1985; cf. Wills 2000). However, Pueblo Bonito's huge quantities of valuable, imported goods and their concentration with the site's two paramount burials contradict the conclusion that the Chacoan hierarchy was corporate-based. This latter evidence is instead consistent with a network-based political-economic strategy (Blanton et al 1996) or an individualizing chiefdom (Renfrew 1974).

The contradictory inferences derived from Pueblo Bonito's architectural data as opposed to its artifactual and mortuary data can be explained by organizational change. Pueblo Bonito's two paramount burials were among the site's earliest burials, dating to approximately A.D. 1020. Akins (Chapter 8) states that these burials coincided with large-scale construction in Chaco Canyon and the use of great kivas. But renewed construction at Pueblo Bonito did not begin until 1040, and the greatest building did not occur until 1075 (Windes, Chapter 3; Stein et al., Chapter 4). Furthermore, this eleventh-century construction markedly increased the amount of civic space (kivas and great kivas) at Pueblo Bonito (Metcalf, Chapter 6).

This chronological information suggests that initially the Chacoan hierarchy was network-based, with an emphasis on differential access to personal wealth and the accumulation of prestige goods as seen cross-culturally in individualizing chiefdoms. Through time this network-based hierarchy was transformed into a corporate-based hierarchy with an emphasis on monumental construction and group ritual (in kivas and great kivas) as seen cross-culturally in group-oriented chiefdoms. This organizational shift explains the contrast between Pueblo Bonito's early and late material remains (Judd 1964; Wilcox 1999:130). The numerous valuable artifacts and relatively crude masonry architecture of early Bonito are the remains of a network-based hierarchy or individualizing chiefdom. The relatively few valuable artifacts and the technically sophisticated masonry architecture of late Bonito are the remains of a corporate-based hierarchy or group-oriented chiefdom.

Another, and possibly related, organizational change might also have characterized the Chacoan hierarchy. The site's earliest burials are predominantly male. At approximately A.D. 1030, burials become predominantly female and continue to be so throughout the rest of the site's use as a mausoleum (Akins 1986). This gender shift might signify a transformation of the Chacoan hierarchy from one dominated by males to one dominated by females and matrilocal kin groups (Farmer, Chapter 5; Neitzel 2000; Peregrine 2001).

FUNCTION

Pueblo Bonito had two major functions whose relative importance changed through time. In its initial stage, the site's primary function was as a residence. Although people continued to live in Pueblo Bonito throughout the rest of its history (Windes, Chapter 3; also see Wills 2000), the importance of the residential function was eventually eclipsed by the site's role as a ceremonial center. Bustard (Chapter 7) presents two kinds of evidence that Pueblo Bonito's early function was as a residence. One is the site's Stage I layout, which is typical of Pueblo I–II residential structures throughout the northern Southwest. The other is the presence of domestic features in a handful of Stage I rooms.

Pueblo Bonito's early residents were probably high-status members of Chacoan society. Akins (Chapter 8) dates Pueblo

Bonito's two paramount burials—men whose high status was inherited—to A.D. 1020. The older of these men was 50 years old when he died, so an ascribed social hierarchy must have been in place by no later than A.D. 970. Architectural evidence suggests that this hierarchy might have been in place even earlier, perhaps since the beginning of Stage I construction. In comparison with rooms at other, contemporary residential sites in the northern Southwest, Pueblo Bonito's Stage I rooms are larger and multistory.

For Pueblo Bonito's initial stage, we have suggestive evidence that the site already held ceremonial significance. This evidence includes the structure's location next to Threatening Rock (Marshall, Chapter 1) and some of its architectural alignments (Stein et al., Chapter 4; Farmer, Chapter 5). Clear evidence for a shift toward a ceremonial function appears at approximately 1020, when some habitation and storage rooms in the site's northern and western sections began to be used as elite family mausoleums. By 1050, the site had been transformed into a major ceremonial center, a function that would retain its primacy until the site was abandoned.

This transformation by 1050 is evidenced by the site's many kivas and great kivas, its astronomical alignments, its caches of ritual artifacts, and its continued use as an elite mortuary. Furthermore, by 1050 the site's layout was no longer similar to those of contemporaneous residential sites in the northern Southwest. In addition, rooms with domestic features decreased in number, indicating a shift in room function. By 1075, domestic features had all but disappeared from the site, to be replaced by suites of featureless, spatially segregated rooms. This shift suggests specialized use by large corporate groups (Bustard, Chapter 7).

Elucidating what kinds of ceremonial activities took place at Pueblo Bonito and who participated in them is a task that can easily veer from the inferential to the speculative. It is clear, however, that several different kinds of rituals were conducted at the site. The two burial groups are the results of formal mortuary rites that probably varied depending on the deceased's status. Some kinds of rituals must have also been involved in the interment of the site's relatively small number of isolated burials. Turner and Turner (1999:111–131) argued that Pueblo Bonito's burials exhibit evidence of cannibalism. If this is true, then some of Pueblo Bonito's mortuary rites, and perhaps other ceremonies as well, might have involved human sacrifice and even ritual cannibalism (cf. Akins, Chapter 8).

The site's astronomical alignments offer convincing evidence for scheduled rituals, some of which might have been conducted in conjunction with ceremonies at other canyon sites (Farmer, Chapter 5). Scheduled rituals were probably conducted in kivas and might have varied depending on timing, purpose, and whether the setting was a great or a regular kiva. Rituals involving the caching of sacred artifacts might also have been scheduled, and these, too, might have varied according to the location of the cache and the kinds and quantities of the artifacts.

The nature of Pueblo Bonito's ceremonies apparently changed through time. The clearest example of such a shift occurs at approximately 1085, Lekson's (1986) Stage VII. This final building stage produced almost entirely civic structures (Metcalf, Chapter 6), but unlike previous civic buildings, these kivas were mostly small and located at the plaza's edges (Windes, Chapter 3). Furthermore, Stage VII construction reoriented Pueblo Bonito's plan to emphasize equinox as well as solstice alignments (Farmer, Chapter 5). A key part of this reorientation was the building of a wall that enclosed the site's plaza, separating it both physically and visually from the area to the south. The only access to Pueblo Bonito's interior became a single doorway located at the wall's midpoint and centered between the structure's two platform mounds. The doorway was also aligned with one of the great kiva walls in Pueblo Bonito's plaza and with the central axis of Casa Rinconada on the canyon's south side. On the summer solstice this alignment parallels the approximate direction of sunlight 30 minutes prior to the sun's apex, the time of the Fajada Butte sun dagger event and the Casa Rinconada sun patches.

Farmer (Chapter 5) argues that a series of interlocking rituals involving coordinated sunrise, midday, and sunset observations on the solstices and equinoxes were conducted at Fajada Butte and at Pueblo Bonito, Casa Rinconada, and perhaps other canyon great houses. If this scenario is correct, then the coordination of rituals at Pueblo Bonito and Casa Rinconada would have been formalized at approximately 1085 with the construction of Pueblo Bonito's south wall and its single doorway.

Several suggestions have been made about who participated in Pueblo Bonito's ceremonies. These ceremonies were probably orchestrated by the site's inhabitants. As the highest-ranking members of Chacoan society, their responsibilities were probably religious as well as political and economic. Their priestly role is suggested by their residence and burial in the most important Chacoan ceremonial center. Further suggestions about who conducted Pueblo Bonito's ceremonies have been made by Farmer (Chapter 5), who thinks that at least some ceremonies were run by women's societies, and Mathien (Chapter 10), who thinks that some of Pueblo Bonito's sacred artifacts were used by different clans. Perhaps these clans were headed by the two elite families documented by Akins (Chapter 8).

Large numbers of religious pilgrims, too, might have visited Pueblo Bonito to participate in its ceremonies (Judge 1989). The primary evidence for pilgrims comes from depositional patterns in the site's trash. Although Pueblo Bonito's residential population was small, enormous quantities of trash have been excavated from the site, and much of it seems to have been deposited intermittently (Windes 1989; cf. Wills 2001 for an alternative view of Pueblo Alto). Only Akins

(Chapter 8) addresses the question of pilgrims in this volume. She notes that if there were pilgrims and any died at the site, none was buried there.

The breadth of participation in Pueblo Bonito's ceremonies changed around 1085. If Farmer's (Chapter 5) scenario of interlocking rituals at multiple canyon sites is correct, then more people than just Pueblo Bonito's residents would have been involved, both as participants and as observers. By this time, however, pilgrims would have been unable to enter the site's plaza as they might have done previously. With the construction of the south wall, visitors could observe only activities occurring outside the site, such as the ritual processions described by Farmer.

Another change took place after 1150. By then, Pueblo Bonito was no longer used as a residence, but ritual activities continued to be conducted in its kivas. Windes (Chapter 3) suggests that the participants lived at nearby Hillside Ruin (cf. Stein et al., Chapter 4) and other small sites. Clearly, whatever ceremonies were still being conducted at Pueblo Bonito, they were greatly diminished versions of their predecessors. The priestly elite was gone, and burials were no longer being added to the site's two mortuaries.

In addition to residential, ceremonial, and mortuary functions, two other functions have been proposed for Pueblo Bonito. One is that the site served as a storage facility. The most obvious storage rooms are located in the site's north-central section, where large ritual caches have been uncovered. For these rooms, storage was clearly related to ceremonial activities. Storage may have also occurred elsewhere in the site. The most definitive evidence is the presence of built-in platforms in eight miscellaneous rooms (Bustard, Chapter 7).

Another proposed function for Pueblo Bonito is that of a trading center. If a trading center is defined as a place where goods are exchanged, then Pueblo Bonito does not fit the definition. It was the recipient of a wide variety of imported goods, some from long distances and some in large quantities, but although Pueblo Bonito imported much, it seems to have exported little (Sebastian 1992a; Toll 1985). Thus, the site was a destination for traded goods and not a trading center in the normal sense.

The best answer at present to the question of what Pueblo Bonito was used for is that the site had multiple functions whose relative importance changed through time. It was an elite residence, a ceremonial center, a mortuary, a storage facility, and a destination for trade goods. These functions were all interrelated to varying degrees. For example, the site's role as an elite residence was probably tied directly to its function as an elite mortuary. Its role as an elite mortuary may in turn have contributed to its evolution into a ceremonial center. Pueblo Bonito's roles as a storage facility and a recipient of enormous quantities of trade goods were probably related to the fact that the site was an elite residence and a major ceremonial center.

The conclusion that Pueblo Bonito had multiple, interrelated functions whose relative importance changed through time reinforces the obvious point that Pueblo Bonito is a complex, difficult-to-interpret archaeological site. Arguments about whether it was a residence or a ceremonial center represent intellectual dead ends, because they ignore what is most interesting about the site—its complexity. What happened a millennium ago at Pueblo Bonito is simply too complicated to be understood by pigeonholing the site as either a residence or a ceremonial center. For archaeologists, one of the most significant aspects of Pueblo Bonito is that it does not seem to fit models developed from ethnographic and historic analogs. This lack of fit has been the source of many of the controversies about the site. It also offers archaeologists the opportunity to obtain not just a more nuanced appreciation of Pueblo Bonito and its role in Chacoan society but also a broader understanding of the variety of social forms associated with middle-range societies in general (Feinman 2000a, 2000c; Feinman et al. 2000; also see Mills 2000).

POPULATION

The evidence that Pueblo Bonito served as an elite residence throughout its history raises the question of how many people lived there. Over time, Pueblo Bonito's physical size, as measured by numbers of rooms, increased. Bustard (Chapter 7), however, documents how, after 1050, the vast majority of new rooms were nonresidential. The number of habitation rooms remained small, indicating that the structure's population size did not increase along with its physical size.

Windes (Chapter 3) argues that Pueblo Bonito's population never exceeded 100 people, a figure that is consistent with previously published low estimates (Bernardini 1999; Windes 1984). The claims that few people lived at Pueblo Bonito are convincing for two reasons. First, they are derived from different kinds of data—numbers of hearths and other domestic features and the site's layout. Second, proponents of low peak estimates have a valid point when they say that higher peak estimates derived from room counts alone (e.g., Neitzel 1999:196) are inflated because they fail to consider room function and room abandonment.

Those who argue that Pueblo Bonito's low population estimates are too low note that the site may have had more domestic features, especially in collapsed upper-story rooms, than were recorded during excavations (Reyman 1987a, 1989). If this is true, then Pueblo Bonito's peak population might have been two or three times greater than the lowest proposed estimates. Yet it seems unlikely that the number of unrecorded domestic features was so great that their inclusion in population reconstructions would increase the lowest proposed peak estimates by tenfold or more, to match the levels generated from room counts. In addition, not all rooms with

recorded or unrecorded domestic features had people living in them. Windes (Chapter 3) documents how, throughout Pueblo Bonito's history, large portions of the site, including rooms with domestic features, were abandoned and used for trash deposition as part of a cycle of occupation, abandonment, repair, and reuse.

Another reason Pueblo Bonito's low peak population estimates have been questioned is that they contradict a documented correlation between population size and organizational complexity (Carneiro 1967; Feinman 1995; Feinman and Neitzel 1984; Kosse 1990, 1996: Lekson 1985; Naroll 1956; Tatje and Naroll 1970). Some argue that Pueblo Bonito's population was larger than the low peak estimates because the site was the most important center in a hierarchical society with three status levels. Cross-culturally, the centers of such societies generally have populations ranging from 500 to 4,000 people (Feinman and Neitzel 1984). A conceptual problem exists, however, in the assumption that a positive correlation should exist between Pueblo Bonito's population size and the complexity of Chacoan sociopolitical organization. The problem is that Pueblo Bonito does not represent a discrete settlement. Rather, it is just one structure, albeit the largest, in a community that encompassed many other structures.

When Pueblo Bonito's low population estimates were first proposed, some researchers (e.g., Judge 1989) made analogies between Pueblo Bonito and large Mayan sites with monumental architecture. Mayanist archaeologists defined the limits of these sites by the presence of monumental structures such as pyramids, temples, and palaces and viewed them as the remains of empty ceremonial centers (Sabloff 1990). That interpretation has now been rejected, but not because higher population estimates have been attributed to Mayan pyramids, temples, and palaces. Rather, Mayan centers are now viewed as having been densely occupied because their site boundaries have been redefined as extending beyond the monumental structures. Surveys of these surrounding areas have consistently revealed evidence of dense occupation (e.g., Coe 1967; Willey and Leventhal 1979).

The Mayan analogy still applies to Pueblo Bonito, but in a different way from before. Just as Mayan pyramids, temples, and palaces were individual structures within an urban center, so Pueblo Bonito was one structure in a broader community. The importance of both Mayan pyramid-temple-palace complexes and Pueblo Bonito derived not from how many people lived in them—probably a relatively small number in both cases. Rather, it came from who these people were in terms of their social status and the power they exerted over other members of their society.

To focus on Pueblo Bonito's population in order to draw conclusions about the site's importance or the complexity of its society is misleading. It is analogous to using the population of the White House, where the United States president lives today, in order to draw conclusions about the importance of the White House or the complexity of contemporary American society. Relatively few people live at the White House, but they include one of the world's most powerful people, making this structure one of the world's most important places. And just as the White House is only one structure in the capital city of the United States, so Pueblo Bonito was only one structure in the major settlement cluster of Chacoan society. Inferences about importance and complexity can be made only by considering the broader communities of which these structures are a part.

For Pueblo Bonito, this broader community consisted minimally of the great-house cluster, sometimes referred to as the Pueblo Bonito complex or downtown Chaco, located in the center of Chaco Canyon. These boundaries, however, are probably much too conservative. More likely, the settlement of which Pueblo Bonito was a part encompassed all of Chaco Canyon. If so, then a conservative estimate for its population would be between 2,000 and 6,000 people (Drager 1976; Hayes 1981; Lekson 1984; Neitzel 1999; Pierson 1949; Schelberg 1982; Windes 1984). Pueblo Bonito might not have housed many people itself, but it was the largest and most centrally located structure in what was the proto-urban capital of Chacoan society. Pueblo Bonito was the focal point of Chacoan society, the center of the center. As such, although its residents were few in number, they were the most important and powerful people in the Chacoan world.

CONCLUSION

Pueblo Bonito is one of the most intriguing archaeological sites in the southwestern United States. It is intriguing because of its enormous size, elaborate architecture, rich burials, and large quantities of valuable artifacts. Together, these characteristics raise questions about how the people who built and used Pueblo Bonito were organized, what the structure was used for, and how many people lived there. These questions have been at least partially answered in the preceding chapters.

The people who built and used Pueblo Bonito were organized in a three-tier social hierarchy. Initially, this hierarchy was network-based, as in individualized chiefdoms. It was subsequently transformed into a corporate-based hierarchy, characteristic of group-oriented chiefdoms. This organizational change coincided with a shift in Pueblo Bonito's function. Throughout its history, Pueblo Bonito served as an elite residence, with the number of permanent residents never exceeding several hundred people. Initially, this residential function was primary, but it was eventually supplanted by the site's role as a ceremonial center.

In comparison with other large Southwestern sites, Pueblo Bonito is an anomaly. It is not just its enormous size, elaborate architecture, rich burials, and fancy artifacts that make

Pueblo Bonito so unusual. It is what these remains signify about the kind of society that left them behind. The one overriding characteristic of prehispanic societies in the northern Southwest is their egalitarianism. Evidence for status differentiation is rare (Feinman 2000a), and when present, it tends to be ambiguous. This ambiguity has been the cause of sometimes heated debates among archaeologists about the degree of complexity found among prehispanic Southwestern societies (see Lightfoot and Upham 1989; McGuire and Saitta 1996). When social hierarchies did develop, they were corporate-based, with an emphasis on communal activities and group rituals as seen cross-culturally in group-oriented chiefdoms.

Pueblo Bonito contradicts this northern Southwest pattern for egalitarianism in several ways. First, the evidence for a social hierarchy is clear and redundant. Second, during Pueblo Bonito's initial stage, the hierarchy was network-based. This emphasis on differential access to personal wealth characteristic of individualizing chiefdoms is unique in the prehispanic northern Southwest. Finally, when Chacoan society was transformed into a corporate-based hierarchy, or a group-oriented chiefdom, the emphasis on group rituals and the construction of monumental architecture was much greater than in other prehispanic Southwestern societies with corporate-based hierarchies.

These differences raise two major questions confronting Chacoan archaeologists today. First, what conditions caused Chacoan society to follow such a divergent evolutionary trajectory in comparison with other prehispanic Southwestern societies? The answer to this question may lie not only in environmental factors (e.g., Dean 1992) but also in the religious realm (Marshall, Chapter 2). Second, why did the Chacoan trajectory shift at approximately A.D. 1050 to a path more similar to that seen in other hierarchically organized Southwestern societies, but in an exaggerated form? Perhaps the conditions promoting the ethos of egalitarianism throughout the northern Southwest were so strong that a network-based strategy could not be sustained.

To understand what made Pueblo Bonito the most important place in Chacoan society, we must continue the kinds of intensive analyses that have been presented in this volume. Yet site-based analyses are not enough. We also need to consider the site in its broader context, and contextual analyses must be carried out at multiple scales (Feinman 1992; Neitzel 1989a, 1999; Neitzel and Anderson 1999). At the lowest contextual level, Pueblo Bonito was the largest structure in the building cluster known as the Pueblo Bonito complex or downtown Chaco. This cluster was in turn part of a larger community comprising all of Chaco Canyon. I have argued here that the canyon as a whole made up a single, dispersed, proto-urban center that functioned as the capital of Chacoan society. Whatever its limits, the inhabitants of this center dominated a society that encompassed an as yet undefined portion of the

San Juan Basin and whose influence extended even farther throughout the northern Southwest.

Determining what kinds of power enabled Pueblo Bonito to dominate Chacoan society, the most complex society ever to develop in the prehispanic northern Southwest, and what kinds of influence it exerted beyond its societal limits requires a consideration of evidence from both Pueblo Bonito itself and from other sites in Chaco Canyon, the San Juan Basin, and beyond. The evidence from Pueblo Bonito highlights the site's ceremonial role, and the ceremonial functions of other great houses have been documented in a series of recent studies (e.g., Kantner and Mahoney 2000). It appears that much of Pueblo Bonito's unifying power was religious, although the site apparently also exerted other kinds of power—economic, political, and perhaps military.

The most obvious evidence for Pueblo Bonito's economic power is its large quantities of goods imported from throughout the San Juan Basin and more distant areas. These goods include special items such as religious offerings, status markers, and perhaps even symbols of office, as well as more mundane objects such as logs and ceramics. Whatever their purpose, the fact that such large quantities of so many different kinds of materials were imported testifies to Pueblo Bonito's ability to control valuable resources from a vast region.

The clearest evidence for Pueblo Bonito's political power is the considerable labor invested in constructing the site. Although the motivation for this construction may have been religious, political skills would have been necessary to obtain materials, mobilize labor, and administer construction activities (Metcalf, Chapter 6). Political skills would also have been necessary to manage water distribution in surrounding agricultural fields (Vivian 1974).

There is suggestive evidence that Pueblo Bonito might also have exerted military power over its society. Marshall (Chapter 2) suggests that Pueblo Bonito's views to the south, east, and west made its location easily defensible. This advantage, however, did not apply to the north, where the cliff face blocked the view completely. It might be that Pueblo Alto, on the mesa top above Pueblo Bonito, functioned in part as a northern lookout for Pueblo Bonito and that its initial construction in 1020 coincided with a heightened concern with defense. Stronger evidence that Pueblo Bonito may have exerted military power over Chacoan society includes the violent death of one of the site's two paramount burials, the defensive configuration of some great houses (LeBlanc 1999:180–182), and signaling stations linking nearby Pueblo Alto with distant great houses (Lekson 1986:231). Though it seems unlikely that armies marched Chacoan roads (cf. Wilcox 1993), the effects of force or the threat of it should not be ignored as a possible contributor to Pueblo Bonito's power (LeBlanc 1999; Turner and Turner 1999; Wilcox and Haas 1994).

Pueblo Bonito's economic, political, and military power was probably linked inextricably to the site's ritual power. The nature of this interrelationship remains to be investigated, as do the ways in which the relative importance of each kind of power changed through time, especially with the shift from a network-based to a corporate-based leadership hierarchy. The evidence that Pueblo Bonito did exert economic, political, and possibly military power suggests that Pueblo Bonito's ritual power might have been neither benevolent nor benign. Rather, as Lekson (personal communication 2001) has observed, Chacoan religion may have been stern, vigorous, and oppressive, not unlike the militant Catholicism of the Crusades or the Inquisition.

Given all this, what was Pueblo Bonito? It was the most powerful place in its world. It was a sacred place—the place where the most important and elaborate ceremonies of the Chacoan religion were conducted. It was the home of a priestly elite composed of two families who, through their religious, political, economic, and perhaps military power were able to make Pueblo Bonito the preeminent Chacoan center. From there these families ruled a complex and far-flung society and influenced more distant areas as well. Pueblo Bonito was the center of the center—the most important structure in the most important settlement in the most powerful society ever to develop in the prehispanic northern Southwest.

Pueblo Bonito was for all intents and purposes abandoned by A.D. 1150. By this time, its residential population had declined to a mere handful of people, and widespread use of the site had ceased. For perhaps as much as five more decades, however, the site continued to be used for ceremonies by its few remaining occupants and by people living elsewhere. Today, the site is a sacred place for Pueblo groups such as the Hopi and Zuni, who identify Chaco Canyon as the place of their ancestors, the place where their ceremonial cycles began (Lekson and Cameron 1995).

Archaeologists will never be able to reconstruct the full grandeur of this structure as it once was. The chapters in this volume tell us much, and further research will undoubtedly reveal more. But secrets are the essence of sacred places even when they are in use. A millennium ago Pueblo Bonito must have inspired awe and a sense of mystery to all who visited it. Its ruins continue to do so today.

ACKNOWLEDGMENTS

Many thanks to all of the volume's contributors, whose research generated the ideas presented here. I am also grateful to Wendy Bustard, Gary Feinman, John Kantner, Steve Lekson, Tom Rocek, and Tom Windes for their useful suggestions for improving earlier versions of this chapter.

References

Abrams, E. M.
  1994   *How the Maya Built Their World: Energetics and Ancient Architecture.* University of Texas Press, Austin.
Adams, E. C.
  1983   The Architectural Analogue to Hopi Social Organization and Room Function: Implications for Prehistoric Southwestern Culture. *American Antiquity* 48(1):44–61.
Adler, M. A., and R. Wilshusen
  1990   Large-Scale Integrative Facilities in Tribal Societies: Cross-Cultural and Southwestern U.S. Examples. *World Archaeology* 22(2):134–143.
Ahlstrom, R. V. N., J. S. Dean, and W. J. Robinson
  1991   Evaluating Tree-Ring Interpretations at Walpi Pueblo. *American Antiquity* 56(4):628–644.
Akins, N. J.
  1985   Prehistoric Faunal Utilization in Chaco Canyon Basketmaker III through Pueblo III. In *Environment and Subsistence of Chaco Canyon, New Mexico,* edited by F. J. Mathien, pp. 305–445. Publications in Archeology 18E, Chaco Canyon Studies, National Park Service, Albuquerque, New Mexico.
  1986   *A Biocultural Approach to Human Burials from Chaco Canyon.* Reports of the Chaco Center no. 9. National Park Service, Santa Fe, New Mexico.
Akins, N. J., and J. D. Schelberg
  1984   Evidence for Organizational Complexity as Seen from the Mortuary Practices at Chaco Canyon. In *Recent Research on Chaco Prehistory,* edited by W. J. Judge and J. D. Schelberg, pp. 89–102. Reports of the Chaco Center no. 8. National Park Service, Albuquerque, New Mexico.
Altschul, J. H.
  1978   The Development of the Chacoan Interaction Sphere. *Journal of Anthropological Research* 34(1):109–146.
Arnold, J. E., and A. Ford
  1980   A Statistical Examination of Settlement Patterns at Tikal, Guatemala. *American Antiquity* 45(4):713–726.
Ashmore, W., and R. R. Wilk
  1988   Household and Community in the Mesoamerican Past. In *Household and Community in the Mesoamerican Past,* edited by R. Wilk and W. Ashmore, pp. 1–27. University of New Mexico Press, Albuquerque.
Banning, E. B., and B. F. Byrd
  1989   Alternative Approaches for Exploring Levantine Neolithic Architecture. *Paleorient* 5(1):154–160.

Barnes, E.
  1994   *Developmental Defects of the Axial Skeleton in Paleopathology.* University Press of Colorado, Niwot.
Baxter, V.
  1980   Pueblo Bonito: A Case Study in Community Design to Utilize Solar Energy. Unpublished M.A. thesis, Department of Landscape Architecture, University of Wisconsin, Madison.
Bernardini, W.
  1999   Reassessing the Scale of Social Action at Pueblo Bonito, Chaco Canyon, New Mexico. *Kiva* 64(4):447–470.
Betancourt, J., J. Dean, and H. Hull
  1986   Prehistoric Long-Distance Transport of Construction Beams, Chaco Canyon, New Mexico. *American Antiquity* 51(2):370–375.
Bickford, F. T.
  1890   Prehistoric Cave-Dwellings. *Century Magazine* 40 (October): 896–911.
Binford, L. R.
  1971   Mortuary Practices: Their Study and Their Potential. In *Approaches to the Social Dimensions of Mortuary Practices,* edited by J. A. Brown, pp. 6–29. Memoirs of the Society for American Archaeology no. 25. Washington, D.C.
Blake, E. R.
  1953   *Birds of Mexico.* University of Chicago Press, Chicago.
Blake, M., S. LeBlanc, and P. E. Minnis
  1986   Changing Settlement and Population in the Mimbres Valley, Southwest New Mexico. *Journal of Field Archaeology* 13(4):439–464.
Blanton, R. E.
  1994   *Houses and Households: A Comparative Study.* Plenum Press, New York.
  1998   Beyond Centralization: Steps toward a Theory of Egalitarian Behavior in Archaic States. In *Archaic States,* edited by G. M. Feinman and J. Marcus, pp. 135–172. School of American Research Press, Santa Fe, New Mexico.
Blanton, R. E., G. M. Feinman, S. A. Kowalewski, and P. N. Peregrine
  1996   A Dual-Processual Theory for the Evolution of Mesoamerican Civilization. *Current Anthropology* 37(1):1–14.
Bonanno, A., T. Gouder, C. Malone, and S. Stoddart
  1990   Monuments in an Island Society: The Maltese Context. *World Archaeology* 22(2):190–205.
Bourdieu, P.
  1973   The Berber House. In *Rules and Meaning,* edited by M. Douglass, pp. 98–110. Penguin Books, New York.

Bourke, J. G.
  1962   *The Snake Dance of the Moquis of Arizona.* Rio Grande Press,
  [1884]   Chicago.
Bradley, B. A.
  1988   *Annual Report of Excavations at Sand Canyon Pueblo (5 MT 765).*
           Report submitted to the Bureau of Land Management, San
           Juan Resource Area Office, Durango, Colorado. Crow
           Canyon Archaeological Center, Cortez, Colorado.
  1993   Planning, Growth, and Functional Differentiation at a Pre-
           historic Pueblo: A Case Study from Southwest Colorado.
           Journal of Field Archaeology 20(1):23–42.
Bradley, R.
  1984   Studying Monuments. In *Neolithic Studies: A Review of Some
           Current Research,* edited by R. Bradley and J. Gardiner, pp.
           61–66. Reading Studies in Archaeology no. 1. Oxford.
Brandt, E. A.
  1994   Egalitarianism, Hierarchy, and Centralization in the Pueblo.
           In *The Ancient Southwestern Community: Models and Methods
           for the Study of Prehistoric Social Organization,* edited by
           W. H. Wills and R. D. Leonard, pp. 9–23. University of New
           Mexico Press, Albuquerque.
Breternitz, C. D.
  1982   Chronology: Dating the Bis sa'ani Community. In *Bis sa'ani:
           A Late Bonito Phase Community on Escavada Wash, Northwest
           New Mexico,* edited by C. D. Breternitz, D. E. Doyel, and M.
           P. Marshall, pp. 61–70. Navajo Nation Papers in Anthro-
           pology no. 14. Window Rock, Arizona.
Breternitz, C. D., D. E. Doyel, and M. P. Marshall (editors)
  1982   *Bis sa'ani: A Late Bonito Phase Community on Escavada Wash,
           Northwest New Mexico.* Navajo Nation Papers in Anthro-
           pology no. 14. Window Rock, Arizona.
Breternitz, D. A., A. H. Rohn Jr., and E. A. Morris
  1974   *Prehistoric Ceramics of the Mesa Verde Region.* Museum of
           Northern Arizona Ceramic Series no. 5. Flagstaff.
Brody, J. J.
  1977   *Mimbres Painted Pottery.* University of New Mexico Press,
           Albuquerque.
Brown, G. M., T. C. Windes, and P. J. McKenna
  2002   Animas Anamnesis: Aztec Ruins, or Anasazi Capital? Paper
           presented at the annual meeting of the Society for Ameri-
           can Archaeology, Denver, Colorado.
Brown, F. E.
  1990   Comment on Chapman: Some Cautionary Notes on the
           Application of Spatial Measures to Prehistoric Settlements.
           In *The Social Archaeology of Houses,* edited by R. Samson, pp.
           93–109. Edinburgh University Press, Edinburgh.
Brown, J. A.
  1981   The Search for Rank in Prehistoric Burials. In *The Archaeology
           of Death,* edited by R. Chapman, I. Kinnes, and K. Rands-
           borg, pp. 25–37. Cambridge University Press, Cambridge.
Bryan, K.
  1954   *The Geology of Chaco Canyon, New Mexico, in Relation to the
           Life and Remains of the Prehistoric People of Pueblo Bonito.*
           Smithsonian Miscellaneous Collections no. 122(7):1–65.
           Washington, D.C.
Bunzel, R. L.
  1932   Introduction to Zuni Ceremonialism. In *Forty-seventh Annual
           Report of the Bureau of American Ethnology, 1929–1930,* pp.
           467–544. U.S. Government Printing Office, Washington, D.C.

Bustard, W.
  1996   Space as Place: Small and Great House Spatial Organization
           in Chaco Canyon, New Mexico, A.D. 1000–1150. Unpublished
           Ph.D. dissertation, Department of Anthropology, University
           of New Mexico, Albuquerque.
  1997   Space, Evolution, and Function in the Houses of Chaco
           Canyon. In *Proceedings of the First International Space Syntax
           Symposium,* vol. 2, pp. 23.1–23.21. University College London.
Byrd, B. F., and E. B. Banning
  1988   Southern Levantine Pier Houses: Intersite Architectural Pat-
           terning during the Pre-Pottery Neolithic B. *Paleorient*
           14(1):65–72.
Cameron, C. M.
  1984   A Regional View of Chipped Stone Raw Material Use in
           Chaco Canyon. In *Recent Research on Chaco Prehistory,* edited
           by W. J. Judge and J. D. Schelberg, pp. 137–152. Reports of the
           Chaco Center no. 8. National Park Service, Albuquerque,
           New Mexico.
  1997   The Chipped Stone of Chaco Canyon, New Mexico. In
           *Ceramics, Lithics, and Ornaments of Chaco Canyon: Analyses of
           Artifacts from the Chaco Project, 1971–1978,* edited by F. J.
           Mathien, pp. 997–1102. National Park Service Publications
           in Archeology 18G, Chaco Canyon Studies. Santa Fe, New
           Mexico.
  2001   Pink Chert, Projectile Points, and the Chacoan Regional
           System. *American Antiquity* 66(1):79–102.
Carlson, J. B.
  1990   America's Ancient Skywatchers. *National Geographic*
           177(3):76–107.
Carlson, J. B., and W. J. Judge
  1987   Romancing the Stone, or Moonshine on the Sun Dagger. In
           Astronomy and Ceremony in the Prehistoric Southwest, edited by
           J. B. Carlson and W. J. Judge, pp. 71–88. Papers of the
           Maxwell Museum of Anthropology no. 2. Albuquerque,
           New Mexico.
Carneiro, R. L.
  1967   On the Relationship between Size of Population and Com-
           plexity of Social Organization in Human Societies. *South-
           western Journal of Anthropology* 23(3):234–243.
Carpenter, J., and G. Sanchez
  1996   *Prehistory of the Borderlands: Recent Research in the Archaeology
           of Northern Mexico and the Southern Southwest.* Arizona State
           Museum Archaeological Series no. 186. University of Ari-
           zona, Tucson.
Carr, C.
  1994   A Cross-Cultural Survey of the Determinants of Mortuary
           Practices. In *The Pueblo Grande Project,* vol. 7, *An Analysis of
           Classic Period Mortuary Patterns,* edited by D. R. Mitchell, pp.
           7–69. Soil Systems Publications in Archaeology no. 20.
           Phoenix, Arizona.
Castleden, R.
  1993   *The Making of Stonehenge.* Routledge, London.
Chang, K. C.
  1958   Study of the Neolithic Social Groupings: Examples from the
           New World. *American Anthropologist* 60(2):298–334.
Chapman, J.
  1990   Social Inequality on Bulgarian Tells and the Varna Problem.
           In *The Social Archaeology of Houses,* edited by R. Samson, pp.
           49–92. Edinburgh University Press, Edinburgh.

Coe, W. R.
1967   *Tikal: A Handbook of the Ancient Maya Ruins.* University Museum, Philadelphia.

Colton, H. S.
1936   The Rise and Fall of the Prehistoric Population of Northern Arizona. *Science* 84(2181):337–343.

Cooper, L. M.
1995   Space Syntax Analysis of Chacoan Great Houses. Unpublished Ph.D. dissertation, Department of Anthropology, University of Arizona, Tucson.
1997   Comparative Analysis of Chacoan Great Houses. In *Proceedings of the First International Space Syntax Symposium,* vol. 2, pp. 22.1–22.11. University College London.

Cordell, L. S.
1984   *Prehistory of the Southwest.* Academic Press, Orlando, Florida.

Cordell, L. S., and F. Plog
1979   Escaping the Confines of Normative Thought: A Reevaluation of Puebloan Prehistory. *American Antiquity* 44(3):405–429.

Creel, D., and C. McKusick
1994   Prehistoric Macaws and Parrots in the Mimbres Area, New Mexico. *American Antiquity* 59(3):510–524.

Cushing, F. H.
1896   Outlines of Zuñi Creation Myths. In *Thirteenth Annual Report of the Bureau of American Ethnology,* pp. 321–447. Smithsonian Institution, Washington, D.C.
1920   *Zuni Breadstuff.* Indian Notes and Monographs 8. Museum of the American Indian, Heye Foundation, New York.

Czwarno, R. M.
1988   Spatial Logic and the Investigation of Control in Middle Horizon Peru. In *Recent Studies in Pre-Columbian Archaeology,* Part 2, edited by N. J. Saunders and O. de Montmollin, pp. 415–446. BAR International Series 421(2). London.

Dean, J. S.
1989   Temporal Aspects of Tsegi Phase Household Organization. In *Households and Communities,* edited by S. MacEachern, D. J. W. Archer, and R. D. Garvin, pp. 196–200. University of Calgary Archaeological Association, Calgary, Alberta, Canada.
1992   Environmental Factors in the Evolution of the Chacoan Sociopolitical System. In *Anasazi Regional Organization and the Chaco System,* edited by D. E. Doyel, pp. 35–43. Maxwell Museum of Anthropology, Anthropological Papers no. 5. Albuquerque, New Mexico.

Dean, J. S., and J. C. Ravesloot
1993   The Chronology of Cultural Interaction in the Gran Chichimeca. In *Culture and Contact: Charles C. Di Peso's Gran Chichimeca,* edited by A. I. Woosley and J. C. Ravesloot, pp. 83–103. University of New Mexico Press, Albuquerque.

Dean, J. S., and R. Warren
1983   Dendrochronology. In *The Architecture and Dendrochronology of Chetro Ketl, Chaco Canyon, New Mexico,* edited by S. H. Lekson, pp. 105–240. Reports of the Chaco Center no. 6. National Park Service, Albuquerque, New Mexico.

Di Peso, C. C.
1968a   Casas Grandes and the Gran Chichimeca. *El Palacio* 75(4):47–61.
1968b   Casas Grandes: A Fallen Trading Center of the Gran Chichimeca. *Masterkey* 42(1):20–37.
1974   *Casas Grandes: A Fallen Trading Center of the Gran Chichimeca.* Northern Arizona University Press, Flagstaff.

Dohm, K. M.
1988   The Household in Transition: Spatial Organization of Early Anasazi Residential-Domestic Units, Southeastern Utah. Unpublished Ph.D. dissertation, Department of Anthropology, Washington State University, Pullman.

Donley-Reid, L. M.
1990   A Structuring Structure: The Swahili House. In *Domestic Architecture and the Use of Space,* edited by S. Kent, pp. 114–126. Cambridge University Press, Cambridge.

Doxtater, D.
1984   Spatial Opposition in Nondiscursive Expression: Architecture as Ritual Process. *Canadian Journal of Anthropology* 4(1):1–17.

Drager, D. L.
1976   Anasazi Population Estimates with the Aid of Data Derived from Photogrammetric Maps. In *Remote Sensing Experiments in Cultural Resource Studies,* edited by T. R. Lyons, pp. 151–171. Reports of the Chaco Center no. 1. National Park Serice, Albuquerque, New Mexico.

Drennan, R. D.
1991   Pre-Hispanic Chiefdom Trajectories in Mesoamerica, Central America, and Northern South America. In *Chiefdoms: Power, Economy, and Ideology,* edited by T. K. Earle, pp. 263–287. Cambridge University Press, Cambridge.

DuBois, R. L.
1989   Archaeomagnetic Results from the Southwest United States and Mesoamerica, and Comparison with Some Other Areas. *Physics of the Earth and Planetary Interiors* 56(1–2):18–33.

Durand, S. R.
1992   Architectural Change and Chaco Prehistory. Unpublished Ph.D. dissertation, Department of Anthropology, University of Washington, Seattle.

Earle, T. K.
1997   *How Chiefs Come to Power: The Political Economy in Prehistory.* Stanford University Press, Stanford, California.
2001   Economic Support of Chaco Canyon Society. *American Antiquity* 66(1):26–35.

Eliade, M.
1961   *The Sacred and the Profane.* Translated by Willard R. Trask. Harcourt, Brace, New York.

Ellis, F. H.
1968   An Interpretation of Prehistoric Death Customs in Terms of Modern Southwestern Parallels. In *Collected Papers in Honor of Lyndon Lane Hargrave,* edited by A. H. Schroeder, pp. 57–76. Papers of the Archaeological Society of New Mexico no. 1. Santa Fe.

Erasmus, C. J.
1965   Monument Building: Some Field Experiments. *Southwestern Journal of Anthropology* 21(4):277–301.

Evans, R.
1978   Figures, Doors, and Passages. *Architectural Design* 4:267–278.

Fairclough, G.
1992   Meaningful Constructions: Spatial and Functional Analysis of Medieval Buildings. *Antiquity* 66(251):348–366.

Feinman, G. M.
1992   An Outside Perspective on Chaco Canyon. In *Anasazi Regional Organization and the Chaco System,* edited by D. E.

Doyel, pp. 177–182. Maxwell Museum of Anthropology, Anthropological Papers no. 5. Albuquerque, New Mexico.

1995   The Emergence of Inequality: A Focus on Strategies and Processes. In *Foundations of Social Inequality,* edited by T. D. Price and G. M. Feinman, pp. 255–279. Plenum Press, New York.

2000a   Dual-Processual Theory and Social Formation. In *Alternative Leadership Strategies in the Prehispanic Southwest,* edited by B. J. Mills, pp. 207–224. University of Arizona Press, Tucson.

2000b   Corporate/Network: A New Perspective on Leadership in the American Southwest. In *Hierarchies in Action: Cui Bono?* edited by M. W. Diehl, pp. 152–179. Center for Archaeological Investigations, Occasional Paper no. 27. Carbondale, Illinois.

2000c   Corporate/Network: New Perspectives on Models of Political Action and the Puebloan Southwest. In *Social Theory in Archaeology,* edited by M. B. Schiffer, pp. 31–51. University of Utah Press, Salt Lake City.

Feinman, G. M., K. G. Lightfoot, and S. Upham

2000   Political Hierarchies and Organizational Strategies in the Puebloan Southwest. *American Antiquity* 65(3):449–470.

Feinman, G. M., and J. E. Neitzel

1984   Too Many Types: An Overview of Sedentary Prestate Societies in the Americas. In *Advances in Archaeological Method and Theory,* vol. 7, edited by M. B. Schiffer, pp. 39–102. Academic Press, New York.

Ferguson, T. J.

1993   Historic Zuni Architecture and Society: A Structural Analysis. Unpublished Ph.D. dissertation, Department of Anthropology, University of New Mexico, Albuquerque.

1996   *Historic Zuni Architecture and Society: An Archaeological Application of Space Syntax.* University of Arizona Press, Tucson.

Ferguson, T. J., and E. R. Hart

1985   *A Zuni Atlas.* University of Oklahoma Press, Norman.

Ferguson, T. J., and B. J. Mills

1988   Wood Reuse in Puebloan Architecture: Evidence from Historic Zuni Settlements. Paper presented at the annual meeting of the Society for American Archaeology, Phoenix, Arizona.

Fewkes, J. W.

1892   A Few Tusayan Pictographs. *American Anthropologist* 5(2):105–129.

1900   Tusayan Flute and Snake Ceremonies. In *Nineteenth Annual Report of the Bureau of American Ethnology, 1897–1898,* Part 2, pp. 957–1011. Smithsonian Institution, Washington, D.C.

Fewkes, J. W., and J. G. Owens

1892   The La-la-kon-ta: A Tusayan Dance. *American Anthropologist* 5(2):105–129.

Fish, S. K.

1999   How Complex Were the Southwestern Great Towns' Polities? In *Great Towns and Regional Polities in the Prehistoric American Southwest and Southeast,* edited by J. E. Neitzel, pp. 45–58. University of New Mexico Press, Albuquerque.

Ford, R. I.

1972   An Ecological Perspective on the Eastern Pueblos. In *New Perspectives on the Pueblos,* edited by A. Ortiz, pp. 1–18. University of New Mexico Press, Albuquerque.

Foster, S. M.

1989a   Analysis of Spatial Patterns in Building (Access Analysis) as

an Insight into Social Structure: Examples from the Scottish Atlantic Iron Age. *Antiquity* 63(238):40–50.

1989b   Transformation in Social Space: The Iron Age of Orkney and Caithness. *Scottish Archaeological Review* 6:35–55.

Fowler, A. P., and J. R. Stein

1992   The Anasazi Great House in Space, Time, and Paradigm. In *Anasazi Regional Organization and the Chaco System,* edited by D. E. Doyel, pp. 101–122. Maxwell Museum of Anthropology, Anthropological Papers no. 5. Albuquerque, New Mexico.

Franklin, H. H., and D. Ford

1982   Attribute Analysis of Cibola and San Juan McElmo Black-on-White Ceramic Types. In *Bis sa'ani: A Late Bonito Phase Community on Escavada Wash, Northwest New Mexico,* vol. 3, edited by C. D. Breternitz, D. E. Doyel, and M. M. Marshall, pp. 935–954. Navajo Nation Papers in Anthropology no. 14. Window Rock, Arizona.

Frisbie, T. R.

1978   High-Status Burials in the Greater Southwest: An Interpretive Synthesis. In *Across the Chichimec Sea: Papers in Honor of J. Charles Kelley,* edited by C. L. Riley and B. C. Hedrick, pp. 202–227. Southern Illinois University, Carbondale.

1980   Social Ranking in Chaco Canyon, New Mexico: A Mesoamerican Reconstruction. *Transactions of the Illinois State Academy of Sciences* 72(4):60–69.

Fritz, J. M.

1978   Paleopsychology Today: Ideational Systems and Human Adaptation in Prehistory. In *Social Archaeology: Beyond Subsistence and Dating,* edited by C. Redman, pp. 39–59. Academic Press, New York.

1987   Chaco Canyon and Vijayanagra: Proposing Spatial Meaning in Two Societies. In *Mirror and Metaphor: Material and Social Constructions of Reality,* edited by D. W. Ingersoll and G. Bronitsky, pp. 313–348. University Press of America, Lanham, Maryland.

Gabriel, K.

1991   *Roads to Center Place: A Cultural Atlas of Chaco Canyon and the Anasazi.* Johnson Books, Boulder, Colorado.

Gillespie, W. B.

1984   The Environment of the Chaco Anasazis. In *New Light on Chaco Canyon,* edited by D. G. Noble, pp. 37–44. School of American Research Press, Santa Fe, New Mexico.

Gilman, A.

1981   The Development of Social Stratification in Bronze Age Europe. *Current Anthropology* 22(1):1–23.

Gnivecki, P. L.

1987   On the Quantitative Derivation of Household Spatial Organization from Archaeological Residues in Ancient Mesopotamia. In *Method and Theory for Activity Area Research,* edited by S. Kent, pp. 176–235. Columbia University Press, New York.

Goody, J.

1972   *Domestic Groups.* Addison-Wesley Modular Publications no. 28. Cambridge.

Gorman, F. J. E., and S. T. Childs

1980   Is Prudden's Unit Type of Anasazi Settlement Valid and Reliable? *North American Archaeologist* 2(3):153–192.

Grebinger, P.

1973   Prehistoric Social Organization in Chaco Canyon, New Mexico: An Alternative Reconstruction. *Kiva* 39(1):3–23.

1978   Prehistoric Social Organization in Chaco Canyon, New Mexico: An Evolutionary Perspective. In *Discovering Past Behavior: Experiments in the Archaeology of the American Southwest,* edited by P. Grebinger, pp. 73–100. Gordon and Breach Science Publishers, New York.

Haas, J.
1982   *The Evolution of the Prehistoric State.* Columbia University Press, New York.

Hall, E. T
1966   *The Hidden Dimension.* Doubleday, Garden City, New York.

Hanson, J., and B. Hillier
1987   The Architecture of Community. *Architecture and Behaviour* 3(3):249–273.

Hantman, J. L.
1983   Social Networks and Stylistic Distributions in the Prehistoric Plateau Southwest. Unpublished Ph.D. dissertation, Department of Anthroplogy, Arizona State University, Tempe.

Harbottle, G., and P. C. Weigand
1992   Turquoise in Pre-Columbian America. *Scientific American* 266(2):78–85.

Hargrave, L. L.
1970   *Mexican Macaws: Comparative Osteology and Survey of Remains from the Southwest.* Anthropological Papers of the University of Arizona no. 20. Tucson.

Hawley, F. M.
1934   *The Significance of the Dated Prehistory of Chetro Ketl, Chaco Cañon, New Mexico.* Monographs of the School of American Research no. 2. University of New Mexico, Albuquerque.

Hayes, A. C.
1981   A Survey of Chaco Canyon Archeology. In *Archeological Surveys of Chaco Canyon, New Mexico,* by A. C. Hayes, D. M. Brugge, and W. J. Judge, pp. 1–68. Publications in Archeology 18A, Chaco Canyon Studies. National Park Service, Washington, D.C.

Hayes, A. C., D. M. Brugge, and W. J. Judge
1981   *Archeological Surveys of Chaco Canyon.* Publications in Archeology 18A, Chaco Canyon Studies. National Park Service, Washington, D.C.

Hewett, E. L.
1936   *The Chaco Canyon and Its Monuments.* University of New Mexico and School of American Research, Albuquerque and Santa Fe.

Hibben, F. C.
1975   *Kiva Art of the Anasazi at Pottery Mound.* KC Publications, Las Vegas, Nevada.

Hill, J. N.
1970   *Broken K Pueblo: Prehistoric Social Organization in the American Southwest.* University of Arizona Anthropological Papers no. 18. Tucson.

Hillier, B., and J. Hanson
1982   Discovering Housing Genotypes. Working paper, Unit for Architectural Studies, Bartlett School of Architecture and Planning, University College London.
1984   *The Social Logic of Space.* Cambridge University Press, Cambridge.

Hillier, B., J. Hanson, and H. Graham
1987   Ideas Are in Things: An Application of the Space Syntax Method to Discovering House Genotypes. *Environment and Planning B: Planning and Design* 14:363–385.

Hillier, B., J. Hanson, and J. Peponis
1984   What Do We Mean by Building Function? In *Designing for Building Utilisation,* edited by J. Powell, I. Cooper, and S. Lera, pp. 61–72. Spon, London.

Hillier, B., A. Leaman, P. Stansall, and M. Bedford
1978   Space Syntax. In *Social Organisation and Settlement: Contributions from Anthropology, Archaeology and Geography,* edited by D. Green, C. Haselgrove, and M. Spriggs, pp. 343–381. BAR International Series (Suppl.) 47 (II). London.

Hodder, I.
1992   A Hermeneutic Circle: The Haddenham Causewayed Enclosure. In *Theory and Practice in Archaeology,* edited by I. Hodder, pp. 213–240. Routledge, London.

Hoge, J. R.
1994   The Iconography of Hopi Lakone Ritual Imagery. Unpublished M.A. thesis, Department of Art History, Virginia Commonwealth University, Richmond.

Holley, G. R., and S. H. Lekson
1999   Comparing Southwestern and Southeastern Great Towns. In *Great Towns and Regional Polities in the Prehistoric American Southwest and Southeast,* edited by J. E. Neitzel, pp. 39–43. University of New Mexico Press, Albuquerque.

Holsinger, S. J.
1901   *Report on the Prehistoric Ruins of Chaco Canyon, New Mexico.* Ordered by the General Land Office, Letter 'P,' December 18, 1900. General Land Office, Washington, D.C.

Horne, L.
1991   Reading Village Plans: Architecture and Social Change in Northeastern Iran. *Expedition* 33(1):44–52.

Hosler, D.
1994   *The Sounds and Colors of Power.* MIT Press, Cambridge, Massachusetts.

Hovezak, M.
1992   Construction Timber Economics at Sand Canyon Pueblo, Southwestern Colorado. Unpublished M.A. thesis, Department of Anthropology, Northern Arizona University, Flagstaff.

Irwin-Williams, C., and P. H. Shelley (editors)
1980   *Investigations at the Salmon Site: The Structure of Chacoan Society in the Northern Southwest.* Eastern New Mexico University, Portales.

Jackson, W. H.
1878   Report on the Ancient Ruins Examined in 1875 and 1877. In *Tenth Annual Report of the United States Geological and Geographical Survey of the Territories,* pp. 411–430. U.S. Government Printing Office, Washington, D.C.

Johnson, G. A.
1982   Organizational Structure and Scalar Stress. In *Theory and Explanation in Archaeology,* edited by C. Renfrew, M. J. Rowland, and B. A. Segraves, pp. 389–421. Academic Press, New York.
1989   Dynamics of Southwestern Prehistory: Far Outside Looking In. In *Dynamics of Southwest Prehistory,* edited by L. S. Cordell and G. J. Gumerman, pp. 371–389. Smithsonian Institution Press, Washington, D.C.

Judd, N. M.
n.d.   Notes on Excavations. Papers of Neil Merton Judd, Box 8. National Anthropological Archives, Department of Anthropology, National Museum of Natural History, Washington, D.C.

1921   A New National Geographic Society Expedition to the Ruins of Chaco Canyon. *National Geographic Society Magazine* 39(6):637–644.

1922   Archaeological Investigations at Pueblo Bonito. *Smithsonian Miscellaneous Collections* 72(15):106–117.

1923a   Pueblo Bonito, the Ancient. *National Geographic* 44(1):99–108.

1923b   Archaeological Investigations at Pueblo Bonito, New Mexico. In *Explorations and Field-Work of the Smithsonian Institution in 1922.* Smithsonian Miscellaneous Collections 74(5):134–144. Washington, D.C.

1924   Archaeological Investigations at Pueblo Bonito. *Smithsonian Miscellaneous Collections* 76(10):71–77, 98–102. Washington, D.C.

1925a   Everyday Life in Pueblo Bonito. *National Geographic* 48(3):227–262.

1925b   Archaeological Investigations at Pueblo Bonito. *Smithsonian Miscellaneous Collections* 77(2):83–91. Washington, D.C.

1925c   Exploration in Prehistoric Pueblo Bonito, Chaco Canyon, New Mexico. *National Geographic Society of Philadelphia Bulletin* 23:82.

1926   Archaeological Investigations at Pueblo Bonito and Pueblo del Arroyo, 1925. In *Explorations and Field-Work of the Smithsonian Institution in 1925.* Smithsonian Miscellaneous Collections 78(1):80–88. Washington, D.C.

1927a   Archaeological Investigations in Chaco Canyon, New Mexico. In *Explorations and Field-Work of the Smithsonian Institution in 1926.* Smithsonian Miscellaneous Collections 78(7):158–168. Washington, D.C.

1927b   The Architectural Evolution of Pueblo Bonito. *Proceedings of the National Academy of Science* 13(7):561–563.

1928a   Prehistoric Pueblo Bonito, New Mexico. In *Explorations and Field-Work of the Smithsonian Institution in 1927.* Smithsonian Institution Publication 2957:141–148. Washington, D.C.

1928b   Pueblo Bonito and Its Architectural Development. Paper presented at the Twenty-third International Congress of Americanists, New York.

1930a   Dating Our Prehistoric Ruins. In *Explorations and Field-Work of the Smithsonian Institution in 1929.* Smithsonian Institution Publication 3060:167–176. Washington, D.C.

1930b   Pueblo Bonito and Its Architectural Development. *Proceedings of the Twenty-third International Congress of Americanists* (New York), pp. 70–73.

1954   *The Material Culture of Pueblo Bonito.* Smithsonian Miscellaneous Collections no. 124. Washington, D.C.

1955   Exploring Pueblo Bonito. *National Geographic Society on Indians of the Americas,* pp. 332–337. National Geographic Society, Washington, D.C.

1959a   *Pueblo del Arroyo, Chaco Canyon, New Mexico.* Smithsonian Miscellaneous Collections no. 138(1). Washington, D.C.

1959b   The Braced-up Cliff at Pueblo Bonito. *Smithsonian Institution Annual Report for 1958,* pp. 501–511. Smithsonian Institution, Washington, D.C.

1964   *The Architecture of Pueblo Bonito.* Smithsonian Miscellaneous Collections 147(1). Washington, D.C.

Judge, W. J.

1979   The Development of a Complex Cultural Ecosystem in the Chaco Basin, New Mexico. In *Proceedings of the First Conference on Scientific Research in the National Parks,* vol. 2, edited by R. M. Linn, pp. 901–906. National Park Service Transactions and Proceedings Series no. 5. Washington, D.C.

1984   New Light on Chaco Canyon. In *New Light on Chaco Canyon,* edited by D. G. Noble, pp. 1–12. School of American Research Press, Santa Fe, New Mexico.

1989   Chaco Canyon–San Juan Basin. In *Dynamics of Southwest Prehistory,* edited by L. S. Cordell and G. J. Gumerman, pp. 209–261. Smithsonian Institution Press, Washington, D.C.

1991   Chaco: Current View of Prehistory and the Regional System. In *Chaco and Hohokam: Prehistoric Regional Systems in the American Southwest,* edited by P. L. Crown and W. J. Judge, pp. 11–30. School of American Research Press, Santa Fe, New Mexico.

Kantner, J.

1996   Political Competition among the Chaco Anasazi of the American Southwest. *Journal of Anthropological Archaeology* 15(1):41–105.

Kantner, J., and N. M. Mahoney (editors)

2000   *Great House Communities across the Chacoan Landscape.* University of Arizona Anthropology Papers no. 64. Tucson.

Kelley, J. C., and E. A. Kelley

1975   An Alternative Hypothesis for the Explanation of Anasazi Culture History. In *Collected Papers in Honor of Florence Hawley Ellis,* edited by T. R. Frisbie, pp. 178–223. Papers of the Archaeological Society of New Mexico no. 2. Albuquerque.

Kempton, W. M., J. S. Boster, and J. A. Hartley

1995   *Environmental Values in American Culture.* MIT Press, Cambridge, Massachusetts.

Keur, J. Y.

1933   A Study of Primitive Indian Engineering Methods Pertaining to Threatening Rock. Manuscript on file, Chaco Archives, Division of Cultural Resources, National Park Service, Albuquerque, New Mexico.

Kidder, A. V.

1924   *An Introduction to the Study of Southwestern Archaeology, with a Preliminary Account of the Excavations at Pecos, and a Summary of Southwestern Archaeology Today, by Irving Rouse.* Yale University Press, New Haven, Connecticut.

1927   Southwestern Archaeological Conference. *Science* 66(1716):489–491.

King, D. S.

1941   Memorandum for Acting Superintendent Charles A. Richey, dated January 28, 1941. Manuscript on file, Chaco Archives, Division of Cultural Resources, National Park Service, Albuquerque, New Mexico.

Kluckhohn, C.

1939   Discussion. In *Preliminary Report on the 1937 Excavations, Bc 50–51, Chaco Canyon, New Mexico.* University of New Mexico Bulletin no. 345, Anthropological Series 3(2):151–162. Albuquerque.

Kolb, M. J.

1994   Monumentality and the Rise of Religious Authority in Precontact Hawai'i. *Current Anthropology* 34(5):521–533.

Kosse, K.

1990   Group Size and Societal Complexity: Thresholds in Long-Term Memory. *Journal of Anthropological Archaeology* 9(3):275–303.

1996 Middle-Range Societies from a Scalar Perspective. In *Interpreting Southwestern Diversity: Understanding Principles and Overarching Patterns,* edited by P. R. Fish and J. D. Reid, pp. 87–96. Arizona State University, Anthropological Research Papers no. 48. Tempe.

Krüger, M. J. T.
1989 On Node and Axial Grid Maps: Distance Measures and Related Topics. Manuscript on file, Unit for Architectural Studies, Bartlett School of Architecture and Planning, University College London.

Larson, D. O., and J. Michaelson
1990 Impacts of Climatic Variability and Population Growth on Virgin Branch Anasazi Cultural Developments. *American Antiquity* 55(2):227–249.

Lawrence, D. L., and S. M. Low
1990 The Built Environment and Spatial Form. *Annual Review of Anthropology* 19:453–505.

Lawrence, R. J.
1983 The Interpretation of Vernacular Architecture. *Vernacular Architecture* 14:19–29.

LeBlanc, S. A.
1999 *Prehistoric Warfare in the American Southwest.* University of Utah Press, Salt Lake City.

Lekson, S. H.
1981 Cognitive Frameworks and Chacoan Architecture. *New Mexico Journal of Science* 21(1):27–36.
1984 Standing Architecture at Chaco Canyon and the Interpretation of Local and Regional Organization. In *Recent Research on Chaco Prehistory,* edited by W. J. Judge and J. D. Schelberg, pp. 55–73. Reports of the Chaco Center no. 8. National Park Service, Albuquerque, New Mexico.
1985 Largest Settlement Size and the Interpretation of Sociopolitical Complexity at Chaco Canyon, New Mexico. *Haliksa'i: UNM Contributions to Anthropology* 4:68–75.
1986 *Great Pueblo Architecture of Chaco Canyon, New Mexico.* University of New Mexico Press, Albuquerque.
1988a The Idea of the Kiva in Anasazi Archaeology. *Kiva* 53(3):213–234.
1988b Sociopolitical Complexity at Chaco Canyon, New Mexico. Unpublished Ph.D. dissertation, Department of Anthropology, University of New Mexico, Albuquerque.
1991 Settlement Patterns and the Chaco Region. In *Chaco and Hohokam: Prehistoric Regional Systems in the American Southwest,* edited by P. L. Crown and W. J. Judge, pp. 31–55. School of American Research Press, Santa Fe, New Mexico.
1997 Points, Knives, and Drills of Chaco Canyon. In *Ceramics, Lithics, and Ornaments of Chaco Canyon: Analyses of Artifacts from the Chaco Project, 1971–1978,* edited by F. J. Mathien, pp. 659–697. Publications in Archeology 18G, Chaco Canyon Series. National Park Service, Santa Fe, New Mexico.
1999 Great Towns in the Southwest. In *Great Towns and Regional Polities in the Prehistoric American Southwest and Southeast,* edited by J. E. Neitzel, pp. 3–21. University of New Mexico Press, Albuquerque.

Lekson, S. H., and C. M. Cameron
1995 The Abandonment of Chaco Canyon, the Mesa Verde Migrations, and the Reorganization of the Pueblo World. *Journal of Anthropological Archeology* 14(2):184–202.

Lekson, S. H., T. Windes, J. Stein, and W. J. Judge
1988 The Chaco Canyon Community. *Scientific American* 259(1):100–109.

Levine, F.
1989 Homestead in Ruins: Richard Wetherill's Homestead in Chaco Canyon. In *From Chaco to Chaco: Papers in Honor of Robert H. Lister and Florence C. Lister,* edited by M. S. Duran and D. T. Kirkpatrick, pp. 45–58. Papers of the Archaeological Society of New Mexico no. 15. Albuquerque.

Lightfoot, K. G., and S. Upham
1989 Complex Societies in the Prehistoric American Southwest: A Consideration of the Controversy. In *The Sociopolitical Structure of Prehistoric Southwestern Societies,* edited by A. Upham, K. G. Lightfoot, and R. A. Jewett, pp. 3–30. Westview Press, Boulder, Colorado.

Lightfoot, R. R.
1988 Roofing an Early Anasazi Great Kiva: Analysis of an Architectural Model. *Kiva* 53(3):253–272.
1994 *The Duckfoot Site,* vol. 2. Crow Canyon Archaeological Center Occasional Paper no. 4. Cortez, Colorado.

Lipe, W. D., and M. Hegmon
1989 Historical and Analytical Perspectives on Architecture and Social Integration in the Prehistoric Pueblos. In *The Architecture of Social Integration in Prehistoric Pueblos,* edited by W. D. Lipe and M. Hegmon, pp. 15–34. Crow Canyon Archaeological Center, Cortez, Colorado.

Lister, R. H., and F. C. Lister
1981 *Chaco Canyon: Archaeology and Archaeologists.* University of New Mexico Press, Albuquerque.

Littlejohn, J.
1967 The Temne House. In *Myth and Cosmos: Readings in Mythology and Symbolism,* edited by J. Middleton, pp. 331–348. University of Texas Press, Austin.

Loftin, J. D.
1991 *Religion and Hopi Life in the Twentieth Century.* Indiana University Press, Bloomington.

Love, D. W.
1977 Dynamics of Sedimentation and Geomorphic History of Chaco Canyon National Monument, New Mexico. In *Guidebook of San Juan Basin III, Northwestern New Mexico,* edited by J. D. Fassett, pp. 291–300. New Mexico Geological Society, Twenty-eighth Field Conference, Socorro.

Lowell, J. C.
1991 *Prehistoric Households at Turkey Creek Pueblo, Arizona.* Anthropological Papers of the University of Arizona no. 54. Tucson.

Lowie, R. H.
1929 Notes on Hopi Clans. *Anthropological Papers of the American Museum of Natural History* 30:303–346. New York.

Lumpkin, C. K.
1976 A Multivariate Craniometric Analysis of Selected Southwestern Archaeological Populations. Unpublished Ph.D. dissertation, Department of Anthropology, University of New Mexico, Albuquerque.

Malville, J. McK., and N. J. Malville
2001 Pilgrimage and Periodic Festivals as Processes of Social Integration in Chaco Canyon. *Kiva* 66(3):327–344.

Manzanilla, L.
1986 Introduction. In *Unidades habitacionales mesoamericanas y sus*

areas de actividad, edited by L. Manzanilla, pp. 9–18. Instituto de Investigaciones Antropologías, Mexico City.

Marshall, M. P., J. R. Stein, R. W. Loose, and J. E. Novotny

1979   *Anasazi Communities of the San Juan Basin.* Public Service Company of New Mexico, Albuquerque, and New Mexico Historic Preservation Bureau, Santa Fe.

Martin, D. L., N. J. Akins, A. H. Goodman, H. W. Toll, and A. C. Swedlund

2001   *Harmony and Discord: Bioarchaeology of the La Plata Valley.* Archaeology Notes 242. Office of Archaeological Studies, Museum of New Mexico, Santa Fe.

Mathien, F. J.

1981a   Economic Exchange Systems in the San Juan Basin. Unpublished Ph.D. dissertation, Department of Anthropology, University of New Mexico, Albuquerque.

1981b   Neutron Activation of Turquoise Artifacts from Chaco Canyon, New Mexico. *Current Anthropology* 22(3):293–294.

1984   Social and Economic Implications of Jewelry Items of the Chaco Anasazi. In *Recent Research on Chaco Prehistory,* edited by W. J. Judge and J. D. Schelberg, pp. 173–186. Reports of the Chaco Center no. 8. National Park Service, Albuquerque, New Mexico.

1987   Ornaments and Minerals from Pueblo Alto. In *Investigations at the Pueblo Alto Complex, Chaco Canyon, New Mexico, 1975–1979,* vol. 3, *Artifactual and Biological Analyses,* edited by F. J. Mathien and T. C. Windes, pp. 381–428. Publications in Archeology 18F, Chaco Canyon Studies. National Park Service, Santa Fe, New Mexico.

1991   Ornaments and Minerals from 29SJ633. In *Excavations at 29SJ633: The Eleventh Hour Site, Chaco Canyon, New Mexico,* edited by F. J. Mathien, pp. 221–241. Reports of the Chaco Center no. 10. National Park Service, Santa Fe, New Mexico.

1992   Ornaments and Minerals from Site 29SJ627. In *Excavations at 29SJ627, Chaco Canyon, New Mexico,* vol. 2, *The Artifact Analyses,* edited by F. J. Mathien, pp. 265–318. Reports of the Chaco Center no. 11. National Park Service, Santa Fe, New Mexico.

1993   Exchange Systems and Social Stratification among the Chaco Anasazi. In *The American Southwest and Mesoamerica: Systems of Prehistoric Exchange,* edited by J. E. Ericson and T. G. Baugh, pp. 27–63. Plenum Press, New York.

1997   Ornaments of the Chaco Anasazi. In *Ceramics, Lithics, and Ornaments of Chaco Canyon: Analyses of Artifacts from the Chaco Project, 1971–1978,* edited by F. J. Mathien, pp. 1119–1220. Publications in Archeology 18G, Chaco Canyon Studies. National Park Service, Santa Fe, New Mexico.

2001   The Organization of Turquoise Production and Consumption by the Prehistoric Chacoans. *American Antiquity* 66(1):103–118.

McGregor, J. C.

1943   Burial of an Early American Magician. *Proceedings of the American Philosophical Society* 80(2):270–298.

McGuire, R. H.

1980   The Mesoamerican Connection in the Southwest. *Kiva* 46(1):3–38.

McGuire, R. H., and D. J. Saitta

1996   Although They Have Petty Captains, They Obey Them Badly: The Dialectics of Prehispanic Western Pueblo Social Organization. *American Antiquity* 61(2):197–216.

McKenna, P. J.

1984   *The Architecture and Material Culture of 29SJ 1360, Chaco Canyon, New Mexico.* Reports of the Chaco Center no. 7. National Park Service, Albuquerque, New Mexico.

1990   Burials at Aztec Ruins National Monument, Appendix A. In Windows to the North Wing: Rooms 202 and 201, Aztec West, Aztec Ruins National Monument. Manuscript on file, Southwest Cultural Resources Center, Southwest Regional Office, National Park Service, Santa Fe, New Mexico.

1991   Chaco Canyon's Mesa Verde Phase. In *Excavations at 29SJ633: The Eleventh Hour Site, Chaco Canyon, New Mexico,* edited by F. J. Mathien, pp. 127–137. Reports of the Chaco Center no. 10. National Park Service, Santa Fe, New Mexico.

McKinney, C.

1941   Letter written from Chaco Canyon, Thursday (January 23, 1941). Chaco Archives no. 2178D, on file, Division of Cultural Resources, National Park Service, Albuquerque, New Mexico.

McNitt, F.

1966   *Richard Wetherill, Anasazi: Pioneer Explorer of Ancient Ruins in the American Southwest.* University of New Mexico Press, Albuquerque.

Metcalf, M. P.

1997   Civic Spaces: Prehistoric Political Organization in the Northern Southwest, A.D. 1000–1300. Unpublished Ph.D. dissertation, Department of Anthropology, University of Virginia, Charlottesville.

Mills, B. J.

2000   Alternative Models, Alternative Strategies: Leadership in the Prehispanic Southwest. In *Alternative Leadership Strategies in the Prehispanic Southwest,* edited by B. J. Mills, pp. 3–18. University of Arizona Press, Tucson.

Mills, B. J. (editor)

2000   *Alternative Leadership Strategies in the Prehispanic Southwest.* University of Arizona Press, Tucson.

Milner, G. R.

1998   *The Cahokia Chiefdom: The Archaeology of a Mississippian Society.* Smithsonian Institution Press, Washington, D.C.

Mindeleff, V.

1891   A Study of Pueblo Architecture: Tusayan and Cibola. *Eighth Annual Report of the Bureau of Ethnology,* pp. 3–228. Washington, D.C.

Minge, W. A.

1991   *Acoma: Pueblo in the Sky.* University of New Mexico Press, Albuquerque.

Minnis, P. E., M. E. Whalen, J. H. Kelley, and J. D. Stewart

1993   Prehistoric Macaw Breeding in the North American Southwest. *American Antiquity* 58(2):270–276.

Montgomery, B. K.

1993   Ceramic Analysis as a Tool for Discovering Processes of Pueblo Abandonment. In *Abandonment of Settlements and Regions,* edited by C. M. Cameron and S. A. Tomka, pp. 157–164. Cambridge University Press, Cambridge.

Montmollin, O. de

1989   *The Archaeology of Political Structure: Settlement Analysis in a Classic Maya Polity.* Cambridge University Press, Cambridge.

Moore, J. D.

1992   Pattern and Meaning in Prehistoric Peruvian Architecture: The Architecture of Social Control in the Chimu State. *Latin American Antiquity* 3(2):95–113.

Moorehead, W. K.
1906   *A Narrative of Explorations in New Mexico, Arizona, Indiana, etc.* Andover Press, Andover, Massachusetts.

Morris, E. H.
1919   *The Aztec Ruin.* Anthropological Papers of the American Museum of Natural History, vol. 26, Part 1. New York.
1921   *The House of the Great Kiva at the Aztec Ruin.* Anthropological Papers of the American Museum of Natural History, vol. 26, Part 2. New York.
1924   *Burials in the Aztec Ruin: The Aztec Ruin Annex.* Anthropological Papers of the American Museum of Natural History, vol. 26, Parts 3 and 4. New York.
1939   *Archaeological Studies in the La Plata District.* Carnegie Institution, Washington, D.C.

Moulard, B. L.
1984   *Within the Underworld Sky.* Twelvetree Press, Pasadena, California.

Nabokov, P.
1986   *Architecture of Acoma Pueblo.* Ancient City Press, Santa Fe, New Mexico.

Naroll, R.
1956   A Preliminary Index of Social Development. *American Anthropologist* 58(4):687–715.

National Park Service
1981   *Ruins Stabilization.* National Park Service, U.S. Department of the Interior, Washington, D.C.
1987   *Chaco Culture: Official Map and Guide.* Chaco Culture National Historical Park, National Park Service, U.S. Department of the Interior, Washington, D.C.

Neitzel, J. E.
1989a   The Chacoan Regional System: Interpreting the Evidence for Sociopolitical Complexity. In *The Sociopolitical Structure of Prehistoric Southwestern Societies,* edited by S. Upham, K. G. Lightfoot, and R. A. Jewett, pp. 509–556. Westview Press, Boulder, Colorado.
1989b   Regional Exchange Networks in the American Southwest: A Comparative Analysis of Long-Distance Trade. In *The Sociopolitical Structure of Prehistoric Southwestern Societies,* edited by S. Upham, K. G. Lightfoot, and R. A. Jewett, pp. 149–195. Westview Press, Boulder, Colorado.
1991   Hohokam Material Culture and Behavior: The Dimensions of Organizational Change. In *Exploring the Hohokam: Prehistoric Desert People of the American Southwest,* edited by G. J. Gumerman, pp. 177–230. University of New Mexico Press, Albuquerque.
1994   Boundary Dynamics in the Chacoan Regional System. In *The Ancient Southwestern Community: Models and Methods for the Study of Prehistoric Social Organization,* edited by W. H. Wills and R. D. Leonard, pp. 209–240. University of New Mexico Press, Albuquerque.
1999   Examining Societal Organization in the Southwest: An Application of Multiscalar Analysis. In *Great Towns and Regional Polities in the Prehistoric American Southwest and Southeast,* edited by J. E. Neitzel, pp. 183–213. University of New Mexico Press, Albuquerque.
2000   Gender Hierarchies: A Comparative Analysis of Mortuary Data. In *Women and Men in the Prehispanic Southwest: Labor, Power, and Prestige,* edited by P. L. Crown, pp. 137–168. School of American Research Press, Santa Fe, New Mexico.

Neitzel, J. E., and D. G. Anderson
1999   Multiscalar Analyses of Middle-Range Societies: Comparing the Late Prehistoric Southwest and Southeast. In *Great Towns and Regional Polities in the Prehistoric American Southwest and Southeast,* edited by J. E. Neitzel, pp. 243–254. University of New Mexico Press, Albuquerque.

Neitzel, J. E., and R. L. Bishop
1990   Neutron Activation of Dogoszhi-Style Ceramics: Production and Exchange in the Chacoan Regional System. *Kiva* 56(1):67–85.

Nelson, B.
1995   Complexity, Hierarchy, and Scale: A Controlled Comparison between Chaco Canyon, New Mexico, and La Quemada, Zacatecas. *American Antiquity* 60(4):597–618.

Nelson, B. A., D. L. Martin, A. C. Swedlund, P. R. Fish, and G. J. Armelagos
1994   Studies in Disruption: Demography and Health in the Prehistoric American Southwest. In *Understanding Complexity in the Prehistoric Southwest,* edited by G. Gumerman and M. Gell-Mann, pp. 59–112. SFI Studies in the Sciences of Complexity, Proceedings vol. 16. Addison-Wesley, Reading, Massachusetts.

Nusbaum, J. L.
1922   *A Basket-Maker Cave in Kane County, Utah.* Museum of the American Indian Miscellaneous Paper no. 29. Heye Foundation, New York.

Ortiz, A.
1969   *The Tewa World: Space, Time, Being, and Becoming in a Pueblo Society.* University of Chicago Press, Chicago.

Osman, K. M., and M. Suliman
1994   The Space Syntax Methodology: Fits and Misfits. *Architecture and Behaviour* 10(2):189–204.

Palkovich, A. M.
1984   Disease and Mortality Patterns in the Burial Rooms of Pueblo Bonito: Preliminary Considerations. In *Recent Research on Chaco Prehistory,* edited by W. J. Judge and J. D. Schelberg, pp. 103–113. Reports of the Chaco Center no. 8. National Park Service, Albuquerque, New Mexico.

Palmer, J. W.
1994   Copper Bells from Anasazi Sites. *Blue Mountain Shadows* 13:44–45.

Palmer, J. W., M. G. Hollander, P. S. Z. Rogers, R. M. Benjamin, C. J. Duffy, J. B. Lambert, and J. A. Brown
1998   Pre-Columbian Metallurgy: Technology, Manufacture, and Microprobe Analyses of Copper Bells from the Greater Southwest. *Archaeometry* 40(2):361–382.

Parsons, E. C.
1939   *Pueblo Indian Religion.* 2 vols. University of Chicago Press, Chicago.

Peebles, C., and S. M. Kus
1977   Some Archaeological Correlates of Ranked Societies. *American Antiquity* 42(3):421–448.

Peponis, J.
1985   The Spatial Culture of Factories. *Human Relations* 38(4):357–390.

Pepper, G. R.
1899   Ceremonial Deposits Found in an Ancient Pueblo Estufa in Northern New Mexico. *Monumental Records* 1(1):1–6.
1905   Ceremonial Objects and Ornaments from Pueblo Bonito, New Mexico. *American Anthropologist* n.s. 7(2):183–197.

1906   Human Effigy Vases from Chaco Cañon, New Mexico. In *Anthropological Papers Written in Honor of Franz Boas,* pp. 320–334. G. E. Steckert, New York.

1909   The Exploration of a Burial Room in Pueblo Bonito, New Mexico. In *Anthropological Essays: Putnam Anniversary Volume,* by his friends and associates, pp. 196–252. G. E. Steckert, New York.

1920   *Pueblo Bonito.* Anthropological Papers of the American Museum of Natural History no. 27. New York.

Peregrine, P. N.

2001   Matrilocality, Corporate Strategy, and the Organization of Production in the Chacoan World. *American Antiquity* 66(1):36–46.

Pierson, L. M.

1949   The Prehistoric Population of Chaco Canyon, New Mexico: A Study in Methods and Techniques of Prehistoric Population Estimation. Unpublished M.A. thesis, Department of Anthropology, University of New Mexico, Albuquerque.

Pinkley, F.

1938   *The Saga of Threatening Rock.* Southwestern Monuments, Supplements for April, pp. 347–379. U.S. Department of the Interior, National Park Service.

Plimpton, C. L., and F. A. Hassan

1987   Social Space: A Determinant of House Architecture. *Environment and Planning B: Planning and Design* 14(4):439–449.

Plog, F.

1975   Demographic Studies in Southwestern Prehistory. In *Population Studies in Archaeology and Biological Anthropology: A Symposium,* edited by A. C. Swedlund, pp. 94–102. Society for American Archaeology Memoirs no. 30. Washington, D.C.

Powers, R. P.

1984   Regional Interaction in the San Juan Basin: The Chacoan Outlier System. In *Recent Research on Chaco Prehistory,* edited by W. J. Judge and J. D. Schelberg, pp. 23–36. Reports of the Chaco Center no. 8. National Park Service, Albuquerque, New Mexico.

Powers, R. P., W. B. Gillespie, and S. H. Lekson

1983   *The Outlier Survey: A Regional View of Settlement in the San Juan Basin.* Reports of the Chaco Center no. 3. National Park Service, Albuquerque, New Mexico.

Quackenbush, A. D.

1934   NM/CHAC-4940 [map]. Department of the Interior, National Park Service, Chaco Canyon National Monument, Office of the Engineer, San Francisco.

Quilter, J., and A. B. Vargas

1995   Monumental Architectural and Social Organization at the Rivas Site, Costa Rica. *Journal of Field Archaeology* 22(2):203–220.

Rapoport, A.

1969   *House Form and Culture.* Prentice-Hall, Englewood Cliffs, New Jersey.

1979   Cultural Origins of Architecture. In *Introduction to Architecture,* edited by J. C. Snyder and A. J. Catanese, pp. 2–20. McGraw-Hill, New York.

1980   Vernacular Architecture and the Cultural Determinants of Form. In *Buildings and Society,* edited by A. D. King, pp. 283–305. Routledge and Kegan Paul, London.

1990   Science and the Failure of Architecture: An Intellectual History. In *Environment and Behavior Studies: Emergence of Intellectual Traditions,* vol. 11, edited by I. Altman and K. Christenson, pp. 79–109. Plenum Press, New York.

Rautman, A. E.

1998   Hierarchy and Heterarchy in the American Southwest: A Comment on McGuire and Saitta. *American Antiquity* 63(2):325–333.

Reed, H. E., and J. R. Stein

1998   Testing the Pecos Classification. In *Unit Issues in Archaeology: Testing Time, Space, and Material,* edited by A. F. Ramenofsky and A. Steffen, pp. 41–51. University of Utah Press, Salt Lake City.

Reinhard, K. J., and K. H. Clary

1986   Parasite Analysis of Prehistoric Coprolites from Chaco Canyon. In *A Biocultural Approach to Human Burials from Chaco Canyon,* by N. J. Akins, pp. 177–186. Reports of the Chaco Center no. 9. National Park Service, Albuquerque, New Mexico.

Renfrew, C.

1973   *Approaches to Social Archeology.* Edinburgh University Press, Edinburgh.

1974   Beyond a Subsistence Economy: The Evolution of Social Organization in Prehistoric Europe. In *Reconstructing Complex Societies: An Archaeological Colloquium,* edited by C. B. Moore, pp. 69–85. Bulletin of the American School of Oriental Research no. 20. Chicago.

2001   Production and Consumption in a Sacred Economy: The Material Correlates of High Devotional Expression at Chaco Canyon. *American Antiquity* 66(1):14–25.

Reyman, J. E.

1976   Astronomy, Architecture, and Adaptation at Pueblo Bonito. *Science* 193(4257):957–962.

1978a   The Winter Solstice at Pueblo Bonito. Part 1. *Griffith Observer* 42(12):16–19.

1978b   Pochteca Burials at Anasazi Sites? In *Across the Chichimec Sea: Papers in Honor of J. Charles Kelley,* edited by C. L. Riley and B. C. Hedrick, pp. 242–259. Southern Illinois University, Carbondale.

1979   The Winter Solstice at Pueblo Bonito. Part 2. *Griffth Observer* 43(1):2–9.

1987a   Review of *Recent Research on Chaco Prehistory,* edited by W. J. Judge and J. D. Schelberg. *Kiva* 52(2):147–151.

1987b   Priests, Power, and Politics: Some Implications of Socioceremonial Control. In *Astronomy and Ceremony in the Prehistoric Southwest,* edited by J. B. Carlson and W. J. Judge, pp. 121–147. Papers of the Maxwell Museum of Anthropology no. 2. Albuquerque, New Mexico.

1989   The History of Archaeology and the Archaeological History of Chaco Canyon, New Mexico. In *Tracing Archaeology's Past,* edited by A. L. Christenson, pp. 41–53. Southern Illinois University Press, Carbondale.

1990   Rediscovered Pseudo-Cloisonné from Pueblo Bonito: Description and Comparisons. In *Clues to the Past: Papers in Honor of William M. Sundt,* edited by M. S. Duran and D. T. Kirkpatrick, pp. 217–228. Papers of the Archaeological Society of New Mexico no. 16. Albuquerque.

Roberts, F. H. H., Jr.

n.d.   Papers of Frank H. H. Roberts, Jr. Boxes 1 and 2, Miscellaneous Collections no. 4851. National Anthropological Archives, Department of Anthropology, National Museum of Natural History, Washington, D.C.

1927   The Ceramic Sequence in the Chaco Canyon, New Mexico, and Its Relation to the Cultures of the San Juan Basin. Unpublished Ph.D. dissertation, Department of Anthropology, Harvard University, Cambridge, Massachusetts.

1929   *Shabik'eshchee Village: A Late Basketmaker Site in Chaco Canyon, New Mexico.* Bureau of American Ethnology Bulletin 92. Smithsonian Institution, Washington, D.C.

Roberts, J. M.

1956   *Zuni Daily Life.* Laboratory of Anthropology Monograph no. 2, Notebook no. 3. University of Nebraska, Lincoln.

Robinson, W. J., and M. Rose

1979   Preliminary Annual and Seasonal Dendroclimatic Reconstruction for the Northwest Plateau, Southwest Colorado, Southwest Mountains, and Northern Mountains Climatic Regions, A.D. 900–1969. Manuscript on file, Chaco Culture National Historical Park Archive, University of New Mexico, Albuquerque.

Rohn, A. H.

1965   Postulation of Socio-Economic Groups from Archaeological Evidence. *Memoirs of the Society for American Archaeology* 19:65–69.

1977   *Cultural Continuity and Change on Chapin Mesa.* Regents Press of Kansas, Lawrence.

Romney, A. K., W. H. Batchelder, and S. C. Weller

1987   Recent Applications of Cultural Consensus Theory. *American Behavioral Scientist* 31(2):163–177.

Romney, A. K., S. C. Weller, and W. H. Batchelder

1986   Culture as Consensus: A Theory of Culture and Informant Accuracy. *American Anthropologist* 88(2):313–338.

Rothschild, N. A., B. J. Mills, T. J. Ferguson, and S. Dublin

1993   Abandonment at Zuni Farming Villages. In *Abandonment of Settlements and Regions,* edited by C. M. Cameron and S. A. Tonka, pp. 123–137. Cambridge University Press, Cambridge.

Ruppert, H.

1983   Geochemische Untersuchungen an Türkis und Sodalith aus Lagerstätten und Präkolumbischen Kulturen der Kordilleren. *Berliner Beiträge zur Archäometrie* 8:101–210.

Sabloff, J. A.

1990   *The New Archaeology and the Ancient Maya.* Scientific American Library, New York.

Saile, D. G.

1977   "Architecture" in Prehispanic Pueblo Archaeology: Examples from Chaco Canyon, New Mexico. *World Archaeology* 9(2):157–173.

Saitta, D. J.

1997   Power, Labor, and the Dynamics of Change in Chacoan Political Economy. *American Antiquity* 62(1):7–26.

Samuels, M., and J. L. Betancourt

1982   Modeling the Long-Term Effects of Fuelwood Demands on Pinyon-Juniper Woodlands. *Environmental Management* 22(3):133–135.

Schaafsma, C. F., and C. K. Riley (editors)

1999   *The Casas Grandes World.* University of Utah Press, Salt Lake City.

Schaafsma, P.

1999   Tlalocs, Kachinas, Sacred Bundles, and Related Symbolism in the Southwest and Mesoamerica. In *The Casas Grandes World,* edited by C. F. Schaafsma and C. L. Riley, pp. 164–192. University of Utah Press, Salt Lake City.

Schacht, R. M.

1981   Estimating Past Population Trends. *Annual Review of Anthropology* 10:119–140.

1984   The Contemporaneity Problem. *American Antiquity* 49(4):678–695.

Schelberg, J. D.

1982   Economic and Social Development as an Adaptation to a Marginal Environment in Chaco Canyon, New Mexico. Unpublished Ph.D. dissertation, Department of Anthropology, Northwestern University, Evanston, Illinois.

1984   Analogy, Complexity, and Regionally Based Perspectives. In *Recent Research on Chaco Prehistory,* edited by W. J. Judge and J. D. Schelberg, pp. 5–21. Reports of the Chaco Center no. 8. National Park Service, Albuquerque, New Mexico.

Schele, L., and D. Friedel

1990   *The Forest of Kings: The Untold Story of the Ancient Maya.* Morrow Press, New York.

Schillaci, M. E., E. G. Ozolins, and T. C. Windes

2001   Multivariate Assessment of Biological Relationships among Prehistoric Southwest Amerindian Populations. In *Following Through: Papers in Honor of Phyllis S. Davis,* edited by R. N. Wiseman, C. O'Laughlin, and C. T. Snow, pp. 113–149. Papers of the Archaeological Society of New Mexico no. 27. Albuquerque.

Schlanger, S. H.

1988   Patterns of Population Movement and Long-Term Population Growth in Southwestern Colorado. *American Antiquity* 53(4):773–793.

Schumm, S. A., and R. J. Chorley

1964   The Fall of Threatening Rock. *American Journal of Science* 262(9):1041–1054.

Sebastian, L.

1988   Leadership, Power, and Productive Potential: A Political Model of the Chaco System. Unpublished Ph.D. dissertation, Department of Anthropology, University of New Mexico, Albuquerque.

1992a   Chaco Canyon and the Anasazi Southwest: Changing Views of Sociopolitical Organization. In *Anasazi Regional Organization and the Chaco System,* edited by D. E. Doyel, pp. 23–31. Maxwell Museum of Anthropology, Anthropological Papers no. 5. Albuquerque, New Mexico.

1992b   *The Chaco Anasazi: Sociopolitical Evolution in the Prehistoric Southwest.* Cambridge University Press, New York.

Service, E.

1962   *Primitive Social Organization.* Random House, New York.

Shapiro, J. S.

1997a   Fingerprints on the Landscape: Cultural Evolution in the Northern Rio Grande. In *Proceedings of the First International Space Syntax Symposium,* vol. 2, pp. 21.1–21.21. University College London.

1997b   Fingerprints on the Landscape: Space Syntax Analysis and Cultural Evolution in the Northern Rio Grande. Unpublished Ph.D. dissertation, Department of Anthropology, Pennsylvania State University, College Park.

Shimada, I.

1978   Behavioral Variability and Organization in Ancient Constructions: An Experimental Approach. In *Papers on the Economy and Architecture of the Ancient Maya,* edited by R. Sidrys, pp. 209–235. UCLA Institute of Archaeology, Los Angeles.

Sigleo, A. C.

1970   Trace-Element Geochemistry of Southwestern Turquoise. M.S. thesis, Department of Geology, University of New Mexico, Albuquerque.

Silko, L. M.

1995   Interior and Exterior Landscapes: The Pueblo Migration Stories. In *Landscape in America,* edited by G. F. Thompson, pp. 155–169. University of Texas Press, Austin.

Simpson, J. H.

1850   Journal of a Military Reconnaissance from Santa Fe, New Mexico, to the Navajo Country in 1849. U.S. Senate Executive Document 64, Thirty-first Congress, First Session. Washington, D.C.

Smith, A., and N. David

1995   The Production of Space and the House of Xidi Sukur. *Current Anthropology* 36(3):441–457.

Snow, D. H.

1983   Handedness, Technology, and Symbolism in Anasazi Indented-Corrugated Wares. In *Collected Papers in Honor of Charlie R. Steen, Jr.,* edited by N. L. Fox, pp. 189–221. Papers of the Archaeological Society of New Mexico no. 8. Albuquerque.

Sofaer, A.

1997   The Primary Architecture of the Chacoan Culture: A Cosmological Expression. In *Anasazi Architecture and American Design,* edited by B. H. Morrow and V. B. Price, pp. 88–132. University of New Mexico Press, Albuquerque.

Sofaer, A. P., and R. M. Sinclair

1987   Astronomical Markings at Three Sites on Fajada Butte. In *Astronomy and Ceremony in the Prehistoric Southwest,* edited by J. B. Carlson and W. J. Judge, pp. 43–70. Papers of the Maxwell Museum of Anthropology no. 2. Albuquerque, New Mexico.

Sprague, R.

1964   Inventory of Prehistoric Southwestern Copper Bells: Additions and Corrections I. *Kiva* 30(1):18–19.

Sprague, R., and A. Signori

1963   Inventory of Prehistoric Southwestern Copper Bells. *Kiva* 28(4):1–20.

Steadman, S. R.

1996   Recent Research in the Archaeology of Architecture: Beyond the Foundations. *Journal of Archaeological Research* 4(1):51–93.

Stein, J. R., and S. H. Lekson

1992   Anasazi Ritual Landscapes. In *Anasazi Regional Organization and the Chaco System,* edited by D. E. Doyel, pp. 87–100. Maxwell Museum of Anthropology, Anthropological Papers no. 5. Albuquerque, New Mexico.

Stein, J. R., J. E. Suiter, and D. Ford

1997   High Noon in Old Bonito: Sun, Shadow, and the Geometry of the Chaco Complex. In *Anasazi Architecture and American Design,* edited by B. H. Morrow and V. B. Price, pp. 133–148. University of New Mexico Press, Albuquerque.

Stevenson, M. C.

1887   The Religious Life of the Zuñi Child. In *Fifth Annual Report of the Bureau of American Ethnology, 1883–1884,* pp. 533–555. U.S. Government Printing Office, Washington, D.C.

Stodder, A. L. W.

1989   Bioarcheological Research in the Basin and Range Region.

In *Human Adaptations and Cultural Change in the Greater Southwest,* by A. H. Simmons, A. L. W. Stodder, D. D. Dykeman, and P. A. Hicks, pp. 167–190. Arkansas Archeological Survey Research Series no. 32. Wrightsville.

Stoffle, R. W., M. J. Evans, M. N. Zedeño, B. W. Stoffle, and C. J. Kesel

1994   *American Indians and Fajada Butte: Ethnographic Overview and Assessment for Fajada Butte and Traditional (Ethnobotanical) Use Study for Chaco Culture National Historical Park, New Mexico.* Office of Cultural Affairs, Historic Preservation Division, State of New Mexico, and Regional Ethnographer, Southwestern Regional Office, National Park Service, Santa Fe.

Stuart, D. E.

2000   *Anasazi America: Seventeen Centuries on the Road from Center Place.* University of New Mexico Press, Albuquerque.

Stubbs, S. A.

1950   *Bird's-Eye View of the Pueblos.* University of Oklahoma Press, Norman.

Sullivan, A. P. and M. B. Schiffer

1978   A Critical Examination of SARG. In *Investigations of the Southwestern Anthropological Research Group,* edited by R. C. Euler and G. J. Gumerman, pp. 168–176. Museum of Northern Arizona, Flagstaff.

Swentzell, R.

1992   Pueblo Space, Form, and Mythology. In *Pueblo Style and Regional Architecture,* edited by N. C. Markovich, W. F. E. Preiser, and F. G. Sturm, pp. 23–30. Van Nostrand Reinhold, New York.

1997   An Understated Sacredness. In *Anasazi Architecture and American Design,* edited by B. H. Morrow and V. B. Price, pp. 186–189. University of New Mexico Press, Albuquerque.

Tainter, J. A.

1982   Energy and Symbolism in Mortuary Practices. In *New Uses of Systems Theory in Archaeology,* edited by E. G. Stickel, pp. 63–75. Ballena Press Anthropological Papers no. 24. Los Altos, California.

Tainter, J. A., and D. Gillio

1980   *Cultural Resources Overview, Mt. Taylor Area, New Mexico.* USDA Forest Service, Southwest Regional Office, and USDI Bureau of Land Management, New Mexico State Office, Albuquerque and Santa Fe.

Talayesva, D. C.

1942   *Sun Chief: The Autobiography of a Hopi Indian,* edited L. W. Simmons. Yale University Press, New Haven, Connecticut.

Tatje, R., and R. Naroll

1970   The Measures of Societal Complexity. In *A Handbook of Method in Cultural Anthropology,* edited by R. Naroll and R. Cohen, pp. 766–833. Natural History Press, Garden City, New York.

Teklenburg, J. A. F., H. J. P. Timmermans, and A. F. van Wagenberg

1993   Space Syntax: Standardized Integration Measures and Some Simulations. *Environment and Planning B: Planning and Design* 20(3):347–357.

Toll, H. W.

1984a   Material Aspects of Pueblo Ritual with Regard to Goods Distribution in Chaco. Paper presented at the annual meeting of the Society for American Archaeology, Portland, Oregon.

1984b   Trends in Ceramic Import and Distribution in Chaco

Canyon. In *Recent Research on Chaco Prehistory,* edited by W. J. Judge and J. D. Schelberg, pp. 115–136. Reports of the Chaco Center no. 8. National Park Service, Albuquerque, New Mexico.

1985   Pottery, Production, Public Architecture, and the Chaco Anasazi System. Unpublished Ph.D. dissertation, Department of Anthropology, University of Colorado, Boulder.

1990   A Reassessment of Chaco Cylinder Jars. In *Clues to the Past: Papers in Honor of William M. Sundt,* edited by M. S. Duran and D. T. Kirkpatrick, pp. 273–305. Papers of the Archaeological Society of New Mexico no. 16. Albuquerque.

1991   Material Distributions and Exchange in the Chaco System. In *Chaco and Hohokam: Prehistoric Regional Systems in the American Southwest,* edited by P. L. Crown and W. J. Judge, pp. 77–107. School of American Research Press, Santa Fe, New Mexico.

2001   Making and Breaking Pots in the Chaco World. *American Antiquity* 66(1):56–78.

Toll, H. W., and P. J. McKenna

1987   The Ceramography of Pueblo Alto. In *Investigations at the Pueblo Alto Complex, Chaco Canyon, New Mexico, 1975–1979,* vol. 3, *Artifactual and Biological Analyses,* edited by F. J. Mathien and T. C. Windes, pp. 19–230. Publications in Archeology 18F, Chaco Canyon Studies. National Park Service, Santa Fe, New Mexico.

1997   Chaco Ceramics. In *Ceramics, Lithics, and Ornaments of Chaco Canyon: Analyses of Artifacts from the Chaco Project, 1971–1978,* edited by F. J. Mathien, pp. 17–550. National Park Service Publications in Archeology 18G, Chaco Canyon Studies. Santa Fe, New Mexico.

Townsend, L. K.

1986   Artists' Reconstruction of Pueblo Bonito. In *Mysteries of the Ancient Americas: The New World before Columbus,* pp. 254–255. Readers Digest Association, Pleasantville, New York.

Trigger, B. G.

1990   Monumental Architecture: A Thermodynamic Explanation of Symbolic Behavior. *World Archaeology* 22(2):119–132.

Truell, M. L.

1986   A Summary of Small-Site Architecture in Chaco Canyon, New Mexico. In *Small-Site Architecture in Chaco Canyon, New Mexico,* edited by P. J. McKenna and M. L. Truell, pp. 115–339. Publications in Archeology 18D, Chaco Canyon Studies. National Park Service, Santa Fe, New Mexico.

1992   *Excavations at 29SJ627, Chaco Canyon, New Mexico.* Reports of the Chaco Center no. 11. National Park Service, Santa Fe, New Mexico.

Turner, C. G. II, and J. A. Turner

1999   *Man Corn: Cannibalism and Violence in the Prehistoric American Southwest.* University of Utah Press, Salt Lake City.

Van Dyke, R. M., and R. P. Powers

n.d.   Summary and Conclusions. In *An Archaeological Survey of the Additions to Chaco Culture National Historical Park,* edited by Ruth M. Van Dyke. Reports of the Chaco Center no. 13. Anthropology Projects, Cultural Resources Management, National Park Service, Santa Fe, New Mexico. In press.

Vargas, V. D.

1995   *Copper Bell Trade Patterns in the Prehispanic U.S. Southwest and Northwest Mexico.* Arizona State Museum Archaeological Series no. 187. Tucson.

Vivian, G. R.

1932   Casa Rinconada Excavation Report. Archive 1844, Chaco Culture National Historical Park Archive, University of New Mexico, Albuquerque.

1940   Stabilization of Pueblo Bonito, Chaco Canyon National Monument, Fiscal Year 1940. Report on file, Chaco Culture National Historical Park Archive, University of New Mexico, Albuquerque.

Vivian, G. R., and T. W. Mathews

1965   *Kin Kletso: A Pueblo III Community in Chaco Canyon, New Mexico.* Southwestern Monuments Association Technical Series 6(1). Globe, Arizona.

Vivian, G. R., and P. Reiter

1960   *The Great Kivas of Chaco Canyon and Their Relationships.* School of American Research Monograph no. 22. Santa Fe, New Mexico.

Vivian, R. G.

1970   An Inquiry into Prehistoric Social Organization in Chaco Canyon, New Mexico. In *Reconstructing Prehistoric Pueblo Societies,* edited by W. A. Longacre, pp. 59–83. University of New Mexico Press, Albuquerque.

1974   Conservation and Diversion: Water-Control Systems in the Anasazi Southeast. In *Irrigation's Impact on Society,* edited by T. E. Downing and M. Gibson, pp. 95–112. Anthropological Papers no. 25. University of Arizona, Tucson.

1983   Identifying and Interpreting Chacoan Roads: An Historical Perspective. In *Chaco Roads Project Phase I: A Reappraisal of Prehistoric Roads in the San Juan Basin,* edited by C. Kincaid, pp. 3-1–3-20. Bureau of Land Management, Albuquerque, New Mexico.

1990   *The Chacoan Prehistory of the San Juan Basin.* Academic Press, New York.

1992   Chacoan Water Use and Managerial Decision Making. In *Anasazi Regional Organization and the Chaco System,* edited by D. E. Doyel, pp. 45–57. Maxwell Museum of Anthropology, Anthropological Papers no. 5. Albuquerque, New Mexico.

Vivian, R. G., D. N. Dodgen, and G. H. Hartman

1978   *Wooden Ritual Artifacts from Chaco Canyon, New Mexico: The Chetro Ketl Collection.* Anthropological Papers of the University of Arizona no. 32. Tucson.

Ware, J. A.

2001   Chaco Social Organization: A Peripheral View. In *Chaco Society and Polity: Papers from the 1999 Conference,* edited by L. S. Cordell, W. J. Judge, and J. Piper, pp. 79–83. New Mexico Archaeological Council Special Publication no. 4. Albuquerque.

Warren, A. H., and F. J. Mathien

1984   Prehistoric and Historic Turquoise Mining in the Cerrillos District. In *Collected Papers in Honor of Albert H. Schroeder,* edited by C. H. Lange, pp. 93–127. Papers of the Archaeological Society of New Mexico no. 10. Albuquerque.

Washburn, D. K.

1980   The Mexican Connection: Cylinder Jars from the Valley of Oaxaca. *Transactions of the Illinois Academy of Science* 72(4):70–85.

Washburn, D. K., and D. W. Crowe

1988   *Symmetries of Culture: Theory and Practice of Plane Pattern Analysis.* University of Washington Press, Seattle.

Wason, P. K.
1994 *The Archaeology of Rank.* Cambridge University Press, Cambridge.

Waters, F.
1963 *Book of the Hopi.* Penguin Books, New York.

Weaver, K. F.
1967 Magnetic Clues Help Date the Past. *National Geographic* 131(5):696–701.

Webster, G. M.
1991 Labor Control and Emergent Stratification in Prehistoric Europe. *Current Anthropology* 31(4):335–373.

Weigand, P. C.
1994 Observations on Ancient Mining within the Northwestern Regions of the Mesoamerican Civilization, with Emphasis on Turquoise. In *Quest of Mineral Wealth: Aboriginal and Colonial Mining and Metallurgy in Spanish America,* edited by A. K. Craig and R. C. West, pp. 21–35. Geoscience and Man, vol. 33. Department of Geography and Anthropology, Louisiana State University, Baton Rouge.

Weigand, P. C., and G. Harbottle
1993 The Role of Turquoise in the Ancient Mesoamerican Trade Structure. In *The American Southwest and Mesoamerica: Systems of Prehistoric Exchange,* edited by J. E. Ericson and T. G. Baugh, pp. 159–177. Plenum Press, New York.

Weller, S. C.
1987 Shared Knowledge, Intracultural Variation, and Knowledge Aggregation. *American Behavioral Scientist* 31(2):178–193.

White, L. A.
1932 The Acoma Indians. In *Forty-seventh Annual Report of the Bureau of American Ethnology, 1929–1930,* pp. 17–192. U.S. Government Printing Office, Washington, D.C.

Wilcox, D. R.
1993 The Evolution of the Chacoan Polity. In *The Chimney Rock Archaeological Symposium,* edited by J. M. Malville and G. Matlock, pp. 76–90. USDA Forest Service General Technical Report RM-227, Fort Collins, Colorado.
1996 Pueblo III People and Polity in Relational Context. In *The Prehistoric Pueblo World, A.D. 1150–1350,* edited by M. A. Adler, pp. 241–254. University of Arizona Press, Tucson.
1999 A Peregrine View of Macroregional Systems in the North American Southwest, A.D. 750–1250. In *Great Towns and Regional Polities in the Prehistoric American Southwest and Southeast,* edited by J. E. Neitzel, pp. 115–142. University of New Mexico Press, Albuquerque.

Wilcox, D. R., and J. Haas
1994 The Scream of the Butterfly: Competition and Conflict in the Prehistoric Southwest. In *Themes in Southwest Prehistory,* edited by G. J. Gumerman, pp. 211–238. School of American Research Press, Santa Fe, New Mexico.

Wilcox, D. R., and C. Sternberg
1983 *Hohokam Ballcourts and Their Interpretation.* Arizona State Museum Archaeological Series no. 115. Tucson.

Willey, G. R., and R. M. Leventhal
1979 Prehistoric Settlement at Copan. In *Maya Archaeology and Ethnohistory,* edited by N. Hammond and G. R. Willey, pp. 75–102. University of Texas Press, Austin.

Williamson, R. A.
1977 Archaeoastronomy at Pueblo Bonito. *Science* 197(4304):618–619.

1978 Pueblo Bonito and the Sun. *Archaeoastronomy* 1(2):5–7.
1987a *Living the Sky: The Cosmos of the American Indian.* University of Oklahoma Press, Norman.
1987b Light and Shadow, Ritual, and Astronomy in Anasazi Structures. In *Astronomy and Ceremony in the Prehistoric Southwest,* edited by J. B. Carlson and W. J. Judge, pp. 99–120. Papers of the Maxwell Museum of Anthropology no. 2. Albuquerque, New Mexico.

Wills, W. H.
2000 Political Leadership and the Construction of Chacoan Great Houses, A.D. 1020–1140. In *Alternative Leadership Strategies in the Prehispanic Southwest,* edited by B. J. Mills, pp. 19–44. University of Arizona Press, Tucson.
2001 Mound Formation and Ritual during the Bonito Phase in Chaco Canyon. *American Antiquity* 66(3):433–451.

Wilshusen, R. H.
1988 Abandonment of Structures. In *Dolores Archaeological Project: Supporting Studies. Additive and Reductive Technologies,* compiled by E. Blinman, C. J. Phagan, and R. H. Wilshusen, pp. 673–702. Engineering and Research Center, Bureau of Reclamation, Denver.

Windes, T. C.
1975 Excavation of 29SJ423, an Early Basketmaker III Site in Chaco Canyon: Preliminary Report on the Architecture and Stratigraphy. Manuscript on file, Chaco Culture National Historical Park Archive, University of New Mexico, Albuquerque.
1984 A New Look at Population in Chaco Canyon. In *Recent Research on Chaco Prehistory,* edited by W. J. Judge and J. D. Schelberg, pp. 75–87. Reports of the Chaco Center no. 8. National Park Service, Albuquerque, New Mexico.
1985 Chaco-McElmo Black-on-White from Chaco Canyon, with an Emphasis on the Pueblo del Arroyo Collection. In *Prehistory and History in the Southwest: Collected Papers in Honor of Alden C. Hayes,* edited by N. Fox, pp. 19–42. Papers of the Archaeological Society of New Mexico no. 11. Santa Fe.
1987a *Investigations at the Pueblo Alto Complex, Chaco Canyon, New Mexico, 1975–1979,* vol. 1. Publications in Archeology 18F, Chaco Canyon Studies. National Park Service, Santa Fe, New Mexico.
1987b *Investigations at the Pueblo Alto Complex, Chaco Canyon, New Mexico, 1975–1979,* vol. 2. Publications in Archeology 18F, Chaco Canyon Studies. National Park Service, Santa Fe, New Mexico.
1987c The Pueblo Alto Trash Mound and Comparisons with other Great House Middens. In *Investigations at the Pueblo Alto Complex, Chaco Canyon, New Mexico, 1975–1979,* vol. 3, edited by F. J. Mathien and T. C. Windes, pp. 561–664. Publications in Archeology 18F, Chaco Canyon Studies. National Park Service, Santa Fe, New Mexico.
1992 Blue Notes: The Chacoan Turquoise Industry in the San Juan Basin. In *Anasazi Regional Organization and the Chaco System,* edited by D. E. Doyel, pp. 159–168. Maxwell Museum of Anthropology, Anthropological Papers no. 5. Albuquerque, New Mexico.
1993a *The Spadefoot Toad Site: Investigations at 29SJ629 in Marcia's Rincon and the Fajada Gap Pueblo II Community, Chaco Canyon, New Mexico.* Reports of the Chaco Center no. 12. National Park Service, Santa Fe, New Mexico.

1993b   The 1991 and 1992 Room Test Excavations at Pueblo Bonito. Manuscript on file, accession no. 158, Chaco Collections, National Park Service, University of New Mexico, Albuquerque.

1997   Review of *Pueblo Bonito* by George H. Pepper (reprint). *Kiva* 63(1):87–89.

Windes, T. C., C. Ford, and D. Ford

1994   The Chaco Wood Project: Reanalysis of Pueblo del Arroyo. Paper submitted to the Southwestern Parks and Monuments Association, Tucson, Arizona.

Windes, T. C., and D. Ford

1992   The Nature of the Early Bonito Phase. In *Anasazi Regional Organization and the Chaco System,* edited by D. E. Doyel, pp. 75–85. Maxwell Museum of Anthropology, Anthropological Papers no. 5. Albuquerque, New Mexico.

1996   The Chaco Wood Project: The Chronometric Reappraisal of Pueblo Bonito. *American Antiquity* 61(2):295

Windes, T. C., and F. J. Mathien (editors)

1987   *Investigations at the Pueblo Alto Complex, Chaco Canyon, New Mexico, 1975–1979,* vol. 3, *Artifactual and Biological Analyses.* Publications in Archeology 18F, Chaco Canyon Studies. National Park Service, Santa Fe, New Mexico.

Windes, T. C., and P. J. McKenna

2001   Going against the Grain: Wood Production in Chacoan Society. *American Antiquity* 66(1):119–140.

Wozniak, F. E., D. Brugge, and C. Lange

1993   *An Ethnohistorical Summary of Ceremonial and Other Traditional Uses of Fajada Butte and Related Sites at Chaco Culture National Historical Park.* New Mexico Historic Preservation Division and National Park Service, Southwest Regional Office, Santa Fe.

Yoffee, N.

2001   The Chaco "Rituality" Revisited. In *Chaco Society and Polity: Papers from the 1999 Conference,* edited by L. S. Cordell, W. J. Judge, and J. Piper, pp. 63–78. New Mexico Archaeological Council Special Publication no. 4. Albuquerque.

Zeilik, M.

1984   Archaeoastronomy at Chaco Canyon. In *New Light on Chaco Canyon,* edited by D. G. Noble, pp. 65–72. School of American Research Press, Santa Fe, New Mexico.

1986   Keeping a Season Calendar at Pueblo Bonito. *Archaeoastronomy* 9(1–4):79–87.

1987   Anticipation in Ceremony: The Readiness Is All. In *Astronomy and Ceremony in the Prehistoric Southwest,* edited by J. B. Carlson and W. J. Judge, pp. 25–42. Papers of the Maxwell Museum of Anthropology no. 2. Albuquerque, New Mexico.

Index

Numbers in italic refer to pages with figures.

abandonment, 9, 14, 15, 18, 19, 20, 22, 23,
24–28, 29, 30, 31, 32, 41, 52, 53, 56, 59, 92, 104, 108, 125, 137, 147. *See also* burning; construction sequence; destruction; termination; trash

access, 8, 11, 12, 13, 22, 26, 27, 28, 32, 41, 46, 52, 53, 58, 64, 68, 81–83, 84, 85, 86, 87, 85, 86, 88, 89, 90, 91, 92, 96, 97, 98, 99, 100, 102, 103, 105, 134, 146, 148. *See also* boundary; integration; space syntax

Acoma, 10, 12, 92. *See also* Pueblo Indians

adobe, 43, 44, 46, 49, 50, 52, 53, 54, 56, 57, 58, 59. *See also* pavement

agriculture, 11, 13, 61, 63, 70, 78, 105, 136, 137, 138, 149. *See also* climate; corn; environment altar, 55, 57, 96, 139, 140. *See also* offering; shrine

apartment, 58, 59, 80, 88. *See also* domestic, architecture; living room; residence

archaeomagnetic dating, 14, 15–18, 29, 30

architecture, 28, 32, 46, 48, 49, 50, 52, 53, 57, 58, 59, 72–79, 80–93, 127, 138, 143, 144, 148: alignment, 46, 48, 49, 50, 52, 53, 57, 58, 59, 61, 64, 65, 67, 69, 71, 145, 146; analytical methods, 42–45, 81–83, 88; appearance, 8, 12, 144; civic versus noncivic, 72, 73, 74, 76, 77–78, 79, 145, 146; decoration, 73, 78; design, 33, 52, 56–58, 59, 63; form, 45, 50, 53, 58, 59, 66, 73, 80, 81, 82, 84–92; layout, 8, 145, 147; mapping, 2, *33–35, 36, 37, 38,* 39, 43, 44, 52, 55; massing concept model, 42–45; meaning, 58, 72, 73, 74, 80; monumental, 8, 11, 12, 57, 59, 72, 73, 74, 75, 78–79, 81, 144, 145, 147, 148; patterning, 7, 42, 43, 81, 82, 86, 87, 91; perspective view, *34, 35, 39–42, 45, 47, 49, 51, 54, 55;* photos, *3, 34, 35, 40, 48, 52, 66;* plan, *33, 35, 36, 37, 38, 39, 40, 41, 43, 44, 45, 46, 48, 49, 52, 64, 65, 66, 67, 68, 69, 70, 77, 81, 85, 86, 87, 92,* 146; public versus private, 73, 74, 83, 91, 92; size, 1, 2, 6, 7, 8, 9, 13, 26, 41, 45, 46, 47, 48, 49, 58, 59, 65, 72, 73, 74, 76, 78, 80, 82, 85, 86, 91, 87, 92, 134, 139, 145, 147, 148. *See also* access; adobe; apartment; civic construction effort; construction sequence; domestic; foundations; great house; great kiva; integration; kiva; labor; living rooms; masonry; northeast foundation complex; pavement; repair; renovation; room; small site; space syntax; symmetry; village

arrow, 96, 97, 99. *See also* bow; club; projectile point

Arroyo Hondo Pueblo, 82

artifacts, 2, 7, 22, 28, 32, 56, 127–141, 143, 144, 148: distributions, 107–126, 127–135. *See also* basket; bone; bowl; burials; ceramics; ceremonial sticks; cloth; copper; crystals; cylinder vessels; fossil, shell; grave goods; ground stone; jar; jar cover; jet; jewelry;

knife; lithics; mat; pipes; projectile point; ritual, artifacts; shell; spindle whorls; status, markers; stone jewelry; trade; turquoise

astronomy, 7, 61–71, 145. *See* equinox; Fajada Butte; great kiva; moon; solstice; sun, dagger

Aztec Ruins, 28, 29, 31, 32, 34, 35, 53, 68, 69, 101

Aztecs, 34. *See also* Maya, Mesoamerica

azurite, 98, 99, 100

Basketmaker periods, 62, 64, 71, 78, 129, 130, 131, 132, 134, 137, 138, 141

baskets, 62, 64, 70, 96, 97, 98, 99, 100, 103, 129, 140: turquoise encrusted cylinder basket, 97, 101, 103, 107, 131, 144

Bin. *See* mealing; pit

Bis sa'ani, 19

bone, 2, 108, 109, 110, 117–118, 121, 122, 123, 124, 125: awl, 96, 98, 99, 100; ornament, 97, 99; scraper, 2, 98, 99, 103, 112, 127, 131, 140. *See also* burials

Bonitians, 41, 55, 102. *See also* Bonito phase

Bonito phase, 128, 130, 137: early Bonito, 130, 133, 145; classic Bonito, 131, 132, 133, 141, 145; late Bonito, 102, 133, 135. *See also* chronology; Old Bonito

boundaries, 43, 44, 45, 56–57, 64, 81, 82. *See also* access; integration

bow, 98. *See also* arrow; club; projectile point

bowls, 19, 26, 30, 63, 96, 97, 98, 99, 100, 102, 108, 110, 117, 119–120, 121, 122, 123, 124, 125, 132, 140. *See also* ceramics

burials, 2, 7, 24, 25, 31, 32, 46, 53, 54, 57, 62, 63, 69, 70, 81, 92, 94–106, 107, 108, 109, 119, 120, 121, 123, 124, 125, 126, 127, 130, 133, 135, 136, 138–139, 140, 141, 143, 144, 145, 146, 148: Burial 13, 97, 105, 131, 136, 140, 144, 145, 149; Burial 14, 97, 103–105, 131, 136, 140, 144, 145, 149; biological analyses, 100–101, 103, 104, 105, 136, 138–139, 144; great house, 100, 101–103, 137; locations, *95,* 126; Mesa Verde, 101; northern burial room group, 94–98, 100, 101, 102, 103, 104, 105, 108, 109, 110, 112, 113, 114, 115, 116, 119, 120, 121, 122, 123, 124, 125, 126, 127, 137, 139–140, 144, 145; practices, 101–103; small site, 100, 101–103, 137, 139, 140, 144; western burial room group, 94, 95, 98–100, 101, 102, 103, 104, 105, 109, 110, 113, 114, 115–116, 117, 118, 119, 120, 123, 124, 125, 131, 133, 137, 139–140, 144, 145. *See also* cannibalism; children; grave goods; grave robbers; health; men; nutrition; room, Room 33; women